CRISIS INTERVENTION

ABOUT THE EDITOR

Kenneth France grew up in Jacksonville, Florida; attended Davidson College; and then transferred to Wake Forest University, graduating two years later with honors in psychology. In the clinical psychology program at Florida State University, he earned his master's and doctoral degrees, and he did his internship in the clinical psychology department at the University of Florida. For three years he taught at Francis Marion College in South Carolina, and for the last thirty-six years he has been at Shippensburg University of Pennsylvania, where he was the first recipient of the university's Salute to Teaching and the second recipient of the state's Suzanne Brown Excellence in Teaching Award. In Carlisle since 2004 he has been the training coordinator for the Warm Line, and he is also the trainer for the Caring for You Helpline that began in 2013. In Pennsylvania, South Carolina, California, and Florida, he has worked with a variety of human service programs. Besides *Crisis Intervention*, he has written several other books.

Sixth Edition

CRISIS INTERVENTION

A Handbook of Immediate Person-to-Person Help

By

KENNETH FRANCE, Ph.D.

Department of Psychology
Shippensburg University
Shippensburg, Pennsylvania

CHARLES C THOMAS • PUBLISHER, LTD.
Springfield • Illinois • U.S.A.

Published and Distributed Throughout the World by

CHARLES C THOMAS • PUBLISHER, LTD.
2600 South First Street
Springfield, Illinois 62704

©2014 by CHARLES C THOMAS • PUBLISHER, LTD.

ISBN 978-0-398-08106-5 (Paper)
ISBN 978-0-398-08107-2 (Ebook)

First Edition, 1982
Second Edition, 1990
Third Edition, 1996
Fourth Edition, 2002
Fifth Edition, 2007
Sixth Edition, 2014

Library of Congress Catalog Card Number: 2014014510

Printed in the United States of America
R-3

Library of Congress Cataloging-in-Publication Data

France, Kenneth, 1949-
  Crisis intervention : a handbook of immediate person-to-perso help / by
Kenneth France, PH.D., Department of Psychology, Shippensburg
University, Shippensburg, Pennsylvania. -- Sixth edition.
    pages cm
  Includes bibliographical references and index.
  ISBN 978-0-398-08106-5 (pbk.) -- ISBN 978-0-398-08107-2 (ebook)
1. Crisis intervention (Mental health services) 2. Psychiatric emergencie. I.
Title.

RC480.6.F73 2014
362.2'04251--dc23
                                                              2014014510

To the workers and supporters of the
Caring for You Helpline
in Carlisle, Pennsylvania

PREFACE

Crisis intervention is immediate person-to-person assistance. It helps restore self-determination and self-confidence in people who have exhausted their usual coping resources. The intervenor aids in the search for solutions by encouraging the individual to consider and to clarify thoughts, feelings, and options.

This book furnishes a practical framework for providing immediate problem-solving assistance to persons in crisis. As a handbook it presents core knowledge as well as methods tailored to particular circumstances. You, the reader, can select the concepts that are most relevant to your own helping endeavors.

The book is intended for caregivers whose work involves regular or occasional crisis intervention efforts. The techniques are applicable in crisis centers, hotlines, Internet-based services, victim assistance programs, college counseling centers, hospitals, schools, correctional facilities, children and youth programs, and other human service settings. Users of the concepts include counselors, social workers, psychologists, nurses, physicians, clergy, correctional officers, parole and probation officers, and lay volunteers.

Proponents of various theoretical viewpoints have claimed that crisis intervention is an outgrowth of their particular school of thought. It has been stated that crisis theory is (a) rooted in psychoanalytic theory, (b) derived from person-centered theory, and (c) based upon systems theory. Given crisis theory's shared genealogy, the content of this volume can be applied in good conscience by individuals from a variety of theoretical orientations.

Experts at the Harvard School of Public Health and at the National Institute of Mental Health have called for crisis intervention training to be a standard part of preprofessional education in the human services, as well as a focus of continuing education. Such education is recommended because intervening in crises is a common activity for human service professionals. For example, in their current work settings 60 percent of new professional counselors with master's degrees report using basic crisis intervention skills from twice a month to daily (Morris & Minton, 2012). Since this volume covers both basic skills and a wide variety of specialized topics it is a book that is appropriate for preservice students and trainees, and for apprentice and veteran intervenors.

The volume you are reading has been thoroughly updated with new supporting evidence. Older sources are included if they contribute to our understanding of the field because they (1) are seminal contributions produced by pioneers within the area, (2) offer original conceptualizations that are useful to us now, and/or (3) provide empirical findings that continue to be relevant.

In the sixth edition you will find new material on the following topics: the recovery model for persons who have serious and persistent mental disorders, helpful questions when pulling for options from clients, definitions of suicide and suicide attempt, usefulness of clients' self-perceptions of risk for self-harm, deadliness of suicide methods, probability of death associated with suicide attempts, suicidal persons' internal debate regarding life and death, association between limits on firearm purchases and suicide by firearms, decreased access to firearms resulting in lower suicide rates among college students, depression and suicide, suicide rates of prisoners, suicide by incarcerated juveniles during room confinement, bullying and suicide attempts, decision-making abilities of suicide attempters, subsequent deaths of persons who make nonlethal suicide attempts, lethality of suicidal persons who tried to prevent discovery during a past suicide attempt, media accounts of suicides, supporting journalists in their responses to suicides, interrupting a suicide attempt in progress, no-suicide contracts, benefits of problem solving for suicide attempters, homicide preceding suicide, HIV disease and suicidal behavior, subsequent difficulties of young survivors who lose a parent to suicide, suicide survivors perceived needs and experiences with regard to professional help, criminal justice system responses to rape, negotiating with armed perpetrators, advantages and disadvantages of text chat, integration of law enforcement officers into mobile and school-based crisis intervention, activation of crisis intervention services following law enforcement intervention in domestic violence situations, and client follow-up.

As in the five previous editions, the first two chapters provide core concepts that are fundamental to all intervention efforts, the next three chapters discuss special populations, and the final four chapters address a variety of service-related issues. Specifically, in Chapter 1 you will find a practical discussion of crisis theory and the philosophy of crisis intervention. Chapter 2 gives a down-to-earth presentation of basic communication and problem-solving skills. Chapter 3 discusses suicide prevention, assistance for terminally ill persons, and bereavement counseling. Chapter 4 addresses intervention with crime victims, including rape counseling and negotiating with armed perpetrators. Chapter 5 describes group strategies, family and marital interventions, and disaster relief. Chapter 6 focuses on service delivery issues such as case management, physical facilities, and modes of contact. Effective crisis intervention requires good relations among crisis intervenors and other community members. Chapter 7 addresses community relations issues by discussing citizen support, ethics, and cooperation with other organizations. Chapter 8 offers selection, training, and burnout-prevention procedures that can get intervenors started on the right foot and can decrease the likelihood of subsequent disenchantment. One way to maintain interest and energy is to offer continuing opportunities for growth and development. Chapter 9 reviews the research on crisis intervention and describes how individual intervenors can build upon that knowledge.

The references cited at the end of the book come from the literature of several professions, including psychology, psychiatry, counselor education, social work, education, nursing, law enforcement, and corrections. In addition to reflecting the current professional literature, the book also contains ideas and techniques that have been helpful to me in various settings. Those settings include the following: two university hotlines and a community hotline, an Internet-based crisis intervention service, a school system, a Veterans Administration medical center psychiatric unit, the emergency service of a hospital-based community mental health center, a university counseling center, a small community hospital, a public mental health clinic, a private mental health clinic, and a residential youth facility. In addition to direct-service experiences, I have also used the material in the book while fulfilling various roles in the areas of teaching and training, including the following: trainer for a university crisis service and for a county crisis center; instructor in a university criminology department; law enforcement and corrections trainer; assistant professor in a college psychology department; training coordinator for a crisis service, training coordinator for a victim/witness assistance program; training consultant for hospitals, drug and alcohol programs, ministerial associations, juvenile justice programs, a law school, a school district, and a state mental health department. Currently I am an on-call backup and the training coordinator for a telephone-based peer support organization for persons with serious and persistent mental disorders, and I am the trainer for a bereavement helpline. Since 1978, I have been a member of the psychology faculty at Shippensburg University, where I supervise interns and teach abnormal psychology, helping skills, and crisis intervention.

Every example in the book is based on an actual occurrence I have encountered. But each account contains changes in significant details in order to protect the identity of the participants. All of the client names are fictitious.

You will find that the chapters end with study questions. When instructors, trainers, and supervisors use the book as required reading, they often request written answers to the questions. Reviewing those responses is an excellent way of covering a large amount of material in a brief period of time.

I am interested in knowing what you think of the sixth edition. If you have reactions that you are willing to pass along, please write to me at the Department of Psychology, Shippensburg University, Shippensburg, Pennsylvania 17257.

K.F.

ACKNOWLEDGMENTS

Portions of Chapters 2 and 9 also appear in *Helping Skills for Human Service Workers: Building Relationships and Encouraging Productive Change*, written by Kenneth France, Kim Weikel, and Michelle Kish, and published by Charles C Thomas Publisher, Ltd. I appreciate publisher Michael Thomas continuing to support my writing, including the sixth edition of *Crisis Intervention.*

CONTENTS

CRISIS INTERVENTION

Chapter 1

CRISIS THEORY AND THE PHILOSOPHY OF CRISIS INTERVENTION

Crises are a fact of life. Examples include crises concerning relationship difficulties, the loss of a loved one, assault, abuse, health issues, unplanned pregnancy, career setbacks, natural disasters, and terrorism. No one seeks such experiences, but they happen to us anyway. When we are thrown into crisis, the support we receive often plays a crucial role in determining the ultimate effect of the episode. One approach to preventing debilitation and facilitating growth is crisis intervention—a way of assisting those who find themselves in crisis.

CRISIS THEORY

Definition

Experts (e.g., Al, Stams, van der Laan, & Asscher, 2011; Burgess, 2005; Caplan, 1964; Lanceley, 2003; Hoff & Hoff, 2012; Kalafat, 2002a; Kalafat, Gould, Harris-Munfakh, & Kleinman, 2007; Kleespies, 2014; Roberts, 2005b, 2005c; Vecchi, Van Hasselt, & Romano, 2005; Westefeld & Heckman-Stone, 2003) have defined a crisis as a brief episode of intense emotional distress in which the person's usual coping efforts are insufficient to handle the challenges confronting the individual. Something must change. During this period of transition the person has the potential for heightened maturity and growth or for deterioration and greater vulnerability to future stress. Although resolutions can be quite different, all crises share several core features. Below are *five essential characteristics of crises* that are frequently noted by researchers and clinicians:

(a) Crises are *precipitated* by specific identifiable events that become too much for the person's usual problem-solving skills (e.g., Kalafat, 2002a; Myer & Moore, 2006; Parikh & Morris, 2011; Roberts, 2005b; Vecchi et al., 2005; Westefeld & Heckman-Stone, 2003). Often a single distressing occurrence follows a host of difficulties and simply constitutes the "tipping point." Sometimes the inability to cope also involves lingering difficulties that remain from earlier poorly resolved crises.

(b) Crises are *normal* in the sense that all of us feel overwhelmed at one time or another. It is entirely possible that today's crisis intervenor will be tomorrow's crisis victim. None of us are immune from the possibility of suddenly encountering overwhelming difficulties (e.g., Kalafat, 2002a; Parikh & Morris, 2011).

(c) Crises are *personal.* A situation that throws one person off course may merely create an interesting detour for another. It is the individual's perception and interpretation of circumstances that are crucial, rather than the objective nature of events (e.g., Kalafat, 2002a; Lanceley, 2003; Lewis, 2005; Myer & Moore, 2006; Parikh & Morris, 2011; Roberts, 2005b; Vecchi et al., 2005; Westefeld & Heckman-Stone, 2003).

(d) Crises are *resolved* one way or another within a brief period of time. They are too intense to be long-standing or chronic (e.g., Caplan, 1964; Kalafat, 2002a; Orbach, 2003; Parikh & Morris, 2011; Westefeld & Heckman-Stone, 2003).

(e) The resolution can be *adaptive,* as reflected in the development of new problem-solving skills, or it can be *maladaptive,* as demonstrated through defensiveness or disorganization (e.g., Burgess, 2005; Calhoun & Tedeschi, 2006; Caplan, 1964, 1990; Janoff-Bulman, 2006; Parikh & Morris, 2011; Westefeld & Heckman-Stone, 2003). One way or another, the unbearable pressure will come to an end.

A threat exists when there is the imminent potential that certain goals will become more difficult to achieve. If an event is perceived as a threat, the person usually responds with coping techniques that have proved useful in the past. Despite one's best efforts, there are instances when traditional coping strategies fail to resolve the situation within the expected amount of time. As noted by Caplan (1974), continued failure results in a crisis once the individual perceives that usual problem-solving efforts do not alleviate the situation.

An almost infinite variety of events can precipitate crises; some possibilities include death of a loved one, victimization by personal crime, loss of an important relationship, and illness. Even events generally thought of as being positive may have overwhelming stresses associated with them; such situations include promotion, moving to a new residence, birth of a baby, entering school, graduation, and retirement.

Since crises are personal, individuals facing similar challenges may react very differently. Influences on one's subjective evaluation of stress include both personality traits and the nature of the circumstances. Although any given event may have the potential to create demands beyond one's coping abilities, what overtaxes one person's problem-solving skills may be easily resolved by another individual who is using customary coping techniques. Consequently, it cannot be assumed that a given event necessarily will precipitate a crisis, or will be seen as innocuous, by all persons.

For example, how would you react if someone stole a book belonging to you? For one young man that event precipitated a crisis. He was overwhelmed by the fact that someone would violate him in such a way, even though the theft occurred in a juvenile detention center where he had been sent for burning down a neighbor's house—an act for which he experienced no remorse, believing he had done the family a favor by allowing them to collect money from their homeowners' insurance policy.

A crisis must be understood from the perspective of the person experiencing it, no matter what your own view of events might be.

Development

The concept of crisis is as old as humankind's struggle to deal creatively with the challenges and stresses of life. For example, the term *crisis* is derived from the Greek word *krisis*, which means decision or turning point. And one Chinese word for crisis is a combination of the symbols for danger and opportunity.

Although the idea of crisis has been around for a long time, crisis theory is only a few decades old. Researchers and clinicians (e.g., Flannery & Everly, 2000; Morris, 2011; Myer & Moore, 2006; Parikh & Morris, 2011; Pierpont & McGinty, 2005; Roberts, 2005b; Wallace, 2001) generally recognize that crisis theory came into existence with Erich Lindemann's 1944 report on "Symptomatology and Management of Acute Grief." The article is based on psychiatric interviews with 101 patients who recently had experienced the death of a close relative. Thirteen of the subjects were bereaved survivors of Boston's 1942 Coconut Grove nightclub fire where nearly five hundred persons lost their lives. In writing about his interviews, Lindemann described both the symptoms of acute grief and a therapeutic plan for bereavement intervention.

Although the origins of crisis theory can be traced to Lindemann's study, the area's theoretical foundation comes from Gerald Caplan and his associates at the Harvard School of Public Health (Caplan, 1960, 1964). Caplan's interest in crises resulted from his work with families immigrating to Israel following World War II (Caplan, 1951, 1990). His subsequent writing, research, and teaching are generally recognized as the foundation for most of the crisis theory tenets we use today (e.g., Ball, Links, Strike, & Boydell, 2005; Erchul, 2009; Hopkins & Niemiec, 2007; Morris, 2011; Parikh & Morris, 2011; Pierpont & McGinty, 2005; Wallace, 2001).

STAGES OF CRISIS

Phase One–Impact

A person in crisis evolves through at least two, and sometimes three, phases. The first stage consists of the individual's initial reactions to what suddenly has become an unavoidable and apparently insurmountable problem. Usual coping strategies have failed to solve the difficulties created by the precipitating event.

A person's cognitive perception of this failure influences subsequent responses and coping efforts. According to Martin Seligman and his associates (e.g., Peterson, Maier, & Seligman, 1993), a condition termed *learned helplessness* may result if we come to believe that our efforts will have no effect in producing desired outcomes or in preventing undesirable events. Their hypothesis states that one's perceived lack of control may create motivational, cognitive, and emotional deficits. Motivation declines, as reflected by fewer attempts to solve the problem. Cognitively, one becomes restricted and may focus on a single interpretation of events to the exclusion of other possible explanations. Should conditions later change for the better, this static mental set may make it difficult to perceive that efforts are producing positive results. Emotionally, one feels depressed, sad, and hopeless.

Upon discovering that coping attempts are ineffective, a natural reaction is to wonder about the reason for the helplessness. The answer to the question "Why me?" is the person's attribution for the predicament, and that *attribution* influences the pervasiveness and duration of the motivational, cognitive, and/or emotional deficits.

Seligman and his associates identified the following three dimensions of attribution relevant to learned helplessness: internal-external, stable-unstable, and global-specific.

- *Internal-External.* Making internal attributions means seeing failures as resulting from one's own shortcomings, whereas an individual making an external attribution believes anyone in a similar situation would fail because of uncontrollable environmental factors. With internal helplessness the deficits may be so pervasive that one experiences lowered self-esteem, but the effects of external helplessness are not likely to be so widespread.

- **Stable-Unstable.** When making a stable attribution, one does not expect things to change, whereas unstable attributions mean the person anticipates new developments. Attributing helplessness to uncontrollable stable factors results in longer-lasting deficits, while unstable attributions tend to be associated with briefer deficits.
- **Global-Specific.** Global attributions involve perceiving similarities across a wide range of situations, whereas specific attributions are restricted to more narrow applications. Deficits are more pervasive when attributions for uncontrollable events are global, but there are fewer difficulties when such attributions are specific to the situation at hand.

To the extent that one's attributions for uncontrolled failure are internal, stable, and global, there is an increased likelihood of lethargy, single-mindedness, and depression. To the extent that attributions for uncontrolled failure are external, unstable, and specific, one will have more energy, be more flexible, and experience less depression.

Learned helplessness theory focuses on distressing events that are perceived to be uncontrollable. Often we believe, however, that we have at least some control over negative events, and on those occasions empirical research (Brown & Siegel, 1988) suggests that internal and global attributions seem to decrease depression. Such attributions mean we do not feel helpless; instead we believe we can influence events in a variety of situations.

There is a crucial difference between perceiving the outcome to be inside or outside of one's control. For example, two students receive bad grades in all of their subjects; the first one attributes the grades to low ability, while the second one attributes the poor marks to low effort. The first student is attributing the poor grades to an uncontrollable factor—there is little one can do about low ability. Consequently, that person is likely to be discouraged, inflexible, and depressed. The second student, however, is attributing the unsatisfactory grades to a controllable condition. Since that student believes better grades would result from increased effort, learned helplessness does not occur.

Empirical research (e.g., Brown & Siegel, 1988) indicates we are less disturbed by negative events we think we can influence than by those that seem uncontrollable. The distressful experience of lacking effective control is the essence of the impact stage, where there is a feeling of being overwhelmed against one's will.

Helplessness is one common feeling in such situations; another frequent reaction is anxiety—an emotional signal warning us that dread events are about to occur. If those events threaten to block important desires another unpleasant emotion may arise–frustration. And frustrated people often become angry.

Anxiety, frustration, and anger often lead to increases in activity. Sometimes agitated depression results from combining this energy with hopelessness and with the sense of urgency that occurs when one feels out of control. Unlike the clinically depressed person with psychomotor retardation, an individual experiencing agitated depression may expend lots of energy. Unfortunately, it is the equivalent of spinning one's wheels, and it results in no forward movement.

Since the impact stage tends to be brief, intervenors usually encounter crisis clients after the first phase is over. There are times, however, when the worker is with the person during impact. Such instances include death notification and the initiation of unexpected medical procedures.

EXAMPLE. Mary Anderson came to the emergency room for treatment of a wrist injury. She became agitated when told an x-ray would be needed, and she said she did not want to have the procedure, citing her fear of the possible adverse effects of radiation. Yet the x-ray was taken despite her refusal.

When first seen by the crisis worker, Mary was trembling and crying. She felt distraught over having had the x-ray taken.

Mary said she had become upset and nervous four months earlier when it had come to light that improperly stored radioactive samples had been discovered in a variety of places within the science building where she had been attending classes. Soon after the disclosure she had consulted her family physician who had prescribed a tranquilizer for her. She decided, however, not to take the medication "for health reasons." Instead she continued to be preoccupied with the danger posed by her exposure to the radioactive samples.

Mary's friends thought her concern about the samples was silly. On the evening she came to the hospital, they had encouraged her to go drinking with them in order to get it off her mind. While leaving a tavern she fell and injured her wrist.

Although the worker and Mary discussed several options, she was not ready to decide upon a course of action. Consequently, they arranged a second contact for the following day.

DISCUSSION OF MARY ANDERSON'S CRISIS. When the emergency room physician ordered an x-ray of Mary's wrist, he exacerbated residual emotional difficulties lingering from her poor resolution of the crisis experienced at the time of the disclosure concerning the radioactive samples in the science building. Fearing additional radiation exposure, Mary was sincerely worried about the x-ray. On the other hand, the emergency room physician routinely ordered radiology consults, and he found it impossible to believe that the procedure could cause anyone genuine concern. Nevertheless, his patient experienced a crisis precipitated by an event he did not envision as being stressful.

Mary usually disregarded medical advice with which she disagreed, as she had done several months earlier with the tranquilizer prescription. This time she unsuccessfully tried to use the strategy of declining a recommended procedure. When her coping attempt failed, Mary found herself in the first phase of crisis. She discovered she was helpless to prevent the x-ray; she felt anxious about its effects; and she was angry at the person who ordered it.

The stage was set for this crisis by Mary's failure to cope adaptively with her helplessness, anxiety, and anger following the science building revelations. By the end of the emergency room session she recognized the need to deal with those residual problems, as well as with the new crisis. She vowed to address these issues in a contact planned for the following day.

Phase Two–Coping

During the impact stage, the person feels overwhelmed and out of control. As the pressure continues, the individual makes new attempts to alleviate the situation. That renewed effort initiates the second stage of crisis.

As demonstrated by empirical research (Folkman, Lazarus, Dunkel-Schetter, DeLongis, & Gruen, 1986), during the coping phase the person exerts mental and behavioral effort intended to address the demands that currently seem to exceed the individual's resources. Some combination of those attempts to manage the situation is likely to be successful, and as Caplan (1974) noted, most crises are resolved during this stage.

Caplan (1974) also observed that failure to grasp a solution creates a feeling of urgency. The individual desperately believes that something has to give–and soon. This increase in motivation is crucial; it makes crises different from most other problems in living and worthy of a unique intervention strategy that focuses on the person's heightened readiness for growth.

Caplan (1960) pointed out that crises are brief because of the desperate need for a decrease in pressure; the individual adopts some strategy to resolve the problems, defend against them, or escape from them. In addition to making crises short, clinicians and researchers have noted other effects from the high motivation for resolution:

(a) The distress caused by failure of usual coping methods encourages the person to try new problem-solving approaches (e.g., Caplan, 1964; Corcoran & Allen, 2005; Kalafat, 2002a).

(b) Individuals in the coping phase are more open to influence from others (e.g., Vecchi et al., 2005).

(c) A willingness to consider new options combines with heightened receptivity to increase the likelihood that the person will seek help (e.g., Caplan, 1974; Roberts, 2005b).

(d) When the desired assistance is not readily available, some individuals resort to life-threatening behavior as a dramatic "cry for help." Two-thirds of all "suicide attempts" are actually pleas for attention; they are intended to end in rescue rather than in death (Farberow & Litman, 1970). Although tragedies occur and some of these persons unintentionally kill themselves, the purpose of suicide attempts during the coping stage is to generate assistance rather than to end one's life.

Crises often jar the person's usual thinking patterns. This disruption can take two forms. (1) The individual may misunderstand crucial aspects of the circumstances. (2) The person may narrow attention to a few components of the situation. In either case, important considerations may be ignored. Consequently, both mental confusion and cognitive restriction can hinder one's ability to identify available alternatives.

Maturity is another area that may suffer during a crisis. Individuals may fail to fulfill role responsibilities or may engage in behavior that seems out of character.

Coping efforts can focus on eliminating the source of the discomfort or can defend against unpleasant emotions. *Problem-focused coping* attempts to alter stressful situations, whereas *avoidant coping* seeks to prevent or reduce unpleasant thoughts and feelings. Empirical research on these coping styles indicates that when the possibility of change is available in response to distressing life events, it is helpful for part of one's response to involve efforts directed at solving the problem. In such situations, problem-focused coping is often related to both satisfactory outcomes and decreased psychological distress, whereas coping efforts intended simply to prevent or reduce unpleasant feelings tend to have no positive relationship to successful problem resolution (Ben-Zur, 2005; Lazarus, 1999; McMahon et al., 2013; Stanton, Bower, & Low, 2006).

This line of research supports Caplan's (1964) contention that behaviors initiated to remedy causes of difficulties are preferable to tension-relieving strategies that decrease helplessness, anxiety, or frustration without dealing with their sources. There are several forms of coping that seek tension relief without addressing the actual problem. Here are four categories of stopgap efforts intended to defend one against the unpleasant realities of the crisis:

(a) The problem and accompanying unpleasant emotions can be distorted, denied, or repressed.
(b) Restricted viewpoints can be adopted and unbending attitudes developed, such as believing things will magically work out, or denying any responsibility and putting the blame on others.
(c) The problem can be avoided through the use of alcohol or other drugs.

(d) Psychological difficulties can be converted into physical problems, such as insomnia or headaches.

Although these efforts may diminish the present crisis, such approaches typically are maladaptive because they usually increase future susceptibility to emotional disturbance. For example, the case of Mary Anderson demonstrated how an earlier ill-resolved crisis set the stage for new problems.

Coping attempts that do address causes of the distress are likely to result in both positive environmental outcomes and decreased helplessness, frustration, and anxiety. These adaptive consequences become more likely when one adopts the following kinds of approaches:

(a) The problem and associated negative emotions can be recognized, explored, and understood.

(b) Distressing conditions that cannot be changed can be accepted. Examples include the death of a family member or one's own impending death. Such instances often require redefinition of the problem into workable terms; for example, "How can I keep from dying?" has no earthly solution, whereas, "How can I make the most of the time I have left?" opens the door to many opportunities.

(c) It is adaptive to take small steps. Although there may be a desire to resolve everything at once, unfocused effort dissipates energy, whereas breaking down problems into manageable segments tends to generate progress without overtaxing the person.

(d) The motivation to persevere can be sustained by hope—belief in the possibility that things will get better and that one's efforts can make a difference. By believing that success is possible, a person gains energy for positive change. Optimism also fosters self-confidence that allows for respites from wrestling with the crisis. Time-out periods can be restorative and can help the individual become more productive when it is time to renew problem-solving efforts.

As noted by Caplan (1964, 1974), these problem-focused responses frequently lead to successful crisis resolution and to decreased emotional distress, and such strategies often enhance the person's ability to deal with future difficulties.

EXAMPLE. After one year of marriage, June Harrison decided to separate from her husband Bill. She accused him of beating her repeatedly, squandering her substantial inheritance, and abusing alcohol and other drugs. Following the loss of their apartment due to nonpayment of rent, they spent the next two weeks living in their ten-year-old car. This nomadic existence proved too much for June, so she went to another town to visit the Abbots, who were parents of a high school friend.

Soon after arriving at the Abbots' home she called the crisis center. June told the worker that she felt inadequate and feared being unable to handle the day-to-day responsibilities of living on her own. Although she blamed Bill for her predicament and expressed anger towards him, she became tearful when she first discussed leaving him.

After expressing her concerns and considering several options, June resolved to follow through with the separation. She decided to look into the possibility of returning to work for a former employer, and she planned to register with a roommate referral service so as not to wear out her welcome with the Abbots.

DISCUSSION OF JUNE HARRISON'S CRISIS. June realized her former lifestyle was currently unattainable since her inheritance had been depleted. Once she recognized the reality of her situation she displayed a number of problem-focused coping responses. Those included seeking help from friends, as well as contacting a crisis worker with whom she shared her difficulties, regrets, fears, and hopes. After reviewing important elements of her situation, she broke down the problem into manageable bits and began to tackle them one by one.

Phase Three—Withdrawal

A third phase of crisis evolves if none of the adaptive or maladaptive coping attempts alleviate the distress. Unable to continue facing undiminished pressure, the individual withdraws and stops trying to resolve the problems.

Withdrawal can be voluntary or involuntary. The voluntary form of withdrawal is suicide. Unlike the "cry for help" suicide attempts seen in the second stage of crisis, life-threatening behavior in the third phase is intended to result in death. The end of life is now preferable to one's continued pain-filled existence.

The involuntary version of withdrawal is personality disorganization. Often termed a "nervous breakdown" by lay persons, the *Diagnostic and Statistical Manual of Mental Disorders (DSM)* labels this condition brief psychotic disorder if the duration is less than a month, or schizophreniform disorder if it persists from one to six months. Whatever the name, such a psychotic break can involve disturbed thinking, perceptual distortion, mood disorders, unusual motor behavior, and interpersonal difficulties.

EXAMPLE. At the end of a difficult weekend, Helen Barber brought her brother Harold to the hospital crisis intervention center. She described him as appearing calm one minute then engaging in frantic activity the next. She said he believed evil forces were after him and that he perceived he was in continuous communication with the Virgin Mary. Just prior to leaving for the hospital, Helen asked to pray with Harold. He responded by striking her and accusing her of blasphemy.

During the interview, Harold directed most of his comments to the Virgin Mary, whom he believed was listening to his "prayer." Consequently, Helen supplied the worker with information about recent events. According to her, Harold was an accountant who had been under intense pressure to devise a new budget system before his company's next fiscal year. He was also feeling pressure associated with his upcoming marriage, and he was having second thoughts about going through with the wedding. Helen believed that worry associated with these concerns had caused Harold to have insomnia for the past two weeks, but she did not think his mood changes and delusions began until after he left work on Friday.

The crisis worker arranged for a voluntary admission to the mental health inpatient unit. Upon his arrival there, Harold received antipsychotic medication.

DISCUSSION OF HAROLD BARBER'S CRISIS. Harold's best professional efforts failed to produce a new accounting system within the deadline imposed by his supervisor, leaving him feeling anxious and inadequate. Yet the pressure for performance continued, compounded by the added stress of his impending wedding date and his increasing doubts about the wisdom of getting married. After several weeks of intense distress, he withdrew into a brief psychotic disorder.

Adjustment

Caplan (1964) observed that within two months of the precipitating event most individuals are no longer in crisis. The resolution can lead to a lifestyle that is more, less, or equally effective in comparison to the precrisis state. Factors influencing the outcome include the hazardous circumstances, as well as the person's emotional response, previous experience, personality characteristics, and social supports.

When old styles of coping have become ineffective the individual may turn to fresh approaches. The resulting lifestyles can involve major transitions. For instance, a separated spouse may face life alone—as in the case of June Harrison—or a rural flood victim may move to an urban neighborhood. The person may make these changes by choice or they may be mandated by circumstances. As Caplan (1964, 1976) noted, in either case, adjustment to the new realities often involves a lengthy period of adaptation.

PHILOSOPHY OF CRISIS INTERVENTION

Crisis intervention is a form of support that seeks to help the person develop adaptive ways of confronting challenges which have temporarily overwhelmed the individual's ability to cope. Empowerment of clients to productively resolve their crises can be guided by the following five components that comprise a philosophy of crisis intervention: restoration or improvement of coping, immediacy, client competency, secondary prevention, and a focus on problem solving.

Restoration or Improvement of Coping

Crises are distressing episodes that end with or without outside involvement. Crisis intervention is a technique intended to limit the duration and severity of the episode. The minimum goals are to alleviate immediate pressures and to restore the client to a level of adjustment that is as effective as the person's precrisis functioning, whereas the optimal result is for the crisis to be a growth experience that leaves the individual better equipped to cope with future difficulties. Research (e.g., Calhoun & Tedeschi, 2006; Janoff-Bulman, 2006) indicates that when outcomes following stressful encounters are satisfactory, persons tend to view the difficult episodes as learning experiences that leave them better off than they were before.

Immediacy

Individuals are more receptive to help during crises than they are in less turbulent times. Consequently, as noted by Caplan (1964, 1990), focused assistance during this period of flux and high motivation can have greater impact than more prolonged interventions delivered in a less timely fashion.

The impetus for change comes from the unpleasantness of present circumstances. Removing that tension—as some professionals attempt to do by prescribing tranquilizing medication—decreases one's motivation for adaptive change. As psychiatrist Douglas Puryear (1979) pointed out, anxiety should not be allowed to become intolerable, yet neither should it be eliminated since it can act as a powerful incentive for developing improved coping abilities. For many medical professionals, though, writing a prescription is easy, whereas listening to the patient and engaging the person in problem-solving often requires more time than the expert is able or willing to allocate.

Crisis intervention seeks to encourage productive problem solving as a way of decreasing maladaptive coping and preventing withdrawal. The probability of negative outcomes increases when individuals spend long periods struggling on their own without having the benefit of sharing their thoughts and feelings, considering options, and developing plans.

The availability of immediate problem-solving assistance is a fundamental aspect of crisis intervention because it (a) is the most efficient strategy to take advantage of the person's readiness to work, (b) can prevent maladaptive crisis resolution, and (c) can rescue those individuals who are on the brink of suicide or severe personality disorganization. It is for these reasons that crisis intervention programs go to the trouble of offering immediately available services.

Client Competency

As mental health experts have noted (e.g., Flannery & Everly, 2000; Greene, Lee, Trask, & Rheinscheld, 2005; Kalafat, 2002b; Westefeld & Heckman-Stone, 2003), crisis intervention emphasizes the competency of clients in dealing with problems, and it encourages individuals to do all they can for themselves. By recognizing a client's abilities, the worker can enhance the self-esteem of a person who may be feeling helpless, inadequate, or inferior.

If individuals are capable of rational thinking, intervenors encourage them to make their own decisions. More directive tactics are appropriate only when it becomes apparent that the person cannot independently take the necessary steps.

This emphasis on the person's own restorative powers implies that behavior change is sought through the least disruptive means possible. For example, in most cases psychiatric hospitalization should be advocated only as a last resort—although it is necessary and appropriate in some instances.

The right to refuse service is another implication of the emphasis on client competency. When intervening at the request of someone besides the potential client, the worker cannot assume that a crisis exists or that the designated individual desires assistance. Service refusals may occur in settings such as emergency rooms and intensive care units, and in circumstances such as death investigations, domestic disturbance calls, and requests for help made by friends or relatives. The option of declining crisis intervention assistance is always the person's right, although refusing services may be a decision that has immediate consequences for the individual—such as incarceration of a domestic dispute participant or psychiatric hospitalization of an emergency room patient.

Secondary Prevention

Efforts intended to prevent a problem can occur at three levels. (1) Primary prevention decreases the number of instances of a disorder by counteracting potential detrimental influences before they produce harmful effects. (2) Secondary prevention focuses on existing problems in their early stages, thereby decreasing their duration and severity. (3) Tertiary prevention assists persons who have continuing deficits as they work toward regaining higher levels of functioning.

Primary prevention can avert the development of crises by helping individuals learn coping skills that will keep them from being overwhelmed in stressful situations. For example, getting ready for the demands of labor and delivery is the reason for participating in prepared childbirth programs. Such primary prevention efforts educate participants about the pressures they can expect and help them prepare to deal with those future stresses.

Tertiary prevention can ameliorate the residual effects of crises. Examples include the following: administering psychotropic medication to withdrawal-stage individuals who experience personality disorganization; providing psychotherapy to individuals who have lived through high-lethality suicide attempts; and having crime victims participate in ongoing support groups. The goal of such tertiary prevention endeavors is to reduce chronic deficits and to restore the person to the highest adjustment level possible.

Although crisis avoidance through primary prevention and crisis rehabilitation via tertiary prevention are worthy endeavors, this book takes the commonly agreed-upon view (e.g., Kalafat & Underwood, 2005; Lester, 1993, 1994; Shiho et al., 2005) that *crisis intervention* refers to secondary prevention efforts intended to alleviate ongoing problems before they result in debilitating impairment. Consequently, crisis intervention is a technique that is most appropriate for persons experiencing the coping phase of crisis. Such individuals are ready to receive assistance and are eager to participate in a problem-solving process. Those not in the second phase of crisis often are unable or unwilling to work on developing new coping strategies. For example, clients who have reached the withdrawal stage usually require more extensive assistance, while individuals under stress who have not yet exhausted their coping efforts are not likely to be motivated to participate in crisis intervention.

A person experiencing distress is not necessarily in crisis. Being in crisis means one is ready to abandon usual coping efforts. Conversely, staunch maintenance of maladaptive coping styles is not indicative of crisis, even though the person can suffer unpleasant emotions and can fail to meet important goals. Habitually recurring tension and difficulties are chronic in nature and do not constitute crises.

Clinicians (e.g., Kleespies, 2014) define an emergency as a situation that demands immediate action in order to prevent life-threatening or other dire consequences. The same person can experience repeated emergencies without desiring or instituting any change in coping efforts. For example, a person with schizophrenia develops a paranoid delusion involving his sister and he attempts to kill her. Such an occurrence is an emergency and requires immediate action, but it is not a crisis and crisis intervention is an insufficient response.

Community mental health centers and psychiatric emergency services commonly advertise the availability of crisis intervention. Nevertheless, observers (e.g., Semke et al., 1994) have noted that a majority of the "crisis clients" in these programs are persons who already are receiving mental health treatment. Helping individuals cope with challenges linked to serious and persistent mental disorders is an everyday occurrence for these professionals. Unlike the topics typically explored with individuals experiencing crises, discussions with persons facing emergencies who have serious and persistent mental disorders typically need to address overwhelming challenges arising out of the ongoing mental health issues they have (Ball et al., 2005).

For instance, a mental health center crisis line receives a call from a young man who has been hospitalized six times for schizophrenia. His most recent discharge was five months ago, and he has been living alone since then. Two months ago he returned to college and enrolled with junior standing. Last week, however, he failed all of his midterm exams and he now feels hopeless that he will ever be able to accomplish his goal of graduating. He knows he is impaired by schizophrenia and he fears continued mental disintegration. The possibility of further pain and disappointment seem intolerable to him.

The possibility of suicide should be taken seriously in this case. Wayne Fenton (2000) cites studies indicating that as many as 50 percent of persons with schizophrenia have at least one episode in which they consider or attempt suicide. He goes on to note that among those attempts, there is a higher frequency of violent and deadly actions than among attempts by persons who do not have schizophrenia. Also, unlike most persons who do not have schizophrenia but who die by suicide, Doctor Fenton cites studies that show individuals with schizophrenia rarely bring up the topic of suicide during interactions with clinicians in the days before they kill themselves.

Reviews of the literature (e.g., Harkavy-Friedman & Nelson, 1997a, 1997b; Kallert, Leisse, & Winiecki, 2004) conclude that persons with schizophrenia are a high-risk population for suicide, with 10 to 13 percent of all individuals receiving this diagnosis eventually killing themselves. Montross, Zisook, and Kasckow (2005) observe that many suicide deaths of persons with schizophrenia take place during nonpsychotic, depressed phases occurring within the first ten years of the illness. Those observations are supported by Schwartz and Cohen (2001), who discovered that depression accounted for 50 percent of the variation in suicidal intent experienced by 97 patients with schizophrenia, and that disturbed thought processes were negatively correlated with suicidal ideation. Doctor Fenton (2000) notes that dangerous periods include those following losses, failures, hospital discharge, and family difficulties. And Drake, Gates, Cotton, and Whitaker (1984) note that one particularly dangerous scenario is when such individuals have high expectations for themselves but have come to believe they will never meet their goals due to the limitations of their illness; those persons fear further mental disintegration and are hopeless about the future.

As you can see, the young man fits a high-lethality profile. He needs and deserves emergency services. If crisis intervenors were to follow the guidance provided by Doctor Fenton (2000), their clinical efforts would include the following: not attacking delusional systems (since they may be essential to his self-esteem), recognizing his value and worth as a person, and explicitly asking if he is thinking about suicide. But those and other crisis intervention efforts would not be a sufficient response; the young man requires the full range of tertiary prevention services that can be activated on his behalf.

Workers in crisis intervention programs must be prepared to assist clients who have chronic psychiatric problems. For example, Phyllis Solomon and her colleagues (Solomon, Gordon, & Davis, 1984) studied 363 individuals who received community services within one year after being discharged from a state psychiatric hospital. During that year, 9 percent of the group received crisis intervention services. The mean amount of contact was one hour and the median was 30 minutes.

Since brief contact is the norm, it is important to make the most of time spent with an individual who has long-standing psychiatric problems. When working with such a person, Donald Langsley (1984) asserted that it is useful for problem solving to include exploration of the following four areas: danger, support, cooperation, and self-care ability.

(a) *Danger.* Part of your task is to assess the likelihood of self-harm and harm to others.

(b) *Support.* Another crucial consideration is the availability of both professional and social support. It is important to discover what services the individual is receiving, such as counseling, psychiatric treatment, residential services, or day treatment. One should also attempt to find out whom the person depends on for emotional support and for help with everyday tasks. Often it is necessary to contact sources of both professional and social support in order to ascertain the person's current situation, as well as to obtain assistance in making and implementing plans.

For example, imagine you are interviewing an individual who apparently is experiencing delusions and hallucinations. During the contact you ask whether the person is taking any psychoactive medication, and the reply is evasive. In such instances you need to attempt contact with the client's mental health professionals, as well as with any close family members, friends, or caretakers. The mental health professionals can give information concerning diagnosis, medication prescriptions, and program participation, whereas the other sources can provide comments regarding medication compliance, recent stresses, physical illnesses, and usual coping patterns.

(c) *Cooperation.* Evaluate the individual's motivation and ability to participate in a problem-solving process. In your opinion is the person willing and able to implement a realistic plan?

(d) *Self-Care Ability.* Judge the person's ability to live independently, using your own observations and the opinions of others you contact. Does the person have—and appropriately use—food, clothing, and shelter? If self-care is a problem, consider what degree of supervision the person needs. Determine whether you will have to support a hospital commitment by making a commonsense assessment of danger, support, cooperation, and self-care ability. (Chapter 3 contains a rating scale for evaluating danger, support, and cooperation.)

Empirical research has found a relationship between two of Langsley's factors—danger and cooperation. In their study of psychiatric inpatients, Beauford, McNiel, and Binder (1997) discovered that attacks and fear-provoking threats were twice as likely to come from uncooperative patients (e.g., demanding to be discharged, denying emotional problems) than from cooperative patients (e.g., being actively involved in treatment, engaging in problem exploration). Additional factors associated with inpatient violence were a recent history of violent behavior and being highly agitated or excited.

The medical model is the dominant philosophy among several theoretical orientations that influence emergency mental health services. As clinicians and researchers have noted (e.g., Deemer, 2004), strategies based on this viewpoint are quite different from those arising out of crisis theory.

According to the medical model, the problem is a mental illness whose symptoms often reflect fundamental physiological and character defects. The purpose of intervention is to ameliorate the illness through the use of clinical assessment and diagnostic labeling, which often lead to psychotropic medication and sometimes to psychotherapy.

Common emergency mental health practices under the medical model include the following: (1) interpreting complaints as symptoms of underlying pathology and (2) seeing one's goal as arranging for a disposition of the case, that is, making a referral. Practitioners of emergency mental health often do not view themselves as offering treatment services. Instead, they tend to believe it is their job to decide where such treatment should occur (e.g., Schuster, 1995).

Emergency services programs that take the medical-model approach frequently advertise the availability of crisis intervention. Sometimes, though, crisis clients of these programs receive medical model dispositions rather than crisis intervention.

In addition to the medical model, another approach relevant to emergency mental health programs is the recovery model (e.g, Levine, 2012). With regard to understanding challenges experienced by persons who have serious and persistent mental disorders, the recovery model recognizes the role of biology, interaction with the surrounding social environment, and the individual's own coping efforts. Just as is true with crisis intervention, the recovery model emphasizes the benefits of self-determination and empowerment. Consequently, when those in need of emergency mental health services are able to think clearly, problem solving as conducted in crisis intervention can be a useful recovery model activity. For example, consistent with the recommendations of Donald Langsley discussed earlier, research has found that frequently occurring options considered by such persons include the appropriateness of medication, the need for hospitalization, involvement in organized activities, personal coping strategies that have been effective in the past, and having support arising out of caring relationships (Ball et al., 2005).

It is possible for the same program to offer both emergency mental health services and crisis intervention. In order to accomplish such double duty, staff members must understand the differences between the two modalities and must know when each approach is appropriate.

With both an individual in crisis and a lucid person experiencing a mental health emergency, the intervenor identifies and supports problem-solving skills that can be used to resolve the present difficulties, as well as to enhance future coping efforts. Although the plan developed may include contact with other services, the decision of whether to institute such a referral is made with each individual rather than being a common goal for all clients.

At times, other treatment modalities must be brought into play. Examples of persons in need of additional services include those experiencing long-standing problems such as abuse of alcohol or other drugs, recurring mania or depression, chronic free-floating anxiety (tension without an identifiable source), and habitual assaultive behavior. A brief intervention is an insufficient response for persons who are disoriented, confused, and unable to think rationally. In all of these cases referral is a fitting goal.

Crisis intervention can be a sufficient response for persons who are capable of rational thinking and who have had a recent upsurge in difficulties. It is most successful with essentially normal individuals who are encountering overwhelming problems.

Intervenors must be able to differentiate crises from situations that require tertiary prevention. Including referral as a goal should not be automatic, yet workers must always keep that option in mind.

There is evidence to suggest that many crisis workers naturally make a distinction between clients needing a problem-solving consultant and those needing more active guidance. Marc Daigle and Brian Mishara (1995) analyzed 617 calls placed to two suicide prevention centers in Quebec. The researchers discovered two intervenor styles–"Rogerian" and "Directive." Workers were more likely to use the directive style when clients were at greater risk for suicide, were frequent callers to the service, or were intoxicated.

Focus on Problem Solving

Experts (e.g., Berman, Jobes, & Silverman, 2006; Kalafat, 2002a, 2002b) agree that the central thrust of crisis intervention is to engage the person in a problem-solving process. All of the worker's skills focus on that task.

Individuals in the second phase of crisis are distressed at having failed to resolve their difficulties, and they are receptive to using new coping strategies. Crisis intervention taps this readiness by involving the person in a problem-solving endeavor intended to improve both the individual's emotional state and the distressing circumstances.

The turmoil and confusion of the crisis state actually make it easier to engage the person in creative problem solving. As psychiatrist Norris Hansell (1976) noted, adaptive reorganization and action can result when a client with such flexible thinking comes in contact with a worker who is prepared to facilitate the open consideration of both traditional and novel possibilities.

The person's mood tends to improve when the individual is making decisions and implementing plans. These endeavors result in activities that decrease feelings of helplessness and foster realistic hope. Confused persons find that problem solving moves them toward increased understanding and a sense of order. Those feeling helpless begin to regain confidence in their ability to influence events, and hopeless individuals start to believe that positive outcomes are possible.

Problem solving begins with exploration of the person's reasons for seeking assistance. Careful exploration is essential in order to discover the true nature of the person's concerns, since crisis intervenors attract a diverse array of clients with wide-ranging difficulties.

While attending to the individual's description of events, the worker also seeks to understand how the distressing circumstances have fostered unpleasant emotions. Exploring those reactions enables the client to increase emotional insight by linking negative feelings with the conditions that influenced their development.

Once there is a shared understanding of changes the client desires, the next step is to consider alternatives. Since even the best options have their costs, the discussion eventually covers both the pros and cons of available possibilities. During this part of the interaction, the client's mood often begins to improve as the person develops a growing sense of control associated with considering potential tasks and predicting likely consequences.

The ultimate goal of the initial problem-solving effort is the development of a plan that concretely describes a set of behaviors intended to alleviate specific difficulties. When appropriate, plans involve friends and relatives, as well as professional and institutional sources of support.

Crisis intervention is a brief problem-solving endeavor. Since studies of such treatment modalities have tended to indicate that maximum progress generally occurs within eight sessions or less (Steenbarger, 1994), and since crises are not chronic conditions, eight sessions can be seen as the typical maximum duration of crisis intervention. When programs adopt that position, a natural result is to limit crisis services to a maximum of eight contacts (e.g., Bengelsdorf, Church, Kaye, Orlowski, & Alden, 1993). I believe that in order to go past that number the clinician should clearly specify the expected benefits and should closely monitor anticipated change.

Duration of contacts tends to vary within a fairly wide range, although length is often influenced by the service modality. As researchers have noted (e.g., Cawunder & Mohr, 1982), many telephone interactions last between 20 and 35 minutes. Walk-in meetings frequently go about twice as long. And outreach interventions commonly take two hours or more.

In terms of client age, crisis intervention is appropriate with a wide range of individuals. Clinicians have asserted that crisis intervention is an appropriate modality with children and adolescents (Dunne-Maxim, Godin, Lamb, Sutton, & Underwood, 1992; Pitcher & Poland, 1992; Poland, 1994; Schonfeld & Kline, 1994), adults, and older individuals (Doyle & Varian, 1994).

Clients contacting crisis intervention programs are experiencing a variety of challenges. Typically, about half of all contacts concern relationship issues. Other topics include the following: sexuality, loneliness, self-esteem, finances, alcohol and other drugs, pregnancy, work or school problems, abuse, suicide, health, death, spirituality, and mental disorders (e.g., Barber, Blackman, Talbot, & Saebel, 2004; Boehm, Schondel, Ivoska, Marlowe, & Manke-Mitchell, 1998; Boehm, Schondel, Marlowe, & Manke-Mitchell, 1999).

With regard to the service setting, crisis intervention takes place in a wide range of environments. One survey (Bell, Jenkins, Kpo, & Rhodes, 1994) of hospitals in a large metropolitan area indicated that 85 percent of trauma centers and 74 percent of other hospitals offered crisis intervention, and that emergency rooms offered crisis intervention more than any other social service. As noted in the preface, additional service settings include crisis centers, hotlines, Internet-based crisis services, victim assistance programs, college counseling centers, schools, correctional facilities, children and youth programs, and other social service agencies.

SUMMARY

Crises are distressing turning points in which the failure of traditional problem-solving strategies can propel individuals toward growth, defensiveness, or withdrawal. Although the essential concept of crisis is thousands of years old, crisis theory is a relatively recent development. Part of that theory describes a series of crisis stages. The first phase consists of the person's initial reactions to failing in attempts to handle disturbing circumstances. Common responses include helplessness, anxiety, frustration, and anger. Following the initial impact, the individual enters a second phase characterized by renewed coping efforts instituted out of intense desire for the situation to end. Intervenors use this heightened motivation to foster adaptive problem solving, although the desperation can also lead to maladaptive defenses. If none of the attempted solutions are effective, a final phase results in which the person stops trying to resolve the difficulties. This withdrawal can come about voluntarily through suicide or involuntarily via personality disorganization.

Crisis intervention seeks to limit the severity of crises and to restore or improve coping. Such immediate assistance increases the likelihood of adaptive coping by taking advantage of the person's readiness to work. Intervenors draw upon the individual's own resources before considering the need for more directive guidance. Crisis intervention is a secondary prevention approach intended to aid persons in the coping phase of crisis. Consequently, arranging a referral is not a routine goal. Instead interventions focus on problem solving—accomplished by exploring thoughts and feelings, considering alternatives, and developing a plan (which may or may not involve a referral).

STUDY QUESTIONS

1. Think of a crisis you have had or someone you know has experienced. Briefly describe the situation and explain how it demonstrates the five essential characteristics of crisis. (All of the remaining questions relate to the crisis you select.)
2. In what stage was the crisis resolved?
3. The high motivation for change during crises makes such episodes short and has four other effects. Name those four effects and briefly discuss each with regard to your crisis example.
4. Name four maladaptive and four adaptive approaches to coping. Discuss the relevance of each to your crisis example.

5. Should your example have continued into the withdrawal phase, what are two dangerous ways in which it could have ended?

6. Name the minimum and optimal goals of crisis intervention. Apply them to your example by describing possible outcomes.

7. When should crisis intervention be available? Discuss the timeliness of any assistance provided in your example.

8. In crisis intervention, who should be the first to bring up possible options? How did resolution of the crisis in your example relate to the person's own resources and abilities?

9. Name the three levels of prevention. Classify any prevention efforts in your example and explain the reason for each classification.

10. If the person had been having chronic difficulties, what would have been four areas for a crisis worker to assess? In fact, how was the person functioning with regard to those four areas?

11. If the person had contacted an emergency mental health program that did not use crisis intervention principles, what would have been the goal? (Give a specific example as well as the overall goal.)

12. If the person had contacted a crisis intervention program, on what central task would the intervenor have focused? Briefly describe—with concrete examples—how each phase of that process might have happened.

Chapter 2

BASIC CRISIS INTERVENTION SKILLS

The tradition in crisis intervention is to draw upon the inherent problem-solving skills of clients. Consequently, crisis intervenors use the least amount of control necessary. Yet experts (e.g., Catenaccio, 1995; Leenaars, 2004; Lester, 2005a; Neimeyer & Pfeiffer, 1994) agree that crisis intervention is not "nondirective." Workers guide interactions, contribute their own common sense, and provide appropriate information.

Crisis intervenors can be thought of as problem-solving consultants. The worker collaborates with the client in exploring concerns and feelings, considering alternatives, and developing a plan. And throughout the interaction the staff member conveys the expectation that it is the *client* who will accomplish the major tasks and resolve the crisis. By emphasizing the client's abilities in this way, the intervenor encourages increased confidence, hope, and self-control.

The worker conveys the belief that although clients may be rocked by distressing circumstances, they are capable individuals who will cope with their difficulties and return to an even keel. Intervenors facilitate this stability and realistic self-confidence when they use effective communication and a positive relationship to guide clients through a problem-solving process.

EFFECTIVE COMMUNICATION

David Johnson (2014) has asserted that most verbal messages from would-be intervenors fall into one or more of the following five categories: advice, analysis, sympathy/reassurance, interrogation, and reflection. Each of these categories represents different intentions on the part of senders, and each has different effects on the interaction.

Advice

The intent of advice is to tell the other person what to do. Although it does provide a course of action, advice is likely to have more far-reaching effects on the client. For example, workers who make statements such as, "You should not see her again" are not only dictating a solution, they are also saying that they are better able than the client to decide what should be done. When intervenors establish themselves as the decision-makers they move the focus of the exchange to their ideas and they decrease the client's willingness to freely discuss issues.

Advice can easily turn out to be a "no-win" situation for the giver.

- *Advice rejected.* If the advice seems inappropriate to a client, the person may conclude that the worker does not understand and may reject the advice. In such cases, the intervenor fails to impose a solution while also demonstrating a lack of appreciation for the individual's predicament. Sometimes a client may confront the worker with the inappropriateness of a suggestion, and at other times a client may politely listen with no intention of ever implementing the advice.
- *Advice accepted.* Having advice accepted seems like a better outcome. However, when clients come away with an imposed solution, they may have second thoughts and never act on the idea.
- *Advice doesn't work.* In those instances when clients try to put the plan into effect but fail to achieve the desired results, the worker may be blamed for making a bad suggestion.
- *Advice works.* Even if advice is accepted and works, there still can be unwanted effects. The next time advice-using clients have problems they may depend on workers to resolve the difficulties instead of relying on their own resources.

Since a crisis intervenor empowers clients to address their issues, experts (e.g., Hoff & Hoff, 2012; Kalafat, 2002b; Mishara et al., 2007a) believe that advice is seldom appropriate. Those experts also note, though, that advice may be needed in life-threatening situations. The world's most famous non-directive therapist agreed with that point of view. A magazine writer once asked Carl Rogers how he would respond if, during a session, a suicidal client wanted to leap to his death out of Doctor Rogers' office window. Rogers told the writer that he would not let the person jump (Hall, 1967). If the choice is between suggesting that the man step away from the window or watching him go out it, advice is the appropriate response.

Analysis

Analysis is intended to explain the underlying cause of the concern. As with advice, analysis changes the focus from what the client has to share to insights the worker has to give.

When interviewers analyze, they determine the reasons for events, and then announce the "real" source of the difficulties. For example, "You are having trouble because your expectations are too high." Following such pronouncements, discussion of feelings declines and intellectual explanations increase.

Sympathy/ Reassurance

Among lay persons, sympathy and reassurance probably are the most frequently used and least effective responses. When making a sympathetic statement, the intent is to lessen the other person's feelings of loneliness. But sympathy actually moves the discussion to the speaker's feelings. For example, "*I am sorry* about the way things are going for you." Sympathy may also foster other negative effects, such as the person feeling pitied or doubting the speaker's sincerity.

The intent of reassurance is to decrease distress, and this response can be appropriate if it is based on facts. For example, it may be helpful for a medical professional to tell an accident victim that x-rays indicate there are no broken bones. Most reassurance, however, is not backed up by facts. False reassurance, such as, "I'm sure things will work out," is likely to demonstrate that the speaker does not really understand the person's concerns. Consequently, false reassurance is counterproductive and should be avoided. For instance, rather than telling a terrified rape victim that assailants never return, the worker should assist in the development of concrete plans for increasing the person's safety.

Interrogation

Interrogation takes place when the worker asks questions or tells the client what to discuss. Although this technique usually produces information, it may limit the interaction to topics specified by the interviewer. Consequently, increases in interrogation usually lead to decreases in open communication.

There are instances when crisis intervenors are expected to gather large amounts of specific information. For example, some community mental health centers have crisis workers conduct intake interviews—a procedure that usually requires several pages of information from the client. Although such data collection duties are not directly related to crisis intervention, they may be necessary for program funding or for other vital reasons.

There are two ways of minimizing the interference from information-gathering endeavors. (1) Intervenors can conduct an initial crisis intervention interview and schedule a subsequent contact for data collection. (2) Workers can obtain much of the information via a self-administered questionnaire.

Interrogation in crisis intervention is appropriate when the client needs direction in knowing what to discuss. Once the worker decides to interrogate, however, there still are degrees of control that can be used.

Open-ended probes and questions specify broad areas to be discussed. For example, "Tell me what happened yesterday." "What was your reason for coming in today?" "How are you doing with your new assignment?" (Open-ended questions usually begin with the words "What" or "How.") When responding to open-ended probes and questions, clients retain considerable freedom in selecting the exact nature and amount of information they reveal.

Closed questions specify the precise information needed. For example, "Is this the first time you have been to our agency?" "Did you call him?" "Have you talked with Mr. Brown?" "Does your wife agree?" (Closed questions often begin with the words "Is," "Did," "Have" or "Does.") Closed questions request a small bit of information; since a simple "Yes" or "No" may suffice they are not very economical in generating discussion. When confronted with sequential closed questions, clients often fall into a pattern of brief, limited responses. Consequently, individuals become less likely to tell their own stories or to bring up new topics.

In one situation certain closed questions are especially risky. When making a proposal, workers invite problems when they use any of the following introductions: "Will you," "Can you," "Would you" or "Could you." Such phrasing allows a very simple reply—"No." It is better to avoid these questions unless you are positive the answer will be "Yes."

Funnel sequences of interrogation move from open to closed questions. Initial requests for information are general in nature. The interrogation then becomes increasingly specific and focuses on more restricted areas. Here is an example of a funnel sequence. "How have things been going?" "What happened this morning?" "Did you have some difficulty?" This technique is appropriate when clients feel comfortable discussing the topic.

The freedom associated with open-ended interrogation usually gives clients ample opportunity for wide-ranging discussion. Consequently, they may bring up most necessary information on their own, thereby decreasing the amount of detailed probing needed. Gaps that do remain can be filled through the use of appropriate closed questions.

Inverted funnel sequences move from the specific to the general. For example, "Were you accepted?" "How did they let you know?" "What are you going to do now?" This strategy is especially useful when the other person is reluctant to talk or needs guidance in discussing the desired topic—circumstances that frequently arise during interactions with children and adolescents. Hesitant clients often become more willing to open up after handling a few closed questions that are easy to answer.

Although both open and closed questions have their place, there are several types of interrogation that should be avoided.

Leading questions seek agreement rather than a genuine response by the individual. For example, "You've been in this situation before, haven't you?" Such questions are biased; it is easier to give one answer than another.

Multiple questions ask two or three things before giving the person a chance to respond. For instance, "Were you able to talk about it or were you too afraid?" (Questions containing "or" almost always are multiple in nature.) When faced with multiple questions, clients may become confused or they may simply answer the last question asked.

"Why" questions require individuals to analyze themselves. For example, "Why didn't you come to see us earlier?" Such questions can be intimidating. If clients perceive "Why" questions to be threatening they may attempt to defend themselves by responding with rationalizations or by fabricating answers. Crisis intervention experts agree that "Why" questions are inappropriate (Mishara et al., 2007a).

Reflection

Reflection means using fresh words and simple language to summarize the essential aspects of a message communicated by another person. When workers reflect, they convey receptiveness and attentiveness while most of the interchange continues to originate with the client. This "active listening" technique demonstrates the worker's involvement in the interaction, whereas passive listening, in which there is little or no responding, can be interpreted as disinterest or inattention.

A good reflective statement has three effects. (1) It communicates understanding. (2) It gives the client an opportunity to change the worker's perception. (3) It provides the person with a chance to bring up new information. For example, "There was more work than you could handle by yourself" is a statement that might convey understanding and interest while giving the client the freedom to revise what has been communicated or to continue sharing and exploring new thoughts and feelings.

When trying reflection for the first time, novices commonly feel they are "doing nothing." But reflection is "doing something" for two reasons. First, it is has an effect. The other person frequently expands upon the message reflected by further discussing thoughts and feelings. Second, reflection takes effort on the part of interviewers. They must hear, understand, remember, summarize, and rephrase the message received. Performing all of these functions with 100 percent accuracy is an impossible task. Fortunately, reflection is a technique that allows workers to be human and make mistakes. If an interviewer misunderstands, it becomes obvious when the intervenor incorrectly reflects the client's message. Typically, the client's response is to correct the worker's perception and clarify the issue. Consequently, even when interviewers miss the mark, they still can be fostering good communication. Nevertheless, workers should strive to be as accurate as possible.

In addition to enabling clients to see whether their messages are understood, reflection can assist individuals in changing their behavior. By conveying understanding and acceptance, workers encourage clients to explore as well as to organize ideas and emotions. Once clients accurately assess the situation they are in a better position to decide upon a course of action.

Reflection can take place at several emotional levels:

- *Factual reflection* occurs when workers summarize objective information communicated by the sender. Such a reflection demonstrates a superficial understanding and usually encourages the client to continue surveying the situation.
- *Surface feeling reflections* include both facts and feelings. This type of reflection recognizes emotions at about the same intensity as they were communicated by the client. When hearing such reflections clients tend to feel fully understood, and they often begin discussing the situation in greater detail. So it is not surprising that experts (e.g., Tidwell, 1992) recognize such reflection as a standard part of crisis intervention.
- *Underlying feeling reflections* include emotions not expressly stated by the sender. By reflecting underlying feelings, the interviewer has the potential to move the interaction toward a deeper level of understanding; exploration may become more detailed and intense. At this level, the client often is not aware of the emotions being communicated—until the worker reflects the verbal or nonverbal behavior that signals their existence. Despite the possible benefits, underlying feeling reflections are risky for two reasons. (1) They are essentially educated guesses. (2) Even when these statements are completely accurate, the client may not be ready to accept the validity of such reflections.

Interviewers generally communicate most effectively when they match or slightly exceed the depth of feeling conveyed by the client. Consequently, the surface feeling reflection is one of the best all-purpose responses for crisis workers to use.

EXAMPLE. The following message from a client can be reflected at several levels: "After spending two weeks in the hospital I don't know how I'm going to pay our regular household bills, much less all of these medical bills. I knew going into the hospital would cost some money, but I never dreamed it would be this much!"

- *Factual reflection.* "Having to go to the hospital has put quite a strain on your family budget."
- *Surface feeling reflection.* "Right now you are really worried about your financial health."
- *Underlying feeling reflection.* "As you face all of these bills you are doubting your ability to be a good husband and father."

Nonverbal Communication

Often we communicate a willingness to listen more by what we do than by what we say. For example, patience is a crucial trait for anyone wanting to hear and understand what others have on their minds. Interviewers must be willing to let clients talk. Even when workers think they know what a client is going to say, they ought to assume ignorance. When a person does say the unexpected the intervenor should be willing to let the person bring up topics that had not been anticipated at the beginning of the interaction.

Occasionally there is silence. In such instances workers should not jump in and fill these pauses. Both the interviewer and the client may need some time to absorb and consider what has been discussed.

During silences and throughout the interview an open posture conveys receptiveness. A worker communicates this interest through a slight forward lean with arms relaxed and not folded across the chest.

Another nonverbal expression of interest is the head nod, sometimes combined with an "mmhmm" or "uh huh." When appropriately interspersed among reflections, these acknowledgments can help to convey continuing attention.

Frequent eye contact tends to be desirable, although looking directly at a client throughout the interaction probably will lead to the person feeling uncomfortable. Unflinching eye contact suggests too great a desire for intimacy, and clients may perceive it as an infringement on their privacy. Conversely, too little eye contact can imply that the worker is not interested in the client or is not being honest.

How much eye contact on your part is appropriate? The answer, regardless of your cultural background or setting, is always less than 100 percent. You do not want to stare down your client. Consequently, the seating arrangement should be at an angle, rather than head-on, so that it is possible for you to comfortably look away and break eye contact. Looking at the person 70 to 90 percent of the time is appropriate for clients who feel comfortable with frequent eye contact. Two of the factors affecting such comfort are the person's cultural background and gender. Generally men tend to desire less eye contact than women, and Asian Americans, Latino Americans, Native Americans, and African Americans tend to prefer less eye contact than Americans with European heritage.

Just as the worker's nonverbal behavior is important, the client's nonverbal communication can also be rich in meaning. Although it is necessary to focus on the person's words, those words must be understood in the context of the nonverbal signals accompanying them.

Unfortunately there is no dictionary of nonverbal behavior that reliably and validly translates the meaning of these signals. Consequently, in attempting to assign meaning to nonverbal events, an intervenor should consider what preceded the behaviors, what occurs with them, and what follows the actions. In most cases, the greatest communication value is found in departures from the client's normal ways of talking and moving, such as a sudden decrease in eye contact or increase in rate of speech.

Compared to verbal comments, nonverbal communication is less susceptible to either conscious deception or unconscious censoring. As a result, it often provides information that clients do not realize they are communicating. Although they hear what they are saying, most individuals do not know what they are doing with their bodies when they are talking. Consequently, clients may communicate messages that they have no intention of sending and that they are unaware of having given.

While interpretation must be tentative and must be considered within the context of the interaction, there are some frequently occurring ways in which common messages are communicated nonverbally.

Anxiety

Speech Behavior

- faster speech and less silence
- repeating phrases
- frequent changes in train of thought and not completing sentences
- shifting voice volume
- stuttering

Body Messages

- more gesturing
- increased sweating and face flushing

- frequent shifting of seating position
- foot or finger tapping

Anger

Speech Behavior

- fast and loud speech
- short durations with brief pauses

Facial Expressions

- frowning
- tensed lips
- chin and head thrust forward
- wide eyes

Grief, Sadness, and Depression

- slow speech
- frequent pauses
- sighing
- crying

Control

- increase in speed or volume of speech when the interviewer tries to talk
- increase in speed or decrease in volume of speech when discussing embarrassing topics

Coldness and Distance

- not smiling
- little or no eye contact
- removing corrective glasses or wearing sunglasses
- closed posture (leaning back, arms folded across chest, or legs crossed high up)

Warmth and Openness

- smiling
- making eye contact
- removing sunglasses
- open posture (leaning forward, uncrossed legs, and arms not folded)

Interest and Attention

- timely "mmhmms"
- appropriate head nods (Both "mmhmms" and head nods work best when done occasionally. They become distracting when done too much.)

Hearing Difficulty

- head turned to one side
- staring at your lips

DEVELOPING A POSITIVE RELATIONSHIP

When talking with a worker, persons in crisis often wonder how much they should reveal about themselves. Although they want assistance in solving problems, they may distort or omit aspects of the situation in order to protect private information.

A positive relationship between the client and the worker can decrease distortion and increase open sharing. Such frank communication becomes more likely if the client feels understood, senses that the worker cares, and believes that the intervenor can be trusted. Consequently, a fundamental task in crisis intervention is to establish rapport by demonstrating the following three interpersonal skills: *empathic understanding* of the client's emotions and thoughts, *warm positive regard* for the individual's worth as a human being, and *genuineness* in what one says to the person. Those three interpersonal skills, identified by Carl Rogers, have long been recognized as being a fundamental part of crisis intervention (e.g., Lester, 2005a, 2005b).

Empathy is the cornerstone of a positive relationship. An individual generally finds it easier to communicate with someone who demonstrates understanding. The key word in the prior sentence is *demonstrates*. Empathy involves both sensitivity to the client's feelings *and* the ability to communicate one's perceptions to that person. Such communication is recognized as a fundamental aspect of crisis intervention (e.g., Joiner et al., 2007). Worker empathy has been shown to be positively and significantly related to a variety of productive outcomes during the interaction, such as individuals becoming less sad, helpless, hopeless, confused, depressed, and desperate (Mishara et al., 2007b). Workers can best convey empathy by working on accurately understanding the client and then reflecting the person's thoughts and feelings.

When interacting with an empathic worker, clients often become better able to examine issues in detail. Such contemplation is frequently a prerequisite for effective behavior change.

Nonpossessive warmth means accepting others as human beings, separate from any evaluation of their behavior. The goal is to view clients as unique individuals with their own values and experiences.

A nonjudgmental attitude is the key to warmth. When clients perceive the worker is not judging their disclosures, they feel less threatened and are less likely to make excuses for behavior. Instead they become more willing to explore issues and consider alternatives.

Accepting what another person says is not the same as expressing agreement. It simply means recognizing that clients have a right to their own ideas, feelings, and values.

In most instances persons in crisis are responsible for their own behavior; consequently, workers do not try to dominate clients. Instead, the demeanor of an intervenor who communicates warmth usually conveys the following message: "I care about you. I hope things work out for you. But I am not going to tell you what to do."

Occasionally, workers encounter persons they do not agree with, like, or believe. Such feelings are a natural part of being human. When intervenors discover they are reacting in a judgmental way, they must recognize their prejudicial attitudes and consider the source of their feelings. If this introspection suggests that one has been overly hasty in evaluating the person or has stereotyped the client, then one should suspend judgmental conclusions until there is more information.

All of us experience instances, however, in which we believe our adverse reactions are justified. In such a situation, one option is to focus on the job of assisting in the client's clarification of issues, consideration of alternatives, and development of plans. Although a good relationship may be difficult to achieve, it is important to continue to be honest and to remember that clients are responsible for their own behavior.

Empirical evidence suggests that well-trained crisis workers demonstrate extra care in following accepted crisis intervention techniques when they encounter clients with whom they disagree (France, 1975a; Kalafat, Boroto, & France, 1979). "Playing it by the book" is a legitimate response to a negative personal reaction toward a client.

Workers must know their own feelings and must beware of prejudices. An inappropriate way of handling a judgmental attitude is to deny its existence. When interviewers refuse to recognize their own prejudices they may unintentionally communicate disapproval through their verbal and nonverbal behavior.

Warmth means being accepting and nonjudgmental. Nevertheless, a crisis worker must also respond as a rational person who has common sense. Ultimately, the worker may have to be a source of feedback for what is reasonable and realistic. Although an intervenor should recognize a client's emotions and beliefs, the crisis worker must also encourage the person to consider the consequences of careless behaviors or unreasonable ideas. For instance, if a client overlooks major aspects of the situation, the interviewer should bring those topics into the discussion.

Such input from the intervenor ought to be delivered in a caring and supportive way. Empirical research (Waldron, Turner, Barton, Alexander, & Cline, 1997) has shown that when therapists are judgmental, dogmatic, controlling, or condescending, clients tend to have poorer adjustment following therapy.

Genuineness requires that workers mean what they say. It does not compel interviewers to share everything they are thinking, although it does oblige them to be honest in what they do say to a client. Behavior displayed by genuine workers is a real aspect of themselves and not part of an intervenor facade.

None of us are perfect, and one sign of a genuine worker is being ready to admit one's mistakes. When interviewers do not hear or do not comprehend a client's statement it is better to say, "I didn't understand what you just said" and to ask for clarification rather than to pretend the client has been heard clearly and understood.

Another aspect of being genuine is never making a promise you or your organization cannot keep. Crisis intervenors must be willing to admit the limitations of their involvement, and they must work within those limits.

Genuineness fosters rapport even when the truth may not be what clients want to hear. If the individual believes the worker is being straightforward the person is more likely to trust the intervenor, and it becomes easier to discuss the situation in an open manner.

PROBLEM SOLVING

The central task of crisis intervention is guiding the client through a series of problem-solving steps. Intervenors accomplish this essential activity by using both good communication skills and the rapport of a positive relationship. Throughout the interaction workers should be honest, patient, and caring. And they should frequently offer fresh, jargon-free summaries of client messages.

Problem solving can be seen as having the following three phases: exploring the situation, considering alternatives, and developing a plan.

Exploration

The first phase involves exploring the circumstances and determining how the client is feeling. Some refer to this endeavor as *ventilation*–a metaphor meaning the open expression of emotions and thoughts.

An excellent way to begin is by encouraging clients to share whatever concerns them. Although the most important issue sometimes is not the one clients choose to discuss first, intervenors should avoid interruptions and should rely on active listening during the early going. For example, making a request such as, "Tell me your reason for contacting us" or "What led to you coming in today?"–then letting the client talk–is often an efficient method for generating a large amount of information.

As originally noted by Caplan (1964), when exploring pressures the client faces, workers should encourage the person to describe specific events and examples. Intervenors usually can elicit a detailed account by using reflection and a judicious amount of interrogation.

Individuals overwhelmed by crises sometimes display muddled thinking. When that happens the worker may need to encourage the person to focus on one or two topics. For instance, if a client has trouble identifying a specific precipitating event it may be productive to explore the person's functioning in important areas such as career and family roles.

EXAMPLE.
Worker: What led you to come in this morning, Mrs. Baker?
Sarah Baker: I just can't sleep. I toss and turn all night, then I'm tired all day at work. I feel like I'm becoming a zombie.
Worker: You're feeling exhausted, and you need to get your rest at night.
Sarah: That's right. I just can't stand going on like this anymore. It's getting so that I feel tired no matter what I'm doing.
Worker: Not sleeping is exasperating. It sounds like there was a time when you weren't having trouble sleeping.
Sarah: There was–but not for the last three weeks. I just wish I knew what started it. I've tried to figure out the reason for it, but I just keep drawing blanks.
Worker: Well, let's work some more on that. Think back to three weeks ago and tell me how things were going at work and at home around that time.
Sarah: Let's see–that was the middle of October. Well, my job was going OK–

I'm a teller and my responsibilities haven't changed in the last six months. At home I've just been trying to keep up with the housework.
Worker: Working at the bank and keeping the household running sounds like quite a job.
Sarah: I guess I'm managing. Of course, it was a lot easier before my husband got so busy as a rescue squad volunteer. He used to help out at home with the dishes and the vacuuming. Now since he's become a shift supervisor he says he doesn't have time to do those things anymore.
Worker: When did you have to assume those additional responsibilities?
Sarah: Well it was around a month ago when he got promoted, and a few days after that when he decided to cut back at home.
Worker: About the same time you started having trouble sleeping.
Sarah: Yeah. I guess that's right. I never put the two together. But it's silly to lose sleep over having to do the dishes. And besides, I think it's good for him to do what he's doing with the rescue squad.
Worker: There are quite a few sacrifices you seem to be making for the good of the rescue squad.
Sarah: Well, I am doing more housework. Really though, I guess I miss him being gone three evenings a week instead of just one.
Worker: You feel left out.
Sarah: I just wish he would be as considerate of me as he is of them. I don't mean I want him to quit–I just wish they weren't quite so important to him.
Worker: You want to be sure you are important to him.
Sarah: Yeah. . . .
DISCUSSION OF SARAH BAKER'S CRISIS. When Sarah could not identify a reason for her sleeplessness the worker asked her to discuss her roles at work and at home. The resulting description of her household duties proved to be a fruitful area.

While exploring the nature of the situation, workers should be sure to reflect the client's feelings. (Failing to address negative feelings bypasses one of the primary motivations for change.) After giving the unpleasant feelings center stage, the focus can later move to considering adaptive ways of dealing with the sources of those distressing emotions.

The intervenor should encourage the client to discuss important events in conjunction with the behaviors and emotions they evoke. Such discussion moves the interaction toward the goal of the exploration phase, which is to summarize a logical sequence of events and responses, thereby clarifying the recent occurrences that have resulted in the crisis state. When examined in this way, the ineffective behavior and intense emotions associated with the crisis are no longer bewildering to the client. Instead, they can be seen as human responses to intense pressure.

Since the exploration phase concentrates on immediate concerns, workers should not focus on personality development. It is fruitless to address ingrained behavior patterns for which modification would be an arduous task. As clinicians have asserted (e.g., Leenaars, 2004), the goal in crisis intervention is not to reshape the client's personality. Instead, the identified problem needs to be one that appears amenable to change.

Although the client initially may have described the problem in one way, during the exploration phase the worker may need to assist the person in reformulating the difficulty. For example, defining Sarah Baker's concern as changes in the relationship with her husband was a reformulation of the problem she originally described as sleeplessness.

An accurate conceptualization of the difficulty is a prerequisite for efficient problem solving. The concern should be described in a way that makes it appear manageable, and the description needs to make sense to the client in light of recent experience.

As Chapter 1 defined the term, there is no *crisis* unless the client perceives a danger or a loss. In line with this viewpoint, several crisis services espouse the philosophy that the person making contact is the client. Even if the request for assistance is initiated on behalf of another, the individual initiating contact is the person with whom the worker begins the problem-solving process. Often the resulting plan involves interaction between the center and the supposed person at risk. In a significant number of cases, however, the third party fails to perceive a hazard that requires intervention, and the problem-solving activity reverts to the initiator of the contact. This scenario highlights the importance of a traditional counseling concept–*ownership* of the problem. A client must "own" a problem if there is to be any progress; individuals will not work on solving difficulties for which they deny responsibility or involvement.

Problem exploration should last as long as important facts and feelings continue to emerge. Workers need to move the discussion toward new considerations if the interaction seems to be going in circles and focusing on material that already has been covered. Often such cycling indicates that enough issues have been explored and that it is time to move on to the next phase.

By the end of the exploration stage emotions should have been recognized and related to recent events. In addition, the client and worker should now share a mutual understanding of existing pressures, as well as changes desired in those circumstances. Once the central challenges of the situation are recognized, it is time to begin deciding what to do about them.

Considering Alternatives

After the exploration phase has identified aspects of the crisis that can be modified and outcomes that are preferred, the worker leads the client through a fresh consideration of options and their probable consequences. The goal is to discover a few possibilities that are likely to produce the desired results.

As alternatives are considered, positive emotions such as confidence and hope may develop. When clients display such feelings, it is important to recognize them. Not only does such recognition contribute to creating an atmosphere of realistic optimism, but it can also have other effects. For example, Barbara Frederickson has described the "broaden-and-build theory of positive emotions," for which there is empirical support (e.g., Fredrickson & Branigan, 2005; Fredrickson, Tugade, Waugh, & Larkin, 2003; Tugade, Fredrickson, & Barrett, 2004). She maintains that positive emotions enhance coping by facilitating efforts at broadening thinking and building resources. While experiencing positive feelings, thinking tends to be creative, flexible, and inclusive. Rather than closing doors on possibilities, the person tends to want to explore a variety of alternatives. Having considered an array of options, the individual is prepared to make informed choices and to initiate actions that can have long-lasting adaptive consequences. The powerful effects of positive emotions can speed recovery from a crisis and can increase the likelihood of the episode becoming a growth experience.

With regard to helping the client focus on options, often there is a natural progression from exploration to a consideration of possible solutions. In some cases, however, there needs to be a decision regarding what aspect of the crisis to tackle first. Two principles can be helpful in making that decision:

- First, it is best to divide problems into manageable segments. Small steps increase the likelihood of favorable outcomes and provide a sense of accomplishment at the completion of each task. Such systematic organization of efforts often adds structure to the person's life and may be a welcome relief from the chaos of recent events.
- Second, it is productive to begin with a difficulty that is real, yet has a good chance of being resolved with relative ease. Focusing on a problem that allows immediate progress often leads to an early success experience. When clients encounter such concrete evidence that they can influence events, the usual results are enhanced self-confidence and a renewed sense of control.

Once the worker and client select a problem, there are three open questions the intervenor should consider asking. Each of the questions can be modified to take into account specifics of what is being discussed. What must not be modified is changing any of these initial open questions into a closed question. Closed questions should also be avoided in any follow-up intended to generate options. For example, it might be much better to ask, "What actions on your part have encouraged the kind of atmosphere you want in the relationship?" rather than "Do you want to stay in the relationship?" Asking such a closed question when pulling for options implies the issue is binary, which may oversimplify matters into a false dichotomy.

Here are the three open questions that can serve as starting points for generating options.

- *"What have you tried so far to deal with _____?"*

It is enlightening to review past attempts at coping with the difficulty. Although failures can be recognized, the emphasis needs to be on efforts that have shown some promise. For example, as a follow-up question you might eventually ask, "With regard to _____, what resources have been helpful and still might have more to offer?"

A related strategy is to survey coping techniques the person has used to address similar issues in the past. (This is an essential activity if the individual claims nothing has worked in the present crisis.) For example, you might ask, "When things were going well with regard to _____, what were you doing to encourage that success?" Occasionally it might also be appropriate to focus on the prevention side of that topic, for instance, "When dealing with _____ in the past, what have been some tendencies you have needed to guard against?"

If a client acknowledges that difficult situations have been handled before, there is the implication that the current predicament can also be dealt with successfully. Such a review of past triumphs changes the focus away from the exploration phase emphasis on what has been lost or changed, to a more upbeat recognition of personality strengths that the individual retains in spite of the crisis. Thus, without offering any false reassurance, a problem that is perceived as all-embracing and overwhelming can be circumscribed and placed within the context of life's stable elements.

Discovering successful efforts and recognizing current assets may enhance the client's self-esteem while also providing valuable problem-solving information. As in the exploration phase, it is a good idea to identify concrete behavioral examples.

- *"What have you thought about trying?"*

After surveying past problem-solving approaches, the worker may need to discover other strategies the client has considered. These are ideas the person has thought about but has not actually attempted.

• *"Right now, what other possibilities come to mind?"*

Having surveyed past attempts and ideas, the intervenor may put moderate pressure on the client to generate new options. If your initial attempt with this third question does not generate any promising alternatives, there are related questions you can ask. Here are three. (1) "Imagine it is impossible for you to do anything we have discussed so far. What would be some other options?" (2) "Imagine you had no 'history' or 'baggage' to deal with. What might you be free to do?" (3) "What would happen if you just kept on doing what you are doing now?"

An additional variation on the third considering-alternatives question is brainstorming, in which the person identifies multiple possibilities in rapid succession without critically evaluating any of them. In my own experience, I have found brainstorming to be an effective technique with adolescents. They often seem to enjoy naming outrageous alternatives, with the result being increased rapport derived from the nonjudgmental atmosphere of the discussion.

When using the considering-alternatives questions it is important to recognize them as tools. Their purpose is to generate options. There is no need to continue with the questions once sufficient possibilities have been identified. If the intervenor decides to use the three questions, though, it is important to ask them in order. For example, do not ask the second question unless the first question has already been explored.

Notice that there has been no mention of intervenors offering possible solutions. I believe suggestions have their place in crisis intervention, although only after the intervenor has made a concerted effort to get the client to generate options.

If the crisis worker has a viable alternative in mind that the client has not mentioned, it can be presented for consideration. When the option is one used by a previous client, I sometimes use the following sort of introduction: "Recently I worked with an individual who had a situation similar to the one you are facing now. That person tried. . . ." I then describe the coping attempt and its resulting outcome.

The goal of the considering alternatives phase is to identify two or three promising options—or, as Chip and Dan Heath (2013) say, until the person falls in love at least two times. For alternatives that are to be closely examined, workers should encourage the client to describe the likely positive and negative outcomes associated with each idea. Positives include what might be gained by the action with regard to this and other issues, and negatives include what it might cost in terms of effort, resources, or lost opportunities. Such examinations should be open, with no pressure to make a snap decision on what course to take. Chip and Dan Heath (2013) cite research indicating the best options tend to be ones that promote desirable conditions and prevent undesirable ones. The most meaningful conditions to promote and prevent are ones that will have important residual ripples well into the future.

Another option-evaluation strategy the Heath brothers (2013) suggest is to ask, "What would need to be true in order for this possibility to be a good idea?" Responses to that question can also lead to developing a plan for implementation that incorporates "rumble strips."

Most of us have been on roads that have rumble strips. Sometimes they are on the edge of a traffic lane, sometimes they are on the center line, and sometimes they are on the approach to an intersection. Their purpose is to get our attention and to encourage us to ask ourselves, "Is this what I want to be doing?" Within the context of problem solving, rumble strips often are deadlines or other boundary markers, but there are many possibilities. For example, let's say a young woman has decided to work on improving her relationship with her boyfriend. She has concluded that a tendency she needs to guard against is making negative assumptions about motivations for his actions. If working on the relationship is to be successful, she will need to avoid jumping to negative conclusions about motivations for his behavior. For example, if she finds herself believing he did not like a meal because he failed to request additional servings, her negative attribution for his behavior could be a rumble strip for asking herself, "Am I inappropriately jumping to a conclusion that he did not like the meal."

During the considering alternatives phase it can be perfectly acceptable to merge options into a new hybrid possibility or for the client to develop a new of way of conceptualizing an issue and what to do about it. For instance, in response to the previously mentioned question of, "What actions on your part have encouraged the kind of atmosphere you want in the relationship?" a young man might realize that he has never really thought about the sort of atmosphere he wants in the relationship. One result of that insight could be a plan to identify qualities he wants, as well as those the other person desires.

When discussing options, clients may display a wide range of emotions, including doubt, impulsiveness, and dependency. Some seek to avoid the anxiety associated with decision making by rejecting all alternatives; others handle the stress by impulsively grasping the first option discussed; and some seek to avoid responsibility by asking the worker to decide what should be done. The potential difficulties of rejecting all possibilities (known as the "Why Don't You, Yes But" game in Transactional Analysis terminology), impulsiveness, and dependency can be handled by firmly encouraging the client to consider anticipated pros and cons of the major alternatives. This approach usually results in potential difficulties being pinpointed and adaptive choices being highlighted, without the worker making decisions for the client.

Nevertheless, when the crisis worker has knowledge of stumbling blocks that clients may encounter, it is appropriate to share the information with them. For example, "Because of the waiting list at the mental health center, it will be two months before you can see a therapist there. You may want to consider other counseling resources."

A potential solution must be consistent with the person's values, beliefs, and personality if the client is expected to follow through with the strategy. The most carefully designed plan is worthless if the individual is not committed to implementing it. Sooner or later the client will decide not to follow an unwanted course of action; sometimes that decision is made during the session and other times it occurs when the time comes for implementing the strategy.

If a client needs assistance in thinking through an option, the worker may want to consider role-playing, a long-standing cognitive-behavioral technique for investigating potential problem-solving approaches. By participating in such pretend scenarios, the person can consider how practical an option seems to be and can discover areas in need of further planning.

Clients can role-play themselves and they can also play the parts of other persons involved in the situation. The latter technique is based on the Gestalt Therapy "no gossiping" rule that says one cannot talk about a person who is not present (Perls, 1970). Consequently, the client imagines the other person is in the room, talks to the individual, supplies a predicted response, and essentially holds a "conversation" with the person. Sometimes called the "empty chair" technique, empirical research (Shahar et al., 2012) has demonstrated that the approach is an effective therapeutic strategy. In my own experience, I have found the technique to be especially helpful in making issues concrete and in getting the client to view the circumstances from others' perspectives. By considering those additional viewpoints, the person often becomes better able to decide upon a course of action.

EXAMPLE.
Worker: You say you are going to break off the relationship with your boyfriend. Let's pretend we are at your place, he has just arrived, and he is standing at your door. What are you going to say to him?
Nancy: I would tell him . . .
Worker: Remember we're pretending he is standing at the door. Talk to the door as if you were talking to him.
Nancy: David, how could you leave town for a week and not tell me where you were going? I heard you went back to Memphis and were seeing your old girlfriends. Well, if you think you can come back to me, you can forget it!
Worker: Now go stand at the door and pretend you are David.
Nancy: (at the door) Let me come in and tell you what happened.
Worker: Now stand next to your chair and respond to him as yourself.

Nancy: (standing next to her chair) You can just stay right where you are and tell me.

Worker: OK, Nancy, let's stop pretending now. It sounds like you really mean it about not taking him back.

Nancy: I do mean it. I've had it with him. He can't treat me like this and expect to come back.

Worker: What do you think he expects?

Nancy: He probably expects me to back down. I guess he thinks I can't make it without him.

Worker: If you don't take David back will you be able to get along without him?

Nancy: I know it will be rough for a time. I will be all right though.

Worker: It seems as though you expect David will try to change your mind. Let's do some more pretending. What else might you say to him?

Nancy: (standing next to her chair) David how could you just pick up and leave for a week and not tell me anything? I heard you were in Memphis running around with some of your old girlfriends. Well, you can forget it if you think you're coming back to me!

Nancy: (at the door) Come on. Let me in, and I'll explain it all to you.

Nancy: (standing next to her chair) You just stay where you are and tell me.

Nancy: (at the door) You know how I get the urge to travel sometimes. I tried to call you, but either the line was busy or you weren't available. Come on, Nancy. You know I don't care about anyone but you. Let me come inside.

Worker: Let's stop pretending. If David said that, how would you respond?

DISCUSSION OF NANCY BROWN'S CASE. The worker used the "empty chair" approach to role playing (although in this situation the client was standing). The exercise clarified Nancy's commitment to her decision and helped her consider issues that might result from her choice.

Empirical research (Dunkel-Schetter, Folkman, & Lazarus, 1987) has found that persons experiencing highly stressful situations often receive more social support than those in low-stress circumstances, and crises often are resolved with the help of friends and family members. But those individuals can also be part of the problem, as demonstrated in Nancy Brown's case. So before including others in a plan, the intervenor should assess their degree of involvement in the person's difficulties. Such exploration is crucial, according to experienced clinicians (e.g., Leenaars, 2004).

Many individuals who contact crisis services already are receiving psychotherapy or other mental health treatment. An important person in these clients' lives is the therapist. When the client is in therapy, the crisis worker and the therapist should not work at cross-purposes. To this end, ethical guidelines (e.g., American Psychological Association, 2002) note that one should discuss the multiple-intervenor issue with the client and that it may be appropriate to contact the other clinician.

When a crisis intervention program is part of a mental health center, there can be close collaboration with other center components in developing treatment plans for clients already receiving assistance. Although such coordination should be a top priority, maintaining lines of communication can be difficult at times. For example, the clinical director of one mental health center mandated that crisis workers handle all night and weekend contacts involving center clients without contacting therapists.

Workers are likely to meet with varied success when they attempt to consult professionals who are not associated with the crisis organization. The next two examples, both involving psychiatrists, demonstrate the range of attitudes that exist.

In one case a psychiatrist phoned a crisis service in the middle of the night and stated that a patient had called his answering service, saying she was going to kill herself. (It turned out that the woman was in therapy with another psychiatrist who was on vacation, and the physician requesting assistance was "covering" his colleague's patients.)

The crisis team did an outreach to the client. When the next shift came on duty at the center, a worker attempted to contact the physician who had made the referral. He was "not available" and the crisis staff member left a message. Later the physician's receptionist called and said, "Doctor _____ has no information on your patient."

In another case (Harold Barber described in Chapter 1), the client produced a prescription bottle that listed the name of a psychiatrist in a city one hundred miles away. A worker called the physician's home number, and the doctor took time to discuss the client with the worker, even though it was a Sunday afternoon. Although the psychiatrist had seen Harold only once, the information he provided proved to be valuable in developing a treatment plan.

The intervention with Harold Barber also is an example of a case involving psychoactive drugs. As described earlier, Harold received antipsychotic medication due to the degree of his personality disorganization. Although medicine was appropriate in Harold's case, whenever psychoactive medication is considered, it is an option that should be carefully examined. Unfortunately such thoughtful consideration is sometimes absent. Psychiatrist Douglas Puryear (1979) asserted that the most frequent misuse of psychoactive medication is the prescription of drugs that are not medically necessary. In his opinion, medical practitioners should beware of too often prescribing drugs in response to frustration, unhappiness, moderate anxiety, and other "normal" emotions. Rather than being deficient in their levels of psychoactive chemicals, Puryear says individuals experiencing such unpleasant emotions are lacking human caring and support; they don't need a prescription; what they do need is someone who will listen and will assist them in confronting their problems.

By the end of the second problem-solving phase the interviewer and client should have discussed two or three options in detail and should have considered the likely advantages and disadvantages associated with those possibilities. Although none of the alternatives may be perfect, the final task is to choose one option, or a combination of several possibilities, and plot a course that has a good likelihood of success.

Developing a Plan

The goal of the first crisis intervention contact is the development of a strategy for coping with the crisis. This objective is the reason for all of the worker's efforts regarding communication, rapport building, and problem solving.

When clients have faith in the plan that is developed, they experience fewer negative emotions because they devote much of their mental and physical energy toward accomplishing tasks they believe will be productive. This positive activity can also have the following beneficial effects: *order* can come to what has been a chaotic situation as clients work on a logical series of tasks; a sense of *self-control* and enhanced *self-esteem* can result when clients attribute tangible progress to their own efforts; and realistic *hope* can grow as they plan courses of action, then experience success.

These beneficial effects can result from productive efforts that focus on relatively small aspects of the situation. An end to the stress is not a prerequisite for effective coping. Although, in the best of circumstances, carrying through with the strategy will modify the source of the crisis.

A good plan has four characteristics. These traits make any plan effective, regardless of the strategy's specific details. For example, if ten workers were to intervene with the same hypothetical client they might develop half a dozen different plans. All of those plans would be effective if they had the following traits:

(a) The plan should be *negotiated*, not dictated. It is more likely that the tasks will be consistent with the individual's personality, values, and attitudes if the plan is the result of collaboration, rather than being a mandate from the worker. Clients should not leave the interaction feeling that they have been pressured toward a certain direction; instead they need to come away believing that they have chosen a course of action. As demonstrated by a review of empirical literature (Deci & Ryan, 1987), compared to coercion, perceived self-control has a variety of advantages, including less anxiety, more optimism, higher self-esteem, and—most importantly—greater persistence in attempting to implement the plan.

(b) Although it is acceptable to have some long-term goals, most of the plan should focus in the *present.* It ought to be possible for the client to start implementing the plan today or tomorrow. The focus in crisis intervention is on immediate problems that are going to be resolved one way or another within a matter of weeks. Strategies will fail if they depend upon distant events, such as long waiting lists or appointments scheduled months into the future.

(c) The plan needs to be a series of *concrete* steps directed toward problem resolution. Tasks should be defined in behavioral terms so there will be no doubt about what needs to be done or when each objective has been achieved. The plan should specify the responsibilities of each participant, including the client, the worker, the worker's organization, and other sources of support.

(d) Expectations that are specified in the plan must be *realistic.* In the worker's judgment, it should be likely—not just possible—that the plan will succeed. If planned tasks are to be of any use, participants must be capable of following through with them. For intervenors this means limiting promises to actions that can be accomplished by your own staff members. For clients, an important issue is dependency; some persons in crisis require more assistance than others. Consequently, workers should be as active as is necessary, and they should be willing to allow situational dependency. Although the intent is not to treat clients as though they were incompetent, neither should intervenors deny clients an important source of support. Crisis workers need to take a middle road; they should be willing to provide all of the assistance that is needed, without performing tasks that clients could do themselves.

To the extent possible, attempts should be made to identify difficulties that are likely to be encountered in implementing the plan. Through discussion or role playing, the intervenor and client can look for trouble spots and can modify the plan as necessary. This "anticipatory planning" prepares the client to expect difficulties so that when the person encounters roadblocks, they do not come as a complete surprise.

Although the chances of positive outcomes increase when the worker and client engage in anticipatory planning, devise small steps, and follow other effective problem-solving guidelines, a client *must* be motivated in order for crisis intervention to be successful. Most persons in crisis are willing to work toward problem resolution, although the commitment of some individuals may be questionable. When the latter is the case, the intervenor can assess the client's motivation for adaptive change by examining several areas:

• Past effort to deal productively with the crisis usually indicates higher motivation than an absence of adaptive coping attempts.
• Client-initiated contacts tend to be more productive than requests for as-

sistance resulting from pressure by others.

- The client offering ideas during the interaction suggests more interest than does an inability to generate options.

If the desire for crisis intervention seems questionable a worker may want to make the first step of the plan one that can be easily achieved by the client and, at the same time, can be accomplished only by the client. When the person follows through, subsequent contacts can build on that initial success.

EXAMPLE. Carol Patterson called the Council on Aging in order to obtain information on how to receive a psychiatric evaluation. Since it was a holiday, the office was closed, and she heard a recorded message that gave the number of the crisis center. She called the crisis intervention program and told the worker that she needed a psychiatric evaluation in order to convince her landlord that she was sane. Carol claimed he was trying to evict her because he believed she was "mentally off" and too messy. She reported that a year earlier she had moved from a twelve-room house into her current four-room apartment. Although she said she had sold "most" of her furniture, she believed she had kept more than she needed. In addition, she said she usually felt too tired to clean when she arrived home from work.

Apart from her difficulties with the landlord, Carol also reported problems with her employer for whom she had worked seventeen years. She said her supervisor was trying to make her quit, even though she only had a short time until she was eligible for retirement.

With Carol's permission the worker called her priest who had known her for ten years. He said both her apartment and the yard behind it were full of junk and infested with roaches. Several months earlier she had agreed to allow the church maintenance worker to throw away some of her excess possessions. When the man arrived, however, she refused to allow him to remove anything. Her priest said the landlord and the justice of the peace had arranged for her to be evicted on a date that now was one week away. He also reported they had agreed not to evict Carol if (1) she was receiving mental health assistance, and (2) the apartment was clean.

The worker and his partner made an outreach to Carol's apartment in order to further evaluate the situation. Behind her part of the building was a very large, neatly stacked pile of junk; it was indeed an eyesore, especially to the residents of neighboring apartments. Carol answered the door but refused to allow the crisis team inside. She said it was too messy and so crowded that there was no place to sit down. Carol remained guarded but polite during the brief discussion with the workers.

Subsequent conversations with the landlord and the justice of the peace confirmed her priest's account of their positions.

The first step in the plan developed with Carol was for her to come to the mental health center for a psychiatric evaluation. The worker scheduled an appointment that was two days later.

She arrived at the appointed time and received the psychiatric evaluation. The psychiatrist perceived no mental health problem and encouraged Carol to cooperate in allowing her priest to have her apartment cleaned.

Further contacts among the crisis staff, Carol, and her priest resulted in a plan that called for a group of church members to clean her apartment on Saturday. This time when the cleaning day arrived, Carol allowed the work to proceed.

By the eviction deadline her apartment and yard were sufficiently neat so that her landlord allowed her to stay. The final step in the plan was for Carol and her priest to hold further discussions centering on her problems at work. DISCUSSION OF CAROL PATTERSON'S CASE. The plan was *negotiated.* Although the worker and Carol agreed that her job difficulties were important, they decided to focus on the more pressing issue of her impending eviction. The initial step in the plan was to obtain what Carol had first requested—a psychiatric evaluation. This task also served as a test of her motivation.

Although some of Carol's behavior certainly was eccentric, changing her personality traits was not the intent of the intervention. Instead, the plan focused on her *immediate* difficulties, with the paramount goal being the prevention of her eviction. Speed was essential if Carol was to keep her apartment; the necessary tasks had to be completed within one week.

The plan was simple and *specific.* The first step was to obtain a psychiatric evaluation, and the second task was to have Carol's apartment cleaned.

Early in the intervention it became apparent that any *realistic* chance of success would require a high degree of activity on the part of the crisis staff. The first hurdle was arranging a psychiatric evaluation. Initially, the worker only promised to try setting up an appointment, since it normally took from three to eight weeks to obtain such service at the mental health center. After negotiating with three different mental health representatives, the worker finally obtained a satisfactory appointment time.

Having succeeded in arranging mental health assistance, the next step was to persuade Carol to allow the cleaning of her apartment. With the "prestige suggestion" of the psychiatrist setting the stage, Carol agreed to let her priest arrange for the cleaning to be done. The worker previously had cleared this strategy with the priest who then organized a group of parishioners to accomplish the gargantuan task.

Although the intervention was active, it was as unobtrusive as possible. After the first two steps were completed, the worker arranged for subsequent support to come from Carol's priest who already was part of her social network.

INTERVENTIONS INVOLVING LONG-STANDING ISSUES SUCH AS ALCOHOL AND OTHER DRUGS[1]

In a study of psychiatric emergency services in nine California general hospitals, Steven Segal and Elisabeth Dittrich (2001) found that for one-third of the patients, substance use contributed to the presenting problem. At times crises can relate to long-standing patterns of maladaptive behavior. When that is the case, crisis intervenors may want to encourage movement toward new adaptive efforts. One way to do that is to use the basic skills already discussed and to consider ideas associated with two concepts—motivational interviewing and stages of change. In the research literature, those concepts are most often associated with alcohol and other drugs, but they can be applied to any chronic difficulty that a person has the potential to change.

Motivational Interviewing

Psychologists William Miller and Stephen Rollnick (Miller & Rollnick, 2002; Miller & Rose, 2009) have investigated and advocated a style of intervention they call motivational interviewing. Their approach puts the focus on what the person with the difficulty has to say. In fact, *expressing empathy* (which often can be done through reflection) is the first principle of their technique.

Here is an example of empathy with an individual having alcohol-related difficulties. The person says, "My boyfriend and I can't drink around each other. If I drink with him I get very angry. We get in big fights about nothing. One time he called me the wrong name. If I hadn't been drunk, I would have shaken it off. But I really flipped out. I smacked him across the face in front of a lot of people. Then he took me home because I was an embarrassment to both of us." The listener reflects, "Drinking together has led to episodes that you regret."

The second principle is *highlighting differences* between the person's current behavior and the individual's own desires for the future. Two ways of identifying these discrepancies are to reflect remarks that (1) suggest the person recognizes there is a problem, or (2) is concerned about issues related to alcohol or other drugs.

Here is an example that focuses on the existence of a problem. The person says, "On Halloween we got dressed up in costumes and went to a party. In the beginning we were having fun. Then I got drunk. I tried to do something with a girl who had a boyfriend. That was a mistake. The next day I

---

1. Most of this section is taken from *Straight Talk on Alcohol and Other Drugs / a web site for college students* by Kenneth France and Benjamin Dourte (http://www.alcoholandotherdrugs.com).

said I wasn't going to drink anymore. But that only lasted about a month. Then I started getting drunk again." The listener responds by saying, "There are things you've done when drunk that you don't want to do again, so you tried to give up drinking."

A second way to highlight differences is to focus on comments that indicate worry or apprehension the individual is having. For instance, a person says, "I've been arrested for underage drinking a few times. Now I'm nineteen, but I can't drive for another year. I have enough money for a car, but I got slapped with another underage drinking charge. If I get arrested again, I won't be allowed to drive until I'm twenty-four. And I really don't want to wait five years until I can drive. My biggest fear right now is getting another underage drinking charge." The listener reflects, "You dread getting arrested again for drinking."

The third motivational interviewing principle is *avoiding arguments.* Drs. Miller and Rollnick have reviewed the scientific literature on alcohol and other drugs and have concluded that there is no evidence to support the idea that arguing with people helps them to change. On the other hand, there is lots of evidence to support the nonconfrontational approach that motivational interviewing takes.

Rolling with resistance is the fourth principle. With this guideline, Drs. Miller and Rollnick emphasize that it is the other person's problem. Any decision for change is up to that individual. Consequently, reluctance to change is to be expected, and when it occurs, it is simply acknowledged. Rather than trying to push a course of action, motivational interviewing calls for the listener to encourage the other person to generate options and to explore advantages and disadvantages of those possibilities.

The final principle is *supporting self-confidence.* The objective here is to encourage the person to develop a realistic belief in his or her ability to handle challenges and to eventually succeed in making a change. Reflection again comes into play as the listener looks for opportunities to highlight comments that communicate (1) intention to change and (2) optimism about making progress.

Here is an example that focuses on intention to change. "Last month I had two friends killed in a car accident caused by alcohol. They weren't drinking. But their car was hit by a guy who had been drinking. He ran a red light and smashed into them. They died in the hospital later that night due to internal injuries. After that I made a pact with myself—I'm never again going to drive after I've been drinking." The listener reflects, "After the deaths of your friends, you became determined not to get behind the wheel when you're under the influence of alcohol."

The idea of reflecting optimism is shown in the following exchange: "I felt like I was spending too much time partying and that I got out of control too often. Now I don't go out during the week, and I work on the weekends. So

I don't party that much anymore. I work to make money, but I also do it because it takes me out of being tempted with going out every weekend. I've removed myself from that scene and from the people I was around who did that all of the time. When I do go out to have a good time, I don't have to get totally trashed. I can have a couple of drinks and that's it." The listener says, "Your new style feels good, and you believe you can stick with it."

It is possible to encourage motivation to change by understanding thoughts and feelings, highlighting discrepancies, avoiding arguments, rolling with resistance, and supporting self-confidence. Those activities have been examined in empirical research (Miller, 1996; Morgenstern et al., 2012) and have been found to be associated with both decreased client resistance and lasting positive change, whereas confronting clients by disagreeing or arguing with them has been associated with higher client resistance and either lack of positive change or negative change.

Stages of Change

As just noted, sometimes efforts at changing are successful and sometimes they aren't. Intervenor actions can influence change, but ultimately the most important factor is the person's readiness to change—what Miller (1996) has called "making up one's mind." For a number of years, the topic of how individuals intentionally change aspects of themselves has been the focus of research by psychologists James Prochaska, John Norcross, and Carlo DiClemente (1994) and by social worker Janice Prochaska (Prochaska & Prochaska, 1999). James Prochaska's interest in self-change arose out of his anger and disappointment at not being able to help a person who was dependent on alcohol and who frequently was depressed. That person was his father. Mr. Prochaska consistently denied that he had a problem with alcohol. None of his family's attempts to change him were successful, and he refused professional help. When James Prochaska was a junior in college, his father died.

Now, years later, James Prochaska and his colleagues have developed a widely accepted theory of self-change that is relevant to alcohol and other drugs, as well as to many other areas. Regardless of the particular focus of change, the basic elements of the process seem to remain the same. There are stages that individuals tend to go through, and there are different strategies that they tend to use as they pass through the various phases. First, we'll take a look at what Prochaska and his colleagues have to say about the stages of change, and then we'll consider different strategies that can help people to change.

There appear to be six stages of change. Being in one stage does not necessarily mean a person will advance to the next level. When change does occur, though, it usually develops in ways described by the stages.

- *Precontemplation.* Although others may believe that the individual needs to change, a person in the precontemplation stage denies responsibility for these perceived difficulties and intends to continue on the current course. The issues that others see as problems are viewed by the individual as trusted ways of coping and as being under control. Any unwanted patterns that do exist are seen as being caused by others, and they are viewed as being the ones who must change. On occasions when those in the environment successfully pressure the person into new behavior, that change evaporates as soon as the external pressure stops. When others confront the person regarding problematic behavior, the individual may minimize the behavior or may offer rational, but flawed, explanations (although the brighter and more extroverted the person, the more convincing the rationalizing may seem). In addition, negative feelings may be swallowed (internalized)—a trait that is associated with depression. Nevertheless, in the person's mind, the disadvantages of changing outweigh the advantages.
- *Contemplation.* During this stage, the person tries to understand how things got to be the way they are and acknowledges that change is necessary, with the intended effort being in the future. Sidetracking can occur in any of the following ways: requiring certain success before being willing to act, waiting for perfect conditions, or, toward the other extreme, rushing into impetuous action.
- *Preparation.* Now the individual becomes increasingly certain that changing is the right decision and makes final arrangements necessary for taking action, including firming up a specific, realistic plan. Before moving to action, though, the person must decrease the number of disadvantages associated with changing and must increase the number of advantages associated with changing, so that the advantages clearly outweigh the disadvantages. (The rule of thumb is two new advantages for every abandoned disadvantage.)
- *Action.* At this time the individual takes public action. Potential difficulties include the following: inadequate preparation, giving up if there is no quick fix, and, at the opposite end of the continuum, maintaining efforts that are only partially successful.
- *Maintenance.* While gaining strength from a successful new style, the person in the maintenance stage also acknowledges a vulnerability to the old ways. Consequently, the individual makes the sustained effort necessary to avoid brief lapses and to prevent relapses. When a slip occurs, the person should acknowledge it and should make a plan for remedying the situation that led to it. The individual must prepare for and withstand social pressure from others in the environment who continue to act in the old way.

• *Termination.* The old behavior does not tempt the person, who now has no fear of relapse. The individual is confident and comfortable with the new style. Reaching the termination stage is possible for people who have had difficulties with alcohol or other drugs. Research by Prochaska and his associates has shown that 17 percent of former alcohol-dependent persons and 16 percent of former cigarette smokers are in the termination stage. These individuals now completely abstain from use and are no longer tempted by their old habits.

When a relapse occurs in the action or maintenance stages, most individuals return to contemplation or preparation, rather than going all the way back to precontemplation. Here are some facts about relapse.

• A slip does not constitute a relapse.
• Complications are the norm, rather than the exception.
• Among self-changers, 20 percent or less are completely successful on the first try.
• It is normal to recycle several times.
• It is helpful to see recycling as an opportunity to learn from your mistakes.
• Using available support increases your chances of avoiding subsequent relapses.

Strategies for Bringing About Change

In order to start a self-change effort there is only one basic requirement—being open to learning new information. As progress is made through the different stages of change, Prochaska and his colleagues have found that certain strategies tend to become most helpful at different times. Listed below are the stages of change, with the most common strategies listed for each stage. It can be helpful to think about which stage of change a person is in and to consider whether some of the strategies listed for that stage might be appropriate to discuss with the individual.

• *Precontemplation*—information gathering and community involvement.
• *Contemplation*—information gathering, community involvement, expressing feelings, and acknowledging your true values.
• *Preparation*—community involvement, expressing feelings, acknowledging your true values, and making a commitment.
• *Action*—community involvement, making a commitment, using alternatives, dealing with your surroundings, rewarding good effort, and enlisting social support.

- *Maintenance*—using alternatives, dealing with your surroundings, rewarding good effort, and enlisting social support.

In that list of stages and strategies, there are nine different approaches named. Here are brief descriptions of those strategies. The phrase in parentheses is the term that Prochaska and his associates use for the strategy:

- *Information Gathering.* (Consciousness-Raising) (Used during precontemplation and contemplation.) Information gathering involves input from others, such as personal experiences or research findings. It also includes observing, recording, and analyzing your own behavior, thoughts, and feelings. The resulting increased awareness is a prerequisite for meaningful action.
- *Community Involvement.* (Social Liberation) (Used during precontemplation, contemplation, preparation, and action.) Community involvement is tapping public ways in which your environment can be supportive, such as realizing there are others who share similar interests and discovering relevant societal rewards.
- *Expressing Feelings.* (Emotional Arousal) (Used during contemplation and preparation.) Expressing feelings can result from insights you discover, as well as from exposure to real or fictional accounts (movies, television shows, or novels) that touch relevant issues in your life.
- *Acknowledging Your True Values.* (Self-Reevaluation) (Used during contemplation and preparation.) Acknowledging your true values means coming to the heartfelt conclusion that you must change your behavior in order to become the kind of person you want to be.
- *Making a Commitment.* (Commitment) (Used during preparation, action, and maintenance.) Making a commitment involves believing you have what it takes to follow through with the plan you have developed.
- *Using Alternatives.* (Countering) (Used during action and maintenance.) Using alternatives occurs when you think and act in ways that are more productive than your old approach.
- *Dealing With Your Surroundings.* (Environmental Control) (Used during action and maintenance.) Dealing with your surroundings includes the following: identifying challenging situations you must face and preparing to cope with them; avoiding problematic circumstances and people that you can do without; and using physical reminders (notes, lists, or sayings) to help keep you on task.
- *Rewarding Good Effort.* (Rewards) (Used during action and early maintenance.) Ways of rewarding good effort include self-praise and enjoyable consequences that you provide yourself, as well as reinforcers from others.

• *Enlisting Social Support.* (Helping Relationships) (Used during action and maintenance.) Enlisting social support means developing or strengthening relationships with individuals who honestly convey understanding and caring.

REFERRAL

As in Carol Patterson's case, making a referral often is an essential aspect of crisis intervention. Because of the red tape involved in Carol's situation, the crisis worker made the mental health appointment for her. In other instances, it may be appropriate to give the basic information to clients and have them make their own arrangements.

When providing a referral to a community resource, essential facts to give the client include four categories of general information and two kinds of information relevant to the particular individual:

General

- name of the organization or professional;
- address (and directions if needed);
- phone number (and whether the telephone is likely to be answered by a person or by an automated message);
- hours of operation;

Specific

- relevant services offered;
- any restrictions (such as fees, geographical area served, or other eligibility requirements).

All of the information must be correct. It is much better to say, "I don't know," than to make inaccurate statements about a community resource.

Workers making referrals ought to describe relevant services usually provided by the organization or professional, although they should never promise that a specific service will be offered to a particular client. As noted previously, the only promise you can make is one that will be carried out by your own staff. (Remember that in Carol Patterson's case the worker promised to try to arrange a mental health appointment for her.) It is appropriate to discuss community resources in terms of their usual functioning and expected performance. Nevertheless, staff members of other programs always retain their prerogatives, including whether or not to offer assistance, what services to implement, and when services will be delivered.

It is easy for a client to fall between the cracks separating one agency's services from another's. Bureaucratic intricacies, eligibility requirements, and other pitfalls mean the crisis staff's responsibilities do not necessarily end once a referral has been made. If there are problems it may be appropriate for a worker to act as a troubleshooter and advocate. The kind of activity demonstrated in Carol Patterson's case often is necessary if clients are to receive assistance when they need it.

Sometimes referral is the primary objective of the intervention. In these instances, one contact with a follow-up probably is sufficient, although such clients still need to feel that they participated in developing the course of action. Consequently, even when referral is the goal, exploring the problem and considering alternatives may be necessary if the referral is to be one that the client wants and is likely to use.

When the person is not in crisis but requires assistance, referral often is the most appropriate action a crisis worker can take. For example, referral frequently is the goal with psychotic individuals, although reaching that objective may take extra effort. When working with psychotic persons who have schizophrenia or are paranoid, intervenors may find the following tactics to be useful:

- With face-to-face contacts a good way to minimize interfering stimulation is to conduct the session in a quiet room that is free from interruptions—while always having access to immediately available assistance.
- An even, calm voice usually is best.
- It may be helpful to discuss concrete realities on which you both can agree.
- Be willing to offer guidance in directing the conversation while avoiding confrontation as much as possible.
- Do not participate in discussions of fanciful topics. If you can't follow what the person is saying, confess your lack of comprehension.

EXAMPLE. Ben Harrison had a diagnosis of schizophrenia, and he was a patient in the partial hospitalization program of a mental health center. On the morning of the contact, Ben and his parents had argued about whether or not he was going to move out of the family home.

Although he had already rented an apartment, Ben had now decided not to move from his parents' house. But his mother believed she and his father could not stand to have him living with them anymore, and she told him he had to leave. A shouting match ensued, and Mrs. Harrison called the police.

The police officers arrived, perceived no violation of the law, and had the dispatcher call the mental health center crisis service. Since Ben already was a client in the center's partial program, one of the crisis workers talked with his therapist about Ben and about her availability to meet with the family. The team then left the center, met the officers at a convenience store, and spoke with them about the situation. Upon arriving at the Harrison home the team found that Ben had left to go to a nearby restaurant. The workers told the Harrisons they would talk with Ben.

The following interaction took place after one of the workers (wearing a hospital name tag) entered the restaurant and sat down at the rail next to Ben.

Worker: Hello Ben, my name is Ken France. I work with the crisis intervention service.

Ben Harrison: What do you want?

Worker: Your parents are worried about you and they asked me to see how you're doing.

Ben: I just came here to have some breakfast. I have a right to eat where I want. They can't stop me.

Worker: It looks like you have a pretty good breakfast there.

Ben: Yeah. It's usually pretty good here.

Worker: So, you come here often.

Ben: That's right.

Worker: I like their strawberry pie.

Ben: Me too, but I don't get it that often because it costs so much.

Worker: It sounds like you have to watch your finances.

Ben: Don't play games with me! Don't play games with me! You know how much money I have. Don't play games with me!

Worker: Well Ben, I'm sure some of the people at the mental health center know how much money you have, but I don't know about your income.

Ben: I have plenty of money. I have plenty of money. Here, just look at this. (He proceeded to show the worker a checking transaction register listing a balance of about $47,000.)

Worker: You certainly do have a lot of money.

Ben: My father thinks he can tell me what to do. He can't tell me a thing. I've got my own money.

Worker: What are you going to do when you leave the restaurant?

Ben: I'm not going to the hospital! You can't make me go to the hospital! I know my rights. All I'm doing is sitting here eating breakfast, and you can't make me go to the hospital!

Worker: You're right, Ben. I don't know of anything you've done for which you could be put in the hospital against your will.

Ben: I never want to go back there. I never want to go back there. Have you ever had shock treatment? Well I have. Well I have. I tell you it's no fun. I never want to go back there and you can't make me.

Worker: I don't want to take you to the hospital. I just want to see how you are doing.

Ben: I'm doing fine.

Worker: What are you going to do after you leave the restaurant?

Ben: I guess I'll go back to my parents' house.

Worker: Your mom told me that you and your parents had an argument this morning.

Ben: My mother is a wonderful person. She's a wonderful person. I have to stay home to take care of her. My father won't take care of her. I have to stay home.

Worker: She said you had planned to move into an apartment this afternoon but that you had changed your mind.

Ben: I'm not leaving. I have to stay to take care of my mother. She's a wonderful person.

Worker: She seems like a very nice person. Who is your worker at the mental health center?

Ben: Judy Martin.

Worker: How do you like her?

Ben: She's OK.

Worker: I think it might be a good idea for Judy and you and your mom to talk about where you're going to live.

Ben: OK, I'll do that. I'm not leaving home, though, and I'm not going to the hospital.

Worker: I'll ask Judy to give you a call.

Ben: OK.

Worker: When do you think you'll be home?

Ben: I like to have a slow breakfast. This is a nice place.

Worker: It is a nice restaurant. When do you think you'll be leaving?

Ben: I guess in about twenty minutes.

Worker: If it's OK with you, I'll tell your mother that you'll be home in about half an hour.

Ben: That's OK.

Worker: And I'll see if Judy can give you a call later in the morning. If she can't I will be back in touch with you.

Ben: OK.

Worker: Well, I like your choice of restaurants for breakfast. They have good coffee here.

Ben: Yeah, they do.

Worker: Bye, Ben.

Ben: Bye.

DISCUSSION OF BEN HARRISON'S CASE. The purpose of the interaction with Ben was to assess his condition and to determine the most appropriate form of intervention. The exchange focused on concrete matters and avoided confrontation as much as possible. Although Ben was mildly agitated, his condition did not appear to warrant emergency hospitalization. Instead, the most appropriate action seemed to be for him to talk with his therapist from the mental health center's partial hospitalization program. After Ben consented to that plan the workers went back to see his mother and father. The Harrisons agreed that Judy would be a good person to mediate the dispute. Later that morning she met with Ben and his parents.

CLOSING

Following development of the plan it is time to bring the contact to a close. Effective endings require tact and preparation. For example, skillful intervenors stop reflecting and suggest that new topics be saved for a subsequent contact (if those new concerns do not affect the plan already developed).

In preparing for the closing, the intervenor should anticipate a brief recapitulation. This ending summary helps consolidate the session's content and fosters a sense of accomplishment.

The final summary can contain the following components:

- the worker's description of the difficulties, including how different aspects of the situation are related;
- the worker's listing of any questions that remain to be considered;
- the worker's review of decisions reached, combined with a statement that gives credit to the client for progress made;
- the *client's specification* of the tasks in the plan. (It is crucial that the client be the one to describe the plan. Often, this restatement identifies areas that need to be clarified. It also ends the interaction with the client describing a set of circumstances that encourage realistic hope.)

A good way to bring an initial face-to-face contact to a close is to give the client a physical reminder of the session. Examples include the following: agency cards and pamphlets, articles, and written information on resources. Such gifts further reinforce the impression that progress is being made.

SUBSEQUENT CONTACTS

As noted in the previous chapter, one problem-solving interaction often is sufficient, although as many as eight contacts may be necessary. If multiple sessions are part of the plan, some clinicians (e.g., Rudd, Mandrusiak, & Joiner, 2006) advocate negotiating an intervention contract. Such agreements suggest clients are responsible persons, thereby further enhancing self-esteem.

The components of an intervention contract can include the following:

- behavioral goals of the intervention (either the Observation Scales described in Chapter 9 or a more general statement, such as "Our efforts will focus on increasing your skills in managing the family finances");
- the client's responsibilities (such as keeping appointments, openly exploring difficulties, and attempting to implement agreed-upon plans);
- the duties of workers and their organization (such as continuous availability, keeping appointments, actively listening to the client, encouraging problem-solving activity, and maintaining confidentiality);
- the maximum duration of the contract (for example, eight sessions over a period of eight weeks);
- provision for follow-up contact (for instance, "Someone from our program will make a follow-up call to you six weeks after your last session; the purpose will be to see how you are doing").

The primary function of subsequent contacts is to monitor progress in implementing the plan. A good way to begin is with a review of tasks undertaken since the last contact. The worker should praise successful efforts in order to emphasize that progress is taking place. If a client has difficulty perceiving that positive changes are occurring, the intervenor may suggest that the person keep a diary in order to collect evidence that demonstrates the good days are becoming more frequent, while the bad days are decreasing in number.

When a client does encounter difficulties in implementing tasks the worker should explore the unsuccessful coping attempts and should examine possible reasons for the trouble. If necessary, the intervenor and client can revise the plan and specify new tasks. Workers should expect such adaptive alterations to be part of most multiple-session cases.

As efforts toward problem resolution continue, the intervenor should recognize and praise the client's positive characteristics, such as striving, venturing, patience, and tolerance. When unhelpful actions occur, the worker must decide whether it is best to confront or ignore the behavior. Examples of such misguided client effort include (1) maladaptive distortion and denial and (2) manipulative attention-seeking efforts that are disruptive, socially inappropriate, or contrary to the agreed-upon plan.

Crisis intervention clients frequently decide to terminate with little or no warning. Once feelings of distress recede, individuals may believe they have achieved sufficient progress toward resolving difficulties.

When clients fail to keep a scheduled interaction, contacting them can be appropriate. If they desire further services the crisis intervention should continue. When they believe enough progress has been achieved, however, the intervenor should not attempt to force further problem-solving efforts upon them—except for those persons who have entered the withdrawal phase of crisis. In these cases the worker may need to provide additional assistance to prevent life-threatening behavior or to address personality disorganization.

For clients who maintain contact the worker should eventually bring up the topic of termination. There are two events that can signal the need for this discussion—the client believing enough progress has been made or when one interaction remains in the original contract.

Clients have a variety of opinions about termination. Some accept it with no visible reaction while others see it as an important event. When clients believe termination is significant they may interpret it as a loss or view it as an achievement. The latter is more likely when workers use the Observation Scales discussed in Chapter 9.

During the final interview workers should continue to use their usual communication techniques, rapport-enhancing skills, and problem-solving strategies. In addition, intervenors can direct the discussion toward the following four topics: recent effects of the crisis, long-term impact, remaining tasks, and future contact.

- *Recent Effects.* The worker can ask the client (1) to recall the factors that prompted the request for assistance and (2) to describe how those circumstances have changed. This recapitulation is likely to enhance the belief that it is possible to cope with difficult events in life.
- *Long-term Impact.* The intervenor can explore other insights learned and can review newly developed or rediscovered coping skills. Such evidence of positive adaptation can lead to a sense of improved problem-solving abilities and enhanced personal growth.
- *Remaining Tasks.* The interviewer can survey any remaining problem areas, with an emphasis on the client's ability to plan and implement problem-solving strategies.
- *Future Contact.* Although the worker should recognize the client's skills, the door ought to be left open for additional assistance if the need should arise. Also, the intervenor ought to alert the individual about any anticipated follow-up contact (discussed below).

Sometimes clients want to continue using a crisis service for months or years on end. In such situations workers must remember that continuing past eight contacts usually means the interactions no longer constitute crisis intervention.

Three to eight weeks after termination is an appropriate time for a follow-up contact. When an organization uses follow-ups, the worker ought to mention them during the initial interaction and during the termination session (if there is one).

Most follow-ups occur via the telephone, and either clients or workers can initiate them. Having clients call back leaves the responsibility with them and recognizes their competency. Nevertheless, staff members should place the call if appropriate workers are on duty only at certain times or if an expected call has not come in from a particular client.

Experts (e.g., Garland & Zigler, 1993) have noted that follow-up offers benefits for both the client and the crisis intervention program. Client benefits include the following: maintaining motivation to work on tasks agreed upon at termination, assessing the person's current state in relation to the concerns that led to the intervention, and letting the person know that support is available if it should be needed again. Program benefits from follow-up contacts include the following: discovering changes attributed to the intervention, assessing the effectiveness of referrals (if the client received any), and finding out the person's attitude toward the program. Empirical research (Fiester, 1979; Fiester & Fort, 1978) suggests that client satisfaction is primarily related to the following two factors: (1) the perceived degree of problem resolution, and (2) the program's availability and accessibility.

Follow-up contacts are usually short. In just a few minutes the worker can cover the following five areas:

- *Goals.* Check on the intervention goals in terms of progress toward achieving and maintaining them.
- *Adjustment.* Briefly explore the person's current ability to cope with life.
- *Referral.* If a referral was part of the plan, ask the client whether contact was made and whether the requested service was provided.
- *Feedback.* Encourage feedback by asking three questions. What is the person's general opinion of the program? How difficult was it to obtain service from the program? What positive or negative reactions does the individual have to specific aspects of the intervention?
- *The Future.* The worker can end the contact with two comments—an expression of praise for ongoing progress and a statement on the continued availability of support.

SUMMARY

Crisis intervenors use effective communication and a positive relationship to guide clients through a series of problem-solving steps. Workers emphasize client initiative and competence, and they employ the least amount of control necessary.

Interviewers tend to communicate most effectively when they avoid advice, analysis, sympathy, and reassurance, and rely instead on reflection and on a judicious amount of interrogation. In addition to understanding clients' words, intervenors should remember that nonverbal communication can also convey valuable information.

Workers *enhance rapport and trust* by using the interpersonal skills of *empathy, warmth,* and *genuineness*. Crisis intervenors also remember to pair respect for the client with a willingness to provide feedback on what is reasonable and realistic.

The crucial crisis intervention activity of *problem solving* can be seen to have three phases. (1) The first phase is *exploring the person's thoughts and feelings*. After achieving a shared understanding of important issues, the worker and client move to the second phase. (2) *Considering alternatives* involves pulling for options from the client, which can be facilitated by one or more of the following three questions (tailored to the specifics of what is being discussed): *What have you tried . . . ? What have you thought about trying? Right now, what other possibilities come to mind?* After considering several viable possibilities, the intervenor and client move to the final phase. (3) *Developing a plan* involves deciding on a course of action that is *negotiated, focused in the present, specific,* and *realistic.*

When working with individuals who are engaging in long-standing maladaptive behavior which they have the potential to change, it may be appropriate to use techniques associated with motivational interviewing. It can also be helpful to consider the person's stage of change, as well as strategies that have been found to be effective in that stage.

Referral should be part of a plan only when it is appropriate and likely to be used. If information is provided on community resources, it must be complete and accurate.

At the close of a problem-solving session it is productive to review insights, decisions, and plans, then emphasize that the progress made was due to the client's efforts. If subsequent crisis intervention contacts are anticipated, an intervention contract can clarify the purpose and nature of future sessions. During each subsequent interaction the worker should monitor the client's efforts toward implementing the plan. At termination, discussion can include the short- and long-term impact of the crisis, as well as strategies to be used in the future. A good way to close a case is with a follow-up contact— an interaction that demonstrates caring and support for the client while generating valuable feedback for the program.

STUDY QUESTIONS

1. Jennifer has a neighbor who is harassing her. She has become completely exasperated following his latest tactic of ringing a cowbell out-

side her window around 6 a.m. every morning. You advise her to file "disturbing the peace" charges against him. What are the potential hazards you run in giving advice to Jennifer?

2. Among lay persons, what are the most frequently used and least effective responses to a person experiencing difficulties?

3. Respond to the following comment with an open-ended question. "I had a nervous breakdown a couple of years ago, and now I'm afraid it's about to happen again."

4. When is it appropriate to use an inverted funnel sequence of questions?

5. Reflect the content and feelings of the following statement. "I just found out from the doctor that I am pregnant. The father and I broke up a month ago, and if my parents find out they'll kick me out of the house. What should I do?"

6. You are talking with a client who speaks rapidly, changes the topic frequently, and stutters. What feeling might give rise to that nonverbal behavior?

7. How should you respond if a client says to you, "I processed so many creedsteds today, I feel like one myself"?

8. What is the goal of the exploration phase of problem solving?

9. A client says, "I've done everything I can to get my roommate to do her part of keeping the place up, but nothing works." If you are just beginning to consider alternatives what is your response?

10. The client from the previous question eventually says, "I know, I'll just kick her out." You believe that action would not be wise at the present time. What is your response?

11. With her son having received a letter of acceptance from his top-rated college, Karen has been talking to you about the difficulty she will have in meeting future financial obligations on her current salary. She has worked at the same company for ten years and has not had a promotion, although the boss often praises her good performance. Yesterday the company posted an availability notice for a supervisory position. Karen wants to ask for her boss's support in applying for the opening, but she is having misgivings about how to discuss the topic with him. What cognitive-behavioral technique could Karen use to explore possibilities? Describe how you would implement the technique.

12. What is the primary goal you seek to achieve during the initial crisis intervention contact?

13. Imagine that you have just concluded your first contact with the client in questions 9 and 10. Describe the plan that emerged and how it exemplifies the four traits of an effective plan.

14. A client says the following. "After I've been drinking awhile I tend to say things that I later wish I hadn't said. I am much more critical of peo-

ple than I would be if I were sober. But when I'm drunk I don't really care much about how other people feel, so I go ahead and say things that tend to be hurtful. The next day I wish I had kept those thoughts to myself, but the damage has been done and I am in trouble again. Many times I have put myself in predicaments. I've even lost several friends because of my insensitive remarks. I don't really trust myself anymore when I am drinking." Give an example of a response you would make if you were using motivational interviewing. State which of the techniques your response demonstrates.

15. Describe a real example of a person trying to change with regard to issues concerning alcohol or other drugs. State the stage of change represented in your example, as well as the change strategies being used.

16. Assume that a referral is part of your plan for the client in questions 9, 10, and 13. Name the hypothetical community resource and provide all relevant information, as if you were giving it to the client.

17. When you discover you are interacting with a psychotic person, what guidelines do you keep in mind?

18. What would you say at the close of the interaction to the client in questions 9, 10, 13, and 16?

19. During the final summary at the end of a contact who should describe the plan?

20. What is the primary purpose of subsequent contacts?

21. Due to marital difficulties Brian contacted a crisis program several times. Six weeks have gone by since termination, and it is time for the follow-up telephone call that he agreed to receive. What benefit might such a call have for Brian?

Chapter 3

SPECIAL POPULATIONS: INTERVENTIONS ASSOCIATED WITH SUICIDE AND DEATH

Crises may involve death or the possibility of death. Sometimes the issue is suicide, sometimes a terminal illness, or perhaps bereavement. Crisis workers must be prepared to intervene in all of these situations.

The Centers for Disease Control and Prevention define suicide as death resulting from self-directed injurious action associated with any intensity of intent to die as a consequence of the action (Crosby, Ortega, & Melanson, 2011). They define a suicide attempt as nonfatal self-directed behavior that has the potential to injure and is associated with any intensity of intent to die as a consequence of the action. The attempt may or may not actually cause injury. The U.S. Department of Veterans Affairs has also adopted these definitions (Brenner et al., 2011).

Suicidal behavior is recognized as the most frequent mental health emergency (e.g., Bongar & Sullivan, 2013), and the suicide prevention movement has provided much of the impetus for crisis intervention. The American Association of Suicidology operates nationwide evaluation systems for certifying both crisis intervention centers (American Association of Suicidology, 2012) and individual crisis workers (AAS Individual Certification Committee, 2005).

For many crisis intervention programs, 6 to 36 percent of the contacts are likely to involve suicidal persons (e.g., Barber et al., 2004; Cornelius, Simpson, Ting, Wiggins, & Lipford, 2003; Mishara et al., 2007a; Shrivastava et al., 2012). Compared to interventions for other reasons, research indicates that an interview with a suicidal individual tends to be more intense and it tends to last longer (Cawunder & Mohr, 1982; Mishara et al., 2007a). When responding to these clients, workers must use the basic skills discussed in Chapter 2, as well as special assessment and intervention techniques.

SUICIDE LETHALITY ASSESSMENT

Suicide lethality is the risk of the person killing himself or herself in the immediate future. Experts note that since suicidal behavior and suicide are such rare events, accurately predicting them in a specific individual is impossible (Berman, 2006; Berman et al., 2006; Bongar & Sullivan, 2013; Bryan & Rudd, 2006; Jobes, Berman, & Martin, 2005; Kleespies, 2014; Rudd & Joiner, 1998). Nevertheless, estimating the risk of suicide currently existing for a person is possible, and experts (e.g., Berman, 2006; Berman et al., 2006; Bongar & Sullivan, 2013; Bryan & Rudd, 2006; Jobes, Rudd, Overholser, & Joiner, 2008; Kleespies, 2014; Roberts & Yeager, 2005; Witte et al., 2010; Van Orden et al., 2010) agree that assessing the degree of risk is a mandatory activity with suicidal clients. Not to do so violates legal standards of care and is inconsistent with clinical practice guidelines (e.g., Berman, 2006; Berman et al., 2006; Bongar & Sullivan, 2013; Leenaars, 2004; Morris & Minton, 2012). In their current work settings, 54 percent of new professional counselors with master's degrees report judging and responding to risk of client self-harm between twice a month and daily (Morris & Minton, 2012).

Empirical research demonstrates that the factor which best discriminates between individuals who kill themselves in the near future and those who do not is whether the person is thinking about committing suicide (Britton, Ilgen, Rudd, & Conner, 2012; Brent, Perper, Moritz, Allman, et al., 1993; Shafii, Carrigan, Whittinghill, & Derrick, 1985; Trautman, Rotheram-Borus, Dopkins, & Lewin, 1991). This fact, which seems so obvious, sometimes gets lost in discussions of how to identify individuals who are at risk for suicide. Clearly, the single most accurate way of determining if a person is running such a risk is to explore whether the individual is considering suicide.

After conducting an empirical investigation that revealed clinicians overestimated "suicidality" about half the time, Thomas Joiner, David Rudd, and Hasan Rajab (1999) recommended that intervenors pay attention to what the individual says. The authors stated that the person's self-report should be the most important source of information.

Exploring self-perceived risk is strongly supported by Peterson, Skeem and Manchak (2011). Once during the person's hospitalization and once later in the community, researchers asked 147 individuals with a substance use disorder and another mental health diagnosis about their self-perceptions of risk for self-harm during the next two months. Participants rated themselves on a 5-point scale ranging from "no concern" to "greatly concerned" relevant to how much concern they believed their therapists should have about them harming themselves during the next two months. In addition, researchers documented recent self-harm prior to the assessment, obtained scores on the

Brief Symptom Inventory 6-item Depression scale, and ascertained self-harm during the two months after each assessment. Findings included the following. Recent self-harm did *not* predict self-harm during the next two months. For each increase of one point on the BSI Depression scale, there was a 16 percent increase in the likelihood of self-harm during the following two months. What was more impressive, though, was that for each increase of one point in the person's perception of self-harm risk there was a 77 percent increase (controlling for BSI Depression scores) in the likelihood of engaging in self-harm during the next two months. Another finding was that participants who judged there was no risk of self-harm were more often correct than were those who said there was some degree of risk. The authors concluded that the participants' self-perceptions of risk were unsurpassed by any other assessment device with regard to the ability to accurately predict self-harm during the next two months.

Sometimes clients themselves bring up the topic of suicide. In other instances the intervenor may suspect that the person is contemplating self-destruction. Whenever workers have such suspicions, it is appropriate to ask about suicide. For example, during an encounter with a client who communicates a depressed mood, one appropriate response may be to ask, "Are you thinking about killing yourself?"

When intervenors are able to develop good rapport, there is a high correlation between the life-threatening behavior of individuals and their self-reported suicidal intent, as demonstrated in an empirical study by Douglas Robbins and Norman Alessi (1985). These researchers also observed that the reliability of such self-reports may be greatest when the topic of suicide is discussed during a one-to-one interaction rather than in the presence of family members.

Exploring possible suicidal thoughts tells clients that the intervenor is taking them seriously and is interested in their well-being. Consequently, clients who are thinking about suicide generally answer the worker's question by discussing their self-destructive thoughts, while persons who are not suicidal are still likely to appreciate the intervenor's interest and caring.

Asking clients if they are thinking about committing suicide is not easy to do, but if workers sidestep the topic, suicidal persons may interpret the interviewer's reticence as a cue to avoid the subject. Some intervenors do not bring up the topic of suicide because they believe if they do, clients who previously had not considered suicide might see immediate death as a new and desirable option. As a variety of experts (e.g., Berman et al., 2006; Gibson, Breitbart, Tomarken, Kosinski, & Nelson, 2006; Greenstone, 2005; Schwartz & Rogers, 2004; Strentz, 2012) have noted, however, there is no evidence to support the belief that exploring suicide lethality increases the likelihood of self-destruction.

Available empirical evidence (e.g., Hendin, Maltsberger, Lipschitz, Haas, & Kyle, 2001; Michel, 1987; Shafii et al., 1985) suggests that 65 to 85 percent of all individuals who kill themselves communicate their suicidal intent prior to their deaths. Research indicates that only 16 to 30 percent of all persons who communicate suicidal intent actually go on to engage in life-threatening behavior (e.g., Kovacs, Goldston, & Gatsonis, 1993; Reinherz et al., 1995). For every twelve to fifteen self-harm related hospital emergency room visits in the United States there is one suicide (Claassen et al., 2006). For each suicide death in the United States the number of suicide attempts decreases with age, with the approximate number of attempts for each age group as follows: teens, 50; twenties, 20; thirties, 14, forties, 10; fifties, 6; sixties, 3; seventies, 2 (throughout the lifespan the mortality rate from attempted suicide is about 3- to 4-times higher for males than for females) (Friedmann & Kohn, 2008). The fact that many more people threaten or attempt suicide than kill themselves is the basis for the myth that when persons threaten suicide or engage in a nonfatal suicide attempt they just want attention and there is no real danger. To the contrary, communicating any sort of suicidal intent increases lethality far above the base rate. Intervenors can assess the degree of increased danger by exploring four acute risk factors (suicide plan, emotions, suddenness, and object loss) and one predisposing factor (past suicide attempts).

Suicide Plan

Thomas Joiner, David Rudd, and Hasan Rajab (1997) compared 196 suicide "attempters" to 134 suicide "ideators" and found that having a plan for suicide was more frequently associated with "attempters" than with "ideators." Doctor Joiner (e.g., 2000, 2005) believes the existence of a suicide plan often discriminates between persons who consider suicide and those who actually try to kill themselves. Clinicians, in general, are in tune with that belief. For example, Gregory Carter and his colleagues (Carter, Safranko, Lewin, Whyte, & Bryant, 2006) studied the cases of 3,148 deliberate self-poisoning patients, including 920 who were referred for psychiatric hospitalization. The researchers investigated the reasons for those referrals. Almost 60 percent of the variance in the hospitalization decisions was accounted for by the patients disclosing that they had been thinking about and planning for suicide.

When working with a suicidal person it is crucial to explore the topic of a plan for suicide. But there is evidence that crisis phone workers only engage in such exploration with about half of their suicidal callers (Mishara et al., 2007a). Since you are reading this, you now know that is an important mistake to avoid.

When a person has thought about preparations for suicide, the worker can assess the degree of danger by evaluating the plan with respect to the following three elements: deadliness, availability, and concreteness.

Deadly methods are those that often preclude medical treatment. Death is the most likely result for the following: shooting, hanging or suffocation, drowning, stepping in front of a moving vehicle, inhaling poisonous gas (such as carbon monoxide), and jumping from a high place (Elnour & Harrison, 2008). On the other hand, methods that allow medical intervention tend to be less deadly. For instance, although drug overdosing or wrist cutting can kill a client, such methods tend to be less lethal because they allow more opportunity for emergency medical attention.

Empirical research (Cooper et al., 2005; Michel, 1987) has shown that isolation from potential help increases the deadliness of any means. Consequently, the worker should discover whether the plan involves choosing a time and place that decrease the possibility of intervention. Examples include the following: selecting a remote location, locking a door to prevent access by would-be intervenors, and acting during a time when contact with others is unlikely. In residential settings this lack of contact may be imposed rather than sought out. For example, a study by Jenny Shaw and her colleagues (Shaw, Baker, Hunt, Moloney, & Appleby, 2004) reported that 84 percent of prison suicide victims they studied were alone in their cells at the time of their deaths. In a study of suicides among confined juveniles (Hayes, 2005), 75 percent had been placed in single-occupancy rooms, with 50 percent confined to their rooms at the time of their deaths.

Available methods increase the suicide risk, so the intervenor may need to explore whether the individual has deadly resources. For instance, if a person threatens to commit suicide with a firearm, the worker should ask whether the individual has access to a gun and ammunition. Such availability increases the chances of a lethal outcome. David Brent and his colleagues (1988) found that adolescents who actually committed suicide were more than twice as likely (74% vs. 34%) to have firearms in the home than were individuals in a matched group of suicidal teenage inpatients who were still alive. Other similar matching studies with adolescents (Shah, Hoffman, Wake, & Marine, 2000) and with middle aged and older populations (Conwell et al., 2002) have also found that the deceased individuals were significantly more likely to have had firearms in their homes than were the matched control participants.

In a similar vein, Azrael, Hemenway, Miller, Barber, and Schackner (2004) found that firearms accounted for 71 percent of the 153 youth suicides they studied. Out of those 109 deaths, 83 percent occurred at home with guns that were stored unlocked. The researchers also looked at 26 suicides they viewed as being impulsive (such as suicides following arguments with parents regarding issues that had not led to arguments the day before). Out of those 26 deaths, 24 of them were due to firearms, leading the authors to conclude the easy access to guns can turn temporary turmoil into irreversible tragedy.

In a review research on the link between suicide and the availability of firearms, David Brent and Jeffrey Bridge (2003) concluded that compared to control participants, suicide victims are much more likely to have had firearms in their homes, and those weapons are likely to have been used as the means of death.

Within the United States, availability of firearms varies from state to state. Andrés and Hempstead (2011) found that there were significantly fewer male suicides by firearms when the state had laws requiring permits to purchase firearms and restrictions on minors purchasing firearms. Laws targeting specific groups (persons with issues relating to mental illness, alcohol, or drugs, and those having convictions for misdemeanors or domestic violence) had much less of an impact on male suicide by firearms. (The authors said they focused on males because they account for almost 90 percent of suicide deaths from firearms.)

When the availability of deadly means varies from one setting to another, the prevalent modes of suicide also differ. In the United States, where guns can be easy to obtain, death by firearms accounts for almost 60 percent of the suicides (e.g., Pierpont & McGinty, 2005). On the other hand, in Southern Trinidad, 81 percent of suicidal deaths result from a different readily available means–paraquat, an agricultural poison (Hutchinson et al., 1999).

Sometimes, though, the switch to a different means of suicide can be associated with a decrease in the rate of suicide. That seems to be the case with college students in the United States. Allan Schwartz (2011) conducted research that involved five years of data from the National Survey of Counseling Center Directors. During one or more of the five years, 645 institutions of higher education were represented in the survey, with 98 percent of those being 4-year schools in the United States. Participating directors reported 156 suicides by females and 424 suicides by males. Among the women 10 percent of the suicides were by firearms, and among the men 31 percent of the suicides were by firearms. Among all 20- to 24-year-olds during a similar time period in the United States, 31 percent of female suicides were by firearms, and 52 percent of male suicides were by firearms. Doctor Schwartz reported that the overall suicide rate for the students was 7 suicides a year per 100,000 students, which was substantially lower than the rate of 12.1 suicides a year for all 20- to 24-year-olds. He concluded that the lower suicide rate resulted primarily from less use of firearms as the means of suicide, which was a consequence of decreased availability of firearms among college students. His study cites other research noting that 4.3 percent of students report having a firearm at college, compared to 38 percent of households in the United States having at least one firearm. Additional research cited in his study notes that among 20- to 24-year-olds who attempt suicide the probability of death is 80 percent when a firearm is the means employed (compared to less than 1 percent when the means is ingesting a substance).

In the United States the transition from adolescence to adulthood often involves college. In Israel that transition almost always involves mandatory service in the Israeli Defense Force. Gad Lubin and his colleagues (2010) report that during the early part of the twenty-first century the suicide frequency for 18- to 21-year-old Israeli Defense Force soldiers was 28 per year. Many of those suicides were by military-issued firearms when the soldiers were on weekend leave at home. As part of a suicide-prevention program, in 2006 the Israeli Defense Force ordered that when going on such leave soldiers had to store their firearms at their base. In the two years after that change of policy, weekend suicides by firearms among 18- to 21-year-old soldiers decreased from 10 per year to 3 per year, with no statistically significant change in weekday suicides. Overall there was a 40 percent decrease in the suicide rate. As with U.S. college students, decreased availability of firearms was associated with a markedly lower rate of suicide.

The most frequent means of suicide in correctional facilities is hanging, a deadly action that can be arranged in many ingenious ways, including sitting or kneeling rather than suspending oneself (e.g., Fruehwald, Frottier, Eher, Gutierrez, & Ritter, 2000). In part because of the many available ways of accomplishing it, hanging or self-strangulation has been found to account for over 90 percent of jail and prison suicides (e.g., Shaw et al., 2004; Hayes, 2012) and over 98 percent of suicides among confined juveniles (Hayes, 2005; 2009).

Concrete plans heighten the potential for suicide. Michel (1987) compared 50 individuals who had attempted suicide and survived to 50 persons who had killed themselves. The deceased individuals had demonstrated significantly more planning than those who remained alive. And in a study (Brown, Overholser, Spirito, & Fritz, 1991) of 112 adolescents who had attempted suicide, 57 were classified as impulsive suicide attempters and 29 were categorized as premeditated attempters. Those who had contemplated suicide and had planned their attempts demonstrated greater depression and hopelessness than the impulsive attempters. One aspect of research conducted by Tracy Witte and her associates (2010) was to examine initial call and follow-up information on 380 suicidal callers to 16 participating centers in the National Suicide Prevention Lifeline. The researchers found a significant positive correlation between making plans to hurt or kill oneself and believing that one was going to die by suicide. In light of such research, a vague threat such as, "I'm going to take an overdose," probably is associated with lower lethality than a detailed and specific statement, such as, "I've been saving my prescription pain medicine, and tomorrow, after everyone has gone to work, I'm going to take the pills."

Empirical investigation also indicates that plans are more lethal when they involve final arrangements (Michel, 1987). Examples include giving away possessions and putting financial matters in order.

Although there is a natural hesitancy to talk about suicide plans, clinicians (e.g., Jacobs, Brewer, & Klein-Benheim, 1999; Rosenberg, 1999) agree that the intervenor must explore such ideas in a straightforward manner. For instance, one way to begin is with the question, "How do you plan to kill yourself?" Following such an opening the worker then can use reflection and further interrogation to elicit information necessary for assessing the plan's deadliness, availability, and concreteness.

Unfortunately, workers cannot relax if they fail to discover a well-thought-out plan because some suicidal individuals act on impulse—a danger that may be especially high with young persons. That view is supported by Thomas Simon and Alex Crosby (2000). They studied 16,262 ninth through twelfth grade students throughout the United States. The researchers found that 15 percent of those who reported having attempted suicide during the previous 12 months also said they did not plan such an attempt. Similarly, in a study of nearly lethal suicide attempts among persons aged 13 to 34, Simon et al. (2001) found that in 24 percent of the cases, the time between deciding to kill oneself and making the attempt was less than five minutes. Lacking a well-thought-out plan does not necessarily prevent a person from attempting suicide.

Emotions

Most persons who kill themselves are depressed (e.g., DeJong, Overholser, & Stockmeier, 2010). After surveying studies that investigated mortality associated with major mood disorders, David Clark and Ann Goebel-Fabbri (1999) concluded that the estimated lifelong risk of suicide among persons having major mood disorders is probably 15 percent.

Overholser, Braden, and Dieter (2012) compared 148 individuals who had killed themselves to 257 persons who had died from natural causes. At the time of their deaths, 19 percent of those who died from natural causes had a depressive diagnosis, compared to 70 percent of those who died by suicide. Research by Timothy DeJong and his associates (2010) found that each of the following indicators of depression is likely to occur in three-quarters or more of persons who kill themselves: depressed mood, anhedonia (loss of interest in enjoyable activities), fatigue, a sense of guilt or worthlessness, and difficulty concentrating.

A typical depressive episode involves the individual being on an even keel, then the mood worsening and eventually reaching bottom, followed by a gradual recovery. For individuals who become severely depressed, one consideration may be the point to which they have progressed in the depressive episode. There is some research that indicates a potentially dangerous time in a serious bout of depression is when the person seems to be improving, and several explanations have been offered for this increase in suicidal thought and actions (e.g., Cassells, Paterson, Dowding, & Morrison, 2005; Lanceley, 2003). One possibility is that the person has a bipolar disorder, with the observed improvement actually being hypomania or mania. Another potential explanation is that once deciding upon suicide as the means of coping, the person may experience a sense of relief—knowing that the pain will soon end. A third perspective focuses on the ability of depressed persons to take action. When at the depths of their despondency, profoundly depressed individuals do not have the energy to implement a suicide plan. As the depression begins to lift, however, more energy becomes available while distressing feelings still linger. When thoughts of suicide return, there is now an increased likelihood of the person acting on them.

Ongoing agitation combined with despondency can also increase lethality. When clients feel helpless to change their situations and at the same time they show the restless expression of hostility, guilt, or anxiety, they are in danger of acting upon self-destructive impulses. This may be especially true with children and adolescents. For example, in a study that compared a group of normal adolescents and young adults to a matched group of hospitalized suicide attempters, the attempters were found to be far more hostile, depressed, and hopeless than the control subjects (Simonds, McMahon, & Armstrong, 1991). Hospitalized suicide attempters with highly lethal intent have been shown to have more trait anxiety than those with low-lethality intent (Chance, Kaslow, & Baldwin, 1994). And Cohen-Sandler, Berman, and King (1982) collected evidence to suggest that displays of aggression in young persons can be a key factor differentiating those who are merely depressed from individuals who are both depressed and suicidal. That point was strongly supported by the findings of a study which gathered information from persons who had known 49 young people in Utah who died by suicide. Moskos, Olson, Halbern, Keller, and Gray (2005) found that respondents frequently reported the individuals had experienced temper outbursts, with anger being the most commonly recognized emotion in the youths prior to their deaths.

It is also true, however, that persons who choose suicide may become calm. Agitation and distress may decrease once these individuals decide on death as the means of controlling their destiny. Consequently, sudden calmness can be like the eye of a hurricane, a bad sign that indicates impending destructiveness.

Numerous empirical studies indicate that hopelessness increases the risk for suicidal thinking and behavior (e.g., Beautrais, 2004; Dori & Overholser, 1999; Furr, Westefeld, McConnell, & Jenkins, 2001; Dieserud, Roysamb, Ekeberg, & Kraft, 2001; Hetrick, Parker, Robinson, Hall, & Vance, 2012; Johnson, McMurrich, & Yates, 2005; Joiner & Rudd, 1996; Rudd, Rajab, & Dahm, 1994). For example, in a study of psychotherapy outpatients, Beck, Steer, Beck, and Newman (1993) found that hopelessness was the emotion that was most closely associated with suicidal thinking. And Beck, Brown, Berchick, Stewart, and Steer (1990) found that, as a group, outpatients who eventually died by suicide had scored significantly higher on the Beck Hopelessness Scale than outpatients who remained alive or who had died from natural causes.

When persons feel hopeless it is easier for suicide to become the only apparent solution. Believing there is no other viable option also indicates profound helplessness. Such clients think that their efforts are futile and that circumstances cannot change for the better. These individuals see death as a means of regaining control over what happens to them. Escape from life and surrender to death may become the person's only strategy.

In a study (Hendin, Maltsberger, Haas, Szanto, & Rabinowicz, 2004) that asked 26 therapists to describe a patient of theirs just before the client's death by suicide, a majority of the individuals displayed intense hopeless (58%) and rage (69%). But the most frequently occurring emotion (85%) and the one that best distinguished the deceased persons from a set of nonsuicidal clients (0%) was desperation. The authors describe that emotion as intolerable anguish combined with an immediate need for relief.

Israel Orbach (e.g., Orbach, 2003; Orbach, Mikulincer, Blumenson, Mester, & Stein, 1999) and James Zimmerman (1995) believe the experience of an irresolvable problem is a central element in child suicide. They suggest that hopelessness in the face of overwhelming demands tends to characterize suicides in childhood. Such children feel trapped. They believe they are incapable of changing distressing conditions, and they see no end to their insurmountable difficulties. Consequently, death becomes a means of escaping from problems they feel powerless to solve.

Related to the emotion hopelessness is the sense of "burdensomeness" discussed by Thomas Joiner, Michael Brown, and others (e.g., Brown, Dahlen, Mills, Rick, & Biblarz, 1999; Joiner et al., 2002; Joiner et al., 2007; Ribeiro, Bodell, Hames, Hagan, & Joiner, 2013; Stellrecht et al., 2006; Van Orden et al., 2010). In their investigations of this concept, Thomas Joiner (e.g., 2000, 2005) and his colleagues have found support for the idea that compared to persons who attempt suicide but do not die, "completers" are more likely to perceive themselves as being a burden to loved ones. Other researchers have also found supporting data for the role of burdensomeness in suicidal ideation (e.g., Bryan, Clemans, & Hernandez, 2012; Monteith, Menefee, Pettit, Leopoulos, & Vincent, 2013). Milton Brown and his colleagues (Brown, Comtois, & Linehan, 2002) studied 75 chronically suicidal women who had engaged in deliberate self-injury within the previous eight weeks. The researchers classified the self-injury episodes as either with (suicidal) or without (nonsuicidal) the intent to die. In terms of reasons for those episodes, participants attributed about one-third of the suicidal episodes to making others better off, whereas they attributed less than 8 percent of the nonsuicidal episodes to that reason.

Suddenness

John Riskind and his colleagues (Riskind, Long, Williams, & White, 2000) have proposed a "looming vulnerability" model. It suggests that when harmful events rapidly escalate they become more disturbing. If there has been a sudden upsurge in difficulties, the risk of suicide is higher. Evidence for such upsurges comes from a study by Cooper, Appleby, and Amos (2002), in which the investigators gathered data from informants who knew individuals selected for the study. One set of subjects was comprised of persons who had recently died by suicide, and the other set was a matched group of control participants. In the week prior to the index date (the day of death for the suicide victims), individuals who had killed themselves had both a much higher number of setbacks and more severe setbacks than the control participants.

In a previously mentioned holistic approach to understanding suicidal crises, Herbert Hendin and his colleagues (2001) examined specially prepared reports written by the therapists of 26 individuals who had killed themselves. The researchers concluded that most of the deceased persons had demonstrated their suicidal crisis via two or three of three markers. (1) For 21 of the 26 patients, there had been an intense emotional response to a *precipitating event*, such as the loss of a crucial relationship or a significant career setback. (2) All of the patients were depressed; 22 of them communicated a *desperate need for relief from their anguish*. Other acute feelings included feeling abandoned, anxious, enraged, guilty, and humiliated. Longstanding emotions included feeling rejected, hopeless, lonely, and unworthy. (3) Verbal *communication of suicidal thoughts* came from 17 of the patients.

Other empirical research has also shown that suicidal thinking tends to increase during acute stress. Among a group of 425 of ninth through twelfth graders, Huff (1999) found that the degree and "recency" of stress accounted for 80 percent of the variation in suicidal thinking. During a time of rapidly worsening circumstances, there may be a period of several days in which the person is ready to commit suicide. For example, Marttunen, Aro, and Lon-nqvist (1993) conducted psychological autopsies on 53 adolescent suicide victims. During the month prior to death, 70 percent of the victims had experienced a stressor that had contributed directly to the suicide, with almost half of those stressors occurring during the person's final 24 hours of life. Likewise, Azrael et al. (2004) found that in the 153 cases of youth suicide they investigated, 75 percent of the deceased individuals had been experiencing a major life crisis. In a similar study, Earle, Forquer, Volo, and Mc-Donnell (1994) examined the mental health program records of 93 outpatients who had committed suicide. Responses from the individuals' therapists indicated that 74 percent of the deceased patients were experiencing acute stress at the time of their deaths. The most common stressor was family relationships (28% of the 93 individuals), with other stressors having frequencies of 1 percent to 11 percent. In decreasing order of prevalence those other stressors were as follows: illness or death of a parent; housing problems; another person's death; health problems; court involvement or a jail term; difficulty with job, status, or self-concept; financial problems; change in mental health program or therapist; another person's suicide; sexual difficulties; being a crime victim; pregnancy; and illness of a friend.

An especially deadly combination is acute stress combined with use of alcohol and/or other drugs, as demonstrated in a study by Lindsay Hayes (2012) that focused on suicides in jails (holding facilities that usually keep individuals less than seventy-two hours and detention facilities that typically keep persons less than two years). At the time of their death, 20 percent of the suicide victims had been under the influence of alcohol and/or other drugs.

In a study that compared adolescents hospitalized after suicide attempts to normal high school students, Adams, Overholser, and Spirito (1994) found that the hospitalized adolescents reported more major life stressors (such as criminal justice involvement or a parent remarrying) and more exit events (such as bereavement or moving to a new area). Although there were no significant differences between the two groups with regard to chronic stressors (such as family financial problems or persistent interpersonal conflict), among the suicide attempters chronic stressors did account for 15 percent of the variation in suicidal thinking.

Apparently, long-term problems put one at greater risk when there is a sudden upsurge in difficulties. For example, abusers of alcohol and other drugs, as well as individuals with other chronic difficulties, have been noted to be at increased risk for suicide (e.g., Cooper et al., 2005; Earle et al., 1994). And when dependence on alcohol is combined with ongoing depression, the risk may be even higher. For example, Cornelius et al. (1995) studied patients seeking an initial evaluation at a psychiatric facility. When alcohol-dependent depressed persons were compared to nondepressed alcohol-dependent persons and to depressed individuals who were not alcohol-dependent, higher incidence of suicidal ideation was the factor that best distinguished the group having both alcohol dependence and major depression. In the previously mentioned longitudinal study by Helen Reinherz and her colleagues (1995), when 18-year-olds who had attempted suicide were compared to 18-year-olds who had not attempted suicide, the attempters were 17 times more likely to have a history that included both depression and substance abuse or dependence. In interviews with 357 adolescents who had attempted suicide in the past and were now seeking crisis intervention, Rotheram-Borus, Walker, and Ferns (1996) found that 28 percent of them reported using alcohol or other drugs prior to attempting suicide.

Higher suicide lethality characterizes young persons who have ongoing problems. As mentioned in the section on emotions, the suicide risk increases when the young person in difficulty is also impulsive—often demonstrated by substance abuse or by a history of altercations. For example, in a longitudinal study of adolescent outpatients, Kovacs et al. (1993) concluded that for teenagers diagnosed with a mood disorder, a coexisting conduct disorder and/or substance use disorder increased the risk for attempting suicide. And King, Hill, Naylor, Evans, and Shain (1993) evaluated 54 adolescent girls who were inpatients on a psychiatric unit. The researchers found that alcohol use, depression intensity, and severity of family dysfunction were intercorrelated and, to varying degrees, each was predictive of suicidal thinking. The authors describe the prototypical adolescent girl at risk for suicidal thinking to be a person who has longstanding low-level depression, whose oppositional style of interacting contributes to recurring conflicts with her parents, who feels a sense of loss and fears being rejected and abandoned as a result of those conflicts, and who consumes large quantities of alcohol during those stressful episodes.

Some adolescents impulsively attempt suicide when they first encounter difficulties; however, most suicide attempts by teenagers occur after the failure of less drastic coping attempts. A frequently observed (e.g., Curran, 1987) pattern is (1) rebelling, (2) withdrawing, (3) running away, and (4) attempting suicide. All of these behaviors represent efforts to gain control over aversive situations.

Object Loss

According to psychoanalytic theory, an *object* is an activity, relationship, or possession in which an individual invests interest and energy. Clinicians and researchers (e.g., American Academy of Child and Adolescent Psychiatry, 2001; Bongar & Sullivan, 2013; Cassells et al., 2005; Gould & Kramer, 2001;

Gould, Shaffer, & Greenberg, 2003; Greenstone, 2005) agree that lethality increases when the precipitating stress involves a recent or impending object loss. In the previously reported study by Adams et al. (1994) that compared adolescents hospitalized after suicide attempts to normal high school students, the hospitalized adolescents reported more exit events (such as bereavement or moving to a new area). And in a review of the literature, Heikkinen, Aro, and Lonnqvist (1993) concluded that the risk of suicide is increased by distressing life events. Examples include the following: loss of physical abilities through illness or accident; loss of self-esteem and status due to financial setbacks, unemployment, or criminal charges; loss of security resulting from a change in residence or promotion; and loss of an important relationship due to strife, rejection, relocation, separation, divorce, family disruption, or death.

In their study of 656 youth suicides, Hoberman and Garfinkel (1988) found the following precipitants within three days of the death: arguments (15%), loss of a relationship (9%), legal difficulties (9%), disappointments (9%), job problems (9%), school difficulties (6%), threats of separation (5%), and target of assault (2%).

Moving to the other end of the age continuum, De Leo and Ormskerk (1991) reviewed characteristics of suicide among older persons and noted several common motives for life-threatening behavior. Included in the list were chronic illness, death of a loved one, loss of independence, interpersonal conflict, and social isolation. Illness is frequently part of the lives of older suicide victims. In a study of 1,022 suicides by persons 20 years old and older, Heikkinen, Isometsa, Aro, Sarna, and Lonnqvist (1995) found the most frequently occurring life event at any age level was physical illness in victims age 70 and older. Among men, 63 percent experienced physical illness in the three months preceding death, and for women age 70 and over the figure was 40 percent. Likewise, in an investigation by Howard Cattell and David Jolley (1995) of 100 persons over age 65 who died by suicide, the most frequently identified difficulty was physical illness. Among the sample studied, 65 percent were in ill health when they chose to kill themselves.

In a previously mentioned research program that asked 26 therapists to describe a patient of theirs just before the client's death by suicide, Maltsberger, Hendin, Haas, and Lipschitz (2003) found that in 21 of the 26 cases there was a precipitating event linked to the person's death. Examples included loss of a romantic relationship, destruction of a career, business setbacks, death of a loved one, life-threatening illness of a child, unwanted change in mental health treatment, and an argument with an important individual in the person's life.

In all these examples of object loss, the thwarted person experiences frustration and pain. For the high-lethality individual, as Shneidman (2001) noted, the pain becomes intolerable, and the person concludes that suicide is the only sure means of pain relief. A similar line of reasoning comes from the United Kingdom, where psychologist Mark Williams (2002) has suggested that suicidal actions are a "cry of pain" in response to entrapment (believing there is no escape). In Israel, researchers (Orbach, Mikulincer, Sirota, & Gilboa-Schechtman, 2003) empirically investigated such mental pain and concluded that common features include the following six factors: the perception of irreversibility, lacking control, feeling empty, experiencing overwhelming emotions, feeling unable to respond to the situation, and believing oneself to be strangely changed. In a follow-up study (Orbach, Mikulincer, Gilboa-Schechtman, & Sirota, 2003) comparing hospitalized suicide attempters to nonsuicidal psychiatric patients and to nonpatients, the suicidal individuals scored significantly higher on all six factors.

There can be many sources of pain and a sense of entrapment. Sean Cleary (2000) described questionnaire results from 1,569 New York State ninth through twelfth grade students who thought about suicide in the past 12 months, then described suicidal thoughts/behavior and victimization they had experienced (among other health risk behaviors). Indicators of victimization included the number of days the student did not go to school because of feeling unsafe, the number of threats or assaults experienced, and the number of times the student's property had been deliberately damaged or stolen. Indicators of suicidal thoughts/behavior included whether the person had considered suicide or made a suicide plan, and how many times the individual had attempted suicide. Compared to nonvictimized students, suicidal thoughts/behaviors occurred more than twice as frequently among victimized students.

Sometimes victimization comes in the form of bullying. Among a group of adolescents they surveyed, Rigby and Slee (1999) used peer nominations to determine that 16 percent of the boys and 9 percent of the girls were perceived to be victims of bullying. With regard to suicidal thinking, Rigby and Slee found that being bullied and lacking social support accounted for about 15 percent of the variation in boys and 19 percent of the variation in girls. As a group, bullying victims demonstrated more suicidal thinking than nonvictims, but the differences were relatively small. One way of interpreting these findings is that for a given individual, being the victim of bullying can contribute to suicidal thinking but that there is a great deal of variation from one person to the next. Hinduja and Patchin (2010) drew similar conclusions based on their survey of middle school students. The researchers reported that victims of bullying (both traditional and in cyberspace) were 1.7 (traditional) to 1.9 (cyber) times more likely than nonvictims to have attempted suicide, but the authors also concluded that being a victim of bullying accounted for only about 6 percent of the variance in suicide attempts.

Loss of a key relationship is a common occurrence among suicidal teenagers. In one comparison (Kosky, 1983) of suicidal to nonsuicidal young persons, more than 80 percent of the suicidal youngsters had lost a key relationship through death or divorce, while such losses had been experienced by only 20 percent of those in the nonsuicidal group. And in the Simonds et al. (1991) study, 36 percent of the suicide attempters had experienced the recent breakup of a romantic relationship whereas only 5 percent of the nonsuicidal subjects had recently suffered such a loss. In the previously mentioned Moskos et al. (2005) research, among 41 adolescent males who had died by suicide, problems relating to romantic relationships were the most commonly experienced stressors.

Compared to nonsuicidal adolescents, suicidal teenagers have more difficulties in important peer and family relationships. A study (Miller, King, Shain, & Naylor, 1992) of hospitalized suicidal adolescents found that these individuals perceived more emotional distancing among family members and felt more isolated at home than did other psychiatrically hospitalized teenagers or normal adolescents in the community. Compared to nonsuicidal high school students, suicidal adolescents have also been found to experience more stresses associated with sexual relations and with achievement expectations (Rubenstein, Heeren, Housman, Rubin, & Stechler, 1989).

David Brent and his colleagues (Brent, Perper, Moritz, Baugher et al., 1993) compared 67 adolescent victims of suicide to 67 matched control subjects. During the year prior to their deaths, the deceased adolescents experienced significantly more interpersonal conflict (especially conflicts with parents), interpersonal loss (most commonly the loss of romantic relationships), and external stressors (such as legal concerns and disciplinary problems).

Furr et al. (2001) also found similar contributing factors among the college and university students in their survey. The researchers noted the following causes of suicidal thinking and behavior (listed with the percentage of suicidal students who cited each one): hopelessness (49%), loneliness (47%), helplessness (37%), girlfriend/boyfriend problems (27%), money problems (26%), and parental problems (20%). The number of factors listed by students tended to increase with the severity of the suicidal thinking/behavior. Nonsuicidal depressed students attributed their depression to an average of 3.6 factors; nonattempting students who had considered suicide attributed their suicidal thinking to an average of 4.0 factors; and students who had attempted suicide attributed their suicidal behavior to an average of 4.6 factors.

As noted above, relationship difficulties are common among young suicidal persons. That is also true of adults. In the previously cited research by James Overholser and his associates (2012), the two stressful life events that best distinguished between persons who had killed themselves and those who had died from natural causes were relationship problems (36% vs. 17%) and legal difficulties (63% vs. 37%).

Encompassing many of the previously identified examples of object loss, Thomas Joiner (e.g., 2005) believes that suicidal individuals have lost a sense of belongingness and a feeling of being competent. Support for the importance of a sense of competence also comes from a study conducted by Timothy DeJong and his colleagues (2010). The researchers compared 50 individuals who had attempted suicide and survived the attempt to 50 persons who had killed themselves. The two greatest differences between the groups were that significantly more of the deceased individuals had experienced financial stress (52% vs. 18%) and job stress (56% vs. 20%). Feeling stressed because of job or financial pressures implies a challenge to one's competence in those areas.

Sometimes part of the loneliness experienced by suicidal individuals can arise out of discomfort others feel in being with them. It is frightening to hear a person talk about committing suicide, and individuals often respond defensively by reassuring the individual or by changing the subject. Such reactions are likely to be interpreted by the suicidal person as rejection or lack of concern. Even when the individual understands the discomfort of those who are close, the defensiveness of others may leave the person with no one in whom to confide. Consequently, such isolation further increases lethality.

Being imprisoned can cause widespread object loss. One is cut off from crucial relationships and forced to face a future that is full of uncertainty. So it is not surprising that the first month of incarceration is the most dangerous 30-day period for suicide attempts, with more individuals attempting suicide on the first day than at any other time (e.g., Fruehwald et al., 2000; Shaw et al., 2004). In his study of jail suicides, Lindsay Hayes (2012) found that 23 percent of the victims died within 24 hours of being incarcerated. In the previously mentioned survey of suicides among confined juveniles (Hayes, 2005), all of the deaths occurred within the first four months of confinement, with 4 percent taking place during the first 24 hours and over 40 percent during the first 72 hours. Overall, the suicide rate for prisoners is much higher than the rate for the population of the country in which the prison is located. In a study of prisons in 12 countries (Australia, Belgium, Canada, Denmark, England and Wales, Finland, Ireland, The Netherlands, New Zealand, Norway, Scotland, Sweden) the suicide rate for male prisoners was 3 to 6 times higher than the rate for nonincarcerated males, and the rate for women was 6 to 56 times higher than the country's rate for nonincarcerated women (Fazel, Grann, Kling, & Hawton, 2011).

PAST SUICIDE ATTEMPTS

Compared to individuals who have never tried to kill themselves, persons who have made past suicide attempts are at greater risk for depression, as Hutchinson, Tess, Gleckman, and Spence (1992) found in their study of institutionalized adolescents. Likewise, in an investigation of psychotherapy outpatients, Beck, Steer, and Brown (1993) found that of the variables studied, the report of a past suicide attempt was the factor most closely correlated with current suicidal thinking. In a similar vein, Lewinsohn, Rohde, and Seeley (1994) found that among the variables studied in their sample of high school students, the best predictor of a future suicide attempt was the adolescent having made a past suicide attempt. Pfeffer et al. (1993) conducted a six to eight year follow-up of individuals who had experienced psychiatric hospitalization as children and during that hospitalization had been classified as suicide attempters or suicide ideators. Compared to nonpatient controls at follow-up, the attempters were six times more likely to have attempted suicide again and the ideators were three times more likely to have done so.

A past suicide attempt is also associated with increased risk of subsequent death by suicide. A study that focused on persons age 60 and over revealed that of 42 individuals who had killed themselves, 19 percent had made a previous suicide attempt, compared to 4 percent having made a suicide attempt among a control group of 196 patients visiting medical practices (Conwell et al., 2000).

Several studies have included examination of subsequent suicides of persons who made suicide attempts that did not end in death. In a study that followed up on 302 individuals who had made a medically serious suicide attempt requiring at least 24 hours of hospitalization, Beautrais (2004) found that within five years, 37 percent of the participants had made at least one additional suicide attempt and another 6.7 percent of them had died by suicide. Gibb, Beautrais, and Fergusson (2005) collected data on all individuals during a ten-year period who were admitted to a hospital due to attempting suicide (ending the data collection 10 months after the last admission). Among the 3,690 patients, 28.1 percent were admitted for another nonfatal attempt, and 4.6 percent died by suicide. An average 3.88 years after they made a suicide attempt in Denmark, researchers (Christiansen & Jensen, 2007) followed up on 2,614 individuals. Official statistics indicated that 2.33 percent had died by suicide, and another 8.04 percent had died due to other reasons. The suicide rate of the suicide attempters was 58-times greater than the rate (.04%) for a matched group of control subjects during an average follow-up of 4.14 years. Death from other causes was 3.22-times greater for the suicide attempters than for the control subjects (2.49%). Choi, Park, and

Hong (2012) studied emergency room patients in Seoul, South Korea over a 30-month period. Compared to the suicide rate among all Koreans, subsequent death from suicide was 82-times greater among suicide attempt patients admitted to the hospital, 54-times greater for suicide attempt patients who were discharged, 21-times greater for nonsuicidal patients who were admitted, and 11-times greater for nonsuicidal patients who were discharged.

In fact, there is widespread agreement among clinicians and researchers (e.g., Apter & Wasserman, 2003; Berman et al., 2006; Boergers & Spirito, 2003; Bongar & Sullivan, 2013; Bryan & Rudd, 2006; Cooper et al., 2005; Gould & Kramer, 2001; Greenstone, 2005; Modai et al., 2002; Joiner et al., 2007; Montross et al., 2005; Pfeffer, 2001; Ribeiro et al., 2013; Simon, 2007; Stellrecht et al., 2006; Tidemalm, Elofsson, Stefansson, Waern, & Runeson, 2005; Van Orden et al., 2010) that when an individual currently is considering suicide, lethality is higher for persons who have previous suicide attempts or who have rehearsed the plan to make sure it would work. Thus, a past history of attempts by the individual is a factor that predisposes the person to be at greater risk for suicide (Joiner, Walker, Rudd, & Jobes, 1999; Rudd & Joiner, 1998).

As previously noted in the section on deadliness of a plan for suicide, isolation increases the potential lethality of any means for suicide. Consistent with that observation, Amy Wenzel and her colleagues (2010) found that among a group of now-deceased persons who had been hospitalized for a suicide attempt or for suicidal thinking, those who had actively tried to conceal their suicidal actions were three times more likely to eventually die by suicide than those who had not tried to conceal their life-threatening actions. So if a person reports a past suicide attempt, a possible topic to explore is whether the individual took action to prevent being discovered. Trying to conceal life-threatening action during a past suicide attempt increases lethality for the current episode.

Suicide attempts or suicides among friends and family members also predispose the person to be at greater risk for suicide. Gould, Fisher, Parides, Flory, and Shaffer (1996) found a family history of suicidal behavior for 5 percent of 147 control subjects, compared to 17 percent for 120 suicide victims who had died by suicide before age 20. In the previously mentioned study by John Simonds and his colleagues (1991), 50 percent of the suicide attempters had a family member who had attempted suicide, whereas a family history of suicidal behavior existed for only 14 percent of the control group. Likewise, as part of the previously mentioned follow-up project by Cynthia Pfeffer and her colleagues, Pfeffer, Normandin, and Kakuma (1994) included an examination of whether the individual's mother had attempted suicide. The investigators found the following percentages with regard to mothers attempting suicide: 48 percent for former child psychiatric inpa-

tients who had attempted suicide, 26 percent for former child psychiatric inpatients who had considered suicide, 8 percent for former child psychiatric
inpatients who had not been suicidal, and 14 percent for normal children.
And in a study by Mohammad Shafii and his colleagues (1985), 30 percent
of the adolescents who died by suicide had been exposed to suicidal behavior on the part of an adult family member, compared to 12 percent for nonsuicidal control subjects.

When a parent or other adult relative has attempted suicide, the greater
danger may result from modeling, from a hereditary predisposition toward
depression, or from both learning and genetics. Two studies suggest that the
more important factor may be learning. In the Shafii et al. (1985) study just
cited, although 30 percent of the deceased individuals had been exposed to
suicidal behavior on the part of an adult family member, 60 percent of those
who killed themselves had known a sibling or friend who had engaged in suicidal behavior, compared to 12 percent for control subjects.

The learning/heredity issue was addressed in a different way by Brent,
Kolko, Allan, and Brown (1990). Within a psychiatric inpatient population of
individuals having mood disorders, they compared 42 suicidal adolescents to
14 nonsuicidal adolescents. In terms of exposure to suicidal thinking, behavior, or deaths on the part of family members, 57 percent of the suicidal patients had such exposure whereas only 14 percent of the nonsuicidal patients
had such experience. And further analysis of the data indicated that exposure to suicidal behavior on the part of a relative contributed to the difference between the groups, whereas a family history that included suicidal behavior did not. Consequently, both Shafii et al. (1985) and Brent et al. (1990)
suggest that seeing other persons model suicidal actions may be more important than any hereditary factor.

On a broader scale, the idea of modeling is also supported by the work of
Elmar Etzersdorfer and Gernot Sonneck (1998). Those researchers suggest
that persons who are in the midst of a suicidal crisis and are experiencing
ambivalence can be encouraged to choose death by media accounts of suicides. Etzersdorfer and Sonneck focused on suicide deaths in the Vienna,
Austria subway. Such deaths had been reported by the media in dramatic
ways that included front-page headlines and pictures. In response to the continuing suicides and coverage of them, a committee formed by the Austrian
Association for Suicide Prevention involved both human service professionals and media specialists in creating and launching a campaign to help journalists learn about potential harmful consequences of certain reporting styles
and to suggest alternative journalistic approaches to suicides.

Recommended guidelines stated that a media account might encourage
suicide to the extent that it reported details of the deadly means, glorified the
person's life, saw the action as romantic, and attributed the suicidal state to

generic difficulties (such as receiving bad news). The guidelines also stated that seeing suicide as desirable could be increased to the extent that the media account was a lead story, prominently used the term "suicide," included a picture of the deceased, and implied that the action was heroic. In terms of alternative ideas for news accounts, the guidelines recommended that stories include helpful resources for persons experiencing similar stressors to those that had troubled the deceased, as well as background information about suicide and suicide prevention resources. Etzersdorfer and Sonneck reported that many members of the media decided the guidelines were worth a try. In the months that followed there were fewer news accounts of suicides and those that did appear were more moderate.

In the six months prior to the committee's efforts there were 19 suicides in the Vienna subway, whereas during the next six months there were three suicides. In subsequent research Niederkrotenhaler and Sonneck (2007) found that during the year following implementation of the guidelines, for areas of Austria in which participating newspapers reached 67 percent of the population there was a significant decrease in the overall suicide rate (estimated to be 47 fewer suicides that year), whereas there was no significant change in the suicide rates in parts of Austria where participating newspapers reached a minority of the population.

In his article on media coverage of suicide, Steven Stack (2003) emphasized that the response of the Austrian press included fewer articles, with accounts that did appear being briefer than before and located inside the newspaper rather than on the front page. Based on that information and on his analysis of other research, he concluded that while changing the quality of media coverage can help, substantial benefit might result from reducing the amount of coverage devoted to suicides. His conclusion is supported by other reviews of the literature (e.g., Gould, Jamieson, & Romer, 2003) and by the organizations named in the next paragraph.

With regard to reporting on suicide, there are media guidelines available on the web at the following URL: www.ReportingOnSuicide.org. Those guidelines were created in a collaborative effort by a number of organizations, including the U.S. Centers for Disease Control and Prevention, the National Institute of Mental Health, the Substance Abuse and Mental Health Services Administration, the American Association of Suicidology, the National Suicide Prevention Lifeline, the Suicide Prevention Resource Center, and the Annenberg Public Policy Center.

Media professionals have information available to them that, when implemented, has the ability to prevent suicides. Unlike the Austrian press, though, the U.S. Surgeon General has concluded there is no evidence that American media professionals have changed their practices in response to the recommended guidelines (Stack, 2003), and other researchers have also found a lack of impact (Tatum, Canetto, & Slater, 2010). Likewise, advocates of similar guidelines (produced by the Suicide Prevention Resource Center and available at http://www.sprc.org/library/at_a_glance.pdf) found that few U.S. newspapers followed the recommendations (Edwards-Stewart, Kinn, June, & Fullerton, 2011). Researchers in Hong Kong described a similar lack of guideline use by the press there (Au, Yip, Chan, & Law, 2004).

In an insightful review of research on media guidelines and suicide reporting, India Bohanna and Xiangdong Wang (2012) made a number of empirically supported observations regarding ways to increase the use of media guidelines relating to suicide. Of crucial importance is the integral involvement of targeted media in the development of guidelines. One strategy is to share information and relevant resources that can be used by journalists as part of their own research into the most life-promoting ways to handle suicides. Supporting journalists in coming to their own conclusions about how to engage their audience in creative and life-affirming ways is more likely to be effective than simply telling them what to do (much like the core crisis intervention concept of supporting client competency rather than simply giving advice). One option is to provide reporters with information regarding the previously discussed research by Gernot Sonneck and his colleagues, showing clear evidence that (1) limiting coverage of suicides, and (2) including certain elements and not others in accounts that do appear are approaches associated with lower suicide rates in media consumers. Abstracts of the two previously cited articles are available at the following URLs.

http://link.springer.com/article/10.1023%2FA%3A1009691903261
http://www.ncbi.nlm.nih.gov/pubmed/1746473

As with the lack of a suicide plan, clinicians and researchers (e.g., Kleespies & Dettmer, 2000) have noted that the absence of a previous suicide attempt by the person does not necessarily mean the individual is a low risk for suicide. Often the first attempt is the one that kills the person. Empirical research (e.g., Hoberman & Garfinkel, 1988; Isometsa & Lonnqvist, 1998; Marttunen, Aro, & Lonnqvist, 1992) indicates that 56 to 80 percent of suicide victims die as a result of their first attempt.

Many demographic variables have been related to suicide. Examples include the following: age, sex, race, marital status, occupation, and socioeconomic status (e.g., Bongar & Sullivan, 2013; De Munck, Portzky, Van Heeringen, 2009; Kleespies, 2014; Levinson, Haklai, Stein, & Gordon, 2006; Purselle, Heninger, Hanzlick, & Garlow, 2009; Vijayakumar, John, Pirkis, & Whiteford, 2005). Although there are population trends associated with all of these factors, researchers and clinicians (Beck, Rush, Shaw, & Emery, 1979; Spirito et al., 1993) have pointed out that such information is not very useful when the goal is to assess the lethality of a specific person and that it is more appropriate to focus on the thoughts, feelings, and behaviors of the individual being evaluated.

INTERVENING WITH SUICIDAL CLIENTS

Experts (e.g., Berman et al., 2006; Lanceley, 2003; Leenaars, 2004) agree that it is safest to take all suicidal individuals seriously and to believe that death is possible. Never brush off an incident as just a manipulation or a gesture. In fact, experts recommend that intervenors avoid using the term *gesture* in this context, since it minimizes the importance of the person's actions (American Academy of Child and Adolescent Psychiatry, 2001; Crosby et al., 2011; Heilbron, Compton, Daniel, & Goldston, 2010; Rudd & Joiner, 1998).

Clients are responsible for their own behavior, and they may choose to commit suicide. Nevertheless, if suicide is to be the means of escaping problems, the choice should be made in a stable state and only after thorough consideration of alternatives. Most clinicians (e.g., Berman, 2006; Berman et al., 2006; Leenaars, 2004) assert that it is the responsibility of crisis workers (1) to do all they can to keep the client alive long enough for this stable state to be achieved and (2) to help the individual explore alternatives to suicide. Although attracted to death for a time, most suicidal individuals do not continue to seek death. For example, in a study (Garrison, Addy, Jackson, McKeown, & Waller, 1991) that assessed 1,073 adolescent students in the fall for three consecutive years, each year 43 to 58 of the individuals reported high levels of suicidal thinking during the previous week. Only one student, however, had high levels of suicidal thinking during each of the three evaluations. In a similar study, Myers, McCauley, Calderon, and Treder (1991) made assessments at 12-month intervals to evaluate suicidal thinking and behavior of 7- to 17-year-olds diagnosed with a major depressive disorder. Of the 50 individuals who were suicidal at the initial assessment, only eight also were suicidal during each of the three subsequent evaluations.

The goal in crisis intervention is to help the person survive the present episode in order to be alive long enough for the almost inevitable change of heart to take place. To enhance their chances of success, intervenors should attend to the following five considerations: interrupting a suicide attempt in progress, determining appropriate intervention, decreasing the availability of lethal means, problem solving, and recognizing the potential for homicide.

Interrupting a Suicide Attempt in Progress

Any self-injury or concrete actions already taken to produce self-injury by a suicidal person must be seen as serious developments. In such instances the first priority is to interrupt the suicide attempt. For example if on the phone with a person who has a loaded gun, one initial option is to ask the person to move to a different room from the gun or to put the firearm in a safe place in a separate room. If self-injury has already occurred, arranging medical attention is a top priority. In such cases, crisis workers ought to be as active as is necessary in securing needed medical attention.

In order to know whether there is a need to interrupt a suicide attempt in progress, the intervenor must ask whether a suicide attempt is already underway. In a study of crisis intervention phone services, Brian Mishara and his colleagues (Mishara et al., 2007a) found on calls with suicidal individuals in which it had been determined that the person had developed a plan for suicide involving a specific method, only 19 percent of the time did the worker explore whether a suicide attempt was already in progress. For calls in which it was determined that a suicide attempt was currently underway, about one-third of the workers did nothing to interrupt the attempt.

If a suicide attempt is already in progress it is necessary to actively intervene. Not doing so can have disastrous consequences. In one instance a caller to a crisis center told the worker that her husband had taken several barbiturates and had consumed a fair amount of alcohol. The worker, who was a nurse, told the caller to put a blanket on him and to take him to the hospital if he had problems. The caller interpreted this advice to mean that her husband would be all right; unfortunately, though, he died during the night from the deadly barbiturate-and-alcohol combination. This tragic episode demonstrates that it is better to err on the side of over activity than to risk such terrible consequences.

For example, it does not take much acetaminophen to kill a person. The minimum lethal dose is only 7.5 grams, the equivalent of 15 extra-strength Tylenol® tablets. And, without treatment being initiated within 12 to 16 hours of ingestion, 25 or more grams (50 500-mg tablets) almost always ends in death. Research (e.g., Bland, Newman, & Dyck, 1994) has found that in North America, drug overdose is the most common means of suicide attempt, with acetaminophen being the drug most commonly ingested. Furthermore, acetaminophen use in intentional self-poisoning has been increasing (e.g., Olfson, Gameroff, Marcus, Greenberg, & Shaffer, 2005). Nevertheless, many persons are not aware of the danger of an acetaminophen overdose, as demonstrated by Myers, Otto, Harris, Diaco, and Moreno (1992). They surveyed 169 suburban high school students and found that 40 percent underestimated how deadly an acetaminophen overdose can be. In a follow-up study involving 569 rural adolescents, half of the participants thought it would take 100 or more 500-mg tablets to cause death (Harris & Myers, 1997). In a similar vein, researchers (Shone, King, Doane, Wilson, & Wolf, 2011) interviewed 266 young people (16–23 years old) and found that 64 percent of the participants did not know what acetaminophen was, even though a third of those who had never heard of it had actually used acetaminophen during the previous month.

Such lack of knowledge was relevant to the case of 14-year-old Krista, whose parents brought her to a crisis center and said she had taken an unknown quantity of acetaminophen-based cold tablets. Realizing the possible risk Krista faced, the crisis worker suggested that they take her to the hospital emergency room. But her parents refused, saying she wasn't that sick. Nevertheless, the worker insisted that she be taken to the emergency room. Following an initial examination there, she was admitted to the intensive care unit.

Intervenors need to be willing to be assertive in interrupting a suicide attempt in progress. Such interruption can include arranging medical evaluation and treatment of individuals who have engaged in life-threatening behavior. Helping the person to survive the episode must be the first priority.

In addition to referring clients to medical resources, the referral process also operates in the other direction. For instance, crisis workers in hospital settings often are called upon to evaluate suicide attempters after the patients have been judged "medically clear." Frequently, such individuals appear to be better able to cope than they really are. Consequently, before concluding that no further assistance is needed, one must carefully assess the circumstances that have changed for the better. If there has been no real change, the person may simply repeat the life-threatening behavior.

Determining Appropriate Intervention

Advantages of Death, Disadvantages of Life, Advantages of Life, Disadvantages of Death

Experts (e.g., Berman, 2006; Bongar & Sullivan, 2013) note that clinical and legal standards of care require intervention plans to take into account the person's risk for suicide. Research indicates that over 94 percent of highly suicidal individuals engage in an internal debate in which they weigh the advantages and disadvantages of life and death (Harris, McLean, Sheffield, & Jobes, 2010). It is necessary to explore a suicidal client's desire for death. Discussing advantages of death in a nonjudgmental way allows the expression of frustrations that the person believes death will alleviate. By encouraging the open discussion of suicidal ideas, the intervenor demonstrates understanding and a willingness to face the person's desperation, thereby strengthening the therapeutic relationship. In such a supportive atmosphere, the client and worker can consider the anticipated consequences of the person's death. Researchers have identified common reasons for wanting to be dead. As previously mentioned, Thomas Joiner (e.g., 2005; Ribeiro et al., 2013; Van Orden et al., 2010) believes that suicidal individuals frequently perceive they are a burden to others and have lost a sense of belongingness. David Jobes and Rachel Mann (1999) found suicidal college students' reasons for wanting to be dead often centered on the idea of escape. Those thoughts included fleeing from the past, bringing an end to pain, and avoiding responsibilities.

Starting with the advantages of suicide is a good rapport-enhancing technique. But as described below, eventually the discussion should cover both the advantages and disadvantages of life, as well as death.

Following exploration of death's advantages, the disadvantages of living can be addressed by focusing problem-solving resources on the issues that are overwhelming the person. During problem solving the intervenor should define those difficulties in workable terms, should help the client generate fresh options, and should strive to negotiate a specific, realistic plan that encourages the person to begin working on productive tasks. (Problem solving with a suicidal person is discussed in greater detail later in the chapter.)

Advantages of living also need to be explored. As Linehan, Goodstein, Nielsen, and Chiles (1983) and Osman et al. (1998) discovered, common reasons for living include believing you can eventually cope with life, recognizing your responsibilities and closeness to family members, thinking about connections to friends, and attributing positive characteristics to yourself. In the previously cited study by Jobes and Mann (1999), suicidal college students' top four reasons for living were family connections, general hopes for the future, specific plans and goals for the future, and enjoyable activities. Empirical research (e.g., MacLeod et al., 1998) indicates that compared to nonsuicidal persons, individuals who are suicidal and have recently harmed themselves tend to be less able to think of positive experiences that may happen in the future. In a similar vein, Mann, Waternaux, Haas, and Malone (1999) found that compared to psychiatric inpatients who had never attempted suicide, those who had attempted suicide tended to generate fewer reasons for living. At least one study (Miller, Segal, & Coolidge, 2001) has found that college students independently identify fewer reasons for living than do older individuals. When a client has difficulty generating such reasons, the intervenor can encourage the person to recall reasons that were important in the past and that may become meaningful again. The worker can also take an inventory of the client's strengths, as well as contributions the person has made and can continue to make—if the individual decides not to commit suicide.

Having established rapport and demonstrated understanding, the intervenor ought to explore the disadvantages of death if the person remains suicidal. Within the supportive atmosphere of a therapeutic relationship it is appropriate to confront death fantasies that enhance the desirability of suicide. By increasing the person's anxiety about death the worker can decrease, at least temporarily, the attractiveness of suicide. The previously mentioned research by Marsha Linehan and her colleagues (1983) found that fear of death did differentiate between those persons who had seriously considered—but not attempted—suicide and those individuals who had actually engaged in life-threatening behavior.

In a desperate situation the person may finally decide against suicide due to death-related fears. Such fears include the pain of self-injury, the end of life, and the unknown nature of death. Thomas Joiner (e.g., 2005; Ribeiro et al., 2013; Van Orden et al., 2010) points out that, unfortunately, many suicidal persons have had experiences which have desensitized them to the thought of being dead. (Examples of desensitizing experiences include long-standing exposure to pain and suffering, chronic self-mutilation, and multiple suicide attempts.) When that is the case, there may need to be a consideration of consequences beyond those experienced by the individual, such as the impact on family members and friends.

The finality of death is one disadvantage that often is overlooked by young suicidal persons. For example, Israel Orbach (1988) described the case of a suicidal seven-year-old girl whose romantic notions of suicide were shattered when he asked her to describe what happens when a dog dies. Following her insight into the finality of death, she began to make progress in developing new coping techniques.

As demonstrated by Orbach's client, young persons frequently tend to romanticize suicidal death. For instance, they may believe they somehow will be invisibly present and secretly observing the reactions of others to their death. Clinicians (e.g., Orbach, 1988; Stefanowski-Harding, 1990) agree that it is appropriate to confront such beliefs when considering the disadvantages of death.

As previously discussed, Joiner (e.g., 2005; Ribeiro et al., 2013; Van Orden et al., 2010) believes that suicidal individuals often perceive themselves to be a burden and to be disconnected from friends and loved ones. Joiner also believes that these perceptions usually are mistaken and, when they are accurate, almost always identify conditions that are modifiable. Consequently, deciding to kill oneself due to thoughts and feelings related burdensomeness and lack of belongingness is making an ill-informed decision if it involves ending one's life before (1) determining the accuracy of the perceptions, and (2) giving others opportunities to change.

By encouraging the person to analyze the pros and cons of suicide, the worker may help the individual become more objective about wanting to die. After considering the advantages and disadvantages of both life and death, the intervenor must assess the person's continuing attraction to death. As you would suspect, the risk of suicide is still high if the client continues to see death as being more attractive than life.

From the standpoint of planning appropriate interventions, there are several key ways of classifying individuals who have attempted suicide, as noted in the following three sections and in Figure 1.

Chronically Self-Destructive

First, a substantial number of persons who attempt suicide have chronic difficulties. In the previously mentioned study by Herbert Hendin and his colleagues (2001), among the 26 patients who killed themselves, 9 had ongoing substance abuse and 15 displayed moderate to severe impulsivity. In a survey of 16,644 adolescents, 5 percent of them reported having made multiple suicide attempts (Rosenberg et al., 2005). In a 10-year follow-up study (Sonneck & Horn, 1990) of 581 persons who had attempted suicide, 18 percent had made at least one other suicide attempt and 4 percent had killed themselves. In follow-up of a clinical population (previously referred to in this chapter), Cynthia Pfeffer and her colleagues (1991) reported that among a group of 20 individuals who attempted suicide during a six to eight-year period, half of them made multiple attempts. Similarly, in the previously reported research by Paul Trautman and his colleagues (1991), 45 percent of the 60 suicide attempters had made a previous attempt. Compared to persons who have made single suicide attempts, persons making multiple suicide attempts have been found to experience greater psychopathology and more interpersonal difficulty (e.g., Esposito, Spirito, Boergers, & Donaldson, 2003; Forman, Berk, Henriques, Brown, & Beck, 2004).

Rudd, Joiner, and Rajab (1996) studied military personnel receiving mental health treatment. When 68 individuals reporting multiple suicide attempts were compared to 136 persons who had simply thought about suicide and to 128 participants who had each made one suicide attempt, those who had made multiple attempts displayed more serious thoughts of suicide, more depression, greater stress, and less self-appraised problem-solving ability. The authors concluded that this more severe clinical profile elevated the suicide risk for those who had made more than one attempt. In another investigation in the same setting, Joiner and Rudd (2000) found that for those making multiple attempts, the amount of negative life events was not related to the severity of suicidal thoughts and actions. In other words, relatively mild negative events could just as easily lead the person to be suicidal as

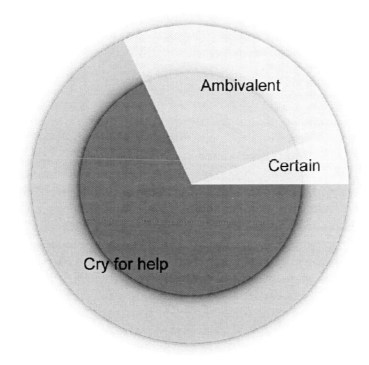

Figure 1
Determining Appropriate Intervention by Assessing Duration and
Intent of Suicidal Behavior
Outer Circle: Chronically self-destructive
Inner Circle: Suicidal crisis

more severe negative events. But the severity of negative events did predict how long the person remained suicidal. The authors hypothesized that such individuals negate support and lack the skills to solve the problems themselves, thereby inviting prolonged periods of feeling suicidal. Unlike those who had made multiple suicide attempts, persons who had simply been thinking of suicide or who had made only one attempt, showed more suicidal symptoms in response to more severe negative events. But the duration of the suicidal episode was almost unrelated to the severity of the negative events. The authors suggested these individuals mobilized and used resources to resolve their difficulties, so that almost regardless of the severity of the negative events, there was a resolution within a brief period of time. These findings and interpretations are consistent with the view that the "ideators" and "one-time attempters" were in suicidal crisis, whereas the "multiple attempters" were chronically self-destructive.

Unfortunately, a common outcome for chronically self-destructive individuals is an early death by suicide. Runeson, Beskow, and Waern (1996) studied suicide deaths among 15- to 29-year-old individuals. The research included eight persons with a diagnosis of schizophrenia, 16 persons with a diagnosis of borderline personality disorder, 13 with a diagnosis of major depression, and eight with a diagnosis of adjustment disorder. The authors calculated the average amount of time from the first communication of suicidal intent or observed suicide attempt to the person's death by suicide. The intervals were as follows: 47 months for those with schizophrenia, 30 months for those with borderline personality disorder, three months for those with major depression, and 0 months for those with adjustment disorder. Within those diagnostic categories, the percentage of individuals for whom the interval was two years or more was as follows: 100 percent for schizophrenia, 63 percent for borderline personality disorder, 31 percent for major depression, and 0 percent for adjustment disorder. Those findings support the view that most of the persons with schizophrenia and borderline personality disorder had been chronically self-destructive, whereas the individuals with adjustment disorder had been in crisis.

Other studies have also found persons with ongoing psychiatric difficulties to be overrepresented among individuals who die by suicide. In a study (King, 1994) of 286 probable suicide deaths over a seven year period, 108 of the deceased persons had received psychiatric care within one year prior to their deaths. Among the recent patients, 85 percent had a history of depression, alcoholism, or schizophrenia and 80 percent were taking psychotropic medication. In the Earle et al. (1994) study of 93 outpatient suicides reported earlier, 77 percent had been hospitalized in a psychiatric facility. Among the 93 deceased individuals, 62 percent had a history of alcohol or drug abuse, 24 percent had a diagnosis of depression, and 32 percent had a diagnosis of schizophrenia.

With regard to chronic mental disorders, psychoses appear to be more problematic than nonpsychotic disorders. In a study of 158 individuals with mental disorders who had attempted suicide, Warman, Forman, Henriques, Brown, and Beck (2004) found that 30.9 percent of the 55 persons with psychotic disorders attempted suicide again within two years, compared to 16.5 percent of those with nonpsychotic disorders.

For persons who have chronic problems such as alcohol or other drug abuse, clinical depression, or schizophrenia, crisis intervention is not a sufficient response. It is true that crisis intervenors may be able to help clients move in positive directions by using core crisis intervention skills, as well as techniques such as those discussed in the "Interventions Involving Long-Standing Issues" section of Chapter 2. Nevertheless, suicide prevention for individuals with chronic difficulties must emphasize long-term rehabilitation that helps them achieve the highest level of functioning possible.

Unfortunately, as clinicians and researchers have noted (e.g., Boergers & Spirito, 2003; Joiner & Rudd, 2000), individuals who are chronically self-destructive often resist help. For instance, in the Earle et al. (1994) study, 30 percent of the outpatient suicide victims were described as being either unwilling or reluctant to accept treatment. And accepting the idea of treatment does not necessarily mean that the person will actually go. For example, Litt, Cuskey, and Rudd (1983) followed up on referral compliance of 27 adolescents who had been brought to a hospital emergency room after a suicide attempt. None of those who had a history of previous suicide attempts complied with the referral, whereas half of those with no previous attempts did seek help from the recommended resource.

Rudd, Joiner, and Rajab (1995) investigated young adults referred to treatment following a suicidal crisis. Compared to the 143 individuals who successfully finished therapy, the 45 persons who dropped out (immediately following completion of the one-day assessment phase or within the initial two days of treatment) had general coping styles that included higher levels of hopelessness, pessimism, and cynicism.

Among suicidal persons who enter therapy, some may continue to demonstrate a lack of cooperation. For example, Trautman, Stewart, and Morishima (1993) studied suicide attempting and nonattempting adolescents who began outpatient treatment in a psychiatric clinic. The mean number of sessions for nonattempters was 5.8, while attempters averaged 4.3 meetings. As a group, attempters dropped out of treatment more quickly and kept a smaller percentage of scheduled visits.

Compared to the studies by Litt et al. (1983) and Trautman et al. (1993), Piacentini et al. (1995) found higher therapy participation rates for adolescent emergency room patients referred to outpatient psychotherapy following a suicide attempt. Among the 143 individuals studied, 91 percent participated in at least one counseling session, and the average number of meetings was 5.9. Although the study was conducted at the same hospital as the Trautman et al. (1993) research, Piacentini et al. (1995) reported using an active style of case management. Within 24 hours of a missed appointment, the family was contacted by phone (or by letter if they did not have a telephone), and a new appointment was scheduled. If two consecutive no-shows occurred, the family received the following communication in a letter: if the next appointment is not kept, the case will be terminated for nonadherence, and, if warranted, a report for medical neglect will be filed. The authors suggested that this "vigorous" case management strategy probably accounted for the higher participation rates.

Some persons stay in therapy and remain suicidal. A study by Jobes, Jacoby, Cimbolic, and Hustead (1997) focused on 73 suicidal college students receiving therapy at a university counseling center. The researchers labeled 18 of the students as "chronic nonresolvers." Those individuals averaged 16.5 therapy sessions and continued to be preoccupied with suicidal ideas, emotions, and behaviors. The remainder of the students were "acute resolvers." They averaged 6.5 therapy sessions that ended with at least three consecutive sessions in which they had no suicidal thoughts or feelings and were judged to be "behaviorally safe."

Receiving therapy, however, does not necessarily preclude another suicide attempt. Anthony Spirito and his colleagues (Spirito et al., 1992) arranged one-month and three-month telephone follow-up contacts with adolescent suicide attempters who received services at a psychiatric hospital or a general hospital. Of the former patients contacted, 6 percent indicated a subsequent attempt at the one-month follow-up and 10 percent reported a subsequent attempt at the three month follow-up. And in a follow-up study with a longer duration, Allard, Marshall, and Plante (1992) recruited individuals who had made a suicide attempt and randomly assigned them to either an experimental group that received intensive outpatient treatment or to a control group. (The control group averaged 1.54 psychiatric contacts during the first year after the attempt, whereas the experimental group averaged 12.35 contacts.) Despite the special effort, 35 percent of the experimental subjects attempted suicide again within two years, compared with 30 percent of the control subjects (a statistically nonsignificant difference).

Cry for Help

Second, information from the Suicide Prevention Center of Los Angeles (Farberow & Litman, 1970) suggests that about two-thirds of all persons who engage in life-threatening behavior do not want to die; instead, they are making a dramatic cry for help.

Some suicidologists refer to such self-destructive events as *instrumental suicide-related behavior* (e.g., Bryan & Rudd, 2006; O'Carroll et al., 1996). Another term sometimes used in this context is *parasuicide*, but there is disagreement on what that word means. Some authors use *parasuicide* to refer to nonfatal self-destructive behavior not primarily intended to end in death (e.g., Chu, 1999; Slaby, 1998), some authors note that *parasuicide* is used to refer both to that behavior and to nonfatal self-harm behavior intended to end in death (e.g., Brown et al., 2002; Leenaars, 2004; Maris, Berman, & Silverman, 2000; Miller & Glinski, 2000; O'Carroll et al., 1996; Plutchik, 2000; Roy, 2001), and other authors simply say it is self-destructive behavior that does not end in death (e.g., Pfeffer, 2001). Some who had been using the term, such as the WHO/EURO Multicenter Study of Parasuicide, have chosen to replace it with terms such as *suicidal behavior* (e.g., Kinyanda, Hjelmeland, & Musisi, 2005; Sayil & Devrimci-Ozguven, 2002). Others recommend that the term should be abandoned altogether (e.g., Crosby et al., 2011; De

Leo, Burgis, Bertolote, Kerkhof, & Bille-Brahe, 2006). That recommendation seems to be well founded.

Many "cry for help" individuals are in the second phase of crisis. Often they have sought help in dealing with the pressures they are facing, but help has not materialized. In an effort to solicit the needed aid, these persons take dramatic, attention-getting action. Crisis intervention can be a sufficient response for persons in crisis who are making a cry for help, so long as the worker begins the intervention by recognizing the client's desperation.

Ambivalent or Certain

Third, research (Farberow & Litman, 1970; Gispert, Davis, Marsh, & Wheeler, 1987) suggests that about 5 percent of those who attempt suicide are completely sure they want to die, while about 30 percent of persons who engage in life threatening behavior are ambivalent and leave their rescue to fate. Many of the individuals in these two categories are in the third phase of crisis. Despair is the predominant emotion. They have given up trying to resolve the difficulties, and they see suicide as offering a way of ending the unbearable pressure.

One concrete indicator of having given up may be a suicide note. In the previously discuss research by Timothy DeJong and his colleagues (2010) that compared 50 live individuals who had attempted suicide to 50 persons who had killed themselves, significantly more of the deceased persons had left a suicide note (52% vs. 20%).

For the suicidal individual in phase three of crisis the potential for life-threatening behavior often lasts several days. In helping the person survive this crucial period, mental health experts (e.g., American Academy of Child and Adolescent Psychiatry, 2001; Berman et al., 2006; Bongar & Sullivan, 2013; Deemer, 2004, Hendin et al., 2001; Leenaars, 2004; Roberts & Yeager, 2005; Silverman, 2005) believe that suicide prevention efforts may need to include hospitalization.

To summarize appropriate interventions with regard to the categories in Figure 1, here are the major points.

- Ongoing services are necessary for individuals who engage in suicidal behavior and are chronically self-destructive.
- Crisis intervention can be a sufficient response for persons who do not have long-standing difficulties, but who, during a crisis, "attempt suicide" in order to communicate a dramatic cry for help.
- Hospitalization needs to be seriously considered for individuals who engage in suicidal behavior and are ambivalent or certain about wanting to be dead (regardless of whether they have long-standing problems).

Hospitalization

Bongar and Sullivan (2013) and Kleespies (2014) noted that legal and clinical standards of care require intervenors to specify and apply criteria for hospitalization of suicidal individuals. One such set of criteria was developed by Bengelsdorf, Levy, Emerson, and Barile (1984). They suggested that when deciding whether to support hospitalization versus outpatient service, the following three factors should be evaluated: dangerousness, support, and cooperation. (These three considerations were discussed in Chapter 1 with regard to problem-solving topics to be included in contacts with individuals who have long-standing psychiatric problems. Danger, support, and cooperation are in both sets, whereas self-care is also included when the assessment concerns a person with chronic difficulties.)

With regard to the following scale, Herbert Bengelsdorf and his colleagues use a total score of nine or below as indicating that hospitalization should be seriously considered. On the other hand, they believe outpatient services probably are appropriate for persons receiving scores of ten or higher. (The numerals indicate the number of points assigned for each item.)

Suicidal/Homicidal Danger

(1) Threatens suicidal or homicidal behavior, has made a recent dangerous attempt, or is unpredictably violent.

(2) Threatens suicidal or homicidal behavior or has made a recent dangerous attempt but at times sees such thoughts and actions as unacceptable, or has a history of unpredictable violence or impulsivity but none currently.

(3) Life-threatening thoughts that are ambivalent in nature, a "suicide attempt" that did not place the person in any medical danger, or inconsistent impulse control.

(4) Some current or past suicidal or homicidal actions or thoughts but clearly intends to abandon them, and has no problem with impulse control.

(5) No evidence of life-threatening thoughts or behavior, and no history of difficulty with impulse control.

Support

(1) Insufficient support from family, friends, or community resources.

(2) Potential support exists but impact is likely to be small.

(3) Sufficient support can be arranged but with difficulty.

(4) Sufficient support can be arranged but there are questions regarding the reliability of some components.
(5) Appropriate support is available.

Cooperation

(1) Unwillingness or inability to cooperate.
(2) Little appreciation or understanding of intervention efforts.
(3) Passive acceptance of intervention efforts.
(4) Ambivalence or weak motivation with regard to intervention efforts.
(5) Initiates request for outpatient services and is motivated to actively participate in treatment.

The Bengelsdorf scale continues to be recognized as helpful way of distinguishing between the need for outpatient services and the need for hospitalization (e.g., Brooker, Ricketts, Bennett, & Lemme, 2007; Horsfall, Cleary, & Hunt, 2010; Links, Eynan, Ball, Barr, & Rourke, 2005; Reilly, Newton, & Dowling, 2007).

With regard to the Bengelsdorf et al. (1984) inclusion of medical danger as a factor, there is empirical research to suggest that intervenors proceed with caution. This caveat is suggested by research findings showing that persons attempting suicide often have a poor understanding of the medical danger associated with the means of suicide attempt they selected. For example, Brown, Henriques, Sosdjan, and Beck (2004) studied 180 suicide attempters age 16 and older who were treated in the emergency room of a large metropolitan hospital. Less than half of them (82) had an accurate understanding of the medical risk associated with the self-injury in which they had engaged. This lack of understanding may be even higher for young people. DeMaso, Ross, and Beardslee (1994) studied 17 teenage suicide attempters receiving service in an emergency room. The investigators found no statistically significant relationship between the degree of suicidal intent and the medical danger of the attempt. Another study (Kingsbury, 1993) set in a hospital emergency room recruited 50 adolescent overdose patients. Their responses to the Beck Suicide Intent Scale indicated that self-reported suicidal intent accounted for only 6 percent of the variance in dangerous actions associated with the overdose. In other words, some of the participants had low-lethality actions but high-lethality intent, again suggesting caution in assigning a psychological meaning to the medical danger associated with suicide attempts.

In light of the empirical evidence cited in the preceding paragraph, intervenors should not dismiss a low-danger attempt if the person expected to die from it. Consistent with this point of view, Strauss, Chassin, and Lock (1995) asserted that for purposes of hospitalization decisions, a method indicating high lethality is one that is capable of causing death or is one that the person believes to be deadly, and other experts have expressed similar beliefs (e.g., Pfeffer, 2001).

Way and Banks (2001) investigated admission decisions regarding 456 psychiatric emergency service patients. The factor most closely related to hospitalization was danger to self. Other related factors were psychosis, self-care ability, impulse control, and depression. Those results are consistent with the findings produced by Bengelsdorf and his colleagues, although the factors studied by the two research teams were somewhat different.

Regardless of the person's score on the Bengelsdorf scale or other measures of suicide lethality, clinicians (e.g., Kleespies, 2014; Roberts & Yeager, 2005) note that hospitalization should be encouraged if the individual continues to express an immediate intent to be dead, while refusing or being unable to productively participate in adaptive problem solving.

Decreasing the Availability of Lethal Means

When working with a person who is considering life-threatening action an immediate objective is to decrease the availability of lethal means. Clinicians and researchers (e.g., American Academy of Child and Adolescent Psychiatry, 2001; Azrael et al., 2004; Berman, 2006; Berman et al., 2006; Bongar & Sullivan, 2013; Brent & Bridge, 2003; Bryan, Stone, & Rudd, 2011; Jobes et al., 2005; Kleespies, 2014; Leenaars, 2004; Silverman, 2005; Stellrecht et al., 2006; Ribeiro et al., 2013) agree that often a primary focus of the interaction should be the removal of weapons, pills, or other means of suicide. Depending upon the situation, elimination of available means can be done by the client, a relative or friend, a crisis worker, or the police. Any of these persons can be effective, so long as the removal is done in a safe and reliable way.

One group of researchers (Kruesi et al., 1999) studied the consequences of bringing up and discussing the issue of decreasing the availability of lethal means. In a project involving the parents of adolescents who had been to a hospital emergency room and had received a mental health evaluation there, the researchers examined the effects of what they termed "restriction education." Parents receiving such education were told they could reduce the risk of death by limiting the availability of deadly means, especially firearms, and they were assisted in developing plans for restricting access to such means. Compared to a group of parents who were not given such information and assistance, those who did receive it were much more likely to take action that involved locking up or disposing of firearms, alcohol, and medication.

Craig Bryan and his colleagues (2011) discussed "means restriction counseling." They emphasized that whenever feasible a plan to decrease the availability of lethal means should result from collaborative interaction with the client. Both safety and effectiveness of the plan must be prime considerations. In addition, appropriate involvement of family members and other sources of support often is a key element. The authors suggested production of a written receipt acknowledging what has been agreed to with regard to the means, as well as a separate document describing the elements of the crisis intervention plan that has been developed. Their article provides examples of both documents.

In cases involving suicidal persons who are armed or threatening to jump from a high place, workers ought to be low-key and deliberate. Intervenors should avoid both esoteric philosophizing and threatening ultimatums. It is better to concentrate on the present realities, such as being scared, cold, tired, or hungry.

Some clinicians (e.g., Carney & Hazler, 1998; Pitcher & Poland, 1992; Range, 2005; Rosenberg, 1999) advocate using an agreement that the person will not commit suicide during the next ____ amount of time, with the ____ being whatever commitment the individual is willing to make. Nevertheless, as crisis intervention and suicide prevention experts (e.g., Berman, 2006; Berman et al., 2006; Bongar & Sullivan, 2013; Clark & Kerkhof, 1993; Egan, 1997; Hoff & Hoff, 2012; Joiner, 2005; Kalafat & Underwood, 2005; Leenaars, 2001; McMyler & Pryjmachuk, 2008; Miller, 1999; Rudd et al., 2006) also point out, workers must beware of placing too much faith in such contracts. For example, one counselor I know elicited such an agreement from a young man who then fatally hanged himself less than an hour later. Such experiences with no-suicide contracts apparently are not unusual. Edwards and Sachmann (2010) found that among the 420 practitioners they surveyed, 154 had used no-suicide contracts. For one-third of that minority, after signing the contract a client had engaged in a "serious suicide attempt" or had died by suicide.

Any value of a "no suicide contract" probably comes from the process that surrounds it. By being courageous enough to hear the person's pain and by offering to work with the individual in order to achieve pain relief, the worker communicates genuine caring for the client. As clinicians have noted (e.g., Leenaars, 2004; Motto, 1999), the potential to prevent suicide arises out of the offer of that authentic relationship.

When a worker does negotiate an agreement that calls for a person to avoid self-harm, the contract needs to specify good-faith actions by the client. Possible examples include deciding on adaptive responses to make if suicidal thoughts return, relinquishing potential overdose drugs, and giving up one's firearms.

Workers are interested in decreasing the availability of means by which clients can kill themselves, but no approach is foolproof. The most powerful measure possible is to hospitalize the client under a suicide watch. But not even this drastic measure works all of the time. I have known four patients who killed themselves while hospitalized under a 24-hour suicide watch, and unfortunately my experience is not unique (e.g., Cassells et al., 2005; Jones, Hales, Butwell, Ferriter, & Taylor, 2011).

As previously mentioned, in correctional facilities suicidal inmates are sometimes placed in isolation with close observation. A study of youth suicides during incarceration found that the most common setting for the death (43 percent of all instances) was during waking hours while the young person was confined to a room (Hayes, 2009). Such restriction is no more foolproof for incarcerated individuals than it is for hospitalized persons, and this isolated confinement can actually facilitate suicide in two ways. First, when separated from others, suicidal individuals may concentrate their thoughts on creative methods of killing themselves. Second, isolation cuts the person off from usual social interaction. Anyone placed in solitary confinement can be expected to feel disconnected and sad. For a suicidal individual such isolation makes it more difficult to distract oneself from depression; consequently, despondency may worsen and suicidal thinking may increase. For example, Bonner (2006) found that prisoners held in isolation had significantly higher amounts of suicidal thinking and depression than did inmates in the general prison population.

Due to the dangers of isolated confinement some corrections experts (e.g., Winkler, 1992) recommend avoiding isolation and instead placing suicidal individuals in a dormitory setting so that at least one other person is housed with the individual. This strategy has two advantages. It provides social interaction that can help to alleviate depression, and it involves the presence of others who can aid in preventing death in the event of a suicide attempt.

Whatever the nature of the intervention, the rare individual who remains bent on suicide eventually will succeed. Seemingly unaware of our imperfect ability to physically prevent suicide, some individuals fear that intervenors will make suicide impossible. When I have found that such a fear is blocking the development of a working relationship, I have said to the client, "If you decide you really want to do it, I can't stop you from killing yourself." As clinicians have noted (e.g., Jobes, 2000), leaving open the possibility of suicide in this way can encourage the person to try new problem-solving efforts, since the option of death still remains.

Problem Solving

When working with a suicidal person there are three possibilities—death, physically preventing suicide, and helping the person choose life. As has been previously discussed, crisis intervenors strive to prevent the first possibility; the second possibility can be a lifesaving technique in the short run, although it is impractical as a permanent solution; and the third possibility is the best one. It involves attempting to engage the person in a problem-solving process.

As previously noted, suicidal persons often feel helpless and out of control. Part of such helplessness comes from repeated failure to resolve the situation, but, as experts have observed (e.g., Berman et al., 2006; Brown, Jeglic, Henriques, & Beck, 2006; Clark et al., 2011; Dieserud et al., 2001; Ellis, 2001; Gould, Shaffer, et al., 2003; Leenaars, 2004; Reinecke & Didie, 2005; Reinecke, 2006; Rudd, 2006; Wagner & Zimmerman, 2006; Williams, Barnhofer, Crane, & Duggan, 2006), often another contributing factor is the individual's own inadequate approach to problem solving.

As conceptualized in this book, the first task in problem solving is to explore thoughts and feelings. Attempting to suppress and avoid unpleasant thoughts and feelings characterized many depressed older patients in a study by Lynch, Cheavens, Morse, and Rosenthal (2004). The researchers found that such efforts were correlated with increased hopelessness and more frequent thoughts of suicide. In a similar vein, Cha and Nock (2009) found that adolescents who had been sexually abused as children were more likely to have thoughts of suicide and suicide attempts if they currently were doing a poor job of understanding and managing emotions.

Considering alternatives, the second stage of problem solving discussed in this book, can also be difficult for suicidal individuals. In a study of 48 adolescent suicide attempters by Kienhorst, De Wilde, Diekstra, and Wolters (1995), the most frequently endorsed (80% of participants) reason for attempting suicide was that circumstances were unbearable so something had to be done, and the person did not know what else to do. It has been empirically demonstrated that poor problem solving such as that is frequently associated with feelings of hopelessness and with suicidal thinking and behavior (Rudd et al., 1994). As indicated by empirical research (e.g., Dixon, Heppner, & Rudd, 1994) the progression seems to be that poor problem solving often results in feelings of hopelessness, which in turn can lead to thoughts of suicide.

Moving from thinking about suicide to attempting suicide can be facilitated by the disinhibitory effects of alcohol. Borges and Rosovsky (1996) compared 40 emergency room patients who had just attempted suicide to 372 emergency room patients admitted for other reasons. Those who had attempted suicide were much more likely to be under the influence of intermediate or high levels of alcohol. Borges and Rosovsky believe their findings suggest alcohol consumption can facilitate high-risk behaviors that would be less likely to occur if the person were thinking clearly in a sober state.

Many suicidal persons display cognitive restriction. And their rigid thinking often leads to difficulties in identifying problems and potential solutions, as demonstrated in empirical research (e.g., Dieserud et al., 2001; Orbach, Bar-Joseph, & Dror, 1990; Westheide et al., 2008).

One study focused on adolescent females and compared 77 emergency room patients who had attempted suicide to 39 nonsuicidal psychiatric outpatients and to 23 nondisturbed individuals (Rotheram-Borus, Trautman, Dopkins, & Shrout, 1990). The factor that best differentiated those who had attempted suicide from the nonsuicidal outpatients and the nondisturbed individuals was skill at interpersonal problem solving. On average, those who had attempted suicide demonstrated less skill at generating options in situations involving interpersonal difficulties.

Another study examined incarcerated adolescent males. There were the following three groups of participants: 15 inmates who had harmed themselves within the previous three days and were currently suicidal, 21 inmates with a history of suicidal self-harm who were not currently suicidal, and 25 inmates with no current or past suicidal intent (Biggam & Power, 1999). When compared to the other two groups in terms of their interpersonal problem-solving ability, the currently suicidal inmates offered more irrelevant ideas and more passive solutions.

Jeffrey Bridge and his colleagues (2012) compared the decision-making ability of 40 adolescents who had attempted suicide during the past year to the decision-making ability of 40 adolescents receiving mental health treatment who had never attempted suicide. Overall ability to identify and use advantageous strategies in a card-selection task was significantly better for those who had never attempted suicide. Those with no history of suicide attempts also learned during the decision-making task and became better at it, whereas those who had attempted suicide did not show such progress.

Marzuk, Hartwell, Leon, and Portera (2005) recruited research participants from among persons currently hospitalized and diagnosed as experiencing a major depressive episode. The investigators assessed the cognitive abilities of the participants and compared the results from 25 patients currently thinking of suicide to those of 28 patients who were not currently having such thoughts. There were significant differences on two tests that required changes in thinking and response patterns, with the suicidal group having average scores indicating more rigid thinking. Within each group the variability among subjects was also different, with the suicidal patients showing two to three times the variability of the nonsuicidal patients. In other words, within the suicidal group some individuals had much worse cognitive restriction than others. That finding highlights the importance of responding to the particular needs of the person with whom you are working.

If clients have failed in earlier coping attempts, which may have included the use of alcohol and other mood-altering drugs, suicide may seem to be the only means of stopping the unbearable pain. When they do think of alternative solutions, suicidal individuals often fail to give sufficient consideration to those possibilities and they tend to overemphasize potential negative outcomes, as demonstrated in research by David Schotte and George Clum (1987).

Children and adolescents may be especially susceptible to such restricted thinking because they have limited experience. It may be easier to see suicide as "the only solution" when one has had just a few years to develop a repertoire of possibilities. After reviewing 22 studies on the topic, Speckens and Hawton (2005) concluded that adolescents engaging in suicidal behavior commonly have trouble with social problem solving and that improving their abilities in that area should be a focus of treatment.

At least one study, however, suggests that for adolescents the deficit in problem solving has more to do with quality than with quantity. Keith Wilson and his colleagues (1995) compared 20 suicidal adolescent psychiatric inpatients to 20 adolescents from families of nonmedical hospital staff. Participants in the two groups did not differ in the number of possible options generated for their own most stressful recent life events. They did differ, though, in their understanding of those events and in their responses to them. The suicidal adolescents showed less understanding of the roles they played in bringing about those difficulties. They used fewer of the strategies they generated and also selected more maladaptive options. The results of this study suggest that suicidal adolescents may need considerable problem-solving support.

Joseph Richman (1994) pointed out that, contrary to adolescents, an older person who is suicidal may actually be the best resource for problem solving. The individual's decades of experience in confronting and dealing with difficulties may provide a rich supply of positive ideas. In order to take advantage of that resource, Doctor Richman recommends attempting to tap into the person's wisdom and using it in grappling with the current issues.

Few suicidal individuals seek death; instead they desire an end to what, for the moment, has become an intolerable life. Rather than wanting to be dead, most suicidal persons simply want an end to their painful situation. As Edwin Shneidman observed (e.g., 1999, 2001), the goal in suicide prevention is to relieve the distress and pain in ways that allow life to continue.

Although intervenors should not use moralizing or intimidation in an attempt to convince suicidal clients to choose life, workers must be prepared to confront restricted viewpoints. Clinicians (e.g., Berman et al., 2006; Ellis, 2001; Jobes, 2000; Leenaars, 2004; Rudd, Joiner, Jobes, & King, 1999) agree that intervenors should express the intention to assist the person in tackling problems and that the interaction should focus on expanding possibilities the client perceives to be available. In such a collaborative problem-solving relationship, the client has the potential to feel valued and to reestablish a sense of control, thereby decreasing helplessness and hopelessness.

Empirical research (Pietromonaco & Rook, 1987) has found that depressed persons frequently encourage their own social isolation because they tend to avoid situations that pose interpersonal risks. But research (Folkman & Lazarus, 1986) has also demonstrated that depressed individuals have a high need for social support. So it is not surprising that suicidal individuals often feel abandoned, disconnected, and lonely (e.g., Berman et al., 2006; Brown, 2006; Stravynski & Boyer, 2001). In one study that compared older individuals who had died by suicide to a matched group of control participants, loneliness characterized more than half of the suicide victims, and it was the feature that most distinguished them from the control participants (Waern, Rubenowitz, & Wilhelmson, 2003). Since withdrawal and social isolation are common problems, clinicians and researchers (e.g., Ribeiro et al., 2013) note that frequently there is a need to reestablish interpersonal relationships. Friends and relatives ought to be included in plans when it is possible and appropriate. And in cases of suicidal minors, intervenors should involve parents or other guardians.

Researchers (e.g., Greenhill & Waslick, 1997; Van Heeringen et al., 1995) have noted that suicidal individuals tend to be less likely than nonsuicidal persons to follow through with problem-solving plans that have been negotiated. For example, among callers to SANELINE who were from London and were experiencing psychosis or depression, 44 percent of those who were suicidal reported being noncompliant with previous treatment recommendations, compared to 21 percent of those who were not suicidal (Fakhoury, 2002). Consequently, as experts note (e.g., Berman, 2006), the intervenor may need to involve others in order to help monitor the client's compliance with the problem-solving strategy that has been negotiated. For instance, it might be helpful to have a friend or relative stay with the person awhile. As noted in Chapter 2, though, before incorporating others into problem-solving plans, there needs to be a clear understanding of what they bring to the endeavor. Potential positive contributions should clearly outweigh any anticipated difficulties.

In some cases, the worker may need to encourage the client to focus on disrupted relationships. For instance, if a client's husband has left her and she sees no possibility of renewing the marriage, ways of coping without him should be discussed. Or if difficulties with a close friend have contributed to the client's suicidal crisis, then that friendship should be explored and alternatives considered. Empirical research supports such intervention efforts. For example, a study by Lewinsohn, Rohde, and Seeley (1996) found that suicidal high school students often displayed a combination of interpersonal problems and negative coping styles. One of the authors' recommendations was that intervenors be prepared to help such individuals deal with inter-personal difficulties.

If loss of sleep is a problem, medical consultation may be appropriate in order to obtain a short-acting tranquilizer. Although drug-induced sleep is not as good as natural sleep, after a night's rest the client may be better able to renew efforts toward coping with the situation. Workers must remember, however, that medication can never substitute for the rapport and problem solving that characterize crisis intervention.

As this section notes, there can be many challenges to engaging suicidal individuals in problem solving. It is, however, worth the effort. For example, Carmen Stewart and her colleagues (2009) found that compared to those having "treatment as usual," suicide attempters who participated in problem solving experienced significant decreases in suicidal ideation and hopeless-ness.

Recognizing the Potential for Homicide

Worldwide 1 percent to 4 percent of individuals who die by suicide engage in homicide immediately prior to their deaths (Large, Smith, & Nielssen, 2009). Clinicians (Jacobs et al., 1999; Lanceley, 2003; Nock & Marzuk, 1999) agree that when working with suicidal individuals it is always appropriate to recognize and explore the possibility of homicide. Both suicide and homi-cide are destructive acts, and empirical research (e.g., Greenwald, Reznikoff, & Plutchik, 1994) indicates that at times thoughts of suicide and thoughts of violence toward others are linked. Consequently, suicide prevention may also need to involve homicide prevention. For example, Brent et al. (1993) found that among 67 adolescents who had killed themselves, nine demon-strated homicidal thinking during the week prior to their deaths, whereas none of the 67 individuals in the matched control group expressed such thoughts. And Asnis, Kaplan, van Praag, and Sanderson (1994) compared 403 psychiatric outpatients with no history of homicidal thoughts or attempts to 92 outpatients who had considered homicide and to 22 who had attempt-ed homicide. Out of the 127 suicide attempts reported by the three groups, 65 percent were by members of the "no homicidal behavior" group, 19 per-cent were by those in the "considered homicide" group, and 16 percent were by individuals who had attempted homicide. Thus, 35 percent of the persons who had attempted suicide had also considered or attempted homicide.

Cohen, Llorente, and Eisdorfer (1998) studied suicides in seven Florida counties over a seven-year period. Within that population, about 3 percent of those who killed themselves first killed someone else. More than three-fourths of those murder-suicides were spousal/"consortial" couples in which the man killed the woman, then himself. (Most of the "55 and older" couples were living together, whereas just over half of those "54 and younger" were separated.) Only 8 percent of the cases involved "nonfamilial" victims. So while friends and relatives can be important sources of support, they can also be potential murder victims. For example, during a call to a crisis service a suicidal man expressed a desire for his girlfriend to come see him. When the outreach team arrived at his house (without the girlfriend), he came to the door carrying a loaded gun, ready to shoot the person he expected to be his girlfriend.

When is intended violence foreseeable? According to state courts that have evaluated the issue, there are the following three primary factors relating to the foreseeability of violence: (1) having a history of violent behavior, (2) threatening an identifiable victim, and (3) having a credible motive for engaging in violence. If none or just one of these factors is present, courts rarely find that violence was foreseeable. When two or three of the factors exist, courts usually rule that violence was foreseeable (Beck, 1998). If a client expresses homicidal thoughts or other serious threats of harm regarding a specific person or group, the worker should consult with a colleague or supervisor. When the danger is judged to be genuine, legal and mental health experts (e.g., Eddy & Harris, 1998; Truscott, Evans, & Mansell, 1995) agree that there is an obligation to protect the intended victim or victims. Appropriate actions can include warning identified targets, notifying law enforcement, and advocating hospitalization.

What results when a clinician warns a person who has been threatened? That question was the focus of a study by Renee Binder and Dale McNiel (1996). Their data came from 22 psychiatric residents who, except for one outpatient case, were reporting on experiences in emergency rooms and inpatient programs. Of 15 potential victims who were warned, 11 already knew threats had been made against them. The most common reaction among the four who did not know was a combination of fearing the patient and being thankful for the warning. Of the 11 who already knew of the threats, nine expressed thankfulness for the warning. Among the 23 threatening patients described in the study who were told of a completed warning or an ongoing effort to warn, 13 had no significant reaction, two were thankful, and eight were angry at the clinician. With regard to effects on the therapeutic relationship, the physicians judged that out of the 23 cases in which the patient knew of the warning effort, there was no effect in 15 cases, a negative effect in five cases, and a positive effect in three cases. The researchers concluded that there are few negative consequences and frequent positive consequences associated with warning potential victims.

When planning an outreach to a suicidal client's location, there ought to be an effort to discover whether a weapon is at the scene. When it is learned that there is a gun or other weapon at the location, arrangements should be made for police to accompany the crisis workers so that the law enforcement officers can disarm the person, if necessary. Although workers may act as consultants to the officers in such cases, removing weapons from the scene is a police activity.

While law enforcement assistance sometimes is necessary for the safety of crisis workers, it has other advantages as well. For example, if there is no response at the client's door, the police can be invaluable in helping the workers to gain entry, either by obtaining a key from a landlord or by actually breaking in—if such drastic action is necessary.

> EXAMPLE. Rose Sawyer called the crisis service saying she was furious with her psychiatrist. She said that during the morning's appointment with him he had announced that he was going to terminate her psychotherapy. She claimed he did not appreciate how much she needed help. In order to prove her point she said she was going to go home and kill her daughter and herself.
>
> As the worker explored her plan, Rose told him that she had a gun in her car and that her daughter would be home alone when she got there. Although Rose said she had been in therapy for some time, she stated she never had tried to kill herself. When the worker requested identifying information, Rose refused to give her name; but the worker persisted in seeking information until he was able to discover what she was wearing, a description of her automobile, and that she was calling from her car while parked at a convenience store.
>
> An assisting worker decided to start calling all of the local psychiatrists in an effort to obtain further identifying information. His first call was to the mental health center, and he quickly described the situation to the receptionist. She remembered a woman from the morning's appointments who fit the caller's description. The worker asked to speak with the patient's psychiatrist, who declined the request. Nevertheless, the receptionist did provide the client's name, phone number, and address. The worker then called the patient's residence, but no one answered.
>
> Next, the assisting worker called the police and reported the situation. He provided the caller's name, as well as a description of her clothing and car; he also said that she was calling from her car in the parking lot of a convenience store and that the sound of traffic could be heard in the background. The police notified their patrolling units to be on the lookout for a car fitting the description parked at a convenience store near a major road. Within ten minutes the police had located a likely car and driver. A plainclothes team of officers then went to the convenience store parking lot. They identified themselves and confirmed that the caller was indeed Rose Sawyer, who still was talking to the crisis worker. Rose allowed the officers to take the gun from her car and agreed to accompany them to the police station where the crisis team met her. In addition, the workers requested participation of a protective services staff member to represent the interests of the daughter.
>
> Rose, the crisis team, and the protective services worker spent an hour devising a plan agreeable to all participants. It called for the daughter to stay with

a friend for several days. Rather than killing anyone, Rose decided to confront the psychiatrist with her feelings of being misunderstood and rejected. During the negotiations the crisis team pointed out that other therapists were available, should the physician stick by his decision to terminate their relationship. Rose agreed to contact the crisis service following her next meeting with the psychiatrist.

By this time the assisting worker was able to contact Rose's husband. He eventually arrived and joined the discussion. Frank Sawyer supported the plan and agreed to be with Rose as much as possible during the next several days. The protective services worker said that his office would continue to monitor the case in order to help assure the daughter's safety.

DISCUSSION OF ROSE SAWYER'S CASE. Rose had a lethal plan. She had decided to go home and shoot herself and her daughter with the gun she had in her car, so her intentions were deadly, available, and specific. Since her difficulties sprang from her fear of losing the relationship with her psychiatrist, the life-threatening episode was *sudden* and it involved an *object loss*. The predominant *emotion* she was feeling was anger. Consequently, lethality was increased by the four factors of a lethal plan, a dangerous emotion, a sudden upsurge in difficulties, and a significant object loss. On the other hand, Rose denied *previous suicide attempts*, suggesting a less than maximum degree of suicide lethality. The worker's assessment of the situation was that Rose might kill herself, but that the danger to her daughter was greater.

Since life-threatening behavior had not yet taken place there was no need for *interrupting a suicide attempt in progress*. In *determining appropriate intervention* the crisis workers decided that everything possible had to be done to prevent Rose from going home with a gun in her possession because they believed there was a strong *potential for homicide*. Consequently, *decreasing the availability of lethal means* was a top priority of the intervention. The crisis workers requested police assistance both in finding Rose and in transporting her. Since there was a weapon at the scene, the crisis staff supported the police decision that law enforcement intervention was more appropriate than a crisis outreach.

Problem solving focused on the safety of the daughter, on Rose's relationship with her psychiatrist, and on preventing Rose from killing herself. The resulting plan included measures that focused on each of those issues.

(a) The workers contacted an appropriate community agency to protect the daughter, and the resulting plan included concrete steps to increase her safety.

(b) If Rose did not succeed in renewing her relationship with the psychiatrist she would seek a new psychotherapist.

(c) Rose's husband agreed to spend extra time with her during the next several days.

TERMINAL STAGE OF ILLNESS[1]

What are we facing when we confront death? There are many different opinions.

I once led a suicide prevention workshop in the large conference room of a hotel. The topic for the second day of the meeting was intervening with suicidal individuals. During a discussion concerning the consequences of suicide we began talking about what happens after death. In addition to considering various religious beliefs concerning existence following death, I brought up the viewpoint that existence ends at death. To demonstrate this idea I asked one of the participants to switch off the room lights. Since the facility also served as a nightclub, he had some difficulty locating the correct controls among the various switches for the lighting system. While he continued to search, I presented the analogy that some believe death is like turning off the lights–it is a quiet, peaceful nonexistence.

Just as I finished describing the analogy the lights dimmed. Rather than the expected darkness, however, the room suddenly filled with swirling and sparkling light from a brilliant mirrored ball in the ceiling. The participants gasped and we all began to wonder whether our discussion had been joined by the preeminent Advocate for the heavenly viewpoint.

Although no one knows for a fact what death is like, most views on what happens after death can be classified into four major categories.

- Death is quiet, peaceful nonexistence. This is the belief I was demonstrating when interrupted by the sparkling light.
- The essence of the personality survives in the form of an immortal soul.
- At some point in the future the body will be reconstituted and restored to life.
- An aspect of the personality will be reincarnated in another life form and live again on earth.

The latter three views all involve religious faith, and faith exists only when there is no proof. In the absence of concrete evidence, even the most religious person can have questions about exactly what death will bring.

Thoughts of death sometimes are expressed directly by a terminal patient. In other cases, the person may indirectly approach troubling topics. For instance, a child may ask, "What would happen to me if a plane crashed into my room?" The best response to such a question is a reflection that clarifies what really is being asked, such as, "You want to know what happens when

---

1. Most of this section is taken from *The Hospital Patient: A Guide for Family and Friends* by Kenneth France.

we die." Making that kind of reflection takes courage, but being willing to frankly confront the topic can help the person share a tremendous burden.

Death can be seen as the release from pain, or one can choose to "risk death" by agreeing to a dangerous medical procedure. Nevertheless, few individuals look forward to death.

Even when life is full of suffering, we know what it means to live. Death is different, however, since it is the unknown. Although death is just as much a part of life as birth, its unknown aspect makes death harder to accept.

The burden of facing the unknown can be lightened by the presence of friends and loved ones. Regardless of what we believe about death, it is reassuring to know that one's life has had significance. It can be comforting to see that contributions we have made will still affect those whose lives continue.

Learning that an individual's condition is terminal is stressful for the ill person and for the individual's friends and family. Common feelings at the time of the terminal diagnosis include shock, disbelief, anger, fear, and despair. Being unable to ward off death, persons may experience feelings of futility or helplessness. There may be dreams and goals for which there now is no hope of ever attaining. Vital relationships will end.

If there is gradual deterioration the person may become tired of the condition, tired of medical treatment, and tired of the pain and discomfort. Likewise, family members may grow weary of lengthy or repeated hospitalizations, weary of seeing the person in pain, and weary of the pressure placed on them.

A slowly worsening medical condition threatens self-worth as the person loses physical abilities and role responsibilities while becoming more dependent upon others. As dependency increases, so may anxiety over a host of questions. What will death be like? Will I face it alone? How bad will my physical condition become before I die? How much pain will there be?

When a person anticipates the end of life as we know it, there is mourning over the loss of relationships and the things of this world. Such mourning may include guilt over the hurt and difficulty one's death will cause those who are close.

Some terminal individuals become so overwhelmed by self-doubt, anxiety, or grief that they withdraw into themselves in unreachable isolation. Others strive to cope by denying the reality of their situation. Eventually, many patients come to terms with these issues and are able to face death with either a sense of resignation or an attitude of acceptance.

Honest communication can initiate problem solving regarding those circumstances that are possible to modify. Even when a person's survival and recovery clearly are impossible, setting limited goals that are within reach provides a realistic sense of hope. Working on such tasks can aid coping in a number of ways. Attention is focused on concrete realities and away from anxieties; there are interactions with others and with the environment that demonstrate the person still is a part of this world; reaching the goals often gives a sense of mastery and control that enhances dignity and self-esteem. Being productive, even in limited ways, may provide a feeling of achievement that helps to ease the loss of traditional work and family roles.

There may come a time when there is little that can be done for the person. Yet, there often are friends and family members who could benefit from care and support. Productive contributions may include listening to their concerns and aiding them with problem solving.

It is adaptive to maintain hope. Rather than hope for recovery, however, it may become hope for the patient to be comfortable and hope for the well-being of those who are close, as they move toward acceptance of the inevitable loss they are going to face.

Helping the terminal individual and others with their immediate needs allows them to cope with the situation one day at a time, but they may also want to start planning for what the future will bring. While still cherishing relationships, the terminal person may seek permission to begin separating from friends and family members. And as those who are close continue expressing affection, they may also begin allowing themselves to gradually detach from the individual.

Family members and friends should have an outlet for sharing their grief and other feelings. With a caring person they may need to search for the meaning or purpose of the patient's impending death. They may also have unpleasant feelings to share, such as fear, helplessness, anger, or guilt.

Some of the negative feelings of those who are close may relate to the medical staff. When appropriate, friends and relatives may need to act on their feelings and be assertive with the staff members in question or their supervisors. At the same time, however, it is necessary to remember that doctors, nurses, and other staff members are only human and that technology has its limitations.

Participating in the choice to end medical treatment for a terminal patient may be one of the most difficult kinds of support to provide. Medical technology has changed the definition of death. Although at one time a person was considered dead when there was no heartbeat or respiration, now machines often can maintain those functions. Consequently, the medical profession has developed the concept of brain death. Key elements in brain death are the following:

- a deep coma causing the person to be unresponsive;
- no independent respiration or spontaneous reflexes for 12 hours; and
- the reason for the coma is known and is judged to be irreversible. (Guidelines, 1981)

A number of burdensome questions may arise when a patient is close to death. Here are some possibilities: When does one conclude that the condition is irreversible? How are the patient's wishes incorporated into the medical plan? What are the financial costs resulting from continuation of "heroic measures" such as respirators and cardiac resuscitation?

Crucial questions like these are best discussed with a person who is coherent and possesses sound judgment. As a rational individual I may specify my desires regarding medical efforts on my behalf through an *advance medical directive* (sometimes shortened to *advance directive*) in which those preferences are expressed in writing. One format for communicating such instructions is a *durable power of attorney for health care.* (It is called "durable" because it continues to be valid even if the person who granted it becomes incompetent.) If I am competent I can delegate the authority to make all medical decisions that I could make for myself, including decisions that may permit me to die of natural causes.

Some terminal individuals are reluctant to grant such sweeping power. If I am hesitant to delegate broad decision-making responsibility, I can be more specific in the authority that I assign to another. For instance, I can specify that the person with my power of attorney can make decisions regarding whether I should have surgery requiring general anesthesia, whether I should have a limb amputated, or whether various specified extraordinary means should be used to maintain my life.

An advance medical directive may help to clarify and define the decision-making process during a difficult time. But whether or not the dying person wants such a document, the individual still may wish to discuss issues associated with the termination of medical treatment. Although entering into such a discussion requires courage, it may be important to give the person an opportunity to express desires concerning the extent of life-prolonging medical efforts.

When effective communication with the patient is not possible, input from other sources will have to suffice. The attending physician and close family members are likely to be the most important contributors when decisions must be made without the patient's participation.

HIV DISEASE

In June of 1981, the U.S. Centers for Disease Control officially identified acquired immunodeficiency syndrome (AIDS). Since that time human immunodeficiency virus (HIV) disease has become a health problem of pandemic proportions. As this book goes to press, HIV disease continues to be a terminal condition for which there is no cure.

HIV infects and kills CD4 positive T (CD4+ T) white blood cells that assist in controlling the immune system's response to infection. When HIV knocks CD4+ T cells out of commission, the body becomes susceptible to both infections and cancers. In most instances it is the repeated attacks of these secondary conditions that eventually kill the person with AIDS.

Clinicians and researchers (e.g., Lewis & Harrison, 2005) note that many HIV-related events can precipitate crises. Common examples include the following: being tested for HIV, being diagnosed as positive for HIV, beginning antiretroviral therapy, developing early symptoms of HIV disease, emergence of advanced HIV disease or AIDS, and the terminal deterioration that eventually follows.

Experiencing any of these events can expose the person to a variety of external stressors. As clinicians and researchers have noted (e.g., Fleishman et al., 2000; Heckman et al., 2004), examples of stressors include the following: being blamed for contracting HIV disease, social ostracism, loss or restriction of employment, eviction, others' fear of contracting HIV disease from the person, elaborate infection control procedures, exhaustion of financial resources, and reliance on public assistance.

Simply being tested for HIV is so frightening that many persons avoid evaluation or, if tested, refuse knowledge of the results. When individuals do learn of positive results, many of them enter a crisis state with common emotions including shock, anger, and dread. Issues of concern may include sexual practices, drug use, whether to tell others, whom to tell, rejection by peers, vulnerability to disease, and the reality of one's own mortality.

Despair about the future may lead to suicidal thoughts and actions. An analysis (Catalan et al., 2011) of 66 studies concluded that HIV infection was associated with significant increases in suicidal ideation and behavior. For example, Lorraine Sherr and her colleagues (2008) surveyed participants at five HIV clinics in the United Kingdom. Thirty-one percent of the individuals reported having thought about suicide during the previous seven days. In a study of women with HIV/AIDS in New York City (Cooperman & Simoni, 2005), 18 percent of the women had attempted suicide within one month of being diagnosed with HIV, and 78 percent of them had considered suicide since receiving that diagnosis. In research that focused on a rural population (Heckman et al., 2002), 38 percent of the HIV-infected participants reported having thought about suicide during the previous week.

Following initial HIV infection (often involving acute illness that lasts one to two weeks and generates symptoms similar to mononucleosis), there typically are asymptomatic periods that span several years. Even in the absence of physical symptoms though, the knowledge that one is infected can be a significant stressor.

Eventually, individuals develop early symptoms of HIV infection and experience conditions that indicate broad loss of health but that are not life-threatening. Nevertheless, each new symptom raises the possibility that one is moving closer to AIDS. The resulting psychological distress can be intense.

A diagnosis of late-stage HIV infection or AIDS is applied once the person develops a condition indicating immune deficiency or when the CD4+ T cell count drops below 200. Being officially diagnosed as having AIDS often precipitates a crisis. Typically, there is an increased desire for health care resources and the person remains vigilant for new symptoms. During late-stage HIV infection, additional crises may result from new physical disabilities, treatment failures, and the realization that death is closer. During this period the risk of suicide may increase. Reviews of the literature (e.g., Gibson et al., 2006; Kleespies, Hughes, & Gallacher, 2000) conclude that HIV/AIDS patients do have elevated rates of suicide.

Clinicians and researchers (e.g., Lewis & Harrison, 2005; Poindexter, 1997) agree that crisis intervention in the form of problem-solving assistance is an appropriate therapeutic response to persons experiencing HIV-related conditions. The particular focus depends upon the current needs of the individual. Problem-solving topics should relate to whatever challenges the person has. As the risk of death increases, those topics may increasingly relate to issues associated with the end of one's life.

BEREAVEMENT

Reactions of Bereaved Individuals

Bereaved persons have their own unique approaches to coping with the death of a loved one, just as they have had their own personal coping techniques in dealing with other problems. Although grieving individuals deal with the loss in their own time and own way, clinicians (e.g., Hilarski, 2005; Horacek, 1995; Parry, 1994) note that there are some reactions that frequently occur:

- Initial responses may include the following: shock, disbelief, a wish to deny the loss, and a desire to undo the tragedy. There may be anger, with the focus on persons associated with the death or on the deceased. In the midst of such emotional turmoil, the bereaved individual may find it difficult to make decisions or to think rationally. For a time the person may feel lost or bewildered, and daily routines may be disrupted with the individual believing that such mundane activities are indicative of life's meaninglessness or worthlessness.

- Once the survivor becomes resigned to the loss, time may be spent in sad reminiscing. The person may regret lost opportunities or may idealize aspects of the relationship. Often, there is a persistent need to search for meaning in the death. The individual may also feel despair over the irrevocability of the loss, leading to withdrawal and to resentment of those who appear to live happily.
- Eventually, the person brackets the relationship as a significant part of the past, then proceeds to address life's new challenges and new relationships. Although such an encapsulation in no way diminishes the importance of the deceased person, it does give the survivor the freedom and the energy to continue a fruitful life.

For many persons these kinds of responses constitute successful ways of dealing with the death of a friend or loved one. The reactions associated with shock and reminiscing do not necessarily indicate the failure of coping mechanisms that may precipitate a crisis state.

Bruce Horacek (1995) discussed the difference between abnormal "chronic mourning" and normal "continuing grieving." He said the former involves grief reactions that are debilitating, whereas the latter is a low-grade grief that does not significantly limit day-to-day functioning. Persons experiencing continuing grieving may feel the lasting presence of an "empty space," but that sense of loss does not prevent them from effectively dealing with the demands of everyday life.

Research has shown that 80 percent or more of bereaved individuals effectively cope with the loss during the first year after the death (Bonanno & Mancini, 2006). The absence of such coping characterizes chronic mourning, which is frequently referred to as complicated or unresolved grief.

Adjustment becomes maladaptive if individuals adopt bereavement as a lifestyle. Often maladaptive grief is accompanied by recurring insomnia, prolonged loss of appetite, and an inability to resume usual work or leisure activities. Persistence of such reactions should signal crisis workers that traditional supports have not been sufficient and that further intervention is necessary.

Clinicians (e.g., Farberow, 2001) note that although children often show similar responses to those of adults, young persons also have other reactions to the death of a loved one. Toddlers (ages 1–2), preschoolers (ages 3–6), school-age children (ages 7–12), and adolescents each have their own characteristic ways of responding.

Toddlers do not understand death although they quickly perceive the absence of a parent or other caretaker. Common results include feeling the loss of love and misbehaving in response to the sudden lack of usual controls.

Preschoolers often see death as reversible. Consequently, they may be angry at the deceased for choosing to leave them. Frequently, they displace such anger to the adults who continue to care for them. When it is a caretaking adult who has died, preschoolers worry about who will provide what that person has been giving the family; for instance, wanting a new mother or a new father is a common wish.

Many preschoolers believe that some misbehavior on their part caused the person's death. In addition to feeling guilty they may also fear that they will be next to die.

School-age children often want to hear a specific account of how the death occurred, as well as details of what happens to a dead body. Other common reactions include denial or fear for their own mortality. During the day school-age children may overreact to minor setbacks or difficulties. When not distracted by the day's activities, they may seek comfort by holding a favorite stuffed animal or by wanting to sleep with their parents.

Adolescence is when we usually confront the finality of death for the first time. Losing a loved one intensifies the existential fears that most adolescents encounter. They worry more about their own vulnerability to accidents, disease, and death. In addition, anger toward the deceased frequently is a strong emotion.

Intervention With Bereaved Individuals

When intervening with bereaved individuals in crisis, workers should be sensitive to the type and amount of support that is desired. Qualitative research (Olsson, 1997) suggests that communicating a willingness to provide emotional support (as opposed to informational or instrumental support) is likely to be the most universally appreciated attitude. When individuals want to discuss the challenges they are experiencing, it can be appropriate to help them face the immediate and long-term tasks necessary for their adjustment. Although support must be tailored to each person's unique needs, research demonstrates adaptive coping is often facilitated by focusing on positive emotions, such as those associated with comforting recollections of the deceased person and with the successful handling of challenges (e.g., Bonanno & Mancini, 2006). It may be appropriate to negotiate specific and realistic plans that address both immediate needs and the establishment of new patterns of behavior that will continue to be productive.

Such an approach can also be applicable to children, although with young persons there are additional considerations to keep in mind. Regardless of the child's age, the youngster should be informed of the death soon after it happens. Such news needs to be delivered in a straightforward manner.

Children above the age of three should be allowed to attend the funeral if they wish to go (e.g., Gallo & Pfeffer, 2003). When children have questions about the proceedings, the events ought to be explained in a calm and factual manner.

In addition to deserving an honest notification of the death and to having a right to attend the funeral, there are other responses to consider depending upon the age of the child.

Toddlers need surviving adults to clearly demonstrate continuing love and support. At the same time, they should also receive firm yet fair discipline.

Preschoolers need to understand that the dead person did not want to leave them. And if they express a desire for the replacement of a lost parent, they should be assured that others will continue to care for them.

It is a good idea to explore their understanding of the reasons for the person's death. A caretaker should confront in a low-key way any self-blame or fears that preschoolers have about a similar fate for themselves and others. Often there will need to be multiple repetitions of the reasons for the death and of the low risk to others.

In response to questions, *school-age children* should receive factual explanations of the death and subsequent events. Adults ought to be accepting of grade-schoolers' needs for comfort and should provide ample opportunity for discussing the youngsters' feelings. At the same time a moderate work routine during the day may keep the young persons from being overwhelmed and may help them cope with the loss in small doses.

Adolescents need to know that concerns about oneself are common responses to the death of a loved one. Rather than hiding these feelings that may have seemed irrational, they should have the opportunity to discuss and explore such reactions.

Often the preceding interventions are sufficient to help young persons cope with the loss. In some instances, however, referral for more extensive assistance may be necessary if depression lasts for months or if there are other signs of continuing difficulty, such as persistent self-blame or continuing preoccupation with the death.

Rights and Obligations of Survivors

At any point during our lives we are members of several groups, such as a family, a church, a school, a business, a club, and a neighborhood. When a member of one of our groups dies, Ellen Zinner (1985, 1987) believes that we have certain rights and obligations. In particular, we have rights to recognition, information, and ceremonial participation.

- *Recognition.* The group has a right to be recognized as having lost one of its members. For example, it is appropriate to publicly announce that a participant in the group has died, and it is appropriate for others to offer condolences to the surviving group members.
- *Information.* The group has a right to be informed quickly and accurately about the death and related events. It is inappropriate to withhold or distort information even if it is for the supposed "good" of the survivors.

    Those closest to the deceased have a right to receive the news first. Such persons include immediate family members, close friends, and roommates.
- *Ceremonial Participation.* The group has a right to participate in ceremonies commemorating the deceased person. In addition to funerals, examples include other memorial services and dedication ceremonies honoring the deceased individual.

    Mental health and education experts (e.g., Dunne-Maxim et al., 1992; Newgass & Schonfeld, 2005; Sandoval & Brock, 1996) have asserted that if the death was a suicide, then ceremonies should avoid glorifying or romanticizing the victim, in order to prevent others from seeking similar recognition through their own suicides. Consequently, funerals and memorial services for suicide victims should be arranged so as to cause minimal disruption in the regular group schedule. Dedications of physical memorials ought to be avoided, as should other tributes, such as creating a scholarship fund or naming an athletic event in honor of the person. (The Maine Youth Suicide Prevention Program has prepared and made available online [http://maine.gov/suicide/docs/Guideline.pdf] *Youth Suicide Prevention, Intervention, and Postvention Guidelines.*)

In addition to rights, survivor groups also have obligations. The primary obligations are acknowledgment and support.

- *Acknowledgment.* Just as outsiders have a duty to recognize the group's loss, surviving members have an obligation to acknowledge the death. Examples include printing a memorial page in the school yearbook and the school band playing at the funeral of a student.
- *Support.* Members have an obligation to offer support to those survivors who were closest to the deceased. Such attention includes sending cards and offering to help with tasks.

    Clinicians (e.g., Sandoval & Brock, 1996) agree that members should have the opportunity to freely discuss their reactions. Such discussion ought to include the open sharing of fears, feelings, and concerns. Special attention should be given to self-blame experienced by members.

Group-based support can be helpful following suicide deaths (e.g., New-gass & Schonfeld, 2005). Survivors are most likely to participate if the meetings take place at the physical location of the group, such as a school or dormitory.

For example, one school counselor (Alexander & Harman, 1988) chose to offer support by meeting all seven classes of which a suicide victim had been a member. With each group she used the "empty chair" Gestalt therapy technique. She gave every student a chance to speak to the victim's empty desk in order to express feelings and to say good-bye.

Philip Hazell and Terry Lewin (1993) described another school-based postsuicide intervention. In a series of 90-minute meetings, 20 to 30 individuals at a time discussed a variety of topics, including the following: possible reasons for the suicide; the validity of various rumors; thoughts and feelings of the participants, including their own suicidal thoughts; and resources available to students who might be thinking of committing suicide. Provisions were made for additional follow-up with individuals who appeared to be in need of further assistance.

There is agreement among mental health and education experts (e.g., Dunne-Maxim et al., 1992; Guthrie, 1992) that normal group activities should resume in a timely manner, with special allowances made for members who need additional support. For example, individual follow-up sessions ought to be available for those members who need them.

SUICIDE INVESTIGATION AND SURVIVOR INTERVENTION

The untimely death of a loved one is a tragic experience that taxes one's coping abilities. And the stress intensifies when there is knowledge or suspicion that the death was a suicide.

Crisis intervenors need to understand the potential difficulties that suicide survivors may face. Workers may also need to be prepared to evaluate whether the death was a suicide, and they should be able to assist the survivors in coping with the loss.

Potential Difficulties for the Survivors of Suicide Victims

Compared to the survivors of deceased individuals whose deaths were not suicides, research (e.g., Bailley, Kral, & Dunham, 1999; Bell, Stanley, Mallon, & Manthorpe, 2012; Seguin, Lesage, & Kiely, 1995) shows that survivors of suicide victims have more intense personal and interpersonal difficulties. Interpersonally, they tend to receive less social support and more blame. As a group, survivors of suicide victims feel much more rejected and abandoned, guilty and responsible, ashamed, and stigmatized. Other reactions include greater shock and disbelief. They also spend more effort searching for an explanation; they may try to understand what the suicide of their loved one means in terms of their traditional views of life, and they may want to discover why the person committed suicide. A variety of researchers concur with these observations (e.g., Cvinar, 2005; Gallo & Pfeffer, 2003; Hung & Rabin, 2009; Jordan & McMenamy, 2004; Mitchell, Kim, Prigerson, & Mortimer, 2005; Mitchell, Kim, Prigerson, & Mortimer-Stephens, 2004; Sethi & Bhargava, 2003). In addition, research has found that losing a parent to suicide is associated with increased risk of death by suicide for surviving children (Geulayov, Gunnell, Holmen, & Metcalfe, 2012).

Farberow, Gallagher-Thompson, Gilewski, and Thompson (1992) studied social support of bereaved surviving spouses. The investigators found that compared to individuals whose spouses died natural deaths, surviving spouses of suicide victims received less companionship and were less supported in their attempts to deal with discouragement.

David Brent and his colleagues conducted several studies that examined the effects of suicide on surviving friends. Brent et al. (1992) compared 58 survivors of 10 adolescent suicide victims to 58 adolescents not exposed to such loss. Among the bereaved individuals, 35 persons had a current psychiatric disorder compared to 17 members of the control group. The most common diagnosis was a major depressive disorder (18 exposed subjects vs. 4 control subjects). Among the bereaved individuals who were depressed, the most typical pattern involved onset within a month of the death and depression continuing at least six months after the suicide. Brent et al. (1995) evaluated 146 friends of 26 adolescent suicide victims. Although past maladjustment was a significant risk factor for future problems, other prominent predictors of psychological difficulties after the death were as follows: seeing the death scene, witnessing the suicide, discovering the body, having advance knowledge of the victim's plans, and talking with the person on the day the suicide occurred. Among the surviving friends, eight individuals developed posttraumatic stress disorder and 38 other persons became clinically depressed. And Brent et al. (1993) studied 28 adolescents who had been on a school bus when a student in the back of the bus committed suicide with a gun. During the first two months after the death, 28 percent of the exposed students experienced the onset of a psychiatric condition (a mood disorder, an anxiety disorder, or posttraumatic stress disorder), whereas only 4 percent of the control subjects developed such a disorder.

For suicide survivors there is also increased risk of difficulties in the more distant future. For a 35-year period, Holly Wilcox and her colleagues (2010) examined experiences of individuals who had lost a parent to death while the survivor was under age 26. Compared to survivors of accident victims and to survivors of parents who died from other causes, survivors of suicide victims were significantly more likely to subsequently experience hospitalization for suicide attempt, depression, or psychosis.

Reed and Greenwald (1991) studied bereaved family members and friends, and compared the reactions of suicide survivors to those of individuals who had lost a loved one to accidental death. Results indicated that the suicide survivors felt more guilty and ashamed, and that they experienced more rejection.

Cerel, Fristad, Weller, and Weller (1999) conducted a similar study in which they compared 26 children who had lost a parent to suicide, to 332 children who had experienced the death of a parent for reasons other than suicide or homicide. Immediately after the death the suicide survivors were twice as likely to be anxious (74% versus 38%). Six months later they were twice as likely to be angry (45% versus 22%). And one year later they were more likely to feel shame (22% versus 1%).

One way to avoid stigma and guilt is to act as if the death was not a suicide. Survivors may unconsciously forget facts that indicate suicide, or they may purposefully try to conceal the real nature of the death. Some survivors have taken actions such as hiding or destroying suicide notes and pressuring officials to label the death as accidental or due to natural causes.

Clearly, there are times when survivors try to avoid the painful fact that a friend or loved one has committed suicide. Eventually, such defensive coping can have detrimental effects. For example, in a classic study of emotionally disturbed surviving spouses and children of suicide victims, Cain and Fast (1966a, 1966b) concluded that avoidance of communicating thoughts and feelings associated with the suicide was one of the most important factors contributing to the subsequent difficulties of their subjects. In many instances a conspiracy of silence quickly surrounded the suicide and severely limited the survivors' resources for ventilation. Often there was little or no opportunity for misconceptions to be corrected, for irrational guilt to be resolved, or for anger to be expressed toward the suicide victim. In short, the lack of communication about the suicide tended to halt the normal bereavement process, thereby planting the seeds for future emotional disturbance.

Cain and Fast found that surviving spouses encountered a variety of stresses following the suicide. Often police or coroner's office investigators considered the possibility of murder and included the surviving spouse as a potential suspect. In some cases there were unpleasant interactions with insurance company representatives. And it was not unusual for ministers to refuse to provide typical funeral services, with burial in church grounds sometimes denied. Nevertheless, the most severe stress appeared to be the blame attributed to the surviving spouses by others—especially their in-laws.

Blame tended to be expressed in two forms—lack of support and active attribution. The typical reaction to a bereaved spouse is for neighbors, friends, and relatives to provide concrete assistance with day-to-day responsibilities such as food preparation, household cleaning, and child care. During these contacts and at other times, there is the opportunity to share grief, guilt, sadness, and other emotions associated with the death. Cain and Fast found that spouses in their study received almost none of this support. In addition, the researchers discovered many cases in which relatives, as well as others in the community, directly accused the survivor of driving the deceased to suicide.

In the Cain and Fast study, surviving children faced the same community reaction confronting their parent plus additional stresses. For example, in most cases the parent refused to openly discuss the suicide with the child. And in about 25 percent of the families, the children witnessed some event indicative of suicide, such as discovering a suicide note, only to have the surviving parent later insist that the death actually was due to an accident or illness.

As with their parents, the surviving children in the Cain and Fast study tended not to have opportunities to share their thoughts and feelings. Furthermore, many of these children had a trusted authority figure tell them that their perceptions of recent events were incorrect. So it is not surprising that the most common difficulty in these young persons was distrusting the accuracy of their perceptions. And, in the absence of an opportunity to openly discuss the circumstances of the death, many of the children also blamed themselves for their parent's demise.

Many difficult challenges confront survivors of suicide victims. Do such persons believe they could benefit from professional help? That was one question investigated by Anne Wilson and Amy Marshall (2010). They surveyed 166 adults who had lost a friend or loved one to suicide. The researchers found that 95 percent of the participants said they had needed professional help following the death, but only 44 percent of the survivors had actually received such assistance. The greatest difference between desired help and received help was with regard to wanting assistance from a crisis intervention team; 20 percent of the respondents said they had wanted such support, but only 2 percent had actually received it. Regarding all varieties of professional help received by the participants, only 40 percent of the survivors reported a great or substantial level of satisfaction with the services. Complaints included the following comments about the professional: appearing afraid of the person's grief, seeming too busy to listen, being judgmental, quickly drawing inaccurate conclusions, and failing to accurately perceive the family's needs. The study indicated significant room for improvement in the professional support provided to survivors of suicide victims, with increased availability of high-quality crisis intervention services being one clearly identified need.

The Role of the Death Response Team

As a means of preventing emotional difficulties in the survivors of suicide victims, some organizations provide a death response team (e.g., Grieger & Greene, 1998; Streufert, 2004). By conducting a psychological autopsy the team evaluates the deceased person's intent to die and produces the most accurate report possible. This distortion-resistant investigation can contribute to realistic coping by the survivors. In the process of investigating the death, the team can also develop positive relationships with surviving friends and family members; thereby paving the way for crisis intervention should it become necessary.

The death response team collects information for the psychological autopsy by interviewing individuals who knew the deceased person. Valuable informants may include the surviving spouse, older children, friends, neighbors, supervisors and associates at work, clergy, and physicians.

As originally noted by Curphey (1961) and reinforced by others (e.g., Ebert, 1987; Werlang & Botega, 2003), the team attempts to reconstruct the recent lifestyle of the deceased by seeking several types of information from informants.

- Basic life history data should be explored. There are several areas to be considered. What was the person's health status just prior to death? What stresses had the individual been experiencing? Was there a history of past psychological problems? Had the person ever tried to commit suicide in the past? Is there a family history of suicide? Is there evidence that the person had been reading about suicide or death? How familiar was the individual with the cause of death; for example, if the cause of death was a gunshot wound, was the person familiar with guns, or, if the individual died from a drug overdose, how knowledgeable was the person about drugs? In the weeks before death had the individual made any "final preparations," such as giving away possessions, discussing death with a member of the clergy, drafting or revising a will, getting insurance policies in order, or paying debts? Precisely what were the person's activities during the 24 hours prior to death?
- It is essential to estimate the emotional state of the deceased during the final days and weeks of life. Were there any indications of depression or hopelessness? For example, had the individual appeared to lose interest in life; had the person shown a recent loss of appetite or experienced a change in sleeping patterns? What were the person's feelings and expectations regarding death?
- Communication of suicidal intent should be explored. Did the person communicate suicidal intent either verbally or in writing? In the absence

of direct communication were there indirect signs of suicidal thoughts through morbid statements such as, "Life is meaningless," "I'm not worth much," "I can't stand it any longer," or "I won't be troubling you anymore"?

Law enforcement officers and officials are responsible for gathering and evaluating physical evidence. For interpretations of such evidence, the death response team usually should rely on crime lab studies, the coroner's report, and the police report. Occasionally, however, team members may observe evidence that can help in the formulation of an opinion. For example, in one Los Angeles case, the team discovered that a mop-head had been stuffed into the bathtub-overflow drain. The team suggested that the blockage was a likely attempt to ensure that there would be enough water for the victim to drown after he lost consciousness from an overdose of barbiturates.

By making contact with the survivors, the death response team establishes lines of communication that can be used during the days and weeks following the initial interaction. But the team should also be prepared to provide crisis intervention during the first meeting. When working with survivors who want problem-solving assistance, the intervenors should encourage them to share their reactions, regrets about the past, and concerns about the future. In this atmosphere of interest and acceptance survivors may show a variety of responses, such as crying, questioning their relationships with the deceased, and expressing resentment over what the deceased's death has done to them.

As in any other potential crisis, the needs of survivors vary from one person to the next. Consequently, the death response team provides or helps to arrange whatever support is needed. In addition to responding to the person's emotional needs, the team may help with concrete matters such as child care, banking, or mortuary arrangements.

Surviving children of a suicide victim should hear a straightforward account of their parent's death (e.g., Gallo & Pfeffer, 2003). This explanation is best done by the remaining parent or guardian, and it should be communicated at a level of understanding that is consistent with the children's degree of cognitive development. Both during and after the interaction, the children ought to have opportunities to share their thoughts, feelings, and questions. Throughout these interactions, the adult should be empathic and should be ready to help the children distinguish between imagination and reality. As the young persons experience their own developing reactions to the suicide and as they cope with the responses of friends and classmates, the surviving children should know that the door always will be open for further discussion of their parent's death.

If the surviving spouse or other responsible adult feels uncomfortable about such tasks, this may be an area for problem solving with the crisis worker. So, after clarifying the adult survivor's own reactions and planning appropriate coping strategies, problem-solving efforts may need to focus on that person's responsibilities to the surviving children. The intervenor can help the individual consider the consequences of discussing or not discussing the suicide with the children, then assist in developing and implementing a plan that will provide appropriate information and support for the young survivors.

The death response team should become involved in the case as soon as the death is discovered since every hour of inactivity diminishes the chances of meaningful interaction with the survivors. Delaying contact can enhance the development of defensive strategies such as denial, avoidance, repression, and withdrawal that may begin as soon as the survivors have knowledge of the death. If intervention is not immediate, these defensive distortions may be firmly entrenched by the time intervenors eventually become involved.

Delay sometimes precludes contact with the survivors. Once a coping style for responding to the death has been adopted, a survivor may refuse to see the crisis team. And even if the person might be receptive to the team, friends or relatives answering the telephone or the door may refuse to tell the survivor of the team's wish to make contact in the belief that they are protecting the person from further anguish.

Immediate intervention diminishes or eliminates all of these potential difficulties. Such payoffs do not come cheaply; they require planning and effort. For example, in one community the police call the crisis center whenever there is an apparent suicide or an "unattended death"—that is, no witness present when the deceased died. Immediately after sending officers to the scene, the police dispatcher calls the crisis service and requests a death response team.

EXAMPLE. The death response team arrived at the residence of John Thomas after receiving a report that he had shot himself in the chest with a shotgun. The workers walked past the police car in the driveway and up to the door where John's brother met them. He said that Mrs. Thomas and Steve, her teenage son, were in the kitchen. Before allowing the team inside, however, he asked if it really was necessary for the workers to talk with his sister-in-law and nephew. The workers assured him that the interview was necessary.

Mrs. Thomas and Steve both were crying and expressing disbelief at the events of the last hour. They told the workers that at around 7:00 that morning they heard a gunshot and rushed into the family room to find John sprawled on the floor. He had died instantly from a gunshot wound to the chest.

Steve blamed himself for his father's death, saying he should have put the gun back in its rack rather than leaving it out overnight. The team learned that he and his father had planned to go hunting, and that Steve had been cleaning their guns the night before. Steve said he always cleaned the guns since his father really did not have much experience handling them.

The workers encouraged both Steve and Mrs. Thomas to share their feelings, which included disbelief, self-reproach, and grief. And the intervenors accepted these reactions without being judgmental.

The team learned that John's brother was going to help with necessary arrangements. But they also offered the services of the crisis center if the family wanted to talk further or needed additional assistance.

Before the workers left, one of the investigating officers called them aside. He said there was a fine film of oil on the barrel of the shotgun.

The team contacted the family physician who reported that John had been in both good health and in good spirits at the time of his last physical exam two months earlier. To the doctor's knowledge, John had no history of emotional problems.

The team also contacted John's business partner. He said that as far as he knew things had been going well. He believed John had been looking forward to taking Steve hunting.

The death response team concluded that John's death had been an accident and that he had not intended to die. It appeared that Steve had left the shotgun loaded and leaning against a table in the family room. Apparently John picked it up by the barrel. Because of the oily film, however, it slipped through his hands, the butt hit the floor, and the gun discharged.

DISCUSSION OF THE THOMAS FAMILY CASE: John's *life history* indicated an absence of significant stresses, emotional disturbance, suicide attempts, ill health, or final preparations. His *emotional state* appeared to be good with no signs of depression or hopelessness. And there had been no *communication* of suicidal intent.

The loaded shotgun's oily barrel, combined with John's lack of knowledge about firearms, appeared to be the unfortunate set of circumstances that led to his death. Although sufficient support seemed to be available for the Thomas family, the workers believed that Steve might have a difficult time coping with his role in the accident. So the team made sure the family understood that help was available should they want it.

SUMMARY

A significant number of crisis intervention contacts involve interactions with suicidal persons. It is always appropriate to ask whether the person is thinking about killing him/herself. When such thoughts exist the worker can **assess the degree of lethality** by exploring the following five factors that empirical evidence has shown to increase the risk of suicide: (1) the **plan for suicide**, including the likely *method*, its *availability*, and the *concreteness* of the plan; (2) **dangerous emotional states**, including *hopelessness, depression, a sense* *of being a burden, sudden calmness, agitation,* and *anger*; (3) a **sudden upsurge in difficulties**; (4) **significant loss**, such as an important *relationship, possession,* or *ability*; and (5) a **past suicide attempt**.

The preceding lethality assessment can occur as the intervenor simultaneously implements *five principles for intervening with a suicidal person*. (1) If the individual has a specific plan for suicide, it is necessary to ask whether the plan is already underway and to **interrupt a suicide plan in progress**. (2) **Determine appropriate intervention** by exploring the person's thoughts on the *advantages of death, disadvantages of life, advantages of life* and *disadvantages of death*. When the contact is taking place in the aftermath of a suicide attempt, assess whether the individual is in *crisis* or is *chronically self-destructive* and explore whether the person was intending to make a *cry for help*, was *ambivalent* about being alive or dead, or was *certain* about wanting to be dead. Usual crisis intervention problem-solving techniques may be sufficient for individuals in crisis who have engaged in life-threatening behavior as a dramatic cry for help. On the other hand, preserving life becomes the primary purpose of interventions with suicidal persons who see death as a means of escape. Hospitalization may need to be considered during these intense, but usually brief, periods of self-destructiveness. Additional suicide intervention principles are: (3) **decreasing the availability of lethal means**, (4) **problem solving**, and (5) **recognizing the potential for homicide**.

Terminal illness often involves burdensome issues such as the uncertainty of death, physical deterioration, the loss of role responsibilities, and the extent of life-prolonging efforts to be taken. These burdens can be lessened by focusing problem-solving efforts on circumstances that can be changed.

HIV disease remains a terminal illness of pandemic proportions. A variety of events can precipitate HIV-related crises. Examples include the following: being tested for HIV, being found positive for HIV, symptoms and illnesses associated with symptomatic HIV disease, the development of AIDS and the terminal deterioration that follows. Crisis intervention problem solving can be appropriate during any of these times.

Bereaved individuals commonly experience shock and disbelief, sad reminiscing, and encapsulation of the relationship. Children and adolescents also have their own characteristic responses that should be considered. Bereaved persons may be in crisis if they show exaggerated reactions, and crises sometimes follow the omission of necessary grief work. Bereavement interventions involve encouraging the open expression of emotions, recalling the lost relationship, and planning for the future. In addition to these kinds of assistance, young persons need their own special forms of support. All survivors above the age of three have rights to recognition, information, and ceremonial participation, and adult survivors have the obligations of acknowledgment and support.

Immediate family members of suicide victims are a high-risk population for emotional difficulties. Because others may blame or ostracize them, some lack the opportunity to share their thoughts and feelings. In addition to these problems, surviving children may have difficulties if a trusted adult denies their interpretations of reality. Death response teams are one form of intervention intended to prevent emotional difficulties in this high-risk group. The team can assess the deceased person's intent to die by collecting data regarding the individual's life history, emotional state, and morbid communication. This distortion-resistant information can become part of the survivor's realistic coping. The death response team also offers assistance with tasks confronting the survivors and remains ready to provide emotional support as needed.

STUDY QUESTIONS

1. In the United States, out of 10 adults in their forties who attempt to kill themselves, how many are likely to die as a result of the attempt?
2. Rank order these individuals from highest (1) to lowest (4) in terms of their suicide lethality. Note which lethality predictors are present in each situation.
   (A) Betsy is a 17-year-old high school student who is angry at her parents for not letting her go on a weekend trip with friends. To make them regret restricting her, she is considering suicide by taking ten of her mother's Valium®.
   (B) Andrew has been working at the same mill for the last thirty years. This week his company announced that it will close the mill and permanently lay off all of the personnel. He is pessimistic about finding a new job because of the large number of people in the area who are looking for work. Due to a chronic illness his wife requires ongoing medical attention; by losing both his salary and his employer's health insurance coverage, Andrew sees no way to provide her with the care she needs—except by killing himself so that she can collect his life insurance.
   (C) While driving in an intoxicated state, Martha lost control of her car and ran into a tree. Her two children died in the accident, and she suffered numerous injuries, including being paralyzed from the waist down. During her hospitalization she tried to kill herself by cutting her neck with a piece of broken glass. Now that she is home she continues to experience guilt over the deaths of her children and hopelessness about her future life in a wheelchair. She also feels

that she will be nothing but a burden to her husband John. He has noticed that the agitation she has been experiencing during recent weeks has been replaced by an air of calmness. Martha has saved her prescription pain medication, and she now has a large enough dose to kill herself. Tomorrow she plans to take the overdose after John has gone to work.

(D) Jim is an unemployed computer programmer who lives at home with his parents. He has low self-esteem. Today he is feeling like killing himself because everyone else around him seems so happy while he is so bored.

3. Allan calls the crisis center and tells you he believes his wife Susan has taken an overdose of prescription medication. He asks you what he should do. What is your response?

4. In terms of enhancing your rapport, what is the best topic to start with when interviewing a suicidal person?

5. When considering the intent of life-threatening behavior as described in Figure 1, page 97, members of what groups are most likely to need hospitalization?

6. You are called to the emergency room to evaluate Pat Brown who suffered severe self-inflicted wrist slashes in a suicide attempt. Pat's parents are present and want to help. During a 20-minute interview Pat lethargically expresses a willingness to accept whatever you suggest. The ER physician wants your recommendation regarding psychiatric hospitalization. Give your response, including the reasons for your opinion and the score Pat achieved on the Bengelsdorf scale.

7. What is your primary responsibility to a client who is experiencing a suicidal crisis?

8. Martin is thinking about shooting himself with his shotgun. What is your immediate objective?

9. Kathy is a suicidal client who feels isolated. What are some possible alternatives to consider as you move toward developing a plan?

10. If Martin in question 8 must be disarmed, who should do it?

11. How does problem solving assist terminal individuals in coping with their situations?

12. Chris has just tested positive for HIV. What feelings and issues should you be prepared to discuss?

13. What are three common stages of response demonstrated by bereaved individuals?

14. John is a 15-year-old who comes to you after the death of Robert, his brother. Among other concerns, he is troubled by the anger he feels toward Robert. Describe your intervention with John.

15. Following the suicide death of a high school student, one of the school's administrators seeks your advice concerning appropriate actions. Current plans include canceling classes on the day of the funeral and planting a tree to honor the person. What do you recommend?

16. After studying emotionally disturbed survivors of suicide victims, what did Cain and Fast conclude about the role of open communication?

17. Your contact with Diane immediately follows her husband's suicide by carbon monoxide poisoning. During the interview she mentions that she plans to tell her school-age children that their father died from a heart attack. What is your response?

Chapter 4

SPECIAL POPULATIONS: INTERVENTIONS INVOLVING CRIME VICTIMS

Erik Erikson (1963) asserted that most of us develop a basic sense of trust and an attitude of autonomy by the end of our preschool years. As we cope with life we assume to some extent that others can be trusted and that we are in control of our lives. If we become the victims of personal crime, however, we often find our trust betrayed and our autonomy overpowered. Whenever our fundamental assumptions about life are threatened in this way, we risk entering a crisis state.

Each of us takes action to prevent crime; precautions range from locking our doors to much more elaborate measures. Regardless of our prevention efforts, though, when an attack comes it almost always comes as a surprise. We didn't think it really would happen to us, whether we are the victims of burglary, auto theft, robbery, assault, or rape.

Other common reactions include a sense of violation and a feeling of vulnerability. Despite the need to repair psychic damage, crime victims often must give first priority to more concrete recovery tasks, such as contacting the police, seeking medical attention, and replacing or repairing damaged property. An intervenor should encourage victims to ask for whatever assistance they need and should help to arrange appropriate aid.

CRISIS INTERVENTION WITH CRIME VICTIMS

Crisis intervention is particularly suited to helping crime victims and their families handle both the emotional shock and the concrete problems that may result from the crime. Crisis services can provide immediate intervention, including aid in expediting assistance needed from other community agencies. Resources to be mobilized may involve transportation, medical attention, child care, crime victim compensation, and vocational rehabilitation.

Just as much of our understanding of crisis theory can be traced to the work of Erich Lindemann and Gerald Caplan, crime victim experts (e.g., Hembree & Foa, 2003) recognize that our use of crisis intervention with crime victims in general and with rape victims in particular owes much to the work of two Boston College professors—Ann Wolbert Burgess (nursing) and Lynda Lytle Holmstrom (sociology).

In the early 1970s, one problem being highlighted by the women's movement was violence against women. In that context, Burgess and Holmstrom decided to focus on an aspect of the problem on which there was little research—the victim's point of view with regard to rape and the responses of criminal justice, social service, and healthcare institutions to rape cases (Holmstrom, 2013). The team started their rape investigation by arranging for a major Boston hospital to contact them as soon as a rape victim entered the emergency room. Within half an hour, the researchers arrived to speak with the victim and to observe what she encountered. They also had subsequent interviews with those victims, and, when there were criminal justice proceedings, went with them to court. The work that Burgess and Holmstrom did with crime victims identified commonly experienced challenges, important issues requiring decisions, and frequently encountered survivor reactions, as well as helpful ways of assisting victims of crime.

Being controlled by a criminal violates the victim's sense of self; the more violated the person feels, the greater will be the resulting distress. Empirical evidence (Freedy, Resnick, Kilpatrick, Dansky, & Tidwell, 1994) indicates that the sense of violation generally is greater when the crime was violent and/or sexual. Most individuals find it disruptive to encounter threats or attacks directed at one's physical well-being. Nevertheless, the severity of the episode is determined by the victim, and to some it is disastrous to lose possessions such as a wallet or a car.

Since it is easy to perceive the personal losses of assault victims, those individuals often receive benevolent treatment from others. But the mere loss of possessions usually generates different responses. Even though victims of purse snatching or auto theft may feel their identities have been profoundly violated, others rarely are interested in how these victims are feeling. Instead, typical topics of conversation are descriptions of the stolen items and catching the criminal.

Whatever the nature of the crime, crisis workers can recognize victims' feelings and engage them in a problem-solving process. Frequently elicited emotions include fear and anger focused on the criminal. When the client expresses blame towards the perpetrator, the worker should reflect and reinforce such statements.

Most victims need to discover a reason for the crime so they can understand it and possibly prevent it from happening again. Although certain "target hardening" techniques do reduce the probability of being a crime victim, there is no foolproof way to guarantee safety. Criminals usually choose their victims arbitrarily or according to factors that are outside victims' control. The chance nature of most crimes and our inevitable vulnerability are factors that victims in crisis may find difficult to accept.

Despite the impossibility of complete safety, it is appropriate to support a victim's choice of prudent crime prevention actions. Examples include the following: installing effective locks, incorporating prevention efforts into daily routines, lobbying for increased street lighting, trimming shrubbery to eliminate potential hiding places for criminals, and organizing neighborhood watch efforts.

Some situations cause automatic reactions. When such situations are immediately preceded by other conditions we may develop a reaction to those conditions that is similar to the automatic response evoked by the original situation. For instance, several years ago I wrecked my car on an icy patch of road. I felt terror as I crashed through the guardrail and down into a ravine. (Fortunately my seat belt saved me from injury.) For the rest of the winter I felt an apprehensive tightness in my stomach when I drove by that spot and whenever my wheels lost traction on any icy road. Seeing that spot and having my wheels lose traction were both conditions that immediately preceded my car crashing through the guardrail—an occurrence that elicited the automatic reaction of terror.

My apprehension associated with that particular spot, and with icy roads in general, developed through a process of *respondent conditioning.* In this type of learning there are the following four components: (1) *unconditioned stimulus*—a circumstance that elicits an automatic reaction, (2) *unconditioned response*—the automatic reaction elicited by the unconditioned stimulus, (3) *conditioned stimulus*—a circumstance that immediately precedes the unconditioned stimulus, and (4) *conditioned response*—the reaction to the conditioned stimulus that develops because the conditioned stimulus precedes the unconditioned stimulus.

In the example of my car wreck, the unconditioned stimulus was crashing through the guardrail. The unconditioned response was terror. The conditioned stimuli were the particular spot and my wheels losing traction on the ice. The conditioned response was apprehension.

Although I still do feel some apprehension when my wheels lose traction on an icy road, I no longer feel any stomach tightness when I drive by the accident site. My lack of reaction to that spot came about through the learning process of *extinction.* In respondent conditioning terminology, extinction means the conditioned stimulus repeatedly occurs without being followed by the unconditioned stimulus. I have driven by that spot many times, and I have never had another wreck there, so the spot no longer bothers me. On the other hand, since I have lost traction on icy roads less than half a dozen times since my accident, I still feel some apprehension when that happens—there has not been as much opportunity for extinction to take place.

As you can see, respondent conditioning can cause distressing feelings to become associated with situations that immediately precede an unpleasant event—a scenario that crime victims often experience. For instance, the distress of a victim assaulted in a parking garage is likely to be high the next time the person enters the garage. Nevertheless, because of extinction, continued use of the garage without a subsequent assault ought to reduce apprehension associated with being there.

Two conditions, however, should maintain high levels of distress associated with the garage—suffering another attack there or completely avoiding the place. Both of those circumstances prevent extinction of the fear response. From a respondent conditioning perspective, it is adaptive for extinction to occur; it ought to be helpful for the victim to experience conditions similar to the circumstances associated with the crime without another crime taking place.

Support for this respondent conditioning hypothesis comes from a study of 163 assault victims. Wirtz and Harrell (1987a) found that victims who had repeated opportunities to reexperience the crime situation without suffering a subsequent assault had less psychological distress six months after the crime than did victims who did not have repeated benign exposure to the crime-related stimuli.

The respondent conditioning model suggests two strategies that crisis workers should keep in mind when intervening with crime victims. First, while recognizing that no crime prevention effort is foolproof, plans should include steps to reduce the possibility of further victimization. Second, within the limits of commonsense safety considerations, it is adaptive for crime victims to return to their traditional activities—especially the routines underway at the time the crime took place.

As victims try to resume their lives, there are likely to be good days and bad days. One way to cope with uneven recovery is to keep a diary. It can document the person's progress and be a source of reassurance on the discouraging days.

A diary can serve another function as well if the person includes a detailed description of the incident. This record can help the victim keep facts straight if court testimony becomes necessary. Since it may be months or years before testimony is required, the diary account can serve as a memory refresher prior to court appearances.

COMMON CRIMINAL JUSTICE SYSTEM EXPERIENCES

When a crime is reported, the victim's involvement with the criminal justice system often complicates the person's recovery. Frequently, the court procedures may make it seem as though the victim is the one to be punished rather than the criminal. Already a victim of the perpetrator, the client may become the victim of the criminal justice system as well.

Most criminal cases are resolved through plea bargaining or dismissal. Yet even when there is no trial, the victim still may be ordered to be present for hearings. Depending on the crime and on the jurisdiction, two or three preliminary hearings may be required before reaching the trial phase. As the process unfolds there will probably be continuances. It is not unusual for the victim to arrive at court, wait several hours, and then receive word that the hearing has been postponed.

Many crime victims experience repeated disruptions in their lives as long as the judicial process continues. They must schedule their daily routines around hearings, which often means transportation expenses and lost time at work. Burgess and Holmstrom (1974) observed that some victims actually have been fired from their jobs due to the amount of time they have been required to spend in court. Nevertheless, if the victim is absent from a hearing, for whatever reason, charges against the accused may be dropped. For instance, Holmstrom and Burgess (1978) cited two rape cases in which the victims had been to several hearings, but in both instances charges were dropped when the victim accidentally missed a court appearance. In light of such potentially positive outcomes for accused persons, defense attorneys commonly use multiple continuances as a means of wearing down victims and other prosecution witnesses.

In the minority of cases that finally do go to trial, the victim's testimony is in public before a group of strangers. In addition to reporters and persons present on official business, more sensational trials tend to attract voyeurs who come for the show. Before all of those assembled, the victim is required to give his or her name and address and then is instructed to provide a detailed description of the crime.

After being questioned by the prosecutor the victim faces cross-examination by the defense attorney, whose goal is to discredit the victim. Common tactics include the following: accusatory questions, forced-choice questions in which neither choice is accurate, sarcastic needling, rapid-fire questioning, and its opposite, marathon questioning concerning minute details. No matter what the victim's response, the defense attorney may try to twist the answer to benefit the defendant.

In addition to taking the witness stand, there are other court-related stresses as well. Examples include the following: confronting accused persons and their relatives, hearing contradictory testimony by other witnesses, and learning the outcome of the proceedings.

COPING WITH THE CRIMINAL JUSTICE SYSTEM

Except in cases of child abuse, for which most states require reporting, the worker ought to support whatever choice the victim makes regarding police notification and follow-through with various legal procedures. Victims should realize, however, that not reporting the crime makes them ineligible for benefits from crime victim compensation programs. For cases in which the crime is reported, Bard and Sangrey (1986) suggested several ways to help the person cope with the criminal justice system.

(a) While being interviewed by the police or prosecutor's office, the victim should seek clarification on any questions or procedures that are unfamiliar, or whose purpose is unclear.

(b) If the victim already has given a complete account to one investigator and a subsequent interviewer begins to cover the same material, the reason for the repetition can be questioned.

(c) To keep abreast of case developments, one strategy is to generate rapport with someone in the appropriate law enforcement or prosecutor's office. Being perceived as a human being, instead of as a case, is likely to elicit more helpful responses.

(d) If recovered property is being held as evidence, the person can inquire about procedures for obtaining its eventual return.

(e) If there are threats or harassment from defendants or their relatives, the victim should report such events to the police.

(f) If the victim can afford it or if payment can be arranged, the person may want to obtain his or her own attorney. Although lawyers retained in such a way have no formal role in the proceedings (unlike the French justice system where attorneys representing victims do have a role), they can help to prepare the victim for the court procedures and, if necessary, can respond to harassment from the defense attorney, the accused, or other parties.

Bard and Sangrey (1986) also suggested several questions that are appropriate to bring up with someone from the prosecutor's office. Where is the courthouse located? Where is the best place to park, and how much will it cost? What will the prosecutor ask me? What do you think the defense attorney will ask me? How long do you expect it to take? Is there any way to be compensated for my costs, such as transportation, child care, and lost earnings? Is the hearing still scheduled for tomorrow?

Although the court process may be traumatic and can produce crises of its own, it is possible for victims to prepare in advance for the stresses usually encountered. Role playing, first-hand observation of a trial, and stress inoculation training are three anticipatory coping methods that may be helpful.

The latter strategy is a coping technique intended to help individuals deal with anticipated stress. Psychologist Donald Meichenbaum (1977, 1985) created the approach and named it "stress inoculation training" because, like an inoculation, the person gains a protective benefit from experiencing a small amount of the stress ahead of time.

Meichenbaum says that you can think of any recurring stressful situation as having four phases.

Warning   I think something bad is going to happen
Impact   I was right; I'm in it now.
Arousal   The stress continues and I begin to worry that I might lose control; I might be overwhelmed.
Reflection For now the stress is over, and I am thinking back on how I handled the situation.

The client can use Meichenbaum's four phases to categorize thoughts associated with the stressful episode. First, the person writes down typical self-statements occurring during the warning, impact, arousal, and reflection stages. Next, the individual makes a new list that is also categorized according to the four phases. The client should include the following kinds of entries in the second list: (1) any statement from the first list that might help to reduce stress, and (2) other statements that probably will reduce stress. (When generating new self-statements for the second list, it is important for clients to record only those thoughts that they truly believe. They should avoid propaganda such as, "This won't bother me a bit.")

Here are some victim/witness self-statements for which stress inoculation training could be helpful.

• I'm scared I'll say the wrong thing.
• If I lose control I could ruin the whole case.

The following example shows how such stressful self-statements can be replaced by stress-reducing thoughts.

Stress Inoculation Training

First Set	Second Set

Warning

What will the lawyers say?	I can talk to the prosecutor's office about what might happen.
How will it feel to be on the witness stand?	I can picture myself on the witness stand answering questions.
Will I be able to answer the questions? Will I be able to tell my story clearly and coherently?	I will review the events in my mind, and I will relate them as I perceived them.

Impact

There's the defendant; I've got to make sure he's convicted.	The court system is responsible for the verdict; it's not all up to me.
Just like before, the defense attorney is badgering me during cross-examination.	I've been through a lot already; I can be strong.
He's making me look stupid because I don't know the answers to his questions.	If I don't remember, I can just say so. I'll just answer the questions as best I can.
He's making me nervous by asking the same question over and over.	It's OK to be nervous. I can still stop and think before I answer.

Arousal

He's twisting my words. He's taking my previous testimony and changing it.	I can stand up to him. If what he says is wrong, I'll tell him so.

I want to cry because he's making me look stupid.	My only responsibility is to state the facts as I know them.
I feel as if I might fall apart.	I can just focus on the answers to the questions.

Reflection

I wish I had handled things better.	I can learn from this experience.
What if I have to go through this again?	If I know I'm right, I should stand up for myself.

The second list of self-statements should not be written in stone. As one client told me, your initial production of that list allows you to "format the approach." Once clients begin to use the technique they can make adjustments as needed. They should throw out statements that don't work and add new statements that do seem to be helpful.

Prior to testifying, victims ought to review any material that is available to them. This includes written accounts they made of what happened, as well as evidence such as photographs, audio recordings, documents, etc. If victims are to be credible as witnesses there should not be inconsistencies between different parts of their testimony or between their testimony and the physical evidence.

When it is part of their responsibilities, victims should bring the best physical evidence available. For instance, if documents are relevant, they should bring originals rather than copies. Or if there are objects involved, they should bring the items (if possible) rather than pictures of them.

The victim's role as a witness begins when the person walks into the courthouse. Along with the victim, all of the other courtroom participants also will be inside the building. Depending on the type of hearing, those participants can include the judge, the attorneys for both sides, the court clerk, bailiffs, jurors, defendants, and other witnesses. In time, most of these individuals will be evaluating the victim's testimony, although their evaluations really begin the first time they see the individual. Often that initial observation occurs while the victim is in the courthouse but before the person takes the stand. The victim should realize that one's off-stand actions may create lasting impressions that can color the way others come to view the individual's subsequent testimony.

Since a wait of several hours is the norm, both adults and children benefit from taking something to read or other material to occupy the prehearing time. During their visits to the courthouse, most victims can also use supportive companionship. The companion may be a friend, relative, former victim, or crisis worker. Such a person should provide the client with an opportunity to share thoughts and feelings while waiting for the proceedings to begin, as well as following events such as the hearing being delayed, the victim's testimony, contradictory testimony by the accused, and the verdict.

The best outcome for crime victims is to realize that they have been through a time of great stress and have survived it. They can take pride in their strength and coping skills.

RAPE CRISES

All of the preceding crime victim considerations apply to rape crises. But empirical evidence demonstrates that rape survivors tend to experience greater psychological distress than other crime victims (e.g., Rauch & Foa, 2004). Consequently, there are additional issues that intervenors should keep in mind; this section and the next one highlight those areas.

Rape occurs when a nonconsenting person is forced into sexual activity (e.g., Cling, 2004; Logan, Walker, Jordan, & Leukefeld, 2006). In order for a charge of rape to be filed, law enforcement authorities in most jurisdictions are likely to investigate for evidence of sexual penetration, threatened or actual use of force, and lack of consent.

Each rape survivor responds in a unique and personal way. Nevertheless, there are certain common reactions. Burgess and Holmstrom (1985) describe the rape trauma syndrome as having an acute phase, followed by a period of reorganization that may involve either chronic or delayed stress.

For days following the attack, the victim may have pain or soreness from the physical trauma, although the damage to emotional well-being can be even more extensive. The survivor may continue to experience a broad range of unpleasant feelings, including fear, anxiety, depression, and bewilderment (e.g., Rauch & Foa, 2004).

Dread of possible HIV infection also is a frequently mentioned issue. In a review of empirical research concerning HIV and rape, Burgess and Baker (1992) reported evidence indicating that a significant minority (21 to 41 percent, depending on when they were interviewed) of survivors spontaneously noted worry about AIDS as a major concern. Worrying about sexually transmitted disease is justified, since as many as 43 percent of rape survivors develop sexually transmitted diseases resulting from the attack (Rauch & Foa, 2004).

Adolescent survivors experience most of the emotional reactions seen in adults. Young persons, however, also tend to suffer extreme embarrassment concerning the attack. These victims have a high need to avoid any notoriety that may result from public disclosure of the crime. Frequently, they want to transfer to another school, and they may become truant if not allowed to make the change, as Burgess and Holmstrom (1974) found in their study of rape victims.

Since fear often is a dominant emotion among rape survivors, the need for security frequently becomes paramount. In order to achieve greater safety the person may visit family, stay with friends, obtain an unlisted telephone number, or change residences. For example, in a study that included 46 rape victims, Wirtz and Harrell (1987b) found that within six months of the assault, 16 of those individuals moved to a new residence.

In some cases, the survivor generalizes fear from the specific rape situation to other similar circumstances. Distressing emotions may become associated with being alone, having sexual relations, or meeting persons who have characteristics similar to the assailant.

At least 60 percent—and possibly as many as 95 percent—of rape survivors do not report the attack to law enforcement authorities (e.g., Logan et al., 2006; Rauch & Foa, 2004; Wolitzky-Taylor et al., 2011a; Wolitzky-Taylor et al., 2011b). For those victims whose rapes are reported, the previously discussed criminal justice system considerations are applicable. Unfortunately, justice system involvement may be especially stressful for victims of rape. It is a sad fact that Holmstrom and Burgess (1978) concluded the ordeal of going to court created as great a crisis for the rape survivors they studied as did the crime itself. Most of their subjects felt nervous and frightened about going to court, although unlike the assault, which usually was relatively brief, the court process lasted months or years.

Once on the stand, the rape victim must give the traditional identifying information. In rape trials, however, the opposing attorneys are also likely to debate intimate details of the survivor's personal life. Although there continue to be efforts to limit the amount of private information victims can be forced to reveal, discrediting the victim continues to be a common defense tactic (Rauch & Foa, 2004). For example, when defense attorneys are restricted by rape shield laws they often respond by introducing more innuendo.

The most frequent strategy encountered in rape trials is for the defense attorney to blame the victim by arguing that the person either consented or simply fabricated the alleged sexual activity. And, as with other crime victims, defense attorneys in rape cases try to twist the victim's responses to benefit their clients. For example, Holmstrom and Burgess (1978) found that if the victim delayed in reporting the incident to the police it would be argued that it must not have concerned the individual very much; however, if the victim immediately reported the crime the charge would be made that the person actually had consented and simply was trying to provide a cover story for family and friends. If the survivor was seriously injured or became hysterical as a result of the rape the person's inability to recall all of the details would be criticized; although if the individual was not injured or was calm after the incident the victim's good memory for details would be attacked as demonstrating that nothing very disturbing must have happened.

For the rape victims studied by Holmstrom and Burgess (1978), cross-examination was the worst part of going to court. Their survivors came to view the defense attorney—who usually was male—as a new assailant. His questions seemed to be weapons intended to make victims say the opposite of what they wanted to say. Survivors came to see the attack of cross-examination as similar to the assault of rape; in both situations they were forced to do and say things against their will.

After all of the court-related stress endured by the victim, the usual criminal justice system decision is that the accusations against the perpetrator are an insufficient basis for conviction. In most cases rape charges are dropped or the defendant is acquitted. Rape cases have the lowest conviction rate of any felony (Rauch & Foa, 2004). Citing reports published during the preceding twelve years, Campbell (2008) concluded that among rape cases reported to the police, an average of 33 percent were referred for prosecution, 16 percent resulted in charges being filed, 12 percent involved a criminal conviction, and 7 percent resulted in a prison sentence. The conviction rate reported by Campbell is almost identical to the one observed by Holmstrom and Burgess thirty years earlier.

Holmstrom and Burgess (1978) studied 115 rape victims. In all but six of the cases the crime was reported to the police. Although an assailant was identified in 68 of the cases, in only 24 of them was there a trial or a guilty plea. Four of the guilty pleas were for the crime of rape and the remaining three were for lesser crimes. Of the 18 cases that went to trial, four resulted in rape convictions. (One case involving two assailants resulted in a trial for one and a plea bargain for the other.)

In the Holmstrom and Burgess (1978) study, the eight cases that resulted in rape convictions were remarkably similar. In all but one there was a non-victim eyewitness to the rape, and in seven of the eight rapes the assailant was a stranger. In all of the cases the victim was a virgin or was having sexual relations with just one person, and in all eight the police were notified immediately after the incident. Although the presence of these characteristics was not sufficient to guarantee a finding of guilt, no conviction was obtained when two or more of these characteristics were missing. Thus, the process of multiple hearings and court appearances, that stretched over an average span of two years, resulted in rape convictions for only a small homogeneous group of cases. In addition to these factors, others that have been found to be related to conviction include how badly hurt the woman was and how well the physical injuries were documented, the absence of risky behaviors on the part of the victim (such as drinking alcohol), and the use of a weapon by the assailant (e.g., Logan et al., 2006; Rauch & Foa, 2004).

If the assailant and the victim knew each other prior to the rape, the justice system frequently does not pursue the case. Decreased legal system interest does not mean there should be less of a crisis intervention response in situations involving an assailant who was an acquaintance of the victim. In fact, the initial dilemmas facing such survivors can be complex. Gayle Ellis (1994) noted that reactions may include a sense of betrayal, questioning of one's ability to judge people, and a more complicated decision regarding whether to report the assault to law enforcement authorities.

CRISIS INTERVENTION WITH RAPE VICTIMS

Crisis intervention is recognized as an appropriate strategy for aiding rape survivors who are thrown into a state of crisis (e.g., Burgess & Holmstrom, 1985; Campbell, 2006; Campbell, Patterson, & Lichty, 2005; Westefeld & Heckman-Stone, 2003; Woody & Beldin, 2012). Workers should help victims differentiate and clarify issues, while remembering that each person will behave in her own unique way. Intervenors must be careful not to engage in stereotyping by assuming they know how the person will respond. (In community-based crisis intervention programs almost all rape victims are female. Consequently, this section of the chapter uses feminine pronouns.)

When working with a rape victim, workers should use the same fundamental skills employed with all clients. One essential endeavor is listening to the person and reflecting feelings. The importance of actively listening to rape victims was demonstrated in empirical research conducted by Sarah Ullman (1996). She surveyed 155 women who had been victims of rape. The type of social reaction that had the most positive effects on distress related to the assault and on ultimate recovery was listening to the woman's feelings and encouraging her to talk.

The task of crisis workers is to meet the needs of the particular individuals they are assisting. Nevertheless, some medical and social service professionals seem to believe their first priority is to determine whether the situation meets a legal definition of rape. Such professionals should remember that it is not their job to evaluate the legal evidence of the case. Their duty is to focus on the type of help being sought.

In some cases, the request for assistance may have nothing to do with rape. For example, parents concerned about the sexual activity of their adolescent daughter may bring her to the hospital to be examined, claiming she was raped. In such a situation the most appropriate response may be problem solving that leads to a family counseling referral. Or, after having intercourse a young woman may become terrified about the consequences. She then may go to the hospital, say she was raped, and request a medical evaluation and a "morning-after pill." As Burgess and Holmstrom (1974) noted, in such an instance it may be appropriate to offer both medical attention and crisis intervention.

Rape forces victims to do something against their will. Following the assault they are likely to encounter additional persons who may try to force them to do things they do not want to do. Police officers may ask them to repeat their story; emergency room staff members want family, employment, and insurance information; physicians may order them to undergo medical procedures; and crisis workers may probe for information. Consequently, one common goal for rape survivors is to regain control of their lives.

Empirical research supports the importance of control for those who have been victims of rape. In their study of 87 clients served by rape crisis counselors at five centers in England and Wales, Nicole Westmarland and Sue Alderson (2013) compared responses to a 15-item questionnaire during the first or second counseling session to those during a session that occurred at least six weeks later. The researchers found the greatest difference was strongly disagreeing with the idea of feeling empowered and in control. Initially 61 percent of the clients strongly disagreed with that statement, compared to 31 percent in the subsequent session.

In order to facilitate self-control the intervenor must respect the desires and wishes of the victim, as well as encourage the person to take responsibility for decision making. Then, as the survivor moves toward recovery, the individual can attribute progress to her own efforts and abilities.

A study by Campbell (2006) compared the experiences of rape victims coming to two hospital emergency rooms. At one facility an advocate from a rape crisis center accompanied victims during their stay in the emergency room, and at the other hospital such advocates were not involved. At the first hospital, 36 of the study participants received medical service, and at the second facility 45 participants had medical attention. Some of the questions by hospital personnel seemed to be unrelated to the woman's medical needs. For example, quite a few recalled being asked why they were with the perpetrator (44% at the first hospital and 58% at the second facility). Looking back on their experience with the medical personnel, 91 percent of those at the second hospital with no advocate said the experience left them reluctant to seek additional assistance, compared to 67 percent of those having an advocate feeling that way. With regard to law enforcement, 17 of the survivors at the first hospital had contact with the police, and 28 at the second facility had such contact. Over 80 percent of the survivors at both sites felt disappointed and violated following their interaction with the police. Among women who did not have an advocate present, 89 percent said the encounter with the police left them reluctant to seek additional assistance, compared to 61 percent of those who had an advocate feeling that way. Overall, the presence of the advocate did seem to have some positive effects. Nevertheless, for most women the medical and legal encounters were stressful and unpleasant experiences that left them feeling less willing to seek further help.

Campbell (2005) also investigated the recollections of the nurses, physicians, and police officers who had interacted with the 81 rape survivors at the two hospitals. In most instances, the recollections of the rape victims about the events that took place in the encounters were supported by the recollections of the professionals. What was different was the evaluation by the two groups concerning the reactions of the victims to those events. For example, while 80 percent of the victims said the medical and law enforcement interactions had left them reluctant to seek additional assistance, a minority of the nurses (41%), doctors (27%), and officers (22%) perceived that to be the case.

When rape victims encounter bureaucracies associated with medical care or the criminal justice system, they face stresses that arise out of interacting with such entities. One set of challenges arises out of the fact that the survivor is an outsider entering a complex organization, and another set results from dealing with a group of people rather than with an individual.

As outsiders, victims often don't understand medical or criminal justice system procedures. But survivors have a right to receive a rationale for what is being done, as well as an explanation of what effect it may have on them. Unfortunately, victims sometimes receive insufficient information. For example, Holmstrom and Burgess (1978) reported that one victim in their study was under the impression that her witness responsibilities would be over after testifying to a grand jury. She was shocked to discover that she might be required to make multiple court appearances.

The second source of stress in medical and justice system bureaucracies is that hospital and court personnel are likely to change from one contact to the next. Consequently, the necessity of repeatedly explaining one's situation to a new staff member becomes a burdensome ordeal for many survivors.

Crisis workers can take steps to help victims understand bureaucracies and to allay institutional depersonalization. For example, intervenors can explain hospital and criminal justice system procedures, they can provide emotional support, and they can be available for subsequent contacts.

When working with rape survivors, intervenors should always encourage self-control and should remain ready to assist victims in coping with the stresses arising out of bureaucratic involvement. In addition, when interacting with a rape survivor, workers must be prepared to address the following

key issues: seeking medical attention, reporting the incident to law enforcement authorities, regaining a sense of safety, interacting with family and
friends, and recalling the assault.

Medical Attention

The physical well-being of the victim is the primary concern if the individual has not yet been evaluated by a medical professional. In such cases
the intervenor should explore the person's interest in receiving medical attention and should be prepared to furnish information concerning available
services. For instance, some hospitals refuse to treat rape victims, and others
notify the police whenever a rape victim receives service. Crisis workers
ought to be aware of hospital policies concerning rape victims and should explain those procedures to the survivor.

In addition to formal policies, there are recurring emergency room circumstances that the victim can expect to encounter. It is helpful to describe
this typical routine so that the survivor knows what to anticipate upon entering the emergency room. For example, most victims end up waiting for
some time before being examined. Factors affecting the length of the wait include the seriousness of the victim's injuries, the number and condition of
other emergency room patients, and the number of available physicians.
Nevertheless, even under favorable circumstances there still may be long de-
lays.

A caring person should accompany the survivor to the emergency room.
This companion may be a friend, a family member, a crisis worker from another agency, or a member of the hospital's own crisis intervention staff.
When there are multiple possibilities for companionship, choosing that person can be a topic explored with the victim.

Medical services delivered to rape victims vary from one setting to another, although frequently offered services include the following: a general examination and treatment of injuries, a prophylactic dose of an antibiotic, and,
for women, a pelvic exam and antipregnancy medication in the form of an
emergency postcoital contraceptive (morning-after pill). The nature and potential consequences of these procedures can provoke questions the survivor
may want to discuss.

A general physical examination can provide reassurance if serious injuries
are not present and can lead to treatment of injuries that do exist. Such an
exam can also serve another purpose as well. The medical professional can
be subpoenaed and a report of the exam can be secured as evidence if criminal charges are brought against the assailant. Although the likelihood of
such events is relatively small, their possibility can exert a powerful influence

on medical professionals. Rather than viewing themselves as practitioners of the healing arts, some medical personnel come to view their role as evidence collectors—or as noncollectors, if they use the possibility of justice system involvement as an excuse for not aiding the person.

When a general physical exam is provided to female victims it often is accompanied by a gynecological examination. If the victim is unfamiliar with the usual procedures involved in such an exam, they should be described to her and there should be an opportunity to discuss the advantages and disadvantages of the procedures. The exact characteristics of the exam will depend upon the particular physician and the needs of the victim. In a typical pelvic exam the patient lies on the examining table with her legs apart and her feet placed in stirrups. The physician examines the external and internal genitalia. The latter procedure may include (a) inserting a speculum (an instrument with two rounded edges) in the vagina and holding apart the vaginal walls, (b) placing two fingers of a gloved hand inside the vagina and pressing down with the other hand on the patient's lower abdomen, and (c) placing one finger in the vagina and another in the rectum while pressing down on the abdomen. As might be expected, such physical intrusions lead many victims to see similarities between the exam and the rape (e.g., Campbell et al., 1999).

In addition to a sense of further violation that may be associated with the procedures, other potential negative consequences include physical discomfort and embarrassment. Nevertheless, a gynecological examination has benefits, such as assessment for internal injuries and for the presence of sperm. In terms of judging the examination's pros and cons, it is the survivor who should make the decision concerning whether or not to submit to a pelvic exam.

For many women, negative feelings arise out of medical treatment for rape. For example, Rebecca Campbell and Sheela Raja (2005) found that of the women in their study who had sought medical attention, over two-thirds reported feeling depressed and/or anxious as a result of that experience.

In general, the decision to seek medical help should be made by the victim. If the person is ambivalent, the worker can encourage consideration of the likely consequences associated with seeking or not seeking medical attention. For survivors who do visit an emergency room and are accompanied by a worker, the intervenor's primary duties are to provide the person with information and support. In addition to discussing the emergency room procedures and describing typical effects of medication, the intervenor may help by obtaining tissues, water, or mouthwash, and eventually may assist with transportation from the hospital.

If the person chooses to receive an initial evaluation by a medical professional there are a number of potential reasons for also seeking follow-up medical contact. Possibilities include: pregnancy testing, HIV testing, and evaluation of any symptoms resulting from disease or injury.

Reporting the Incident to the Police

Often, a third party reports the rape to law enforcement authorities. For example, in the study by Burgess and Holmstrom, of the 94 adult rapes that were reported to the police, only 22 of the reports came from victims (Holmstrom, 1985). If intervenors discover the incident has not been reported, the issue of whether or not to notify the authorities is an appropriate area for discussion with an adult victim.

When the survivor is ambivalent, the pros and cons of reporting the assault can be discussed. On the pro side, reporting the crime opens the possibility for the assailant to face justice; if the perpetrator is apprehended it may prevent additional rapes; and reporting usually is a prerequisite for claims to insurance companies or to crime victim compensation boards. On the con side, the survivor will have to repeat the details of the incident many times to many different people; the person may face retribution from the assailant; and if charges are filed, there may be court appearances over a period of months or years.

Unfortunately, many women who report the incident to the police experience negative reactions as a consequence of doing so. In the previously mentioned study by Campbell and Raja (2005), the researchers also focused on participants who had reported the attack to law enforcement authorities. Each of the following reactions to their encounter with the legal system was endorsed by more than two-thirds of the women: was encouraged not to report the attack, refused to take my report, was told the attack was not serious enough to bring charges, felt guilty, felt depressed, felt anxious, the episode made me distrust others, the episode made me reluctant to seek additional help.

If the authorities have been or will be notified, or if the victim decides to postpone a decision (which decreases any chance of a conviction), the importance of certain physical evidence may need to be discussed. From the standpoint of a law enforcement investigation, clinician and administrator Linda Ledray (1993) noted the following reasons for collecting physical evidence: to show that sexual contact occurred, to demonstrate that force was employed, and to identify the perpetrator. Consequently, the following steps may be advantageous: (a) avoid teeth brushing, washing, bathing, showering, or douching before being examined by a physician; (b) saving, unwashed and air-dried, underwear plus any clothing that was damaged or soiled during the assault; (c) using a comb to check for hair samples left by the attacker; and (d) saving fingernail clippings that may provide skin scrapings from the assailant.

In discussing evidence collection, Ledray (1993) strongly recommended that clinicians who collect evidence should maintain ongoing communication with local law enforcement and prosecuting attorney's offices so that there is a clear understanding as to exactly what evidence is useful. And, although she supports appropriate evidence collection, she noted most rape cases never go to court, yet almost all survivors are in crisis. Consequently, she believes providing crisis intervention may be the most beneficial of all the services supplied to rape victims.

If the survivor decides to report the crime, the intervenor can offer to accompany the person to the police. Although, as in the case of emergency room companionship, the client should be free to accept or reject the worker's offer of assistance.

Regaining a Sense of Safety

Intervenors should help rape survivors explore how safe they feel. Fears ought to be discussed and adaptive actions should be considered. Short-term safety issues include where these clients will go after the crisis contact, how they will get there, how safe they will feel there, and who is available to go with them. For long-term security considerations the worker can negotiate a plan that will focus energy on specific steps such as making daily routines safer, installing new locks, or moving to a new residence. Actions such as these can contribute to feelings of enhanced self-control and can improve security.

Interacting With Family and Friends

Often rape victims wonder whom to tell about the incident, as well as how such persons are likely to react. In addition to considering the pros and cons of possible interactions, the worker may want to help the survivor address these issues through role playing. This technique can be useful in helping the victim decide both whether and how to break the news to family and friends.

The adjustment of rape survivors can be influenced by the reactions of friends and loved ones. If such persons are with the victim at the time of the initial contact it can be beneficial to meet with them. The loved ones of rape survivors often need assistance in dealing with their own distress precipitated by the rape. The standard problem-solving approach is a good place to start. Frequently encountered issues include anger at both the assailant and the victim. Although anger at the rapist tends to be openly expressed, anger toward the survivor may be communicated indirectly.

Once their own reactions have been considered, the focus should turn to how they can best help the victim. Daniel Silverman (1978) suggested that this second phase of the interview ought to begin by addressing any misconceptions that have come to light. The two issues that are most likely to be discussed are (1) that rape is an assault rather than an erotic experience, and (2) that the rapist, rather than the victim, is responsible for the attack. After having confronted any misconceptions, the worker should help the friends or loved ones discover how they can assist the person. A prime consideration is encouraging the survivor to mobilize her own coping skills rather than interfering in tasks that the person prefers to accomplish alone. Although lending a helping hand is appropriate, overprotection is not.

One activity that no victim can do alone is to discuss troubling thoughts and feelings. Consequently, friends and loved ones can be important sources of support when they listen to the survivor, provide empathic understanding, and act as sounding boards as the victim describes concerns and problems. Although the worker has been modeling these skills, the intervenor may also need to discuss basic concepts of effective communication and problem solving. For example, the worker might point out that individuals develop their own unique coping techniques and that supporting the survivor in making independent decisions is preferable to telling the person what to do.

Discussing the Assault

Without forcing the victim to discuss a topic the person is not ready to talk about, it is appropriate to explore what happened during the assault. If the individual does not wish to talk about it, the intervenor can say that the offer to discuss the incident will remain open should the person have a change of heart.

As with suicide, intervenors sometimes feel uneasy about exploring such a sensitive topic. Should it become apparent to the survivor that the worker is avoiding a frank discussion of the rape and its aftermath, the person's shame and embarrassment may increase, or these feelings may develop when they did not previously exist.

During discussion of the assault, the worker should not use the word "rape" unless the client refers to the incident using that term. For example, rather than saying, "Tell me how the rape happened," it is preferable to say, "Tell me what happened tonight."

Although eliciting information about what has occurred may be painful for the victim, it can also be a foundation for rebuilding self-esteem. With clients who are ready to talk about the assault, Burgess and Holmstrom (1974) noted that it is appropriate to explore the following topics: facts and feelings regarding the circumstances, conversation with the assailant, sexual details, physical and verbal threats, struggle with the attacker, and drug or alcohol use by the assailant or by the victim.

Self-blame is a frequently occurring issue. Although there are wide-ranging individual differences when it comes to self-blame, compared to women who don't blame themselves, women who blame themselves tend to have more health difficulties and greater mental distress (e.g., Logan et al., 2006).

The topic of self-blame often arises when workers discover that survivors are ruminating about the assault and are trying to think of how they could have changed the outcome by somehow behaving differently. While noting that it is natural to have second thoughts about the incident, the worker may also want to challenge self-blaming statements. In one study (Katz & Burt, 1988) of rape victims, the intervenor behavior that victims most frequently mentioned as being helpful (65% endorsement) was the worker saying, "It was not your fault."

Two experienced rape crisis counselors have advocated "good-natured" confrontation when survivors take responsibility for the assault. Janet Roehl and Donna Gray (1984) recommended that workers ask the following sorts of questions in order to challenge self-blame.

- At any time during the incident did you invite the assailant to rape you?
- Did you post a sign saying, "Attention! I am alone. Please attack and rape me"?

Most of their clients laugh at the questions and deny any such behavior. Consequently, Roehl and Gray believe the strategy helps victims to abandon self-blame in favor of correctly fixing blame on the assailant.

The worker should also review efforts made by the survivor that demonstrated an attempt to control events. During the assault those actions may have included behaviors such as trying verbally to dissuade the attacker, attempting to physically resist by fleeing or fighting, focusing on characteristics of the rapist for future identification, and thinking about what kind of strategy would most likely help one survive the attack. Bard and Sangrey (1979) cited one veteran police officer as telling a rape victim that since she survived, whatever she did was the right thing to do.

In addition to discussing the assault, there can be some benefit to exploring actions the survivor took after the attack. Depending on when the crisis contact occurs, Burgess and Holmstrom (1974) asserted that relevant topics may include the following: how the person sought help and what resulted from those efforts, interactions with the police, and experiences at the hospital.

Although rape survivors have immediate problems confronting them, they are also likely to encounter adjustment difficulties that may not appear for days, weeks, or months. So, in addition to discussing immediate realities, it may be helpful to engage in anticipatory problem solving. For example, Burgess and Holmstrom (1974) recommended telling the client that the incident often affects several areas of a victim's life, including emotions, sexual attitudes and behavior, social relations, and health. Being prepared to discuss these areas can help the survivor to recognize and deal with potential difficulties.

In most instances, the wrap-up of the initial interview should include the following tasks: having the client describe the plan that has been developed, collecting any necessary identifying information on the victim (including names, phone numbers, and addresses of others with whom the person may be staying), and arranging subsequent contacts. If friends or relatives may be answering the telephone at the client's location there should be an agreement on how the worker will be identified if someone besides the client answers the phone.

ADJUSTMENT FOLLOWING RAPE

No other crisis client is likely to have a more difficult adjustment period than a rape survivor. A variety of issues can challenge the person. Examples include the following: recovering from physical injuries, encountering persons who resemble the assailant, being summoned for court appearances, resuming social relations, coping with negative feelings concerning one's sexuality, and handling the fear of being assaulted again.

A review of the literature (Rauch & Foa, 2004) shows that although emotional distress does lessen during the first three months after the attack, fear, anxiety, and depression often remain elevated beyond that time period. For example, Kimerling and Calhoun (1994) found that at least 25 to 35 percent of victims experience reactions to rape that last for years.

During follow-up interviews conducted four to six years after the rape, Burgess and Holmstrom (1979) found that 74 percent of their subjects believed they had recovered from the incident. Half of those individuals judged that they had made a full recovery within a few months, while the other half said it had taken years to return to normal. The remaining 26 percent of the victims believed that they still had not recovered.

In an empirical study by Resick and Ellis (1982), the best predictor of post-rape adaptation was the person's adjustment prior to the rape. The implication is that survivors who had poor coping techniques before the assault were likely to use those same poor techniques after the assault. What might be some of those particularly bad coping techniques? In one component of a study they did, Frazier, Mortensen, and Steward (2005) remained in contact with rape victims for up to a year after their initial visit to an emergency room. The researchers found that those women who blamed themselves for past negative events they had experienced were more likely to use social withdrawal as a coping technique and that social withdrawal was associated with greater distress during the recovery process. Ultimately, the investigators determined that social withdrawal accounted for 36 percent of the relationship between blaming oneself and feeling distressed. Consequently, crisis workers should recognize and reinforce victim statements that blame the perpetrator, should consider confronting survivor self-blame in a "good-natured" way, and should support appropriate social interaction as the person deals with the challenges of being a rape survivor.

Crisis workers should encourage active coping efforts. The usual crisis intervention problem-solving approach is the most appropriate initial response to problematic events and issues that arise during recovery. Although when working with survivors who begin to experience chronic adjustment difficulties, it is appropriate to refer them for additional services, such as individual psychotherapy or couples therapy.

NEGOTIATING WITH ARMED PERPETRATORS

Most crisis intervention activity with crime victims comes after the perpetrator is gone. There are times, though, when workers may be called upon to provide assistance while the crime is in progress.

EXAMPLE. Edward Olson and his wife Mary were having a heated discussion over family finances. When he threatened to hit her she ran out the back door. Edward chased her down, struck her in the head, and forced her back into the house.

A neighbor who witnessed the assault called the police. When the officers arrived, Edward threatened to kill Mary and their two daughters if the police did not leave.

The officers called for reinforcements and began talking with Edward. While these negotiations were taking place, Mary escaped with their youngest daughter.

Once safely away from the house, Mary told the police of continuing marital problems, noting that she and Edward had been to the crisis center several times. The officers then requested an outreach team from the crisis service.

Upon arriving at the scene, the workers found the house ringed by four police sharpshooters. An additional six officers were stationed about 75 yards from the house, with a crowd of approximately 30 people gathered behind them. A television news crew had positioned itself midway between the six officers and the house. The police had established an open telephone line and were negotiating with Edward over the phone.

One of the crisis workers knew Edward. After discussing the situation with the police, the worker approached the house and called out to him. Edward came to the front door, and they talked for about 10 minutes. During this time, Mary decided to take matters into her own hands. She slipped in the back door and rescued her remaining daughter.

When Edward discovered that his daughter was gone, he became enraged. The crisis worker tried to calm him down while walking slowly across the yard toward the front door of the house. Edward then came out the door, aiming a shotgun at the worker and demanding that he take off his coat to demonstrate that he was unarmed. For the next 20 minutes, the shirt-sleeved worker negotiated in 30-degree weather, as Edward stood five feet away with the shotgun pointed at the worker's stomach.

Eventually, Edward agreed to have the worker and three police officers come into the house to discuss matters. Once inside, the policemen jumped Edward and subdued him.

DISCUSSION OF EDWARD OLSON'S CASE. The crisis worker risked his life in this instance, believing he was doing the right thing. Since what he did worked, it was a successful response to this particular situation. But not all crisis workers would have responded in the same way, and many workers would question whether they should be expected to assume such a risk.

The preceding episode could be described as a spontaneous domestic siege in which there were no substantive demands. In this context, a siege involves a perpetrator holding individuals against their will. It was *spontaneous* because Edward Olson probably did not begin the day planning to hold his wife and daughters at gunpoint. It was *domestic* because the people being held were family members. And there were no *substantive* demands because what he wanted (to control and punish his wife and daughters) was unrelated to anything negotiators could help provide. Those terms arise out of three fundamental ways of thinking about situations that involve negotiations with armed perpetrators.

- *Spontaneous-Planned.* In most instances, an armed confrontation involving authorities is not what that perpetrator intended, and emotions tend to be running high. On the other hand, coldness and the absence of emotion often characterize confrontations that perpetrators purposefully set up.
- *Strangers-Not Strangers.* If the people being held are strangers, as time passes the perpetrator may come to develop a more positive view of them. When those being threatened are persons who already have some sort of relationship with the perpetrator, time usually does nothing to improve those relationships. In fact, spending time terrorizing the victims may be what the perpetrator wants.
- *Substantive Demands-Nonsubstantive Demands.* A substantive demand is something the perpetrator thinks cannot be obtained in any other way

than by bargaining with authorities; examples include publicity and large sums of money. When there are substantive demands, authorities tend to have a fair amount of leverage because they can control or influence resources the perpetrator wants. Nonsubstantive demands involve needs that could be easily met on any other day; examples include food and phone calls. If there are only nonsubstantive demands, the perpetrator may already have what is desired (for instance, the ability to terrify family members).

Negotiating with armed perpetrators is more an art than a science. Patience and common sense are essential traits for negotiators who are successful, with success defined as the preservation of human life. Armed assaults by authorities indicate the negotiation has failed. Nevertheless, the potential for armed rescue gives the authorities power in the negotiations, and such assaults often become the primary strategy whenever there is a murder after negotiations have begun (e.g., Greenstone, 2005; Strentz, 2013; Vecchi et al., 2005). But competent negotiators rarely find the situation has deteriorated that far. Instead, they usually are successful in implementing the philosophy of "contain and negotiate." For example, in a survey by Butler, Leitenberg, and Fuselier (1993), there were no murders or serious injuries in 92 percent of the 268 incidents reported, and Van Hasselt et al. (2006) cited data for 2002–2003 indicating that 82 percent of documented incidents ended without physical injury to the perpetrator or victim. Strentz (2012) noted Federal Aviation Administration documents indicating that out of over 400 hijackings of aircraft under their authority, about 98 percent ended without the use of force. Unfortunately, just as Edward Olson did not pull a gun on his family in order to get something from negotiators, some hijackers have no interest in what authorities might offer. The terrorists who commandeered four airliners on September 11, 2001 are a prime example.

Negotiating with armed perpetrators is a law enforcement or executive branch concern; crisis workers intervene only to the extent that the authorities request them to become involved. Experts (e.g., Augustin & Fagan, 2011; Butler et al., 1993; Lanceley, 2003; Strentz, 2012, 2013) assert that appropriate uses of mental health consultants include the following: assessment of the perpetrator, suggestions concerning negotiation topics, and liaison with mental health professionals and resources. The precise role of crisis workers can be clarified in planning meetings between crisis staff and the police. Such planning should take into account two considerations:

- Regardless of how they participate, crisis workers ought not to be in positions where it is possible for them to injured, killed, or taken hostage.
- The best roles for a crisis worker are observer and consultant. The primary negotiator should be a law enforcement officer.

The most common way in which crisis workers become involved is when the authorities discover that a perpetrator has a history of emotional problems. In fact, a variety of background data is likely to be helpful. Here are several categories of information that experts (e.g., Greenstone, 2005; Lanceley, 2003; Strentz, 2012) suggest may be of use to the primary negotiator:

- *Names:* in addition to the perpetrator's name, the names of the person's children, spouse, relatives, and friends.
- *Criminal Behavior:* the number, nature, and outcome of arrests; previous violence or threats of violence.
- *Emotional Disturbance:* accounts of psychiatric hospitalizations or other mental health services, present and past mental disorder diagnoses, threatened or attempted suicide, recent communication of distress (either directly or by actions such as giving away possessions).
- *Relevant Skills:* educational and occupational history, knowledge relating to weapons and explosives.
- *Affiliations:* memberships in religious organizations, sects, or other groups; relationship to the victims.
- *Habits:* interests, smoking, drug and alcohol use, gambling, sexuality.
- *Immediate Problems:* prescribed medications, medical conditions, finances, legal difficulties, disrupted relationships, any special significance of today's date, other current stressors.

A commonly recommended approach in the United States, the United Kingdom, many countries within the European Union, Australia, and New Zealand (e.g., Greenstone, 2005; Hatcher, Mohandie, Turner, & Gelles, 1998; Lanceley, 2003; Royce, 2005; Strentz, 2012, 2013; Van Hasselt et al., 2005a; Van Hasselt et al., 2005b; Van Hasselt et al., 2006; Vecchi et al., 2005; Zealberg, Hardesty, & Tyson, 1998) is to establish a climate of joint problem solving in which the primary negotiator communicates empathic understanding. Keeping perpetrators talking about their concerns and hopes allows them to ventilate their complaints rather than simply ruminating about those difficulties. Within an atmosphere characterized by rapport and calmness, reasoned consideration of alternatives can help perpetrators decrease irrational thinking and increase their understanding of consequences associated with various options. (Thomas Strentz [2013] notes that there are still countries, such as Russia, in which the objective is to kill the perpetrators, regardless of the consequences for innocent victims.)

Negotiators should avoid abstractions in favor of concrete descriptions of concerns and outcomes. The specific topics depend on the situation. For instance, with individuals who take hostages after a robbery, the emphasis may be on the logical consideration of alternatives, whereas with perpetrators who are emotionally disturbed the focus may need to be on feelings. Whenever perpetrators are depressed and suicidal, negotiators should avoid philosophical discussions in favor of concentrating on here-and-now issues such as being cold, hungry, or scared.

When feasible it is best to begin negotiations by recognizing some of the perpetrator's views in ways that are truthful and realistic. For example, in response to a list of demands, one strategy is to say that those are certainly things that can be discussed. When focusing on specific demands (such as those for money or vehicles) it is advisable to reflect the demands in ways that soften them. For instance, if the person has requested a million dollars, the reflection acknowledging that might be, "You want some money out of this."

Before addressing difficult issues in detail, it may be helpful to set the tone of the negotiations by discussing issues that can be resolved with relative ease. For instance, a good place to start can be on how communication will occur between the perpetrator and the authorities. In most cases, the primary negotiator should be near but not face-to-face with an armed perpetrator. Options include speaking around a corner, beside a closed door, or on the telephone—with the phone probably being the best option. Negotiators should avoid talking over a bullhorn since it may contribute to the perpetrator's sense of power. If possible, the authorities also ought to disperse crowds and otherwise keep any audience to a minimum, since ego-gratifying displays of violence may be less likely if there are few people to observe such behavior.

When the focus eventually does turn to major problems, the negotiators should use the usual crisis intervention strategy of separating concerns into small segments. Negotiation needs to uncover new problem-solving alternatives for the perpetrator.

Perpetrators in premeditated hostage taking often have been failures who now are trying to achieve power through a dramatic act. If confronted, however, they usually deny their own inadequacies. Consequently, it may be best for guidance to be unobtrusive so that the perpetrators believe they are the ones who are generating the reasonable alternatives.

At times, however, it can be necessary for guidance to be fairly direct. For example, when a perpetrator is having difficulty perceiving the likely consequences of a possible course of action, the negotiator should state outcomes which might result from that option.

Thomas Strentz (2012) has asserted that the single best predictor of a positive resolution is the development of a trusting relationship between the negotiator and the perpetrator. To that end, the negotiator should be as truthful as possible (without endangering others) and should communicate the attitude of wanting to bring about an honorable resolution that offers hope.

The problem-solving tactics discussed to this point have not been very different from traditional crisis intervention. There are, however, several useful negotiation techniques that do represent departures from usual efforts (e.g., Strentz, 2012, 2013).

    (a) Negotiators should periodically ask perpetrators whether they are now ready to bring matters to a logical, safe, and peaceful conclusion.
    (b) Authorities need to attempt to limit the amount of information that is available to perpetrators.
    (c) In most cases, friends and relatives should not be at the scene. Such persons can become accomplices, victims of violence, or an audience for macho behavior.
    (d) Negotiators should try to prevent movement of the perpetrator so that authorities do not have to reestablish control at a new site.

Attempts to change the perpetrator's views ought to be gradual. Lengthy negotiation is preferable to rapid movement that risks outright rejection. Whenever the negotiator believes a proposal is about to be rejected, a good strategy is to ask the perpetrator to think about it awhile and to make a decision later.

Since the goal is to move the perpetrator to a new viewpoint on certain issues, two-sided attitude change is best. In other words, acceptance becomes more likely if the negotiator acknowledges arguments on the other side of the issue.

Negotiators should strive not to provoke the perpetrator through actions such as criticism, derogatory comments, impatience, arguing, or emphatic rejection of demands. For example, if the perpetrator reneges on a promise, the negotiator should point out the change, but face-saving violence may result from confronting the person with threats or with accusations that the individual is bluffing. Regarding violence that already has occurred, discussions ought to avoid any deaths that happened at the beginning of the incident, since the possible penalties for those offenses may leave little hope for the perpetrator.

Time generally is on the side of the authorities. Gradual negotiation allows everyone's adrenaline levels to decline and decreases the possibility of rash action by either side. Once the perpetrator becomes engaged in a problem-solving dialogue, violence becomes less likely.

SUMMARY

Despite taking routine crime prevention efforts, a person often reacts with shock and disbelief at becoming a crime victim. The criminal act may destroy the victim's usual attitudes of trust and autonomy, and it is likely to create immediate problems that must be resolved.

Crisis intervention is especially suited to provide emotional support and problem-solving guidance to crime victims whose coping skills have been overtaxed. Whenever a victim blames the perpetrator, the worker should be sure to reinforce such expressions. And while recognizing that it is impossible to be completely safe, the worker ought to encourage prudent crime prevention efforts. Within the limits of common sense, it is also adaptive for victims to return to their traditional routines. As the person attempts to resume a normal life, it can be helpful for the individual to keep a diary that documents progress and that can be used as a memory refresher in the event of court testimony.

Involvement in the criminal justice system often is stressful for the victim. The person's life may be disrupted by a series of distressing events, such as postponements and taking the witness stand.

Intervenors ought to support an adult victim's decisions regarding participation in the criminal justice system. The victim should seek necessary information from law enforcement authorities and should take advantage of resources that are available. There are several strategies that can help the person cope with the stress of a pending trial; those methods include role playing, observing someone else's trial, and stress inoculation training. Prior to testifying, the person should review available material and should prepare to bring any evidence for which the individual is responsible. Once arriving at the courthouse, the victim should realize that one's off-stand behavior can influence the attitudes of other courtroom participants. While in the building, coping is easier when the person has brought something to do during waiting periods and when the individual has the support of a caring companion.

A rape survivor is likely to have intense emotional reactions and urgent safety concerns. As with other crime victims, any involvement in the criminal justice system complicates the individual's recovery. If there is courtroom testimony, the defense attorney is likely to discuss intimate details of the person's life, to accuse the victim of lying about the incident, and to try leading the victim into making statements that will help the defendant. Not surprisingly, survivors often see similarities between the defense attorney and the rapist. After suffering such indignities, most rape victims find that the charges are dropped or that the defendant is acquitted.

Crisis intervention with rape survivors should focus on meeting the individual needs of the particular client. Whatever the person's concerns, workers should foster self-control by encouraging independent decision making. When victims encounter medical or justice system bureaucracies, intervenors can facilitate coping efforts by providing information, emotional support, and the availability of subsequent contacts. In addition, there are *five areas intervenors should be prepared to address with rape survivors*.

(1) A decision regarding *medical attention* is the first priority for victims who have not been evaluated by a medical professional. Workers ought to be prepared to describe relevant hospital policies and typical emergency room procedures. If the client decides to seek medical attention, a companion should accompany the survivor to the hospital. When that companion is the worker, the intervenor's responsibilities are to explain procedures and provide support.

(2) Intervenors should be prepared to help rape survivors consider the pros and cons of *reporting the assault to the police*, and workers ought to be available to accompany the victim to the police station. If the crime is reported, the victim should take steps to preserve any physical evidence.

(3) Workers ought to help rape survivors regain a sense of *safety*. Both short- and long-term changes probably will be necessary to improve the client's security.

(4) Deciding *whether and how to tell friends and family* about the rape is another issue that intervenors should be prepared to help victims consider. If friends or loved ones accompany the survivor, the worker can meet them with the following purposes in mind: assisting them in dealing with their own reactions to the rape, confronting any misconceptions about rape, and aiding them in planning how they will assist the victim. One of the best forms of support they can provide is listening to the person and offering empathic problem-solving assistance.

(5) The worker should *offer to discuss the assault*. If the client expresses self-blame, one option is to confront such expressions in a good-natured way. The intervenor ought to recognize and reinforce any indications that the survivor attempted to control events during and after the assault. Since adjustment problems are common, it is appropriate to discuss areas in which victims sometimes encounter difficulties.

Rape may result in psychological distress that lasts months or years. An intervenor should aid rape survivors in actively coping with whatever difficulties they encounter.

The art of negotiating with armed perpetrators requires patience and common sense. Although crisis workers may serve as consultants, they should not place themselves in positions where they may endanger themselves. The best negotiating strategy is empathic problem solving that focuses on concrete concerns and outcomes. It is useful to employ certain traditional crisis intervention techniques, such as unobtrusive guidance and separating major concerns into small segments. In addition, there are specific negotiation guidelines that should be kept in mind, and, for the most part, negotiators ought to employ a nonprovocative approach that focuses on gradual two-sided attitude change.

STUDY QUESTIONS

1. What sort of assistance should crisis workers encourage crime victims to request?
2. While on his way to work one morning, Ike was mugged in the subway. The assault was a terrifying experience for him. Now every time he gets on a subway he feels anxious. With regard to Ike's situation, identify each of the following: unconditioned stimulus, unconditioned response, conditioned stimulus, conditioned response.
3. What pattern of behavior is likely to decrease Ike's anxiety regarding subways? In respondent conditioning terminology, what is that process called?
4. For what reasons might victims dislike defense attorneys?
5. A crime victim says the following to you. "I testified at a preliminary hearing this morning. I know there are going to be more hearings and probably a trial. But I haven't slept well for days because of worrying about what is going to happen during the times I have to testify. When I got on the stand today, I felt out of place. It was like everyone else knew the routine, yet it was all so foreign to me. The worst part was when the defense attorney cross-examined me. I was afraid I might fall apart, and I worried that I might say something wrong. When it was all over, I really wished I had done better." Describe in detail, including two full sets of self-statements, how you would implement stress inoculation training with this client.
6. Among rape survivors who knew the assailant before the attack, what are some commonly encountered complexities?
7. As a crisis intervention supervisor you discover that one of your staff members begins interventions with rape victims by assessing whether the victim's experience meets a legal definition of rape. What feedback do you give the staffer?
8. A rape survivor is confused about criminal justice system procedures and feels exasperated about having to keep telling her story to new investigators. How do you respond?

9. Karen is an 18-year-old freshman at the university. On her way home from an off-campus party she was raped by two assailants. After the incident she ran to her dorm room where she told her roommate Pam what had happened. Although Karen initially said she did not want to tell anyone else, Pam convinced her to call the crisis center. In responding to Karen's call, what five issues should you be prepared to address?

10. Karen says to you, "I don't know if I want to go to the emergency room or not. What will they do there?" What is your response?

11. When you bring up the issue of reporting the attack to the police, Karen says, "I really don't know if I want to report it or not." What are the pros and cons of reporting that you should help her consider?

12. Karen says, "Since they took my billfold, I'm afraid they know where I live." Name several options that you might explore with her.

13. Karen says to you, "I don't know if I can tell my parents or not." How do you respond?

14. Amy continues to be traumatized by the rape she experienced two weeks ago. She was walking home from work and decided to take a shortcut through a dark alley. The assailant followed her into the alley and attacked her there. Since the assault she has repeatedly blamed herself for it with statements such as the following. "I can't believe I was so stupid. I should have known better than to go down that alley. If I hadn't been so foolish, none of this would have happened to me." What might you say to Amy to challenge her self-blame?

15. What are the crucial tasks involved in the wrap-up of the first crisis intervention contact with a rape victim?

16. You have had several sessions with a rape survivor over a period of two months. Despite your best efforts, the victim and her husband are experiencing continued marital strife. What do you do?

17. The local police request your assistance at a house where a client of your agency is holding a gun on his wife. You arrive to find the police communicating with the perpetrator via a bullhorn. After making your way through the crowd that has gathered, you arrive at the police command post. An officer asks you and the perpetrator's mother to go to the house and negotiate with the man. What do you say to the officer?

Chapter 5

SPECIAL POPULATIONS: INTERVENTIONS WITH GROUPS

In addition to using one-to-one contact, crisis workers can also take advantage of group opportunities. For instance, some programs supplement individual walk in services with scheduled crisis groups. Such groups can be an efficient use of staff time and a means of providing unique therapeutic possibilities.

Many of the techniques used in crisis groups also work with families and with disaster victims. All of these multiple-client interventions involve special considerations.

CONDUCTING CRISIS GROUPS

Membership

Some group leaders select new members by individually interviewing potential participants. Others find a pregroup intake session too cumbersome, however, and they rely instead on other staff members to refer clients directly to the group.

No matter how clients join, crisis groups are intended for persons who are feeling overwhelmed by a sudden upsurge in difficulties. In addition, members must possess the basic communication skills necessary for group participation. Those two requirements mean that crisis groups are not appropriate for individuals whose primary difficulties involve alcohol or other drugs, chronic depression, or severe personality disorganization. Although suicidal clients can be included, it has been noted (e.g., Fournier, 2005) that leaders must affirm the value of life and actively encourage them to consider alternatives to taking one's own life. If the leaders find that the group is not meeting the needs of a suicidal member—or any other participant—they should refer that person to a more appropriate resource.

Most groups operate on a rolling admission plan, so that new members continually join the group. This strategy offers the therapeutic advantage of allowing new participants to encounter other clients who are well on their way to resolving their crises. Seeing such concrete examples of progress can give realistic hope to new members and can facilitate adaptive problem solving.

Leaders

Crisis groups can be emotionally fatiguing on workers, since groups usually last longer than other walk-in sessions and also tend to involve faster-paced coverage of concerns, options, and plans. Due to the potential for concurrent activity, it is difficult for a single leader to perceive everything that is occurring within a group. On the other hand, energy and attention demands are more manageable when there are cotherapists. Because coleaders support one another during the sessions by serving as backups for each other's observations and because they share the responsibility for guiding problem-solving discussions, these workers are less likely to feel fatigued after a meeting than would a single leader under similar circumstances. Consequently, it is not surprising that practically all crisis groups are led by two workers (e.g., Zimmerman, Asnis, & Schwartz, 1995).

When one of the leaders is a woman and the other is a man, problems are less likely to develop if a member wishes to discuss matters with a same-sex worker. Having both a male and a female leader also guarantees that there will be the potential for cross-sex interactions as participants explore their situations and make plans for the future.

Leaders must actively focus the group on the crisis being discussed. To this end, they ought to encourage participation from quieter members, and they should keep more verbal ones centered on the task at hand. Explorations into the distant past should be discouraged in favor of understanding influences that exist in the present. Also, groups should not dwell on negative emotions. For example, if one member effectively conveys a feeling of despondency, it is possible for others to focus on their own sadness and for the entire group to move into a downward spiral of depression. When such situations occur, leaders must move the group away from the attitude that things are bad now and are getting even worse. One way to end such a low-mood contagion is to have the participants consider the consequences of depression. For instance, a leader may point out that assuming matters are hopeless is one way to justify not making the effort necessary to change the situation.

Once a member's problem-solving alternatives take center stage, the leaders should guide the discussion toward the consideration of adaptive efforts. As part of that exploration, the workers may encourage other members to share coping techniques they have found to be successful. But when participants suggest alternatives they have not tried themselves, they may be using the defense mechanism of projection, and the advice may have greater relevance for the sender than for the receiver. When members offer coping ideas that clearly are inappropriate for all concerned, the leaders can encourage participants to explore the likely negative consequences of such actions.

Size, Duration, Frequency, and Number of Meetings

In order for clients to experience the therapeutic advantages of group participation, there should be at least four members. This size makes possible group interactions that focus on persons at various stages of crisis resolution, and it allows each participant to have his or her concerns addressed. On the other side of the size issue, groups must not be so large that participants receive insufficient individual attention. In order for each member's crisis to receive adequate consideration, no more than eight clients should be involved in a session. These dual goals of facilitating group dynamics and attending adequately to each individual can best be met in groups of four to six participants.

The duration of a given session depends both on the number of clients and on the amount of time each needs. In most instances, however, sessions last between one and two hours.

The frequency of meetings depends upon the availability of the leaders and upon the clinical judgment of the staff as to how often the group should meet in order to adequately serve its members. Most crisis groups meet once or twice a week. Regardless of how often the group meets, members should be able to obtain additional crisis counseling whenever they need it. If the group's sponsor is a crisis intervention program, the organization's twenty-four-hour crisis telephone, outreach, and walk-in services can serve as valuable backup systems for participants.

As with other forms of crisis intervention, eight crisis group sessions generally should be a client's limit, although most members need no more than four meetings to fulfill their needs. Even persons with severe problems can overcome many of their difficulties in a limited number of sessions. For example, empirical research (Frey, Motto, & Ritholz, 1983) has shown that suicidal clients referred for long-term group psychotherapy make the most rapid progress during the first six sessions.

Group Problem Solving

Clients come to crisis intervention groups with a wide range of problems and with varied ideas about what workers expect of them during sessions. Consequently, leaders should provide an introductory phase of the meeting that addresses both reasons for being there, as well as responsibilities of group members. One way to begin a session is for members to introduce themselves and to briefly tell what led to their participation. The leaders then can describe the intent of the group and the format of a typical meeting. For example, "The purpose of the group is to help you understand what's been happening in your life, how you've been feeling, and what you can do about it. So that we all can get to know and help each other, we will be focusing on one person at a time. If you are a new member, we will ask you to discuss the difficulties you're facing, how you've been feeling, what you've tried or thought about trying to cope with the situation, and what other possibilities you might explore. With the group's help, by the end of tonight's meeting you will have a plan to assist you in starting to resolve your difficulties. Those of you who have been here before will be telling us about your present situation and will be evaluating the progress you are making in carrying out your plans. Whether this is your first time or you're a veteran of three meetings, participating in the group can help you think about what you're facing and can aid you in discovering new ideas on how to cope with your problems. You should expect to receive constructive feedback from the rest of us when you need it, and you will be getting encouragement from us for the progress you make."

Another way to start the session is for the leaders to introduce the new members and ask them to describe briefly their situations and initial responses. The leaders then can ask the veteran members to introduce themselves and to relate their reasons for seeking help, what progress they have made, and what about the group seems to have helped them. After this introductory phase is over, any member is free to bring up a concern before the group.

In addition to the sense of hope that many participants feel, clinicians and researchers (e.g., Gilbar, 1991) have noted other therapeutic aspects of group participation.

(a) The *common bond* of being in crisis can have two positive effects. (1) Members often greet new participants with acceptance, empathy, and caring. (2) Later, during problem-solving efforts, they frequently provide realistic encouragement for the adaptive coping behavior discussed or demonstrated in the group.

(b) As members explore an individual's crisis, that person is likely to *discover new perspectives.* Interactions with other group members can also help participants to scrutinize their own behavior and consider its effects. Exchanges within the group often reveal styles of interaction that may have been ineffective in the present crisis. When such interactions occur, the leaders can encourage members to give feedback to the person demonstrating the problematic behavior. For example, group members may help the person consider what they understood the individual to have communicated, compared to what the person meant to convey. After recognizing the behavior and its effects on the group members, the leaders can encourage the person to consider whether similar interactions are involved in the crisis.

(c) Members can help each other *develop and test problem-solving strategies.* Once an approach is discovered that seems to hold some promise, the client may be able to try out the new behavior through role playing within the supportive confines of the group.

One-Session Impromptu Groups

Carolyn Holmes-Garrett (1989) describes the creation of a group made up of individuals sitting in an intensive care unit waiting room. Membership consists of everyone in the room, except for those persons who choose to walk out.

As the sole facilitator she introduces herself as a member of the hospital staff and explains that she is there to provide any assistance she might be able to offer, such as responding to questions or obtaining information. If there are no immediate requests, she describes a couple of frequently mentioned topics (for example, how to get information from the medical staff and the names of the doctors and nurses) then says that the visitors may also have other concerns they might want to discuss. At this point, one or more of the visitors usually begin to bring up issues. If that does not happen she initiates a series of one-to-one interactions with the visitors. When she discovers similarities in their situations she points out the connections. Even in the most difficult instances, a group discussion now begins.

Throughout her effort, Holmes-Garrett is careful to demonstrate empathic understanding of the visitors' feelings and thoughts. Common concerns include the following: reasons for loved ones being in the ICU, their length of stay and prognoses, memories of happier times, fears about the future, the demands of maintaining daily living activities, and resources for various kinds of support.

Under the leadership of caring and skilled staff members, such impromptu groups can provide a release for distressing thoughts and feelings, as well as a forum in which to explore and develop adaptive approaches to coping.

As reported by Holmes-Garrett, at the end of the session her participants generally are appreciative of what has transpired.

CRISIS INTERVENTION WITH FAMILIES

Crisis workers often encounter persons who are engulfed by turmoil and distress. If clients display maladaptive behaviors that are a transitory aspect of the crisis, one goal of the intervention is to keep them from adopting those approaches as new ways of handling stress. When the poor coping is chronic, however, workers must remember that crisis intervention is not suited to changing long-standing patterns of maladaptive behavior.

When assessing clients, intervenors may be unsure whether the behavior in question represents a transitory state or a personality trait. One way to discover when certain actions began is to interview family members. They can be excellent sources of information about both enduring patterns and recent changes.

Often an intervenor encounters a family when they bring one member in for help. During such contacts the worker should take advantage of the opportunity and should gather information from all who are present. If others are motivated to work toward behavior change the staff member ought to involve them in the problem-solving process.

Sometimes all or most of the family members realize that their usual coping approaches are not sufficient to handle the present situation. Rather than designating one person as the client, they seek help as a family. In these rare instances, group intervention is the worker's strategy from the start.

Whether a family intervention grows out of discussion concerning a designated client or is the goal from the beginning, workers should explore two questions. First, does a crisis exist? Second, who is motivated to change?

Intervenors must discover whether or not the family is in crisis. There is no crisis if the family's concerns are long-standing problems arising out of traditional interaction patterns. In such cases, the best strategy is to explore their interest in a family therapy referral. As always, if such a referral is to be successful, the clients must truly want it.

When the request for help turns out to involve a sudden upsurge in difficulties that overtaxes usual coping methods, intervenors should assess each family member's motivation to work. For example, a father brought in his family because he was worried about his teenage daughter who was using drugs, staying out all night, and refusing to go to school. And a distraught wife called regarding what she perceived to be the depressed state of her husband, who was preparing to leave her and travel around the country. In these instances, the father in the first example and the wife in the second example were in crisis, but the respective daughter and husband were not. Alterations of circumstances were up to the motivated individuals—those engaged in the immature or irresponsible behavior were not in crisis and did not want to change. Crisis intervention will fail unless intervenors focus on those who are interested in making problem-solving efforts.

Conducting Family Sessions

To succeed with families, workers must take into account traditional roles and values of different members, as well as usual communication patterns. As Parad and Caplan (1960) originally noted, rather than modifying such family traditions, successful crisis intervenors seek to negotiate plans that are consistent with those long-standing attitudes and ways of interacting.

By conducting a group interview with a family, intervenors can discover key beliefs and interaction styles. Such insights become even more likely when workers conduct the session at the family residence.

Family intervenors must be prepared to describe and enforce ground rules for the meeting. Some workers prefer to lay out such expectations at the start of the session; my own preference is to bring up each element when it is first applicable. Regardless of when you choose to introduce them, here are five guidelines for enhancing communication and problem solving among family members:

(a) *All members have opportunities to express themselves.* Leaders should encourage all participants to describe perceptions of the problem, feelings associated with the crisis, and ideas for solutions. Often workers can generate appropriate discussion by simply asking an open question such as, "How have things been going at home?" or "What has been happening in your family?" Once discussion is rolling, leaders need to monitor participation levels. For instance, if one member engages in a monologue (such as talking for more than three minutes) a worker should break in with clarifying statements or questions. During normal exchanges, however, interruptions are not appropriate. If a member does interrupt during one of those times, leaders must protect the speaker's right to continue talking.

(b) *When one person is talking, the responsibility of other participants is to listen and understand.* Although listening and understanding are crucial, they are impossible to observe directly. Consequently, intervenors may want to initiate the following reflection rule: before stating one's own opinions, a participant must first successfully paraphrase in a sentence the essential feelings and descriptions communicated by the person who has just stopped talking. Sometimes the new contributor will need to seek clarification from the previous speaker in order to accurately reflect that person's comments.

(c) *Members talk for themselves and not for each other.* A participant may discuss beliefs about another's feelings or thoughts. When making such comments, however, the speaker must address the person to whom he or she is attributing those thoughts and feelings.

(d) *Family members have a right to their own feelings and opinions.* If a person feels hurt, the victim has a right to that feeling. It is not necessary to defend one's claim of being hurt. By accepting the victim's statement at face value, the group decreases the possibility of rancorous debate concerning whether the person is justified in feeling that way. Rather than entering into such a dead-end discussion, members can focus on exploring what to do about the problem. If resolution appears unlikely, leaders can simply recognize the disparity and move the group to another topic.

(e) *Participants should avoid generalizations in favor of specific assertions about identifiable events.* Workers ought to encourage behavioral descriptions such as, "Last week you did not make your bed once, and each day there were clothes on the floor," and should discourage vague statements such as, "Lately, you've been a sloppy mess." Generalizations like the latter comment may prod the other family member to counterattack, while straightforward accounts help to keep attention focused on the problem.

Workers remain neutral and avoid taking sides. Nevertheless, participants may ask them to force another family member to do something. When pressured like that, one tactic is to focus on those making the demand, especially if they seem motivated to work on changing the situation.

Family members frequently express a good deal of animosity. Consequently, leaders must be prepared to defuse bickering and accusations. Douglas Puryear (1979) suggested that often workers can encourage a more productive atmosphere by using two techniques—*focusing on the attacker* and *plussing.*

By focusing on the attacker, the worker protects the victim of a verbal onslaught while exploring concerns with the person who claims to want change. Here is an example:

Father: (to 15-year-old daughter) I've given you everything you could want and hardly asked for anything in return. But no matter what your mother and I do, it's not enough—still all you do is mope around. And now you

try to kill yourself by swallowing half the medicine cabinet. Well, I'm sick of you.
Worker: You really seem disgusted about your daughter's overdose. It looks like you feel your efforts with her have been a failure.

The plussing technique calls for the intervenor to take an overly optimistic stance—to look for the silver lining in every dark cloud. The worker assumes that the participants are decent individuals and that there is at least some positive motivation in almost any behavior. When plussing, the intervenor introduces novel viewpoints that can increase the self-esteem of both the attacker and the target. Here are two examples of plussing:

Worker: You're probably angry at your daughter for staying out past curfew because you are worried about her.
Worker: You didn't go home after wrecking the car because you were afraid of disappointing your parents.

A family in crisis often focuses its attention on one or more of the children. Such young people can be at a disadvantage in two ways. First, adults often criticize and blame them for producing the conditions that led to the crisis contact. Second, since they have more limited experience than adults, they may doubt that things will ever work out in a positive way. These external criticisms and internal doubts can contribute to feelings of stubbornness and rebelliousness.

One technique for decreasing resistance and increasing cooperation is to highlight the young person's strengths. To this end, the worker can explore both current coping efforts and past successes. Such an inventory of abilities can demonstrate that the individual is worthy of praise and also has the fortitude to persevere through difficult times.

Just as with one-to-one contacts, the goal in family crisis intervention is to negotiate a concrete, realistic plan that will begin moving the clients toward resolution of the difficulties. For example, a family may decide that their efforts during the next week will focus on hammering out a set of responsibilities for each member. Once the participants agree to such a plan, each person should describe his or her individual role.

Intervening in Marital Problems

In the chaos of a marital crisis, workers may wonder what has sustained the relationship to this point. At first glance, it often seems that the best solution is for the partners to go their separate ways. Nevertheless, the dissolution of a marriage should not be taken lightly, even though a partner in crisis may be very dissatisfied with the other person.

> EXAMPLE. Sarah Miller called the crisis service because she was distraught over both her health status and her marriage. Recently she had experienced a miscarriage and the removal of a malignant tumor. In addition to being grief-stricken about her miscarriage, she had also become acutely aware of her own mortality. Her husband had responded to her physical problems by arranging to undergo a vasectomy–to prevent future miscarriages–and by refusing to hold or kiss Sarah, apparently out of fear of catching the cancer. She resented not being consulted about the decision to have a vasectomy, and she felt shut out by her husband. After exploring those issues and considering several options, she decided that marriage counseling was the way to go.
>
> Since the crisis worker supported Sarah's request for counseling, the goal of the intervention became a firm referral. Because she lived outside the agency's service area, the worker–with Sarah's permission–called the crisis center in her community. He described Sarah's situation and told the worker that Sarah would be calling.
>
> Ten minutes after ending her call to the original worker, she was back on the line with him again. Sarah said the worker at the other center had told her to look for a job so that she could become financially independent and separate from her husband. Sarah said when she refused that option, the other worker ended the interaction.
>
> She reiterated her desire to find ways of saving her marriage. The worker responded by obtaining information on marriage counseling services in her community.
>
> DISCUSSION OF SARAH MILLER'S CASE. Sarah Miller's story demonstrates the importance of persisting attachments. Intervenors should beware of concluding too quickly that a marriage is irreparably damaged.

When the future of the marriage is in doubt, the intervenor ought to avoid a survey of past marital difficulties. Such fault-finding discussions are not likely to be productive, and they may increase the clients' distress. Instead, the worker should focus problem solving on current options and their likely consequences.

If the couple chooses to attempt a reconciliation and to try to change long-standing habits, the intervenor should make a referral for marriage counseling. In order to prevent the task of contacting a therapist from becoming another spark for dispute, the worker ought to make sure that the couple decides who will be responsible for arranging the appointment. And, as in any crisis intervention effort, if the staff member promises a follow-up contact, the couple will have additional motivation for accomplishing the negotiated tasks.

It is also true that some clients have no interest in a marriage counseling referral, while others refuse to take action toward either ending or reviving the marriage. In such cases the best the worker can do is help them realize the implications of the choices they are making.

When marriages do end, the events associated with separation and divorce can overtax the coping abilities of either spouse. Granvold (2005) noted that such crises are often associated with events occurring during the following phases: deciding to divorce, transitioning from being married to being divorced, and coping with being divorced. Each phase has many potential distressing events. During the process of deciding to divorce, possible events include the following: infidelity, assault, abuse, financial irresponsibility, abuse of alcohol or other drugs, betrayal of trust, and discussion of separation. While transitioning from being married to being divorced, events may include the following: deciding on property distribution, arranging custody and visitation regarding children, and instituting separation. Coping with being divorced may include dealing with events such as the following: seeing the former partner with someone new, discovering unsettling information about events that occurred prior to the divorce, parenting disputes, financial issues, difficulties involving in-laws, making or maintaining living arrangements, job-related demands, and stressors associated with new or existing relationships. Any of these events have the potential to be associated with intense emotional reactions. If the pressures become too much, crisis intervention is an appropriate technique for enhancing the person's adjustment. As in bereavement counseling, the worker may need to start by helping the person deal with feelings of loss and anger, then eventually assist in developing plans for proceeding with life and its new challenges.

DISASTER RELIEF

Floods, earthquakes, avalanches, fires, tornadoes, hurricanes, and other disasters strike hundreds of communities each year. Although there are injuries, deaths, and property damage, most survivors react with effective coping responses that focus on restoring normal conditions. Other survivors are stunned at first and are uncertain how to respond. Yet after a brief period, a majority of them begin adaptive problem-solving efforts. Empirical research has demonstrated that with most disasters less than a third of the population demonstrates serious maladaptive behavior, such as confusion, inability to act, personality disorganization, or posttraumatic stress disorder (e.g., McFarlane, 2005; Young, 2006).

Administrators, researchers, and clinicians (e.g., Bronisch et al., 2006; Center for Mental Health Services, 2001; Gersons & Carlier, 1993; Jacobs, 1995; Reyes & Elhai, 2004; Roberts, 2005a) generally recognize crisis intervention as being an appropriate response to the emotional and problem-solving needs of disaster victims. When delivered in a timely fashion, such assistance can shorten the duration and lessen the severity of emotional disturbance resulting from the disaster and its aftermath.

Each year, the United States government spends hundreds of thousands of dollars providing crisis intervention services following presidentially declared disasters. If the next twelve months are typical, there will be 45 to 50 locations in the United States that the President will declare disaster areas. Nevertheless, about 90 percent of U.S. disasters do not receive a Presidential declaration and its accompanying financial assistance (Reyes & Elhai, 2004). Typically, the responsibility for disaster relief falls on the shoulders of local and state human service programs.

DISASTER PREPAREDNESS

To be most effective, crisis workers must be available to respond immediately in disaster situations. The ideal intervenor is a person who has been trained in both crisis intervention and disaster relief and who lives in the stricken area. Although few communities have such a ready cadre of crisis workers, some programs have demonstrated that a standby force can be there when crisis intervention organizations include disaster preparedness as part of their mission (e.g., Silver & Goldstein, 1992). Then, when disaster strikes, crisis intervention can occur in coordination with other forms of immediate rescue and relief.

Disaster preparedness requires a carefully designed and tested referral network. Although during a major disaster there are never enough crisis workers to identify everyone in need of crisis intervention, those in crisis will make contact with workers if other relief workers know how to refer victims. To this end, crisis service administrators should negotiate the roles of their programs with others involved in emergency preparedness. Potential contacts include (1) organizations such as emergency management programs, Red Cross, National Guard, law enforcement agencies, fire departments, rescue squads, and ambulance units, and (2) resources such as hospitals, physicians, ministers, and morticians.

As part of an emergency-preparedness effort, agencies should arrange reciprocal inservice training. For example, at a crisis staff meeting, rescue squad representatives can describe their units and how crisis workers can assist them. Likewise, crisis program personnel can meet with the rescue squad staff to discuss the provision of crisis services as part of disaster relief. Following such initial exchanges, joint drills can identify issues that need additional planning and coordination.

Modes of Service

Comprehensive crisis intervention programs offer telephone, walk-in, and outreach services (see Chapter 6). If there is a period of time in which there is the threat of catastrophic events, but little or no actual damage to communication channels, members of the population at risk may use the telephone to seek crisis intervention assistance, as Michal Shamai (1994) observed to be the case in Haifa, Israel during the 1991 Gulf War.

In the United States, most crisis intervention in Presidentially declared disasters is accomplished through worker-initiated interactions done by telephone or outreach (Disaster Technical Assistance Center, 2013). When outreach teams are involved they can help to form community groups. Whether in established neighborhoods or in temporary trailer camps, such groups can foster togetherness and support among residents. Their meetings can serve a variety of functions, including the following: discussion of common problems, consideration of parenting issues, ventilation of pent-up emotions, presentation of information about recent developments, rumor investigation and control, communication of a united stance to political leaders, as well as identification of victims who need crisis intervention assistance (e.g., Shelby & Tredinnick, 1995).

Problem Solving

The problems and feelings of disaster victims tend to change as time passes. During the first hours after the disaster begins, common experiences include the following: finding a place of safety, responding to other victims who request help, receiving medical attention, and locating loved ones. Victims often feel some or all of the following: fear of dangerous conditions; dismay at what has occurred; relief at being safe; confusion over what to do next; satisfaction, regret or shame over the fate of others who needed help; concern over physical injuries; and anxiety about the well-being of loved ones.

As the hours pass, victims may begin to focus attention on obtaining food, clothing, and emergency living quarters. Common feelings include the following: thankfulness for assistance, impatience to return home, dissatisfaction with the decisions made by those in authority, and irritation with emergency living conditions.

After the danger is over, survivors may face some or all of the following tasks: making funeral arrangements, cleaning up, and reestablishing needed utilities such as gas, electric, and telephone services. Emotional reactions at this point may include the following: grief over the death of friends or relatives, shock at the physical devastation, and frustration over the slow restoration of services.

During the time of rebuilding, common endeavors include the following: making repairs, establishing temporary residences, and arranging new construction. Some frequently experienced feelings are helplessness when faced with the enormity of the tasks, anger over shoddy workmanship, exasperation with red tape imposed by disaster-relief agencies, and hopelessness that life will ever return to normal.

Victims may feel exhausted at any point. Common circumstances that can drain energy include the following: prolonged efforts to avoid succumbing to the disaster itself, sleepless nights in a crowded shelter, long hours spent in cleanup efforts, and weeks of trying to obtain appropriate services from government agencies and private contractors.

Crisis workers should provide whatever assistance that is necessary to establish rapport and initiate adaptive problem solving. Such assistance may include helping to secure essentials, such as food and a place to sleep, or engaging in small acts of kindness such as bringing a drink of water to a person waiting in line. As is true with all crisis intervention efforts, problem solving should recognize the strengths of clients and build on their past successes. On those occasions when victims are immobilized and do not know where to begin, intervenors can help them make and implement plans.

A minority of disaster victims need mental health assistance. (Notice I am making a distinction between crisis intervention and mental health treatment.) Since intervenors and researchers (e.g., Kroon & Overdijk, 1993) have found that disaster survivors generally do not view themselves as being psychologically disturbed, victims often accept crisis intervenors more readily if the workers do not identify themselves as mental health professionals.

Some survivors may benefit from psychotherapy and others may require hospitalization. In order to facilitate mental health assistance for those who need it, crisis workers should be prepared to assess the potential patient in the following five areas: thoughts, perceptions, emotions, behavior, and interpersonal relations. If the person shows significant disturbances in one or more of these areas the crisis worker should consider referring the individual to an appropriate mental health resource.

(a) *Thoughts.* The victim may demonstrate disturbed thinking by expressing uncertainty about his or her name and location, as well as what day and time it is. The individual may be unable to remember recent events or may not recognize familiar persons and places. In addition to such confusion, the victim may develop delusions or phobias.

(b) *Perceptions.* Individuals can experience perceptual distortions involving any of the senses. Auditory hallucinations tend to be the most common; for instance, victims may hear voices, or their own thoughts may seem loud to them. Clients can experience visual hallucinations in the form of frightening images or other unsettling distortions. Individuals can feel unusual tactile perceptions that are not the result of physical stimulation. Although less frequent, sometimes hallucinations involve smell and taste.

(c) *Emotions.* Victims may need mental health treatment if they suffer severe emotional problems. Examples include extreme reactions, such as unresponsiveness and apathy over several days, as well as wildly inappropriate feelings, such as hilarity expressed about circumstances that are not funny or rage at inconsequential events.

(d) *Behavior.* A victim sometimes engages in actions that are unusual and disturbing. Examples include the following: prolonged lethargy, periods of extreme agitation, peculiar mannerisms, and self-mutilation. If motor behavior is severely impaired, the person may be unable to perform usual self care tasks such as dressing, eating, or maintaining normal hygiene practices.

(e) *Interpersonal relations.* Some victims develop severe difficulties in getting along with friends and relatives. Others suffer dramatic changes in relationships so that traditional sources of support no longer operate; in extreme instances, the individual may be the only family member who survived the disaster. When the restorative powers of crisis intervention are insufficient, workers should arrange for more prolonged therapeutic support.

Information and Referral

Crisis workers ought to be ready to provide accurate information about appropriate resources. When armed with such knowledge, survivors can combat the rumors and misinformation that spawn in post disaster chaos and confusion. Victims who receive accurate knowledge not only waste less energy and suffer less emotional drain, they also come to see the crisis team as a valuable and credible resource.

Team members should have information on all of the services available in the stricken area. They ought to be able to refer clients to appropriate resources for any of the following needs: food, clothing, housing, home furnishings, medical care, emergency funds, legal assistance, employment advice, income tax assistance, property cleanup, home repair and reconstruction, business and farm rehabilitation, and moving assistance.

Relief Worker Burnout

Crisis intervenors and other relief workers risk physical and emotional exhaustion when they provide disaster assistance. Consequently, program administrators should see the coping and adjustment of staff members as a continuing concern. In addition to the burnout-prevention strategies discussed in Chapter 8, managers should consider other efforts as well. Those include (1) holding daily staff meetings in which intervenors can describe problems and express feelings and (2) scheduling mandatory time-off periods to give workers needed respites.

Confined Disasters

Some catastrophes are terrible in their impact but are limited to an isolated population. These confined disasters include events such as bus accidents, train collisions, airplane crashes, and terrorist explosions. As in mass disasters, researchers and clinicians (e.g., Norris et al., 2006; Roberts, 2005a) agree that crisis intervention is an appropriate response in the aftermath of such tragedies. Also, just as with larger emergencies, timely crisis intervention in confined disasters requires advance planning.

Although many of the issues associated with mass emergencies also apply to confined disasters, experts (e.g., Smith, North, McCool, & Shea, 1990) have noted several features that tend to distinguish the latter calamities.

- The event happens suddenly and without warning. Victims have no time to prepare for it.
- The cause frequently can be attributed to the actions of certain persons. There are likely to be human lightning rods that attract bolts of blame and anger.
- The resulting injuries and deaths tend to be especially gruesome. Even seasoned emergency workers may be stunned by the scene.
- Unlike most mass disasters, where it may take days, weeks, or months to organize intervention efforts, in confined disasters workers may be in contact with victims and their relatives in the minutes and hours following the event.

These final two characteristics combine to make confined disaster relief an especially stressful endeavor for crisis intervenors. As with mass disasters, program managers must attend to the psychological needs of crisis workers and others involved in relief efforts.

Several kinds of intervention can be helpful in confined disasters. Examples include the following: information and referral, systematic outreach to victims and their families, crisis groups, and bereavement counseling. In addition to those generic interventions, more specialized strategies have been developed. If crisis workers are with relatives as rescue and identification efforts continue, Avigdor Klingman (1986) noted that there are several possible roles for the intervenors:

- They can become *information sources.* In this role they tell relatives about procedures and events that are underway.
- They can be *problem-solving consultants* and assist family members in addressing issues that are amenable to resolution. Examples include deciding who else to contact and arranging help with continuing responsibilities at home and at work.

  Often it is helpful to encourage the family to identify a friend who can be relied upon for support. When feasible the workers can arrange for that person to join the family. In addition to providing emotional support, the friend can help with concrete tasks such as transportation or contacting others on behalf of the family.
- Workers can also be *companions*—a role that may include both information giving and problem solving. In cases of victim deaths, workers can accompany the bereaved family members during the notification process. When there is an identifiable corpse it is adaptive for relatives to be allowed to view the person's body. Before this event, however, a worker can explain the procedure and can help the family members decide who will participate in identifying the remains.

After the wait is over, a worker should not break contact with the family until the members are in the care of relatives or friends. And intervenors ought to inform those supporters about the continuing availability of crisis intervention services.

SUMMARY

Crisis groups are an efficient use of staff time, especially when new members continually join through a rolling admission plan. Groups led by male and female cocounselors are less fatiguing than single-leader groups and provide each leader with a reliable backup for his or her observations. Leaders should keep the members focused on problem solving and must respond to sidetracking when it occurs. Most crisis groups involve four to six clients, hold one- to two-hour sessions, and meet once or twice a week. Therapeutic benefits of group participation include sharing a common bond with other individuals in crisis, developing new insights into one's behavior, and having the opportunity to role play potential solutions.

By involving family members in an intervention, workers often can increase the chances of adaptive crisis resolution. Intervenors first discover whether a crisis exists, then focus on those who are interested in change. The best strategies are ones that build upon established patterns of interaction. There are five ***family session guidelines*** that can enhance communication and problem solving: (1) ***participants have a chance to express themselves,*** (2) ***members listen to what others say,*** (3) ***each person speaks for himself or herself,*** (4) ***participants have a right to their feelings,*** and (5) ***it is best to focus on specific events.*** Leaders can reduce hostility by using techniques such as plussing and focusing on the attacker. Workers can support children by highlighting the young persons' past successes and current positive efforts. When marital problems are the reason for the contact, intervenors should consider present difficulties in light of the factors that have sustained the relationship to this point. Discussion ought to focus on identifying options for the future and on considering the likely consequences of those possibilities.

Hundreds of disasters occur each year, and, in most cases, responsibility for crisis intervention services falls on local and state programs. Timely response to community emergencies requires a commitment to disaster preparedness, development and testing of intervention procedures, and adequate worker training. Crisis intervenors assist victims in meeting whatever emotional and problem-solving needs they have; in a minority of cases workers must refer individuals for mental health treatment. Teams should be able to supply information on all available disaster relief and human service resources. In order to cope with the physical and emotional demands on them, workers ought to have daily staff meetings and sufficient time off. Unlike mass disaster relief in which mobilization of crisis intervention efforts usually takes days, weeks, or months, the response to confined disasters may include immediate crisis intervention along with other timely forms of assistance. When workers accompany relatives as rescue and identification efforts take place, the intervenors can serve as information sources, problem-solving consultants, and companions.

STUDY QUESTIONS

1. What is the therapeutic advantage of using a rolling admission plan with crisis groups?
2. You are the leader of a crisis group in a hospital, and you decide to approach your supervisor with a request for an opposite-sex coleader. What do you say to justify your request?

3. Fred and William are participants in a crisis group. William needs one more year of service to become eligible for retirement, but he is having trouble with his supervisor. Fred suggests that he quit. What is your response?

4. Richard is a crisis group member who calls you between sessions to talk about a problem in implementing his plan. What is your response?

5. While participating in a crisis group, Caroline says she wants to confront her neighbor about the loud music coming from his residence. She has thought about what to tell him, although she doesn't know if she really could say it. What is your response?

6. Mr. and Mrs. Franklin and their 12-year-old son Bill come to see you. Bill has just been expelled from school for hitting his English teacher. His parents are appalled at his behavior and subsequent expulsion. Bill claims he is unconcerned. On whom do you focus your initial problem-solving efforts?

7. When Bill starts to explain why he hit the teacher, his father interrupts. What is your response?

8. When Bill continues, he says, "She just kept on me. I'm sorry I hit her. I guess I just lost control." Mr. Franklin then says, "You had no right to do such a stupid thing." What do you say to Mr. Franklin?

9. Mrs. Franklin says to Mr. Franklin, "He's not really sorry for what he did." What is your response to Mrs. Franklin?

10. Later, Mrs. Franklin says to Bill, "Knowing what you did, I feel ashamed to be your mother." Bill says to her, "You've got no right to be ashamed; it had nothing to do with you." What is your response to Bill?

11. At a subsequent point, Mr. Franklin says, "He never does anything right." What do you say to Mr. Franklin, and what are two areas to explore with Bill?

12. Marilyn says that for the past year she has had no interest in having sexual relations. Her husband Brandon says he cannot continue to be married under such circumstances. They both assert that they want to save the marriage if possible. As a crisis worker, what strategy do you adopt?

13. In most cases, who provides crisis intervention services following a disaster?

14. How can rescue squad workers help in the provision of crisis intervention following a disaster?

15. During disaster relief following a flood, a police officer brings Robert Edison to you. The officer says that authorities found the body of Robert's daughter two days ago but that Robert continues to search for her. During the interview, Robert says it was not his daughter that was found (in fact she was positively identified). He says he can even hear his daughter calling to him right now. Robert has not changed clothes,

shaved, or brushed his teeth since the flood struck three days earlier. What strategy do you adopt and why?

16. What impact can you have by providing the flood victims in your community with accurate information?

17. What can you do to avoid relief worker burnout as you provide crisis intervention to the flood victims?

18. A train hit a school bus, killing some of the children on board and injuring others. Families of the students have congregated in the lobby of the local hospital. As a crisis worker on the hospital staff what do you do?

Chapter 6

SERVICE DELIVERY

Several factors influence the delivery of crisis intervention assistance. This chapter discusses modes of service, case management, record keeping, and physical facilities. Issues relating to these areas are relevant to any program offering crisis intervention services, including settings such as mental health emergency units, hotlines, general-purpose crisis programs, suicide prevention centers, rape crisis services, and hospital emergency rooms.

MODES OF SERVICE

Compared to other social service agencies, crisis intervention organizations offer support nearer to the beginning of difficulties and closer to the client's usual life space. All full-service crisis intervention programs provide assistance twenty-four hours a day, seven days a week.

Experts in social work, nursing, psychiatry, and psychology contend that 24-hour crisis services should be part of human service programming (Bengelsdorf et al., 1993; Hoff & Hoff, 2012; Lazar & Erera, 1998; Roberts, 2005b; Semke et al., 1994). The effort necessary to deliver around the clock services can be justified on a number of grounds, including humanitarianism, therapeutic effectiveness, and cost efficiency. From a humanitarian standpoint, it is desirable to assist persons who are overwhelmed by distressing circumstances. And it is therapeutically effective to take advantage of their readiness to risk new ways of coping with life. Although offering immediately available assistance is expensive, it is cheaper than the alternatives. The economic value of crisis intervention can be seen through commonsense logic. For example, is it better for an overwhelmed employee to be fired or for the person to receive assistance in coping with the distressing circumstances? More refined analysis of the cost-effectiveness of crisis intervention has been done by experts. As Herbert Bengelsdorf and his colleagues (1993) demonstrated, allowing persons to deteriorate until they require psychiatric hospitalization always costs more than crisis intervention.

Full-service crisis intervention programs save lives and foster adaptive coping by offering three modes of assistance—telephone, walk-in, and outreach. There also are some organizations that offer services on the Internet. Each mode has its own special considerations.

Telephone

The telephone is a vital link between crisis intervention organizations and the populations they serve. To persons who need assistance, this mode of service offers the advantages of availability and control. When help is only a phone call away, clients can surmount geographic and mobility barriers with relative ease. Telephone callers also have more options than do face-to-face clients; they can remain anonymous if they choose (unless the organization is successful in using caller ID or in having the call traced), and they can end the contact at any point by simply hanging up.

In addition to having advantages for clients, telephone communication can benefit workers by facilitating both psychodynamic transference and the immediate involvement of other staff members. The intervenor's relative anonymity often encourages positive transference—callers attributing characteristics to workers that they would most like to see. Telephone contact also makes it easy for others on the staff to become involved in the intervention. For instance, multiple telephone extensions allow the primary worker to receive supervision and assistance while the call is in progress.

How do programs offer around-the-clock telephone crisis intervention? There are many answers to that question.

Late-night callers to one center hear a recorded message giving them the home phone number of the worker on duty that night. Another agency relies on a commercial answering service during nonbusiness hours, and it is the responsibility of the untrained operator to assess whether contact with the on-call person is warranted. Once deciding that contact is appropriate, the operator attempts to reach the counselor on duty so that the staff member can call the client. A different organization has calls directly forwarded to the cell phone number of the worker on duty that night.

With all of those systems, the worker has no access to case information. The lack of supporting resources is often irrelevant, however, since many callers never succeed in reaching the on-duty counselor.

Unfortunately, the problem of clients reaching workers is not solved by simply taking all calls at the organization's location. One center schedules a single worker for nonbusiness hours. So when face-to-face contacts are in progress, there are long periods when callers receive a recorded message saying the worker is temporarily out of the office. At another agency, an administrative assistant takes calls and attempts to locate a counselor if the client seems to be in need of immediate help.

Although these organizations promote the idea that their crisis intervention services are only a phone call away, this representation often is more a wish than reality. The only sure way to deliver continuous crisis telephone service is for trained intervenors to answer the phones at the location where calls are first received.

Walk-In

When a program offers crisis intervention walk-in services, clients ought to be able to arrange a meeting in advance, although scheduled appointments should never be required, and there never should be a waiting list. Immediately available walk-in contact can be helpful when any of the following situations occur: more than one person wants to be involved in the interaction, an individual is in need of emergency assessment, a caller cannot talk in confidence over the telephone, or a client is in danger of physical harm from another person.

Compared to telephone contacts, face-to-face interactions place workers in greater danger. A survey (Jayaratne, Croxton, & Mattison, 2004) that included 941 social workers serving in public nonprofit settings found that 22.8 percent of them had been physically threatened and 3.3 percent had been assaulted.

Sometimes program administrators expect workers to participate in restraining individuals. The Occupational Safety and Health Administration (2004) and experienced professionals (e.g., Petit, 2005) assert that if physical restraint is necessary, the participating staff should be properly trained and there should be a sufficient number of them to safely implement the procedures in which they are proficient. If there is an insufficient number of such personnel or if the crisis workers themselves have not been adequately trained in the procedures to be used, crisis staff should not be expected to participate in physically restraining violent persons.

Although they face greater danger than when talking on the phone, workers in face-to-face interactions are likely to have more information about the client and more control over the person's environment. Prearranged walk-ins enable intervenors to prepare in advance by reviewing previous contacts and other relevant information. Interactions at the organization's location also allow workers to control the physical setting. Walk-in contacts should take place in a quiet room that is free from interruptions and is safe for both clients and workers. (See the "Room Arrangements" section later in this chapter.)

Compared to telephone counseling, face-to-face interventions require crisis workers to keep in mind three additional communication issues—introductions, body language, and note taking.

- *Introductions.* Workers ought to begin face-to-face interactions by introducing themselves and then, if appropriate, explaining their roles and the purpose of the interview.
- *Body language.* During face-to-face contacts, intervenors can observe facial expressions, hand gestures, and other body movements that may be rich in meaning. Of course, such observations are a two-way street; clients also observe workers. Consequently, intervenors must remember to convey interest and attention through their nonverbal behavior.
- *Note taking.* Sometimes taking notes can become a self-defeating activity. While an individual is speaking about vital issues and conveying important nonverbal messages, the worker must focus on the client rather than become sidetracked by the task of producing a set of notes. When communication is less intense, the intervenor has more time to write. The resulting detailed notes, however, can highlight secondary issues and can falsely minimize important aspects of the interview.

If workers want to recall important content, a good technique is to write down key words to serve as reminders of certain topics. Intervenors always ought to write such notes in full view of clients, and workers should be prepared to show their notes to clients who want to see them.

There are two circumstances in which workers *must* take notes. Intervenors ought to record specific information such as names, telephone numbers, addresses, and dates. Workers should also write down any promises they make on behalf of their organization or themselves, so there will be a written reminder of such commitments.

Immediately after the interaction the interviewer ought to set aside time to record an account of the contact. When a staff member schedules consecutive face-to-face interviews, the worker should arrange a minimum of ten minutes between interactions in order to be able to write a progress note on the previous interview and to prepare for the next session.

Outreach

No action demonstrates more caring than workers going out to see a client. Potential outreach situations include the following: a law enforcement request for assistance, an individual demonstrating a high degree of lethality, and, in general, any circumstance requiring face-to-face assessment of a person who cannot or will not come to the agency.

All of the practices that apply to walk-in contacts also are relevant to outreach efforts. When workers leave their office, however, they know (e.g., Zealberg, Santos, & Fisher, 1993) that they also leave the safety and predictability of that setting. The possibility of outreach workers encountering dangerous situations should never be overlooked or minimized.

Outreach activities demand that staff members be able to function independently. When on their own out in the community, workers do not have ready access to office resources or to support staff that may be available at their agency location.

Because intervenors have less control and less potential support in the community than they do in their own office, outreach requires attention to five issues:

(a) Experts (e.g., Hoff & Hoff, 2012) recommend that outreach be a team endeavor—preferably a woman and a man. Two crisis workers increase the likelihood that someone will be free to summon help should the team find itself in a dangerous situation. If the contact is with a single client, the team approach allows one worker to interview while the other one mobilizes needed resources, such as family members or an ambulance. When there is a single identified client and additional persons at the scene, a two-person outreach makes it possible for one intervenor to work with the client and for the remaining team member to talk with others who are present. The participation of both a man and a woman on the team decreases the possibility of ethical problems. (For example, one outreach team was met at the door by a woman wearing a flimsy nightgown. Whatever she had in mind seemed to be discouraged by the presence of the female worker.)

(b) Good communication is essential from the moment an outreach is considered until the workers are back in their office. The team must have a clear idea of the kind of situation to which they are being summoned. Before the team departs there should be an exploration of whether weapons are at the scene—nothing is more disconcerting to outreach workers than knocking on a door and having it unexpectedly opened by a person with a gun. In addition to seeking information, the team members must also provide information. Outreach workers should keep the appropriate authorities aware of their location and activity so that additional help can be provided if it becomes necessary. A good monitoring arrangement is for the crisis organization and the local law enforcement agencies to develop a system whereby the outreach team keeps the police dispatch center notified of their location and service status.

(c) Crisis workers face imminent danger when they go to a scene where physical conflict is taking place. When called to a violent disturbance the outreach team should always request law enforcement assistance. Once at the scene, the police ought to be the first to make contact with the disputants. After diffusing the situation and removing any weapons, the officers can introduce the crisis workers to the potential clients. If problem solving is to be attempted, accepted practice is to separate the individuals and interview them apart—although the intervenors should try not to lose sight of one another. When the case involves a man and a woman, the male worker can interview him while the female team member interviews her. After both clients have a chance to individually explore the problem and alternatives, the team can bring them together for the purpose of developing a mutually agreed-upon plan.

(d) Outreach workers must carry certain essential materials. Every staff member ought to have an agency identification card that can be presented if necessary. The team should take an up-to-date list of frequently used resources, with basic referral information on each entry. It also is a good idea for workers to give agency business cards to clients and to other appropriate persons encountered during the outreach.

(e) Team members must limit their activities to endeavors for which they are trained. If the demands of the situation are beyond their areas of expertise they should request additional assistance. For example, unless crisis workers are trained health care specialists they should call for an ambulance or rescue squad whenever emergency medical attention is needed. Likewise, unless workers have received specific law enforcement and self-defense training they should not attempt to take a weapon away from an individual. If it is necessary to disarm a person or to remove weapons from a scene, the team should ask for police assistance.

EXAMPLE. Claire Miller was a suicidal client of a crisis center. Based on a prior agreement, her supervisor called the center when Claire failed to arrive at work one morning. A crisis worker telephoned her residence, but there was no answer. He then contacted a neighbor, who reported that Claire's car was in front of the apartment. At the worker's request the neighbor knocked on

Claire's door. There was no response. The worker then contacted the police and asked for an officer to meet the outreach team at Claire's apartment. After arriving and receiving no answer to a knock on Claire's door, the police officer requested the landlord to use her passkey. Upon entering the apartment the intervenors found Claire asleep on the bed. When attempts to awaken her failed the officer called an ambulance. The emergency medical technicians took Claire to the hospital where she received treatment for a drug overdose. DISCUSSION OF CLAIRE MILLER'S CASE. Throughout the intervention the team members recognized the extent of their expertise. Law enforcement assistance facilitated entry into Claire's apartment, and the ambulance crew and emergency room staff performed the medical procedures that were necessary. The coordinated effort probably was a life-saving one, since the emergency room physician speculated that Claire could have died from the overdose.

EXAMPLE. Barry Lancaster had a diagnosis of schizophrenia, and he was a client in the partial hospitalization program of a mental health center. Following a deterioration in his behavior, his sister filed to initiate involuntary hospitalization procedures. The police had the responsibility of bringing Barry to the hospital emergency room for an evaluation. As they usually did in such cases, the officers requested that a crisis team accompany them to Barry's home. After arriving and receiving no response to the doorbell, one crisis worker and one of the two police officers entered the house. As they were making a room-by-room search, Barry thrust a shotgun through the kitchen window from outside the house and opened fire–striking and seriously wounding the officer. While the other crisis worker radioed for additional assistance, the second officer located Barry as he was trying to reload the shotgun. The officer succeeded in removing the gun, only to be slashed by a hunting knife before eventually subduing and handcuffing Barry. DISCUSSION OF BARRY LANCASTER'S CASE. The outreach to Barry's residence followed all appropriate procedures, yet two serious injuries still occurred. In outreach, just as in interventions involving armed perpetrators, workers can take certain precautions, but none are foolproof.

Internet

Crisis intervention on the Internet is currently available in the form of live one-to-one text chat. (It is somewhat ironic that the word *chat*–defined in the pre-Internet era as "light familiar talk"–can now refer to such earnest communication between strangers.) As technology continues to develop at a rapid pace, it is unclear how long text chat will remain as a mode of communication, since it proceeds at such a slow pace. (What might be a 20 minute interaction via telephone can easily take an hour, and possibly up to two hours, via Internet text chat.) For now, though, text chat interactions are the primary form of real-time Internet crisis intervention.

Because exchanges typically are so slow, it is possible to carry on simultaneous one-to-one interactions with multiple chatters. In most cases, a veteran worker can handle two chatters at the same time.

Text chat interaction tends to be a condensed version of what might take place during a telephone contact. For example, workers can use the same problem-solving sequence—exploring thoughts and feelings, considering alternatives, and developing a plan. Also, just as telephone interactions can, the Internet can encourage positive psychodynamic transference, as well as client control and ease of contact.

Internet-based crisis intervention has the potential to help chatters from many different regions and countries. (During my seven years as a volunteer Internet counselor, I interacted with chatters from across the United States, as well as from Australia, Canada, India, Singapore, South Korea, the Philippines, Uganda, Kenya, South Africa, Germany, and the United Kingdom.) Chatters also come from a wide socioeconomic spectrum. Although most chatters make contact via their own computers, that is not always the case. For example, in the United States many public libraries offer access to the Internet, and it is not uncommon for individuals who do not have telephones, much less computers, to use those public facilities in order to obtain crisis intervention services over the Internet.

Often the problems that chatters discuss involve universal dilemmas, such as relationship issues revolving around themes of trust, honesty, mutual respect, and fidelity, for which Internet-based crisis intervention can be a sufficient response. It also is possible, however, for the chatter to want and need face-to-face contact with an appropriate resource person. When that is the case, securing relevant information on available services needs to be a focus of the interaction.

Existing as a service within the Internet means there are several million other sites available. Sorting through the possibilities can seem daunting at times, but it is clearly beneficial for an Internet-based crisis intervention program to maintain a wide-ranging compilation of resource pages. Forwarding the URL of one of those pages allows the chatter to open that resource while still online with the worker. Of course such investigation by the chatter further slows the interaction.

Other common reasons for extended pauses between exchanges include composing a long response, having difficulty typing, computer or connection difficulties, incoming phone calls to the chatter, and the chatter needing to attend to children or other pressing responsibilities. And sometimes there are lengthy pauses with no explanation.

Although slowness is often encountered, some exchanges can be so rapid that comments temporarily get out of sequence. For example, just as the worker enters a response, a comment arrives from the chatter. The worker's response then appears in the transcript after a chatter statement to which it does not relate. When such out-of-sequence exchanges occur, the participants almost always seem able to figure out what was intended.

What the parties cannot decipher is the nonverbal behavior that accompanies the process of typing the message. Consequently, to help supplement the meaning of their words, experienced chatters often include typed symbols (e.g., :-) designating a smiley face) or preformatted graphics as a way of communicating some of that unseen and unheard information. Nevertheless, compared to face-to-face or telephone interactions, the reduced availability of nonverbal communication is commonly seen as one of the challenges of text chat (e.g., Taylor & Furlonger, 2011).

Depending on the nature of the log-in process for the service, another category of information that may not be available to the worker is anything that could identify the chatter. While some crisis intervention organizations that provide telephone services automatically obtain the phone number of each caller, similar technology is not currently available for Internet contacts. Since most chatters know that fact, they also know that if they do not provide identifying information they will be anonymous.

At the service with which I was associated, chatters were not required to provide any identifying information about themselves. Nevertheless, about half of them gave their name, mailing address, email address, and phone number. (Of course, we had only the chatter's word to indicate that the information was correct.) There were chatters, though, who contacted the service precisely because they knew it was possible for them to be anonymous. I interacted with several suicidal individuals who said that they contacted us on the Internet rather than calling their local crisis intervention telephone services because they believed their identities would be discovered if they called their local programs. Being able to effectively limit the sharing of identifying information is one component of the enhanced power and control that chatters frequently experience (e.g., Taylor & Furlonger, 2011).

Although it is possible to obtain identifying information on a chatter from the person's Internet service provider, such efforts must be initiated by law enforcement authorities.

When chatters provide email addresses it is possible for the service to send them transcripts of the interactions. Most of the time chatters appreciate receiving that record. Nevertheless, workers must also be sensitive to circumstances in which sending a transcript could be problematic, such as when the computer is shared by family members and the chatter does not want others to be aware of what was discussed during the contact.

CASE MANAGEMENT AND RECORD KEEPING

There is one guiding principle for crisis intervention case management—workers assist those clients they are trained to help, and they refer or discontinue contact with individuals whom they are not prepared to aid. For every intervention, staff members must decide which of those responses is appropriate.

Crisis intervention workers often need to coordinate their efforts with other clinicians. For example, such coordination is essential for intervenors on the staff of mental health emergency services. Outpatient counselors and partial-hospitalization therapists frequently ask their clients to contact the crisis service if problems occur at night or on the weekend. And during those same nonbusiness hours, inpatient units often rely on crisis workers to screen potential emergency admissions.

A crisis worker's response to a client already receiving service should be based upon a plan developed with the primary clinician. When the client's difficulties relate to long-standing problems, the worker should act in support of the existing treatment plan. Depending upon the circumstances, it may be appropriate to listen empathically, make an outreach, tell the client to bring up the concerns at the next regularly scheduled therapy session, or make some other response that has been agreed upon with the primary therapist. Although none of those efforts constitute crisis intervention, they are appropriate if the staff has received the training and supervision necessary to implement them.

When a person contacts a crisis intervention program and needs a form of assistance not offered by the organization, the best response is to make a referral to the appropriate resource. For instance, crisis workers should refer persons who demonstrate health problems, involvement with alcohol or other drugs, chronic depression, or schizophrenia. After making a referral, it is appropriate to monitor the effort by asking for two bits of follow-up information from either the client or the resource. (1) Did the client make contact? (2) Is the person receiving the service requested? A negative or equivocal answer to either question may necessitate further intervention on the part of the crisis staff.

The issue of referral can also arise once an individual approaches eight contacts with a crisis service. If the client needs further assistance, it may be best to refer the person to a more appropriate resource. When—for one reason or another—such a referral does not take place, the staff must carefully consider how to handle further contacts by that individual. If contact is allowed to continue, intervenors must examine its purpose and nature since efforts that surpass eight interactions generally do not constitute crisis intervention.

For clients who are in crisis, effective case management provides guidance for workers involved in subsequent contacts, thereby increasing the likelihood that the staff will carry out their responsibilities in the plan. Although the exact management procedures should reflect the requirements of the particular program, every crisis organization needs a system for monitoring a client's progress. Workers should know what actions are anticipated and when events are expected to occur.

Part of one center's case management system is a bulletin board with the days of the week across the top and the time of day in two-hour blocks down the left-hand side. There is an envelope on the board for each time period. For every action expected with a client, the worker—who negotiated that part of the plan—places a note in the envelope for the period during which the event is expected to take place. (For example, a client calls on Saturday afternoon and requests assistance in arranging a mental health appointment. Since the mental health center does not open to schedule appointments until 8:30 a.m. Monday morning, the worker writes a note requesting a staff member to contact the mental health center on behalf of the client and places the slip in the Monday 8:00 a.m. to 10:00 a.m. slot.) Whenever a plan calls for the client to contact the center at a future time, the worker places a note in the slot for the time period during which the interaction is expected. Likewise, if the plan calls for a worker to initiate a subsequent contact with a client, the intervenor who negotiated that arrangement places a note in the appropriate envelope.

Another crisis service maintains a "change of shift book" in which staff members enter case management information. Before going on duty a worker is expected to read all of the entries made in the book since his or her last shift.

In both of the organizations just described, the staff establishes a chart for each client with whom a plan is developed. The file begins with the current plan for the client and continues with progress notes made after each interaction.

For effective case management to be possible, intervenors must write a progress note for every contact with an identified client. Experts (e.g., Berman, 2006; Bongar & Sullivan, 2013; Kleespies, 2014) assert that such record keeping is also necessary in order to comply with accepted legal standards of care.

There are many appropriate ways to organize client information, so long as the entry contains the essential features of the interaction and plans for the future. One format is to describe (1) the client's concerns and feelings, (2) alternatives that were considered, and (3) plans that were made. Another method is to record (1) the client's subjective account of the situation, (2) the worker's objective observations of the person, (3) the worker's assessment, and (4) what is planned for the future.

In addition to providing an account of what happened, optimal case management requires that workers obtain identifying information. By the end of the first interaction it should be possible for the staff to initiate a contact with the new client. To this end, it is necessary to know the person's name, phone number, and location.

Not all crisis intervenors agree with the preceding paragraph. Some (e.g., Barber et al., 2004; Ben-Ari & Azaiza, 2003) believe the client's ability to remain anonymous should be assured.

Those who advocate asking for identifying information contend that clients who call the organization are seeking help. In order to offer the best possible assistance, the worker needs to be prepared for a variety of events, including the following: being disconnected, needing to arrange an emergency outreach to the client's location, negotiating a worker-initiated call in the plan, the client failing to make a prearranged contact, and the staff making a follow-up call. The only way to be ready for those possibilities is to obtain identifying information.

In my own experience with a variety of crisis intervention organizations, most clients comply with a request to supply identifying information. For the minority of individuals who decline to give such data, the worker can accept that decision and maintain the client's anonymity—with one exception. In life-threatening situations it is the duty of workers to do all they can to obtain the client's name and location. For example, at one crisis program for which I worked, a person called and said she had taken a drug overdose. Although she refused to give her name, address, or telephone number, she did mention having been employed at a particular restaurant. While the worker who took the call continued talking with the client, I telephoned the restaurant, described the caller to the manager, and obtained the needed information. Following an outreach to her residence, an ambulance transported her to the hospital.

With suicidal clients, it is a good idea to obtain identifying information on neighbors, friends, and loved ones. When such data is available, workers can ask one of those persons to check on the client, as occurred in the case of Claire Miller.

In addition to meeting the needs of case management, the record-keeping procedures of the organization should be designed to facilitate program evaluation. For instance, there ought to be summaries of when and how frequently the service is being used. These statistics allow maximum staff coverage to be planned for the busiest times, and they provide an estimate as to what impact the organization is having on the community. Workers should also collect data on what type of population is contacting the service and on what concerns frequently occur. When such information is available, supervisors can adjust inservice training to address prevalent needs.

Program evaluation efforts facilitate the delivery of quality services. In addition, good records are also necessary to document the organization's activities when such evidence is needed in efforts to obtain financial support for the program.

The detailed progress notes of individual interactions are not conducive to program evaluation or to descriptions of the organization contained in funding requests. So, in addition to a case management filing system, there should be another means of categorizing relevant aspects of each interaction. One efficient format is to use a log sheet on which workers list contacts and record various categories of data. Typical log sheet information includes the following: time the contact began and ended; name of the client; address; mode of service (such as telephone, walk-in, outreach, or indirect contact on behalf of a client); source of the referral (such as newspaper article, friend, physician, emergency room, or school); age of the client; nature of the problem (such as marital conflict, potential suicide, or rape); and outcome (such as future contact with the program, referral to another service, or no further assistance needed).

Although record keeping is necessary for case management, program evaluation, and funding justification, it can also serve a fourth purpose—feedback to individual workers. In order for intervenors to receive supervision based upon records they produce, each log entry, progress note, or other written account should include the identity of the staff member making the notation.

SERVICE FACILITIES

As demonstrated by the use of a bulletin board to keep track of client plans, workers' surroundings at a crisis center can influence the intervention they provide. This section discusses room arrangements, information resources, telephone systems, and mobile equipment.

Room Arrangements

The best way to ensure top-notch case management is for all records and all staff to be centrally located. A permanent, continuously staffed location is essential for any comprehensive crisis intervention program.

Walk-in services require an interview room that is separate from the phone room and is large enough to seat six or eight persons. The room ought to be quiet and free from interruptions—a "session-in-progress" sign can help achieve the latter. There should be no telephones, decorative items, or movable furniture that could be used as weapons. Arrangements such as these are a good start, although the following example demonstrates that they are not sufficient.

One crisis service had an interview room that met all of the requirements just described. As frequently happened during busy times, the two workers on duty had split up; one was in the walk-in room interviewing a married couple, while the other staff member was down the hall in the phone room taking calls. About fifteen minutes into the face-to-face session, the husband began to physically attack his wife. The worker responded by grabbing the man from behind so that he inflicted only minor injuries to his wife. With the worker holding the husband and the husband holding his wife, the man decided to break the impasse by backing the worker into the wall and repeatedly slamming him against it. Unfortunately, several minutes passed until the staff member on the phone finally heard the commotion and summoned help.

In addition to the arrangements already described, crisis intervention facilities should have a system that allows workers to immediately call for emergency backup assistance. For example, one of the simplest approaches is to have a help button installed in each room, with clear procedures specifying the appropriate response to such a request for assistance.

Information and Resources

Every crisis intervention organization needs a manual that details all normal staff responsibilities. One frequent responsibility is making a referral, so the program should also have an extensive and accurate resource file. Each entry ought to contain the resource's name, location, phone number, email address, Internet URL, if and when an automatic answering system greets callers, hours of operation, services offered, eligibility requirements (such as fees and catchment area served), and the date when the listed information was last checked.

Crisis programs must regularly update their resource files, preferably with no more than six months between verifications. Workers need to know what organizations assist clients most readily and what conditions must be met to ensure quick provision of services. Follow-up contacts are often instructive. Staff members can also visit frequently used programs in order to gain information and, if necessary, to smooth out referral procedures.

In addition to a referral file, there are other useful resources to keep on hand. Examples include the following: telephone books and telephone cross-reference directories for all communities served, detailed maps of the service area, and frequently called telephone numbers.

Telephone Systems

The minimum crisis telephone system has lines for incoming calls and one unpublished number for making outgoing calls. Workers should have the capability of calling long-distance, and it ought to be possible for any person in the service area to call the program toll-free.

A variety of telephone accessories can be helpful to crisis workers. One simple option is a cord long enough to enable the worker to stay on the line and still reach files, maps, and directories. Multiple extensions allow the intervenor who answered the phone to obtain help in identifying the client, and these lines also enable the primary worker to receive supervisory assistance during the call. In addition to having equipment that facilitates work with incoming calls, it is advantageous for staff members to have devices that make it easier to call out. For example, a speed-dialing system can lessen the effort necessary to reach frequently called numbers, such as the shift backup or the hospital emergency room. Speed dialing can also include police numbers, although a better arrangement may be to have a direct line to the law enforcement dispatch center, so that all the worker needs to do is pick up a phone to reach the police.

Within most areas of the United States, available phone systems include options for giving the caller's name and number (unless the caller has blocked such sharing). The identifying information can be provided as a visual display for every call or in response to a request (typically by hitting *69 immediately after the call) that activates a recorded message stating the caller's name and number. Programs should consider whether or under what circumstances those technologies ought to be used.

Not all telephone options are desirable. The hold option is one telephone accessory that crisis workers can do without. If the phone system comes with this capability I believe crisis workers should never use it, and crisis intervention experts agree (e.g., Mishara et al., 2007a). The negative psychological impact of being placed on hold is one consideration. I have also seen numerous callers cut off as workers attempted to use the hold function. Consequently, I believe a better strategy is to simply lay the phone down if it is necessary to suspend the interaction.

Mobile Equipment

If outreach is one of the services offered, the organization should have a car equipped with a two-way radio, tuned—by prior arrangement—to the police dispatch band. Every outreach team ought to have a mobile paging device that allows office staff to signal them. And the team should have a cell phone. Having the proper equipment not only increases workers' effectiveness, it also is essential for their safety.

SUMMARY

Comprehensive crisis intervention programs offer telephone, walk-in, and outreach assistance around the clock. Some programs offer Internet text chat. The effort and expense necessary to maintain these services can be justified on the grounds of humanitarian concern, therapeutic effectiveness, and cost efficiency.

Telephone assistance has advantages for both clients and workers. For callers, it provides availability and control. For workers, it encourages positive transference, and it allows supportive involvement of other staff members during the contact. The only reliable way of offering 24-hour telephone coverage is to have crisis workers answer the phones at which calls are first received.

Walk-in services are appropriate when any of the following situations occur: there are multiple clients, a person needs emergency assessment, a caller cannot talk privately on the telephone, or a client is in danger. Although office interviews give workers more control, intervenors are in greater danger during face-to-face interactions. Those contacts also require attention to three communication issues—introductions, body language, and note taking.

Outreach is an appropriate response when persons display high lethality, when police officers request assistance, or whenever an individual in need of face-to-face service cannot or will not participate in a walk-in contact. Since outreach workers lack the resources and support available at their office, intervenors should keep in mind the following five *outreach procedures* when they go out: (1) *always work as a team;* (2) *maintain good communication throughout the contact;* (3) *request police assistance when there is violence;* (4) *carry business cards, agency identification, and resource information;* and (5) *only do what you are trained to do.*

Crisis intervention on the Internet currently is offered in the form of live one-to-one text chat. The content of such interactions tends to be a condensed version of what might happen during a telephone contact, but the time from start to finish is much longer. Because of the slowness, it is possible for experienced workers to simultaneously serve two chatters. Frequently, that service includes the provision of other resources.

The concept of doing what you are trained to do applies to all crisis intervention efforts, and it is the guiding principle of case management. When assisting the clients of other clinicians, crisis intervenors should work in support of previously agreed-upon treatment strategies. For clients who need services other than crisis intervention, the best response is to refer them to appropriate resources. A vital part of all case management is good record keeping. In addition, appropriate records are necessary for program evaluation, funding justification, and staff supervision.

If workers are to provide quality crisis intervention assistance, they must have adequate facility support in four areas—room arrangements, information and resources, telephone system, and mobile equipment. Optimum room arrangements require a permanent location, where workers perform record keeping and case management activities around the clock. When in a walk-in room, workers ought to be able to summon help. Readily available information and resources should include a procedures manual, an up-to-date referral file, telephone cross-reference directories, and maps. Telephone equipment ought to include an unpublished number for making outgoing calls and toll-free numbers for all of the program's service area. Workers can benefit from helpful phone accessories such as a long cord, multiple extensions, speed dialing, and a direct line to the police. Outreach teams need a beeper, a cell phone, and a car equipped with a radio tuned to the police dispatch frequency.

STUDY QUESTIONS

1. Joan is so exasperated with her school performance that she is ready to quit. What is the therapeutic advantage of offering her immediately available crisis intervention services?
2. Who should answer the crisis telephone line and where should they answer it?
3. During an interaction, when *must* you take notes?
4. Howard is a suicidal client. Upon arriving at his home, you find him sitting on the porch with a shotgun. What do you do?
5. Tom is a client you refer for psychotherapy. In following up on the referral, what two bits of information are appropriate to obtain from Tom or from the resource?
6. In what kind of room should workers conduct walk-in sessions?
7. How often should resource information be updated?
8. Jill has called you at the crisis intervention center because she needs to talk with someone about her out-of-control son. But you have been very busy with paperwork and you need to finish one small detail, so you put

Jill on hold for a minute while you wrap up your work. What are problems you risk by putting her on hold?

9. What communication equipment does an outreach team need?

Chapter 7

COMMUNITY RELATIONS

A crisis intervention program is only as good as its reputation in the community. Several factors influence how others view the organization. This chapter examines five relevant issues—service quality, publicity, governing body, relations with other resources, and ethics.

QUALITY OF SERVICE

When potential clients consider initiating contact with a crisis intervention program, a crucial factor that influences their decision is communication from prior users about the nature and quality of the assistance offered. This phenomenon, or the lack of it, can be seen in new organizations. Although crisis programs usually begin with a lot of publicity, the first several months tend to be slow. It takes time for people to hear about the service by word of mouth. Since many clients do tell someone else about the organization, business usually increases as more individuals use the program and communicate their positive reactions to others.

In part because clients do spread the word, programs come to be used by persons who want what the organization offers. If that commodity happens to be immediate problem-solving assistance for individuals overwhelmed by a sudden upsurge in difficulties, then crisis intervention contacts will increase.

On the other hand, if a program encourages its staff to engage in activities that do not constitute crisis intervention, the organization may find itself serving a noncrisis population. For instance, the administrators of one agency encouraged staff members to give advice at the first opportunity and to converse with masturbating callers. In time, over half of the contacts were from obscene callers, with chronically lonely individuals accounting for most of the other calls. Almost none of the service consumers were in crisis.

Program quality exerts a powerful influence on the number and nature of contacts to a crisis intervention program. No amount of community relations effort can overcome the effects of inappropriate staff performance. But if the intent and practice of an organization is to offer bona fide crisis intervention services, then efforts to enhance community relations will pay off in increased support and use of the program.

PUBLICITY

Although many new clients hear about a crisis intervention program through word of mouth, organizations can also use publicity to inform the public about available services. For starters, the telephone number should be listed with the emergency numbers in phone directories. Administrators can take advantage of other "free" publicity by issuing press releases, preparing spot announcements for radio and television, arranging appearances on talk shows, and suggesting feature articles to news organization editors and reporters.

Paid publicity efforts can also be effective. Options include the following: ads in telephone directories; both display and classified ads in newspapers; sign space on buses, taxicabs, and billboards; and business cards, pamphlets, phone stickers, and posters distributed to social service agencies, emergency rooms, physicians' waiting rooms, businesses, factories, churches, and schools. Whenever administrators use such advertising, they must periodically change the material in order for it to continue to attract attention.

The most successful media efforts appear to be news organization articles and ads, radio and television announcements, and telephone directory listings (e.g., Ben-Ari & Azaiza, 2003). Nevertheless, the staff of each organization should evaluate the productiveness of their own publicity efforts. Workers can monitor the effectiveness of various public relations initiatives by asking clients how they heard about the service. Staff members then can enter the information in a "referral source" box on the log sheet or contact record form. By obtaining such data, workers help administrators know which publicity activities to continue or expand and which endeavors to modify or discard.

GOVERNING BODY

Ultimately the quality and effectiveness of a crisis intervention service is the responsibility of the organization's governing body. When this entity is a board of directors, it also has the potential to encourage community acceptance and sustenance of the program. Experts (e.g., Hoff & Hoff, 2012) assert that if a board of directors is to facilitate political support, financial backing, and policy guidance, it should represent a broad cross-section of the community. Some board members may be selected because they have special talents, such as fundraising skills or public relations knowledge. And others may be asked to join because of their backgrounds in business, in government, or in professions such as law, medicine, education, or human services. All should be willing to commit the time and energy necessary to serve as active and informed members of the board.

While diversity is good, uniformity is a different matter. When directors limit control to members who are like themselves, they are asking for trouble. The primary examples of this one-dimensional phenomenon are boards controlled by members of a single profession and boards run by the workers themselves. Having been associated with both kinds of organizations, I have seen the difficulties that result from homogeneous boards. The major problems involve a narrow base of support and consensual validity.

Narrow support. One-dimensional boards preclude broad political and financial backing within the community. And when the programs they control become dependent on limited sources of support, those sources exert undue influence over the organization.

Consensual validity. Since a one-dimensional board shares a common background, members often have the same beliefs on issues facing the organization. Unfortunately, those beliefs may be at odds with standard practices. For example, one organization, whose board was controlled by attorneys, decided that anyone who volunteered should be accepted as a worker and that three hours of training was sufficient for direct-service staff members. Programs with worker-controlled boards have instituted policies such as banning follow-up contact with clients and forbidding workers to bring up the topic of suicide. Such idiosyncratic decisions made by homogeneous boards often lead significant segments of the community to look askance at those organizations.

Candace Widmer (1996) wrote about her experience and data collection as an organization development consultant. She had encountered a number of programs that allowed the same individuals to serve both as service providers and as members of the board. In every instance where that had occurred she said problems had resulted. She described both conflict and confusion relating to supervisory roles, the board's role, and the roles of board members.

Worker-controlled boards create a circular arrangement in which administrators are under the authority of the persons they supervise. Consequently, to paraphrase a board member in one of the organizations studied by Doctor Widmer, supervisors may be bypassed when information is transmitted and issues are discussed. One result of such practices is to leave administrators with little or no authority to manage the program.

An alternative to a worker-run board is a board that has one or two worker positions. This approach is similar to university boards that have student members and corporate boards that have labor representatives. Under such a system, direct service staff members participate in board decisions without detracting from their primary role of providing quality crisis intervention services to clients.

WORKING WITH OTHER SERVICE RESOURCES

For a crisis intervention organization to be effective, board members, administrators, and veteran staff members agree that other resources must see it as a valuable source of aid for persons who are in crisis (e.g., Wiener, Wiley, Huelsman, & Hilgeman, 1994). Other agencies and groups must know about the services available from the organization, and they must believe that the crisis program will be responsive to their referral and assistance needs.

When others know about and respect the program, they refer persons who are in crisis. Likewise, when crisis workers see the need for outside assistance they should ask for help or should refer clients to the appropriate resources. If good relations exist, others usually are responsive to requests for support.

Productive community involvement is likely to require communication with a variety of services. Examples include the following: nonprofit organizations such as Alcoholics Anonymous and the Salvation Army, government welfare agencies, schools and colleges, and individual helping professionals such as clergy, social workers, psychiatrists, psychologists, and counselors. In addition to those resources, there are four categories of resources upon which a worker must be able to rely—legal services, emergency medical services, mental health services, and law enforcement agencies.

Legal Services

When clients face eviction, experience marital problems, or suffer abuse, they may require the services of an attorney. If there is a need for legal services, workers should be prepared to help arrange such assistance.

EXAMPLE.
Worker: Crisis Intervention, this is Ken.
Lucy Sanders: You're not going to believe this. Last month my husband and I got a divorce, but now he won't get out of the house.
Worker: So you both are still living there.
Lucy: Living is hardly the word for it. I mean, he's cursing at me and the children all of the time. And he threatens to kick us out. Things are worse now than they ever were when we were married.
Worker: It sounds like you are exasperated with the situation.
Lucy: That's right. I can't take it anymore.
Worker: Who owns the house?
Lucy: Well, I guess we both do. But Frank won't sell me his portion or get out. And I certainly don't have anywhere else to go. . . .
Frank Sanders (in the background): Don't lie! Don't lie! Don't lie! Can't you be honest with anyone? Can't you be honest with anyone?
Worker: It seems like it's hard for you to talk now.
Lucy: What?
Worker: Would you like to come to our office so you could talk a little easier?
Lucy: Yes. Could I come in this afternoon?
Worker: That would be fine. Do you know where we are?
Lucy: You're in the building next to the hospital, aren't you?
Worker: That's right. Come in the double glass doors, and tell the receptionist that you would like to see a crisis worker.
Lucy: OK. I'll be there this afternoon.

During her walk-in, Lucy and the worker focused on obtaining legal assistance. Rather than returning to the attorney who had represented her in the divorce, she preferred to seek new counsel. Since she had no money to pay a lawyer, the worker gave her information on the legal aid program. While at the crisis center she called the legal aid office and arranged an appointment for the next day.

DISCUSSION OF LUCY SANDERS' CASE. Unlike Sarah Miller in Chapter 5, Lucy had no interest in counseling. She just wanted a property settlement that would terminate her proximity to Frank and would provide her with a place to live. Since her problem was essentially a legal matter, the worker explored the option of obtaining an attorney. Dissatisfaction with the lawyer who had handled her divorce, combined with her lack of money, meant she would be an appropriate client for the legal aid program. Given the difficulty with telephone communication from her home, the worker encouraged Lucy to use a crisis center phone to call the legal aid office.

Emergency Medical Services

If crisis counseling is not a service offered by emergency room personnel, the hospital staff should request crisis intervention assistance for patients who are medically clear but are in emotional crisis. Conversely, crisis workers should arrange emergency medical attention whenever it is necessary, including the use of ambulance services or rescue squads to transport ill or injured clients. (For examples involving emergency medical services, see the following cases: Mary Anderson in Chapter 1, Claire Miller in Chapter 6, and Walter Owens and Elsie Lawson in the present chapter.)

Mental Health Services

Crisis workers should be ready to aid mental health professionals who request assistance in responding to client emergencies. When the possibility of needing such assistance arises, planning should occur. For example, if a therapist suggests that a client should call the crisis center in response to between-session thoughts of suicide, the therapist (with the client's permission) should contact the crisis center and provide the following: identifying information on the client, the likelihood of contact, relevant assessment information developed by the therapist, intervention guidance, and communication preferences with regard to any contacts that occur. Likewise, staff members should seek out mental health resources that will accept referrals of crisis clients in need of long-term treatment.

> EXAMPLE. Mary Nelson called the crisis program because she was worried about her husband Tom. During a brief conversation with the worker she arranged to bring Tom to the center. When they arrived, Tom refused to come into the building, so the first half hour of the interview took place outside. Eventually, Tom agreed to come inside where the remainder of the two-hour interaction took place. Throughout the rest of the interview, Tom paced up and down, methodically kicking each building pillar as he came to it. Frequently he refused to answer questions, and, when he did respond, his statements were short. With help from Mary, the worker learned that Tom was worried about his home's water drains becoming clogged. During the past week, he had spent most of his waking hours looking out the window and watching for rain, which he believed might wash away his house. (Mary maintained that their house had no drainage problem.) In addition to the anxieties regarding his home, Tom feared that he might lose his job at the company where he had been employed for the past twenty-seven years. Mary reported that during the three previous summers he had experienced an episode of depression associated with job pressure at the close of the fiscal year. In terms of his present state, Tom said he felt worthless to his family and hopeless about life, although he denied any thoughts of suicide. During repeated attempts by the worker to negotiate a plan, Tom steadfastly refused to make any decisions. He remained noncommittal on the alternatives of seeing his family physician, seeking outpatient psychiatric help, or entering the mental health inpatient unit. Finally, in response

to his wife's urging, he agreed to an appointment with a psychiatrist. The worker then provided mental health referral information to the Nelsons. Two weeks later a follow-up contact indicated that Tom was receiving psychiatric treatment for depression.

DISCUSSION OF TOM NELSON'S CASE. Tom experienced obsessive delusions concerning the possibility of flooding at his home. He behaved in a passive-aggressive manner and compulsively kicked each obstacle he encountered. Emotionally, he appeared to be in a recurrent episode of agitated depression. His wife was at the end of her rope, and it was primarily through her urging that he agreed to accept a mental health referral. Since Tom's thinking appeared to be too restricted and delusional for effective crisis intervention, the worker supported the option of psychiatric treatment.

Psychiatric hospitalization is an option to consider when a client is so disorganized that productive problem solving is impossible and it appears that the person may be suicidal or homicidal. The decision to hospitalize an individual in a psychiatric unit is the responsibility of the admitting doctor. In many hospitals, however, the medical professionals on duty depend upon the observations and evaluations of crisis workers who have knowledge of the patient. When making a referral for possible hospitalization it may be appropriate for the worker to furnish information (1) on any self-injury or harm to others that the client has threatened or caused, (2) on support available to the person, (3) on the individual's cooperation with those resources, and (4) on the person's self-care ability (see Chapters 1 and 3). Also, the staff member ought to report any observations regarding (1) thinking disturbances, (2) perceptual distortions, (3) emotional difficulties, (4) motor abnormalities, or (5) interpersonal problems (see Chapter 5).

Persons in need of hospitalization often come to the attention of crisis workers because they cause problems for others. So, in addition to working with the potential patient, it may also be necessary for workers to provide crisis intervention to the individual's family or close friends.

EXAMPLE. Walter Owens came to the emergency room with a gash in his forehead that required fifteen stitches. After treating Walter's injury the attending physician requested a crisis consult. Walter told the crisis worker that the wound resulted from his wife Anna striking him in the head with a lamp. He said that seven months ago she was hospitalized on the mental health inpatient unit. Following three weeks of inpatient treatment she entered the partial-hospitalization program and did well during the next several months. Two weeks prior to the assault, however, she stopped taking her medicine and stopped going to the day-treatment program. Walter reported that her behavior then became progressively more disturbed and that her personal hygiene had declined. In terms of current options, Walter said he preferred to have his wife live with him at home. He stated, however, that he no longer could endure her disruptive conduct. The worker explored the possibility of bringing Anna to see her mental health therapist. Although Walter did not believe that she would agree to a mental health center visit, he invited the worker to meet with Anna.

The worker arranged an outreach to the Owens home. When the team arrived, Anna agreed to see them. As the interaction began the workers noticed her strong body odor. She seemed unconcerned about Walter's injury and disinterested in talking with the workers; nevertheless, she did respond with rapid speech whenever a worker asked her a question. Anna said that rather than intending to hit Walter with the lamp, she had been trying to kill a giant fly that was covering his face. She claimed that she had been warned by a message on TV telling her to "beware of the flies." In fact, she said she had received many personal messages from the TV during the past week, as well as transatlantic radio communications that she could hear without a radio. She suggested her experiences would all be clear to the workers if she could "square the circles" for them.

Suddenly, Anna picked up an ashtray and threw it over the male worker's head. In response to a reprimand from Walter, she yelled that a giant bug had been trying to land on the worker. Once Anna settled down again, the team explored with her the possibility of going to see her therapist. Anna rejected that option by saying she no longer wanted anything to do with mental health.

The workers and Walter stepped outside the house and continued the discussion while Anna watched TV inside. Walter decided that he wanted her to have inpatient treatment, and he asked if the crisis workers would help arrange a hospital commitment. The team reviewed involuntary hospitalization procedures with Walter, and he said he wanted to pursue the commitment.

Back at the crisis center, Walter completed the legal petition to have his wife committed. The mental health representative came to the center, reviewed the forms, interviewed Walter, and formally requested the police to pick up Anna for a mandatory evaluation.

The crisis team and Walter met the police at the house, and the officers transported Anna to the hospital emergency room. A physician examined her, and she was committed to the hospital's psychiatric inpatient unit.

DISCUSSION OF THE OWENS CASE. The intervention began with the crisis worker engaging Walter in a problem-solving effort. Since Anna was not likely to come to the center, the worker arranged an outreach to further assess the situation. After it became clear that psychiatric treatment was necessary, the team first explored the option of voluntary participation. When Anna refused further mental health contact, the team agreed to help Walter initiate involuntary-commitment procedures. Commitment was appropriate in this case since (1) Anna was a danger to others, (2) the current support at home was inadequate for her needs, (3) she declined to use other available resources, and (4) she appeared to have inadequate self-care ability. Although the crisis workers had no formal role in the commitment process, they supplied the forms, helped Walter complete the paperwork, contacted the mental health representative, and assisted the police in transporting Anna to the hospital emergency room. Upon arriving with Anna at the emergency room, the team met with physician that would be evaluating Anna and gave him a copy of their progress note on the case. The write-up described (1) Anna's danger to others indicated by Walter's head injury and by the ashtray-throwing incident, (2) the support at home by her husband being inadequate for her needs, (3) Anna's refusal to use additional support that was available, and (4) the inadequate self-care ability suggested by her body odor. The written account also described (1) Anna's delusions of reference relating to the TV messages, (2) her hallucinations concerning bugs and radio signals, (3) her flat affect, (4) her pressured speech, and (5) the strain her behavior was placing on the marital relationship. Following her commitment and two weeks in the hospital, Anna was again stabilized on medication, and she returned home.

Law Enforcement Agencies

Police may request crisis intervention assistance with domestic disturbances, suicidal persons, individuals in need of psychiatric hospitalization, crime victims, and other persons in need of immediate help. In turn, crisis workers may ask for law enforcement involvement when there is a weapon at a scene, when an outreach team needs emergency entry into a residence, or whenever a situation requires the expertise and authority of the police. (As discussed in Chapter 6, a speedy and reliable communications system enhances such reciprocal assistance.)

Cases that involve crisis workers and police officers are best viewed as collaborative interventions in which both have special roles to fulfill. The officers' duty is to enforce the law and to maintain the peace, while the workers' duty is to intervene with persons in crisis and to engage them in a problem-solving effort.

Domestic disturbance interventions highlight the respective roles of workers and officers. The police officers' goals are to restore order (so that no one is injured) and to leave as soon as possible (so they can be available for other calls). If the officers have been trained in conflict resolution, they will try to defuse the situation, mediate the dispute, and make a referral. In many jurisdictions there appears to be room for improvement with regard to activation of crisis intervention services for victims of domestic violence. For example, in a study of five police precincts in Seattle, Kernic and Bonomi (2007) found that following law enforcement intervention in intimate partner violence, activation of crisis intervention services occurred for only 20 percent of the victims, with one precinct below 10 percent.

When crisis workers intervene in a domestic disturbance, their goal is to identify individuals who are in crisis and to collaborate with them in developing a realistic plan. In most cases the crisis team will spend over two hours

with the clients—compared to less than 30 minutes for typical police interventions—as the disputants express concerns, consider alternatives, and map
out courses of action.

Another crucial area for cooperation between law enforcement officers
and crisis workers is intervening with persons in need of psychiatric hospitalization. Sometimes, as in the case of Anna Owens, there is a request for
police assistance. Other times, as with Barry Lancaster in Chapter 6, law enforcement officers ask for help from crisis workers.

Peter Finn and Monique Sullivan (1989) studied eight response networks
that had a track record of successfully handling persons needing psychiatric
hospitalization. The investigators identified three essential functions of the
emergency assistance unit:

• It evaluates mentally disturbed individuals and recommends disposi-
  tions.
• It makes effective referrals to appropriate facilities.
• It provides outreach services as needed.

Often this core emergency unit can be the local full-service crisis intervention program. In Finn and Sullivan's (1989) study this was the case in
Washtenaw County, Michigan and in Erie, Pennsylvania. There are other
similar programs, such as the one in Cuyahoga County, Ohio (Dyches,
Biegel, Johnsen, Guo, & Min, 2002).

Finn and Sullivan also concluded that several key characteristics are crucial to the success of effective networks.

• Written agreements commit each participating program to the network
  and specify each agency's roles and responsibilities.
• Network participants include all of the community programs that offer
  emergency services to mentally ill persons.
• There are benefits for all participating resources. (For example, law enforcement officers have more time for other police duties, encounter less
  danger, and experience improved job satisfaction, whereas crisis workers receive priority when requesting police assistance.)

As Finn and Sullivan (1989) discovered, mutual responsibility is the key to
effective police-crisis worker relations. To this end, law enforcement and crisis service administrators can clarify collaborative policies and procedures
through joint planning meetings. For cases in which both organizations are
likely to become involved, plans should be made for sharing responsibility
rather than having one organization "dump" clients on another. Based upon
a sound understanding of each program's capabilities, techniques, and needs,

representatives of the two organizations can develop guidelines that describe how the law enforcement agency and the crisis service are most likely to be of help to each other.

The Crisis Intervention Team of the Memphis Police Department is a model law-enforcement-based approach for delivering persons to a comprehensive hospital emergency room that provides security, assessment, treatment, and referral for all individuals experiencing difficulties relating to mental health issues, developmental disabilities, or substance use. With such a resource available, the specially trained patrol officers who volunteer to be part of the Crisis Intervention Team (in addition to their regular patrol duties) have been shown to feel increased confidence in their ability to handle emergency situations. That positive attitude is justified. The program has been associated with (1) decreased callout rates for the Memphis Tactics Apprehension and Containment Team (similar to SWAT teams in other communities), (2) decreased officer injury rates, and (3) increased referrals to the mental health emergency service (Dupont & Cochran, 2000). Beneficial results have also been found in other communities using similar programs, including Montgomery County, Pennsylvania, Multnomah County, Oregon, Louisville, Kentucky, Akron, Ohio, and Chicago (Browning, Van Hasselt, Tucker, & Vecchi, 2011; Ritter, Teller, Marcussen, Munetz, & Teasdale, 2011; Steadman et al., 2001; Strauss et al., 2005; Teller, Munetz, Gil, & Ritter, 2006; Watson et al., 2010). Worldwide there are now over 1,000 jurisdictions using the Memphis model for Crisis Intervention Teams (CIT International, 2013).

Some communities have developed programs in which crisis workers and police officers ride together (e.g., Ligon, 2005) or in which the police routinely transfer certain kinds of cases to a crisis worker team (e.g., Corcoran & Allen, 2005). Both approaches have resulted in positive benefits.

In Nova Scotia a program was created that included a 24-hour crisis phone service and an outreach team comprised of a mental health professional and plainclothes police officers. Compared to officers in nearby communities that were not participating in the program, during the second year of the initiative participating officers were spending 21 percent less time on the scene (136 minutes vs. 165 minutes). Even more importantly, compared to police service recipients in nearby nonparticipating communities, individuals receiving the new services during its first year participated in a significantly higher number of outpatient contacts (Kisely et al., 2010).

In the United States there are over 600 jurisdictions that have school resource officers. Appropriately trained law enforcement officers serve as key members of student assistance and crisis intervention teams (James, Logan, & Davis, 2011).

In communities where crisis intervention and law enforcement programs are seeking to maintain good relations and smooth operating procedures, staff members from each program can participate in the preservice and in-service training of the other organization. When a crisis intervention organization offers inservice training to a law enforcement agency, the offer should be for all officers who are interested receiving the training. Many mental health experts (e.g., Lamb, Weinberger, & Gross, 2004) advocate agency-wide efforts in order to reach the largest number of officers possible.

Once the trainers know the makeup of the group that will be attending the session, the staff members should enlist the cooperation of those participants who are most likely to have peer influence. Since law enforcement operates according to a military style of administration, the opinions of the senior officer in the group usually affect the attitudes of lesser-ranking officers. Consequently, it will be to the workers' advantage to have a pretraining meeting with the senior officer who will be present at the training. The crisis staff members can describe the basic content to be presented and can ask for reactions and suggestions from the officer. In many instances the officer's comments will make the presentation more relevant to the experience of the participants.

At the start of the first session the workers can draw the senior officer into the discussion. If they have modified their presentation in light of the pretraining meeting, the ranking officer's comments are likely to demonstrate support for the views being presented. By taking time to arrange a preliminary meeting and by involving the senior officer early in the initial session, the workers create an atmosphere that encourages other officers to accept the validity of the training material.

Police officers typically are interested in learning information that is relevant to the tasks involved in their daily work, so the content of law enforcement training should be practical. If the trainers present a theoretical concept, they must quickly relate it to police applications; otherwise, the leaders will face inattentiveness or even hostility from the participants. The format should provide ample opportunity for discussion, and it should encourage the officers to share their expertise in law enforcement matters. In order for the training content to affect the officers' on-the-job behavior, the sessions must provide them with opportunities for applying the concepts to real-life scenarios. Role playing followed by feedback is an essential training component (e.g., James, Logan, & Davis, 2011; Van Hasselt et al., 2005a; Van Hasselt et al., 2006). By using such simulated experiences, participants try out different approaches and discover what works, as well as what doesn't work.

The officers themselves are the best resource for providing examples to be simulated. The trainers then can give the officer-generated situations to actors who will portray the civilian parts in the role play while the officers play themselves, using the crisis intervention techniques they have been studying. (In one training session I made the mistake of asking a deputy to portray a neighbor in a domestic disturbance scene, with two amateur actors playing the husband-wife disputants. During the role play the "neighbor" jumped one of the intervening officers, and in the ensuing fight the combatants broke all four legs off a heavy wooden table. Fortunately there were no injuries.)

After each role play the intervenors should receive detailed feedback on their performances. Once officers are doing well, video replay with feedback can further enhance their skills. But if a group has far to go before reaching a satisfactory level of performance, simple verbal feedback is better at the beginning. Seeing oneself fail miserably on television can activate defenses and can actually decrease the likelihood of constructive change.

Although planning meetings and reciprocal training efforts can lay the foundation for good police crisis relations, the day-to-day performance of the staff on duty will make or break the relationship. When a law enforcement officer asks for crisis intervention help it is crucial for workers to respond immediately to the request. If the team cannot immediately engage in an outreach being requested, a worker must inform the officer of the delay, then attempt to make alternative arrangements.

Depending upon the situation, the actual request for assistance may come from any of several possible sources—an officer, the police dispatcher, or a potential client at the scene. Workers should always try to talk with the intervening officers before making contact with potential clients. (If notification comes from the dispatcher, the worker can obtain the names of the officers at the scene and the phone number there. If the officers already have left the site, the dispatcher can ask them to call the crisis office or can arrange an off-site meeting with the outreach team.) Once the police and the workers are talking, the first topic should be the officers' description and assessment of the situation. The next order of business ought to be a collaborative decision as to how the hand-off from the police to the crisis team will be made. The options are (a) the crisis team arriving after the police have left, (b) the police leaving soon after the team arrives, (c) the police staying until the situation appears likely to remain calm, or (d) one or more officers remaining at the scene as the crisis workers interview the individuals.

When they arrive at the scene, most outreach teams like to find a police car there, since it is a clear sign that they are at the right place. The presence of the officers also allows for further discussion with them and means that their support is immediately available.

As mentioned in Chapter 6, when there are combatants involved, the workers should talk with each disputant separately. The team can then proceed with the group or individual techniques that are appropriate for the situation.

EXAMPLE. The police dispatcher called the crisis center and requested an outreach team to assist with a family disturbance. Since the intervening officers had already left the scene, the team arranged to see them en route to the residence. During their meeting in a convenience store parking lot the officers told the workers about the situation.

Ron Davis was the 18-year-old son of Nancy and Ted Davis. The previous night had been Ron's high school prom, and he had asked to use the family car. When his father refused the request, Ron took the car anyway. Mr. Davis then reported the auto stolen. Around 7:00 a.m. Ron returned home, a shouting match ensued, and Mrs. Davis called the police.

When the officers arrived, Mr. Davis demanded that they arrest his son for auto theft. The officers encouraged him not to press charges, and they suggested instead that the family use the services of the crisis center. With his wife's urging, Mr. Davis agreed to give it a try, although Ron remained noncommittal.

As the crisis team entered the house, Ron went to the basement, leaving his parents and the two workers in the living room. After introducing themselves to Mr. and Mrs. Davis, the team split up (positioning themselves so they could maintain eye contact with each other); the female member of the team went to the top of the basement stairs to talk with Ron while the male worker spoke with Mr. and Mrs. Davis in the living room. Mr. Davis complained that during the past six months his son had been smoking marijuana, drinking, and frequently staying out all night. He said he had tried to control his son by repeatedly putting Ron on restriction and by threatening him with beatings if he violated the sanctions. Such violations happened often, and Mr. Davis had struck his son on several occasions, resulting in no apparent improvement in Ron's behavior. Seeing that he was losing control over his son, Mr. Davis resorted to calling the police when Ron took the car to the prom. He said he was disgusted with Ron's drug use and other irresponsible behavior, and he demanded that his son permanently move out of the house.

Down in the basement, Ron first refused to talk with the crisis worker. After several minutes, however, he began describing his frustration at being constantly on restriction during his senior year in high school. He said that since his father jumped on him for relatively minor infractions, there was no point in obeying anything his dad said. Ron concluded by wishing he could somehow leave home. Reluctantly, he then agreed to rejoin the others in the living room.

The workers summarized what they had heard, and it appeared the most desirable alternative was Ron living on his own. The team gave the family the task of thinking about where Ron might live, how much it would cost, and how he would get the money for his expenses. The team told each family member to consider these issues individually, then to come together during the next two evenings for fifteen-minute discussions of their thoughts. The workers described guidelines for good communication, and they helped Ron and his parents use the techniques during a practice session on the topic of where Ron might live. The family members agreed to come to the crisis center in three days for the purpose of exploring the feasibility of Ron living on his own. DISCUSSION OF THE DAVIS FAMILY CASE. Although Ron had apparently violated the law, the police were more interested in calming the disturbance than in helping Mr. Davis press charges against his son. The officers had defused the situation of its immediate potential for violence, yet communication was still difficult when the crisis team arrived. The female worker eventually succeeded in getting Ron to talk by using an inverted funnel sequence of questions. Since both father and son claimed they wanted a change in living arrangements, the plan focused on assessing the feasibility of Ron living on his own.

Crisis staff members and law enforcement officers need to maintain good relationships if they are to continue generating productive efforts. For example, programs (e.g., Olivero & Hansen, 1994) have engaged in activities such as administrators sending letters of commendation to intervening officers and their superiors, as well as the crisis intervention organization sponsoring awards ceremonies to recognize publicly the contributions of law enforcement officers.

ETHICS

A crisis worker's primary responsibility is to act in the best interest of the client. Although an intervenor ought to respect the traditions of other organizations, the staff member must make decisions based on what is best for the client, rather than on what is best for community agencies and programs. If a community service does not respond appropriately to a client's legitimate needs in an urgent situation, those needs must take precedence over unruffled relations with that resource.

EXAMPLE. Bob Lawson arrived home after a bad day at work. With his wife Elise and his 16-year-old stepdaughter Susan available as targets, he began venting his frustrations by cursing and criticizing them. His tirade increased in severity until, after a couple of drinks, he hit Elise several times. She then called the police, and an officer came to the house. Elise asked him to arrest Bob. The officer refused and left.

Once the patrol car was out of sight, Bob cursed his wife for calling the police and began beating her again. Susan then called the police. While she was on the phone, Bob hit her, then grabbed the phone and smashed it. Nevertheless, she had identified herself to the dispatcher, and the same officer responded again. Both Elise and Susan asked him to arrest Bob. The officer said, "You can't arrest a man in his own home" and left.

As soon as the officer was gone, Bob began cursing his wife and stepdaughter, then he knocked Elise unconscious. Susan dragged her mother to the car, loaded her into the back seat, and drove to the hospital.

The emergency room physician treated Elise's injuries and requested a crisis intervention consult. At the end of a 30-minute session, Elise decided she wanted to press charges against Bob. She also wanted to find another place to stay since she was afraid to go home.

Elise and Susan returned with the worker to the crisis center. Using one of the center's phones, Elise called the police, described who she was, and said she wanted to press charges against her husband. The desk officer replied that she would have to talk with the patrolman who had been to her house, so she asked for the patrolman to call her at the center. An hour later she had not heard from him, so she telephoned the police department again. The desk officer said the patrolman had been busy and that he would call her as soon as possible. An hour later Elise called again and received the same response. After another hour, the crisis worker telephoned the police department, described the situation, and asked to speak with the patrolman. The desk officer told the worker that the patrolman would call as soon as possible. After another hour of waiting and receiving no response, the crisis worker called the district attorney and described the situation to him. Ten minutes later, an officer—not the patrolman—arrived at the crisis center. He assisted Elise in completing the paperwork necessary for her to press charges against Bob.

Elise telephoned the local shelter for abused women and children, and she made arrangements to stay there. After an exhausting night, she and Susan then departed for the shelter. Later that day, officers arrested Bob on assault charges.

DISCUSSION OF THE LAWSON CASE. Police often do not like charges to be filed in family disturbance cases because the person filing them frequently backs out before the case goes to trial. Nevertheless, Elise had a right to bring charges against her husband. The worker encouraged her to do all she could for herself. When the response of the police department proved to be less than adequate, however, the worker eventually stepped in as an advocate on behalf of Elise.

Unfortunately, the situation experienced by Elise is not unique to her. Fleury, Sullivan, Bybee, and Davidson (1998) studied reasons for differential police contact by 137 women who had abusive partners. Among participants who needed law enforcement assistance at least one more time than the police were called, 64 percent of the women said one of the reasons they did not call was because they did not believe the police would assist them. The authors observed that for many of the participants, such a belief was based on experiences in which law enforcement involvement had resulted in nothing being done to the assailant and in no help being offered to the victim.

Although working with other organizations is difficult at times, ethical practice requires that intervenors use appropriate resources rather than overstep the bounds of their own areas of competence. When a client needs specialized information, the worker should refer the person to the appropriate community resource. For example, only medical personnel should give medical advice, and only legal professionals should give legal advice.

Ethical standards also mandate that clinicians safeguard personal information about clients. Each state has its own laws and regulations on the issue of confidentiality, and workers should be familiar with the rules that apply to their setting—especially conditions that require staff members to break confidentiality. For instance, courts usually have the authority in criminal cases to subpoena client information, and most states require workers to report cases of child abuse.

When staff members gather socially, such as meeting for dinner in a public place, they must be careful not to discuss confidential information. In one program, the crisis staff often ate together in a hospital cafeteria that also served patients and visitors. Frequently the workers discussed center clients during those get-togethers. By violating standards of ethical conduct in that manner the workers risked the release of confidential information, and they demonstrated to the patients (many of whom were former clients) how their own situations might be discussed.

Although workers ought to use common sense in preserving the privacy of confidential material, they should also be willing to disclose relevant case information to qualified service resources if such disclosure is necessary to obtain emergency assistance for the client. When communicating with physicians, attorneys, therapists, police officers, or other professionals, workers should limit revelations to information that is essential to arranging the necessary help. In less urgent situations, clients can sign a release of information form that specifies information to be shared and who will be sharing it.

One technique that I use is to call the potential resource and explain relevant details of the case without identifying the client. If the professional agrees to assist the person, I respond that the individual will be making contact in the near future. I then give the client any information necessary for obtaining the needed service, and I suggest that the person get in touch with the resource.

Individuals who request assistance from crisis intervention organizations become the clients of the program; they are never the clients of individual workers. Intervenors are not betraying client confidentiality when they monitor calls, write progress notes, place identifying information in case files, or conduct client staffings. All of those practices are appropriate ways of disseminating client information within the organization.

The stance taken by crisis intervention organizations within the United States is that when persons endanger their own lives or the lives of others, their rights of confidentiality and privacy are less important than preserving life (Mishara et al., 2007a; Mishara & Weisstub, 2010). In such cases, workers must do all they can to implement effective crisis intervention, as demonstrated by the case of Rose Sawyer in Chapter 3.

SUMMARY

If a program offers quality crisis intervention assistance, persons in crisis often learn about it through word of mouth. Administrators can further promote the program by using both free and paid publicity. In order to know what works for a particular organization, workers should keep records on the kinds of information that prompt clients to use their service.

The organization's governing body has ultimate responsibility for the quality of the program. A governing board that represents a cross-section of the community has the potential to provide effective policy guidance, broad financial backing, and strong political support. On the other hand, a one-dimensional board may result in two negative effects—narrow support that can limit the program, and consensual validity that may lead to poor decisions.

When good community relations exist, other resources make referrals to the crisis intervention organization, and they are responsive to referral requests on behalf of crisis intervention clients. Such two-way referral channels are necessary with a variety of resources, including legal assistance, emergency medical services, and mental health programs.

Effective relationships with law enforcement agencies promote the safety and well-being of clients, workers, and officers. Planning meetings can establish guidelines for how each organization can best help the other, and reciprocal training programs allow the staffs of both organizations to practice and apply relevant procedures. Although such efforts provide a firm foundation for police-crisis relations, it is the day-to-day interactions of the individuals on duty that make or break the relationship. Personnel in each organization should be responsive to requests for assistance from the other agency. Once the decision for a joint effort is made, the officers and workers should discuss strategy with each other. Crisis service administrators can further support collaboration by routinely acknowledging the involvement of the police and by informing them about case outcomes.

Crisis intervenors should act in the best interest of their clients. Fulfilling that obligation means workers may need to serve as a client's advocate when other resources are unresponsive, must not offer advice if they are not qualified to give it, should safeguard the confidential nature of client information, should share necessary case descriptions with appropriate service resources, ought to disseminate client information within the service, and should risk violating an individual's privacy if necessary to preserve life.

STUDY QUESTIONS

1. From the perspective of those responsible for managing a crisis intervention program, what is a good reason for finding out how a client learned of that organization?
2. Who is ultimately responsible for the quality and effectiveness of a crisis intervention program?
3. Why is it important for other service resources to know about and respect the crisis intervention organization?
4. Jan came to see you because she has a "sizzling stomach." She knew it was time to visit the crisis program because the traffic lights sent her a coded message telling her to come. Although she describes her sizzling stomach, as well as difficulties she is having with her supervisor at work, she smiles pleasantly throughout the interview and shows no signs of distress. Periodically she jerks her head to the side. Jan is 26 years old and she lives at her parents' home. She has never received mental health treatment. She is dressed appropriately and appears to have good hygiene. There is no indication of any self-injury or harm to others. Jan is receptive to the idea of psychiatric treatment, and you decide to contact a psychiatrist to lay the groundwork for a referral. With Jan's permission, what information about her will you convey to the psychiatrist?
5. As a staff member at the crisis center you have been asked to organize an inservice training program for one of the local law enforcement agencies. Further cooperation with that agency is the goal of your effort. In planning and conducting the event, what are some issues you should keep in mind?
6. Nathan and Angela have been involved in a family dispute. The police dispatcher requests a crisis outreach to their residence, and you agree to go. What do you do next?
7. Edna is a 69-year-old widow who is being evicted because her apartment building will be torn down to make way for a new shopping center. She calls you in a panic, saying she must be out in two days. Although she claims a social service agency promised to relocate her, they have not yet found her a place to live. What do you do?
8. While at a restaurant a coworker asks you how Edna is doing. What is your response?

Chapter 8

FOSTERING INTERVENOR EXCELLENCE AND LONGEVITY: SCREENING, TRAINING, AND BURNOUT PREVENTION

Staffing is recognized as a crucial factor influencing a crisis intervention organization's quality of service (e.g., American Association of Suicidology, 2012). High quality results when crisis intervenors display the following three characteristics: (1) they are committed to helping people; (2) they possess adequate crisis intervention skills; and (3) they feel confident that they and their coworkers are providing needed service. When these conditions do not exist the result is a high rate of staff turnover and a low level of service. In order to minimize staff attrition and to maximize service excellence, administrators and front-line personnel must give attention to three areas—staff selection, preservice training, and burnout prevention.

SCREENING

Crisis intervenors come from a variety of educational and professional backgrounds. For workers with college experience, common majors include psychology, nursing, social work, sociology, communications, and criminal justice. Professionals who learn crisis intervention skills include nurses, physicians, clergy, parole and probation officers, correctional officers, psychologists, social workers, counselors, and teachers. And persons with neither a college education nor professional credentials may also seek to become crisis workers. With proper selection and training I believe that individuals from any of these backgrounds can learn to be skilled crisis intervenors and others share my opinion (e.g., Caplan, 1964, 1974; Hoff & Hoff, 2012; McGee & Jennings, 2002; Paterson, Reniers, & Vollm, 2009).

Regardless of education and experience, a person seeking crisis intervention training should have the following characteristics: (a) a desire to empower people to address their issues; (b) the potential to empathically understand others; (c) the ability to think logically and to demonstrate mature judgment; (d) a willingness to spend the time required for preservice training, inservice training, and the provision of crisis intervention services; (e) the ability to cooperate with coworkers and with personnel in other agencies; (f) a sensitivity to confidentiality issues and an ability to be discrete; (g) whole-hearted support for the program's mission combined with both an awareness of one's own values and an absence of the need to force those values on others while functioning as a crisis worker; (h) an appreciation for the complexity of human dilemmas and an avoidance of pat, simplistic solutions; (i) an ability to accept supervision combined with both confidence in one's abilities and acceptance of the boundaries of one's role within the organization; and (j) a stable personality with a balance of optimism and realism (Berman & Lindahl, 2001; Clary & Orenstein, 1991; Donegan, Sullivan, & McGuire, 1982; Hoff & Hoff, 2012; Kalafat, 2002b; Kranz, 1985; Madonia, 1984).

Gil Clary and Leslie Orenstein (1991) investigated the first two criteria (a desire to empower people to address their issues and the potential to empathically understand others) by measuring altruistic motivation (the degree to which one is concerned for others) and spontaneous empathic perspective taking (one's proneness to naturally appreciate the thoughts and feelings of others) between the first and second meetings of a preservice training class at a volunteer-staffed crisis telephone service. Comparing 43 trainees who were terminated by trainers to 118 individuals who successfully completed the 40 hours of training, graduates had averaged significantly higher scores on empathic perspective taking. And comparing 47 training graduates who failed to follow through with their nine-month service obligation to 71 graduates who were faithful to their commitment, the completers had generated a significantly higher average score on altruistic motivation. The authors also found that there was no correlation between altruistic motivation and perspective taking, indicating that wanting to help people and empathically understanding others are two separate factors.

Some individuals want to become crisis workers because of their own unresolved psychological difficulties. What happens when such persons respond to clients? Neimeyer, Fortner, and Melby (2001) examined that question. They recruited undergraduate psychology students, suicide hotline volunteers, and clinical and counseling psychology graduate students, then asked them to choose appropriate helping responses to written statements by suicidal "clients." The researchers found that the factor most highly correlated with performance was the participant's own suicidal tendencies (frequency of past suicidal behaviors and self-assessed future suicide risk)—in general, the greater the "helper's" suicidal tendencies, the higher the number of "non-facilitative" responses. As Gerald Caplan (1964) noted, just as the carrier of a communicable disease can spread infection, an intervenor who is psychologically maladjusted may encourage clients to choose unhealthy problem-solving techniques and may try to impose his or her own maladaptive coping patterns on others.

A past episode of emotional disturbance should not preclude subsequent crisis work. But in order to be selected as a trainee or as a staff member the person should not have ongoing psychological difficulties that hamper performance. Problematic issues need to be faced and adaptively dealt with before an individual attempts to help others.

Administrators use a variety of screening devices to select crisis workers. Some require applicants to take psychological tests. Although such assessment can identify clearly inappropriate individuals, personality tests are not very effective in making finer distinctions (e.g., Ansel, 1972; Donegan et al., 1982).

Even when there are significant group differences on relevant psychological measures, the overlap in scores among group members may mean that it is impractical to make screening decisions based on an individual's scores. For example, in the study by Clary and Orenstein (1991) reported above, within the screened out, dropped out, and completed commitment groups, there were large variances in altruistic motivation scores and in empathic perspective taking scores. And the significant differences in group means were relatively small in terms of absolute magnitude. In other words, there was a good deal of overlap among groups, so that some dropouts had higher altruistic motivation scores than some completers, and some terminated volunteers had higher empathic understanding scores than some graduates.

In a slightly different vein, many volunteer organizations use screening interviews and role playing to select trainees (e.g., Kalafat, 2002b). Empirical research (e.g., Sakowitz & Hirschman, 1977) has demonstrated, however, that the aptitude of individuals for learning crisis intervention techniques is not restricted by the level of their pretraining helping abilities. Although there may be a correlation between measured pretraining and posttraining communication skills, Albano and Glenwick (1990) found that the correlation accounted for a minority of the variance in the posttraining scores of workers. In other words, most of the posttraining variance in communication skills was accounted for by something other than the participants' pretraining skill levels. And this other factor probably was the amount of learning that took place in the training program. Further support for the overriding importance of training comes from a study by Lorraine Hart and Glen King (1979) in which trainees selected on the basis of their pretraining crisis intervention skills performed no better than self-selected workers after completion of the same training program.

In addition to their questionable usefulness, there is another problem with screening interviews and psychological testing. Both endeavors are time-consuming. For example, at one crisis center the training coordinator spent more time screening applicants than training the staff.

I believe the most efficient volunteer selection method is to use preservice training as a screening device, and that is the approach I have used in each of the three volunteer training programs I have directed. When a program specifies the skills expected of crisis workers, the trainees can evaluate their own desire and ability to offer those skills. If individuals discover that they do not wish to assist people in this way or that they cannot master the material to be learned, then they can choose to help people in some way other than crisis intervention.

In one training program I directed, each person expressing an interest in becoming a crisis worker received an application. The form asked for a detailed personal history and described the characteristics expected of trainees (cited earlier), and the application stated, "If you believe you have these skills you will be accepted into the training class." Half of the individuals who received forms completed them, and 96 percent of the applicants began the training class. Of the trainees who participated in at least one session, 67 percent became crisis workers.

I screened out only 4 percent of the individuals who completed preservice training, so my own experience supports the finding by Ginsberg and Danish (1979) that most self-selected trainees can learn the necessary skills. Of the trainees who did become crisis workers, 94 percent successfully completed their minimum service commitment of six months, and 80 percent of those remained with the organization past the half-year requirement.

Starting with the application form and continuing throughout training, participants received clear statements of expectations. When individuals concluded they were not suited for crisis work, they were allowed to screen themselves out.

The self-selection method has three advantages. It recognizes the competence of trainees in assessing their own abilities. It is efficient in terms of staff time. And it has unsurpassed accuracy in identifying motivated and capable workers.

When selecting full-time crisis workers, participation in such a preservice class usually is not an option. Experts (e.g., Hoff & Hoff, 2012) have noted that effective alternatives include the successful completion of a college course in crisis intervention and previous service as an intern or as a volunteer crisis worker. Such experiences provide individuals with opportunities to assess their own interests and abilities. In addition, course instructors and program supervisors can serve as valuable employment references.

PRESERVICE TRAINING

Minimum Training

Years of education and supervised experience are not necessary in order for a person to offer quality crisis intervention services. But simply having the time and the desire to help people does not sufficiently qualify an individual to do crisis intervention. Research (e.g., France, 1975a, 1975b; Kalafat et al., 1979) has shown that workers who have not been trained in basic helping skills do not provide the facilitative levels of empathy, warmth, and genuineness necessary for developing a positive relationship. Empirical research (e.g., D'Augelli, Danish, & Brock, 1976; McCarthy & Knapp, 1984) also demonstrates that untrained individuals offer problem-solving assistance that is too directive; they do not explore feelings sufficiently; and they rely too much on controlling techniques such as asking closed questions and giving advice. Likewise, empirical research (e.g., D'Augelli et al., 1978; Doyle, Foreman, & Wales, 1977; Margolis, Edwards, Shrier, & Cramer, 1975) has demonstrated that brief training programs of a few hours in length are insufficient to develop essential communication skills. Based on empirical investigation, researchers (Schinke, Smith, Myers, & Altman, 1979) have concluded that although well designed workshops can increase knowledge of crisis intervention techniques, one or two days of training cannot teach the full range of skills needed by crisis workers.

The American Association of Suicidology states that trainees should receive at least 32 hours of formal training (American Association of Suicidology, 2012), and some programs offer more (e.g., Paukert, Stagner, & Hope, 2004). I believe a significant portion of preservice training should be devoted to communication skills, with time allotted for each trainee to do eight role plays involving specific feedback on the person's performance as a worker.

Even when trainees already possess good skills it is advantageous for them to participate in preservice training. During the training sessions individuals with advanced abilities can serve as models and can provide valuable feedback to other participants.

Training Format

The most efficient way to build necessary skills and attitudes is through practice and feedback. Role playing allows trainees to try out content they have studied, to discover what they do well, and to focus on areas for improvement. Empirical research (e.g., Evans, Uhlemann, & Hearn, 1978; Schinke & Rose, 1976) has demonstrated that training programs emphasizing role playing result in better communication skills than either didactic training alone or didactic training combined with general sensitivity training.

There probably is no better way for a trainer to spend time than by conducting role plays. But time is limited, and role playing is a time-consuming technique. The effective use of this valuable method requires careful planning on the part of trainers.

Role plays lasting three to six minutes provide sufficient practice to learn basic helping skills, and they are long enough for trainers to assess the performance levels of participants. These brief role plays supply ample material for constructive feedback, while the segment of behavior is still small enough for the participant not to be overwhelmed with criticism.

When my trainers and I use brief role plays, the leader asks the "worker" to leave the room, then gives the scenario to the "client." After the client describes the circumstances and feelings in his or her own words, the worker returns and the role play takes place. The interaction is recorded on either audio or video media.

After the trainer stops the role play, the worker describes what he or she liked or didn't like about the interview, then the client gives feedback, followed by feedback from the other participants, and finally from the trainer. While receiving feedback, the worker just listens; following the trainer's comments the person can respond. The trainer either plays the recording following the worker's remarks or gives it to the trainee (to be played later). After the feedback is completed the participants can bring up issues that came to mind during the interaction. The time from the beginning of one role play to the beginning of the next is about 20–25 minutes when the recording is played in the group and about 15–20 minutes when the participant plays it later.

A variation on this technique is to divide the class into groups of three. For each role play there is a worker, a client, and an observer (who writes down the comments made by the worker). This technique can allow either longer role plays or increased role-play opportunities for trainees. It also gives a single trainer the ability to lead a large group of participants.

Having multiple trainers is a better way to increase trainer-trainee contact time. For example, I have helped to institute pyramid systems of trainers at a comprehensive crisis center, a community hotline, a college course, a victim/witness assistance program, a statewide juvenile justice system, a campus crisis telephone service, and an Internet-based crisis intervention program.

If preservice training is accomplished via the Internet, one way of doing live text-chat role playing is through an instant messaging system. The basis for such role plays can be edited dialogs derived from transcripts involving actual chatters. Prior to beginning a one-to-one training session, the trainer can open the dialog. During the role play the trainer can then copy and paste chatter comments from the dialog (editing them as necessary).

As has been noted, though, Internet text chat does not allow nontext-based communication. Since the need for the trainer to be perceived as supportive is crucial, it is a good idea to begin and end each training session with oral communication (by phone or other means) between the trainee and the trainer.

The training session can begin with the trainee and the trainer communicating through the instant messaging system. If telephone contact is to be used, the trainer can then place a call to the trainee.

The initial conversation can provide the opportunity for discussing any questions or issues the trainee would like to raise. Once those have been addressed, the trainer can describe what will be happening in the session they are about to do.

Upon returning to the instant messaging system, the trainer can send a comment such as, "The next statement from me will be as the chatter." The trainer then copies the first chatter comment in the dialog and pastes it into the instant messaging box. The role play can continue until the trainee makes 8 to 12 responses, which generally takes 15 to 25 minutes. The trainer then signals a stop to the role play and encourages the trainee to go back and review the instant messaging exchanges. The trainer takes about 10 minutes to produce a feedback email. That is accomplished by copying the instant messaging role play and pasting it into an email message. After each trainee response the trainer can then enter feedback comments. (In order for those to be easily distinguished, one option is to type them in all capital letters.) At the end of the transcript the trainer can also make some general observations about the role play.

The trainer can attach the dialog on which the role play was based, then send the email feedback and the attached document to the trainee (with the option of sending copies to training and program supervisors). Once the trainee has read the feedback, there can be instant messaging discussion about it. If the trainer wishes to do so, that exchange can also be copied and pasted into an email, then sent to the trainee (with the option of sending copies to training and program supervisors). Another helpful action is to send the trainee the actual transcript on which the dialog was based. The session ends with a second oral conversation. Progress and issues are discussed, and the next session can be scheduled.

Such a session takes about an hour, compared to about 20 minutes to accomplish similar tasks in oral role playing. Just as is true in interactions with chatters, Internet-based training using text chat is much more time-consuming than face-to-face training.

Although role playing is a fundamental skill development technique, it should not be the sole training method. For instance, an efficient way of covering content is through readings. (For an Internet-based program, those can be web pages with text material and audio or video clips.) Study questions on the material can provide springboards into discussion.

Observation shifts can also be helpful. Trainees can observe worker-client interactions and can begin to familiarize themselves with the program's physical facilities, record-keeping procedures, and resource files. (With Internet-based programs, many shifts may be done from the workers' residences. When that is the case, trainees can read transcripts of interactions and can become familiar with the organization's home and resource web pages.)

After completing the group meeting and observation phase of training, the successful trainee should serve several supervision shifts in which the person's work is monitored by a trainer or by another experienced worker. The American Association of Suicidology states that trainees should receive at least eight hours of such supervision and should handle a minimum of three crisis contacts before being cleared for independent service (American Association of Suicidology, 2012).

Research (Doyle et al., 1977) indicates that workers keep on improving their communication skills when they receive continuous supervision for several shifts following group-oriented training. Individuals given appropriate on-the-spot supervision demonstrate significantly higher levels of empathy and are judged by their clients to be more understanding and helpful than trainees who do not have such close supervision.

Feedback

Providing feedback to trainees is the primary purpose of both role playing and supervision shifts. By communicating what they perceive as effective or ineffective, observers encourage trainees to maintain their present behavior or to make appropriate adjustments. Since the intent of feedback is to help the receiver plan future behavior in light of past actions, feedback is effective only if the other person uses it.

Good feedback has several characteristics:

• *Specific and immediate.* The most valuable observations are those that describe specific behavior that the person has just displayed. On the other hand, feedback is ineffective when it judges personality traits, contains vague generalities, or focuses on behavior from the distant past.

• *Small doses.* We all have limits on how much criticism we can absorb at one time. In group training situations trainers can prevent overloading by keeping feedback focused on what the participants actually did in the role play.

If feedback puts the receiver on the defensive the person will attempt to avoid the sender's message rather than try to accept it. For feedback to be a learning tool, senders must pay attention to both the behavior they observe and the messages they send.

BURNOUT PREVENTION

Carolyn Cyr and Peter Dowrick (1991) found that burning out in less than a year was a common phenomenon among crisis intervention volunteers. In a survey of volunteers that included a section on ways of preventing and managing burnout, frequently endorsed factors included the following: realize the limits of your role, realize that clients may not take advantage of available help, and realize that some clients may not profit from your efforts. I agree with the opinions of those volunteers.

A fundamental tenet of crisis intervention is client competency. In most instances, those we assist remain responsible for the actions they take and the resulting consequences. The outcomes they experience arise primarily out of their own efforts, not ours. When a crisis intervenor takes the weight of the world on his or her own shoulders, the worker invariably finds that the burden is too much, with burnout as the most common result. Rather than trying to assume responsibility for those we serve, we must remember that, for the most part, they are responsible for making their own decisions.

In a survey of crisis telephone volunteers who had completed preservice training, John Lammers (1991) found that two factors best predicted length of service—features of the work and interactions with other volunteers. Volunteers tended to stay longer if (1) they saw the work as challenging, interesting, and requiring responsibility, and (2) they worked as a team, solved problems together, and were friends.

Staff motivation can have a profound influence on the quality of care that a crisis intervention organization offers. A program cannot provide effective service if it is staffed by burned-out personnel.

When workers burn out they lose concern for clients. Researchers (e.g., Cyr & Dowrick, 1991) have noted both emotional and behavioral indications of burnout. Emotional signs include feeling irritable, depressed, helpless, hopeless, fatigued, apathetic, alienated, or withdrawn. Behavioral signs include intervening in a "mechanical" way, prematurely discontinuing contacts, giving inaccurate information, putting all crisis telephone lines on "hold," failing to show up for shifts, or simply quitting. Administrators can minimize burnout by giving appropriate attention to the following four areas: case management, staffing patterns, staff meetings, and inservice training and supervision.

Case Management

Crisis workers should serve persons they are trained to assist. If crisis intervenors are expected to help individuals who have long-standing problems, the workers should be trained in behavior change techniques that have been shown to be effective with the particular chronic conditions they are trying to ameliorate. When services are limited to crisis intervention, experts (e.g., Bengelsdorf & Alden, 1987) assert that effective case management requires workers to refer noncrisis clients to more appropriate resources.

The need for such referral includes clients who have sexual problems. Providing sex therapy is beyond the scope of crisis intervention. Although a variety of opinions have been expressed in the literature (e.g., Steley, 1990), I believe that no intervention is necessary in the case of sexually abusive callers who masturbate while a worker talks. In my opinion, the appropriate response to such individuals is to terminate the call.

Baird, Bossett, and Smith (1994) suggested that the worker read a prepared statement before hanging up the phone. Here is a paraphrase of their script. "Right now I'm wondering whether you would be interested in talking to someone face-to-face about your need to make calls like this one. The next time you pick up the phone to start such an interaction, I want you to recall what I'm saying right now and to wonder whether you should contact a counselor to arrange an appointment. Your need for face-to-face therapy will be more and more apparent every time you have a desire to place a call like the one you have made to me. I believe that dealing with your need by deciding to seek therapy will be associated with feelings of confidence that you are making the right decision. At that point we would be happy to supply you with information about available counseling resources. For now, though, I am going to end the call so you can consider what I've said." The staff member reads the script straight through, without responding to any attempted interruptions, then hangs up. This strategy provides limited opportunity for abuse of the worker, while also planting the seeds of ideas that eventually may help to change the person's behavior.

Crisis telephone workers, especially female staff members, commonly feel angry about being used and manipulated by sexually abusive callers. I agree with the assertion by front-line workers that providing stimulation for masturbating callers is not a legitimate role for crisis workers.

Program administrators must appropriately address issues related to non-crisis contacts, including obscene calls. Failure to do so increases the probability of staff burnout. For example, at a hotline mentioned in the beginning of the last chapter, the majority of contacts were sexually abusive calls in which male callers masturbated while talking to female workers. Such callers got what they wanted from the hotline because the program's administrators believed it was better for these men to phone the volunteer workers than to call women in the community.

For this hotline, "loneliness" was the second-most frequent reason for calling. Many of these lonely callers were experiencing recurrent depression, a condition outside the workers' area of expertise. The chronically lonely clients not only frustrated the workers, but many of them used the telephone service rather than develop friendships, become more assertive, or seek therapy. As a result, the phone contacts actually became a detriment to these clients rather than a help.

As you might expect, this hotline had a high rate of staff turnover. Much of the program's difficulty in keeping quality workers was due to the administrators' misguided case management.

Staffing Patterns

In a study of volunteer workers at a suicide prevention center, Brian Mishara and Guy Giroux (1993) found that higher amounts of total direct service time during a shift were significantly related to stress during the intervenor's highest-urgency call, as well as to postshift stress. They also found that postshift stress declined as the number of staff members on the shift increased.

Having at least two staff members on a shift is a good idea for several reasons. Often the work load is more than one person can handle, and some modes of service—such as outreach—require a team approach. When business is slow, two workers are still better than one because there is someone with whom to interact. If administrators do not use a team system and staff members must repeatedly serve crisis shifts alone, this lonely and tiring endeavor makes these workers high risks for burnout. (For Internet-based services in which workers do shifts from home, one option is for staff members to routinely log on to the instant messaging system whenever they are on the Internet. That way, during a shift, there usually are off-duty workers who are immediately available through the instant messaging system.)

The amount of client contact time can also contribute to burnout of crisis workers. Although volunteers who serve once a week may enjoy spending their entire shifts providing direct service to clients, full-time crisis workers who put in forty hours a week soon will burn out if each shift contains little or no respite from direct client contact. For example, one crisis service took on the intake function for a mental health center without increasing the direct service staff. The dramatic rise in walk-in contacts placed considerable stress on the front-line workers. As a result, morale suffered and staff turnover increased.

Just as staff members should not be overburdened, they also ought not to become bored. It is invigorating for workers to use their full potential, and many want to do more than fill crisis intervention shifts. If an organization expects to keep such talented and motivated individuals, administrators must provide other opportunities for service. Although potential roles vary from one organization to another, some common possibilities include case manager, trainer, community liaison, crisis group leader, and shift supervisor. (Research reviewed by Russell and Petrie [1994] indicates that while supervisors need a minimum amount of experience, once that minimum is met, additional direct-service time does not lead to further increases in supervision effectiveness.) When staff members believe their talents are being well used, they tend to be more satisfied and less likely to burn out.

Staff Meetings

Arranging periodic staff meetings is another way of encouraging individuals to maintain both their involvement in the organization and their commitment to helping people in crisis. Depending upon the focus of the meeting, staff members may contribute to case management decisions, learn new information, or express concerns to administrators. Staff meeting activities seeming useful to workers is correlated with both their overall satisfaction in their role and with their intent to continue in their position, as demonstrated in empirical research by Chan Hellman and Donnita House (2006).

Crisis intervenors face the emotional drain of intense tragedies and life-threatening emergencies, as well as the frustration of guiding clients through bureaucratic referral networks. Staff members often cope with these stressors by talking with their coworkers. Various organizations meet this need for sharing through activities such as parties, softball games, picnics, retreats, covered-dish dinners, and rituals like going to the local pizza parlor after the formal staff meeting. Such occasions allow workers to build companionship, release tension, express feelings, and compare their experiences to those of their coworkers.

If staff members meet informally, two considerations should guide those get-togethers. First, workers must not discuss clients in public places. Second, in a twenty-four-hour-a-day program someone must "hold down the fort." Administrators should schedule activities and shifts so that this responsibility is shared rather than always falling on the same individuals.

Inservice Training and Supervision

In a survey of ten representative crisis intervention agencies, Richard McGee (1974) found those programs that demanded high commitment and excellent performance from staff members were also the organizations that had the best services and the fewest morale problems. Inservice training and supervision were two of the ways in which the strong programs fostered those positive outcomes.

The American Association of Suicidology recommends that workers receive at least six hours of inservice instruction per year (American Association of Suicidology, 2012). Such training should focus on needs identified by front-line staff, as well as on priorities set by administrators. When this is the case and the selection of topics is shared by workers and administrators, both groups are more likely to perceive the training as being time well spent.

The American Association of Suicidology also recommends that staff members receive a minimum of one clinical supervision hour for every forty hours on duty or every three months–whichever comes first. This supervision can be done individually or in a group setting (American Association of Suicidology, 2012).

In a survey of crisis intervention volunteers, the previously mentioned research by Cyr and Dowrick (1991) found that effective supervision was the theme of two out of the top three factors the volunteers endorsed as ways of preventing or managing burnout. One factor was supervision support, which included being encouraged by the supervisor and having the supervisor available during the shift, and the other factor was the supervisor demonstrating appreciation of the volunteer through actions such as stating the person's importance to the program and involving the individual in organizational efforts and decisions.

Like Cyr and Dowrick (1991), other researchers (e.g., Russell & Petrie, 1994) have identified qualities that characterize good supervision. Here are some commonly cited themes:

- *Emotional support.* Both administrators and workers believe that emotional support on the part of supervisors is a vital aspect of the supervisory relationship. To be effective a supervisor must be trustworthy and must demonstrate understanding of staff members' feelings, as well as respect for their abilities.

- *Client focus.* Within this supportive atmosphere the most desirable feedback is information that focuses on clients and teaches (1) useful ways of conceptualizing material and (2) appropriate intervention techniques. Supervisors may take a number of approaches, including the following: give positive feedback on effective interventions, suggest alternatives for an ongoing case, discuss issues associated with certain types of clients, or describe relevant work experiences of their own.
- *Modeling.* Good supervisors model the personal qualities and intervention skills that they expect workers to demonstrate. Although supervisors tend not to perceive the importance of their own behavior, most workers say they are influenced by the examples set by supervisors.
- *Availability.* When workers are asked to describe the one essential quality that a supervisor must have, the characteristic getting the most votes is availability. Good supervisors are easy to contact. They welcome interactions with workers, and they willingly give a sufficient amount of time.
- *Flexibility.* There are multiple domains in which staff members need leadership, support, and feedback. By flexibly responding to workers' changing needs, supervisors help them continue to grow and develop.

Russell and Petrie (1994) also noted empirically derived characteristics of bad supervision. Those include the following: disinterest, lack of support, incompetence, and exploitation. With regard to that final negative characteristic, ethical codes (e.g., American Psychological Association, 2002) explicitly prohibit a supervisor from having a sexual relationship with a supervisee.

SUMMARY

The success of a crisis intervention organization largely depends upon effective staffing practices. Key areas are screening, preservice training, and burnout prevention.

Although trainees come from a variety of educational and professional backgrounds, essential qualities include common sense, a desire for training and supervision, a commitment to helping others, and a stable personality. An excellent way of selecting individuals with those characteristics is to use preservice training as a screening device.

Thirty-two hours is the minimum amount of training for a crisis worker, with time enough for eight role plays focusing on helping skills. Effective training components include readings, discussions, role playing, observation shifts, and front-line supervision. During all of these experiences, feedback to participants should be specific and immediate and it should come in small doses.

When workers burn out, they lose concern for those they serve. But there are ways of preventing burnout. Thoughtful case management results in workers assisting persons they are trained to help. Good staffing means there are sufficient staff members to do the job and sufficient jobs to keep the staff interested. Periodic staff meetings give workers opportunities to participate in case management decisions, to learn new information, to express concerns to administrators, and to provide support to coworkers. Relevant inservice training and supervision help keep workers energized, up-to-date, and effective.

STUDY QUESTIONS

1. What professional credentials are required in order to become a crisis worker?
2. What characteristics should a crisis intervention trainee possess?
3. What priority should be given to communication skills training for crisis workers?
4. Note which one of the following feedback statements is more effective, and give the reasons for it being preferable.
   (A) "After you interrupted four or five times the other person stopped talking."
   (B) "I've heard you have a habit of interrupting. Let's see what else you're doing wrong."
5. Catherine has been a crisis worker for two years. During that time she has fallen into a routine of working shifts by herself and talking to many repeat callers who are chronically lonely. She now finds she is downplaying the severity of all clients' concerns, and she dreads going to work. What is Catherine experiencing, and how can it be remedied?
6. For a worker who desires more responsibility, what are some possible roles?
7. John, Karen, Sally, Mike, and Pam are crisis workers who have been very busy lately. Things at the crisis center have become hectic, and some of the workers are feeling emotionally drained. Consequently, at a recent staff meeting John suggested that the workers get together for a monthly night out. What are two important considerations that crisis workers need to address when they meet informally?
8. What are five qualities of good supervision?

Chapter 9

EVALUATION OF CRISIS INTERVENTION

This chapter briefly reviews three areas of research—assumptions of crisis intervention, client outcome, and staff performance. Within each of those domains there are empirical findings relevant to the provision of high-quality crisis intervention services. In addition to knowing what the professional literature has to offer, crisis intervenors can also benefit from evaluations of their own efforts. To this end, the chapter concludes by presenting an assessment approach that any clinician can use to collect relevant evaluation information.

ASSUMPTIONS OF CRISIS INTERVENTION

With regard to persons in crisis it is assumed that they are (1) experiencing increased emotional distress, (2) dissatisfied with their coping efforts, and (3) interested in receiving help. In order to investigate those assumptions Howard Halpern (1973, 1975) compared 89 individuals believed to be in crisis to 89 persons not in crisis. In contrast to his noncrisis subjects, he found those in crisis felt more helpless, anxious, confused, and overwhelmed, and demonstrated greater doubt about their ability to cope successfully in social situations. On the positive side, the individuals in crisis were less defensive and more receptive to help.

An additional assumption of crisis intervention is that the approach works best with persons who are in crisis. Endler, Edwards, and Kowalchuk (1983) collected evidence relevant to this assumption by studying 58 outpatient clients of the Crisis Intervention Unit at Toronto East General Hospital. The researchers measured the transitory condition of state anxiety (the degree of anxiety experienced right now) and the enduring characteristic of trait anxi-

243

ety (the extent to which the person generally feels anxious) during both the first and last crisis contacts. Although participants showed a significant decrease in state anxiety over the course of the intervention, those low in trait anxiety showed much larger decreases than those high in trait anxiety. In other words, both groups experienced reductions in situational tension, but the essentially normal subjects displayed greater reductions than the subjects who were chronically anxious. The investigators concluded that crisis intervention met the needs of low trait anxiety individuals who found themselves in crisis, while additional therapeutic intervention was necessary for crisis clients who had high trait anxiety.

Another Canadian study examined differences between chronically suicidal persons and acutely suicidal individuals placing calls to two volunteer-staffed suicide prevention centers (Suicide-Action Montreal and Carrefour Intervention Suicide, Sherbrooke, Quebec). Brian Mishara and Marc Daigle (1997) collected data on 617 calls. (These are the same 617 calls described in the 1995 study by Daigle and Mishara mentioned in Chapter 1, but that analysis addressed different research questions.) Twenty-five percent of the 263 callers were considered to be "chronic"—meaning they were long-standing repeat callers experiencing recurring difficulties. Fifty-two percent of those frequent callers were known to be taking psychotropic medications, and 60 percent were known to be receiving mental health services. The researchers divided into two categories the response styles used by workers in the 617 calls—226 calls had a "Directive Style" involving frequent investigation and suggestion, whereas 391 calls were determined to have a "Rogerian Style" characterized by frequent acceptance. The researchers divided the Rogerian calls into thirds according to whether they were low, moderate, or high in their use of the responses characteristic of that style. For the minority of both acute and chronic callers who experienced decreases in researcher-rated depression during the call, the moderate and high Rogerian groups had significantly greater reductions than the low Rogerian group. For the minority of acute callers for whom the volunteer believed suicidal urgency had lessened, increases in the proportion of Rogerian responses were associated with significantly larger decreases in suicidal urgency. For chronic callers, increases in Rogerian responses did not lead to significantly larger decreases in suicidal urgency. A similar pattern was found with regard to the rate at which callers developed a plan by the end of the call; acute callers showed significantly increased rates of plan development associated with higher levels of Rogerian responses, whereas chronic callers showed no significant differences in plan development associated with increases in Rogerian responses. The researchers concluded that their findings suggest acute callers may benefit from different types of intervention than frequent callers.

Available research supports fundamental assumptions about persons in crisis and about crisis intervention. Individuals in crisis experience emotional distress, perceive their coping efforts to be ineffective, and want help. Skilled crisis intervention can be sufficient for persons overwhelmed by a sudden upsurge in difficulties, but clients with chronic problems require more extensive assistance.

CLIENT OUTCOME

Researchers have used a variety of strategies to evaluate the effectiveness of crisis intervention. For example, a study (King, Nurcombe, Bickman, Hides, & Reid, 2003) of Australia's Kids Help Line focused on independent ratings of crisis calls. Raters listened to recordings of five early minutes and the last five minutes from 101 calls by persons under the age of 18. Using specially designed scales, the raters evaluated the callers on the following three dimensions: mental state (e.g., anger, sadness, hopelessness, distress, guilt, slowed speech), suicidal ideation (e.g., seeing death as preferable, ideas of nondeadly self-harm, thinking about suicide, and having a plan for suicide), and suicidal urgency (e.g., threating nondeadly self-harm that is not imminent, threating nondeadly self-harm that is imminent, threating suicide that is not imminent and for which the means are unspecified or unrealistic, threating suicide that is imminent and for which the means are unspecified or unrealistic, threating suicide that is not imminent and for which the means are specified and deadly, threating suicide that is imminent and for which the means are specified and deadly). At the beginning of the calls, 93 of the young people were suicidal, compared to 14 at the end of the calls, and on all three measured dimensions (mental state, suicidal ideation, and suicidal urgency) there were significant decreases by the end of the calls.

The remaining studies described in this section are divided into the following three categories of client outcome research: referral follow-up, client surveys, and controlled experimentation.

Referral Follow-Up

One measure of an intervention's effectiveness is whether or not the client follows through with the agreed-upon plan. If a referral was part of the plan, then an indicator of success is the client actually contacting the community resource.

At Suicide Prevention, Inc. of St. Louis, researchers (Murphy, Wetzel, Swallow, & McClure, 1969) interviewed 37 callers who were referred to other resources. Eighteen (49%) of the clients said they had contacted the suggested organization or professional.

Investigators (Buchta, Wetzel, Reich, Butler, & Fuller, 1973) at the Call for Help service of St. Clair County (Illinois) examined the number of callers who were referred to an agency and actually obtained service there. In interviews conducted one month after contact with the crisis service, researchers discovered a referral success rate of 60 percent in the 115 cases studied.

At the Nashville Crisis Call Center, follow-up information was obtained on 51 callers who had been referred to mental health agencies. Of that group, 25 (49%) clients actually contacted the suggested organization (Nelson, 1972).

A series of studies at the Suicide Prevention and Crisis Service of Erie County (New York) shed some light on what makes a referral successful. Investigators found that the best predictor of whether or not callers appeared for walk-in appointments was their *degree of interest* in obtaining a referral for face-to-face contact (Slaikeu, Lester, & Tulkin, 1973; Slaikeu, Tulkin, & Speer, 1975; Tapp, Slaikeu, & Tulkin, 1974; Walfish, Tapp, Tulkin, Slaikeu, & Russell, 1975).

Madelyn Gould and her associates (2012) conducted a study involving follow-up interviews with 376 suicidal callers and 278 nonsuicidal callers to 16 participating centers in the National Suicide Prevention Lifeline. In each instance the crisis intervention worker had referred the caller to a mental health or behavioral health resource. Overall, 42 percent of the callers followed through with the referral (44% of the suicidal callers and 39% nonsuicidal callers). Another 10 percent of the suicidal callers and 10 percent of the nonsuicidal callers contacted a similar resource to which they had not been referred, for an overall utilization rate of 52 percent of mental health resources following the call. A majority of those who did not use a mental health resource said they did not do so because they thought their issues could be handled on their own without treatment. That reason was reported significantly more often than any other reason for not following up. The researchers concluded that workers must recognize and respect callers' self-efficacy when making referrals.

John Kalafat and his associates (2007) conducted research that included information on "nonsuicidal" callers to eight telephone crisis services in the United States. There were 392 callers who were given a new mental health referral. Information gathered during follow-up contacts (occurring 1 day to 52 days after the call) indicated that 33 percent of the callers had made and/or kept an appointment with the resource.

The same research team also collected information on suicidal callers to the eight telephone crisis services (Gould, Kalafat, Harris-Munfakh, & Kleinman, 2007). There were 151 suicidal callers who received a new mental health referral. Information at follow-up indicated 35 percent of those individuals had made and/or kept an appointment with the resource.

Referral success rates ranging from 33 percent to 60 percent, combined with the demonstrated importance of the client's degree of interest in a referral, suggest that crisis workers make many referrals that clients do not want. (Unfortunately, my own experience also supports this conclusion.) In order for a plan to be effective it must result from a *collaborative* effort that takes into account the client's needs, values, and beliefs.

Client Surveys

Several investigators have surveyed clients in an effort to evaluate consumer satisfaction. In Newcastle upon Tyne in northern England, the Crisis Assessment and Treatment Service currently uses a survey based on information gathered through interviews with a sample of 70 individuals who used the service during its first sixteen months of existence (Hopkins & Niemiec, 2007). Although a phone service was part of the organization, the interviews primarily focused on the program's outreach teams. The interviewers explored what qualities recipients valued with regard to outreach service they received at home during a crisis. Investigators discovered the following seven themes: *accessibility* in the form of the teams' quick response; *availability* of caring and responsive service 24 hours a day, 7 days a week; *consistency* in the form of using previously developed information and plans relating to the person, as well as being there when promised—or informing the individual if there was going to be an unavoidable delay; *quality* as reflected in the development of rapport and a therapeutic alliance in support of a focus on solutions incorporating the person's strengths; *choice and negotiation* in the form of respecting the individual's ability to make decisions when the person was ready to do so; clear *communication* by team members in all interactions; active collaboration enabling individuals to anticipate *changes and endings* in service provision.

At a Washington crisis organization associated with both a community mental health center and a hospital emergency room, 104 clients who received single-session interventions were interviewed six to twelve months later. Although 80 percent of the clients described the physicians, nurses, and other emergency room staff as either "helpful" or "very helpful," 85 percent of the respondents rated the crisis workers in those two categories. And on a five-point scale (1=low, 5=high) the average self-rated improvement for clients was 4.00 (Getz, Fujita, & Allen, 1975).

In a campus population survey that included sixty-six callers to the crisis telephone service in Auburn (Alabama), 76 percent of the former clients rated the help received as effective (King, 1977).

Follow-up contacts with 109 clients of the Hennepin County Crisis Intervention Center in Minneapolis indicated that 79 percent were "satisfied" or "very satisfied" with the service provided (Stelmachers, Lund, & Meade, 1972).

David Speer and Mark Schultz (1975) questioned 72 clients at the Suicide Prevention and Crisis Service of Erie County who came to the walk-in clinic after being referred there by a center phone worker. When asked to compare the telephone counseling they had received to the helpfulness of their most recent call to a friend or family member, they judged the crisis telephone worker as being more understanding and helpful.

Of 142 callers receiving follow-up contacts at the Crisis Center of San Antonio Area, Inc., 96 percent rated the assistance as "helpful" or "very helpful," and 98 percent believed the worker had understood their concerns (Preston, Schoenfeld, & Adams, 1975).

At the Telephone Counseling and Referral Service in Austin (Texas) investigators (Slaikeu & Willis, 1978) interviewed 74 callers several days after contact with the agency. On a five-point scale, 80 percent of the clients classified the intervention as helpful. As a group the 74 callers also experienced a significant decrease in the perceived severity of the problem during the days following the intervention. Attributions for this change included the following: the call (43%), action taken by the client (26%), the passage of time (23%), and assistance from another person (7%).

In a study (Beers & Foreman, 1976) of 10 workers at the University of Cincinnati walk-in center, 30 clients evaluated the effectiveness of the crisis intervention. Researchers asked the clients to use five-point scales (1=low, 5=high) to assess how well the worker understood their problems, how much they benefited from the intervention, and whether they would recommend the service to a friend. The workers' average effectiveness score was 3.94.

Donovan, Bennett, and McElroy (1979) studied 43 clients who participated in at least four crisis group sessions at the Harvard Community Health Plan. The researchers collected information at the following three points: prior to the person joining the group, at termination, and one year after termination. All of the clients sought help due to an interpersonal crisis—most frequently marital problems or trouble in other close relationships. Measures taken at termination indicated that the participants were significantly less anxious and more flexible than they had been before the group, and that 91 percent believed the group had been helpful. In response to questionnaires administered one year after termination, 78 percent believed the group had helped to resolve their crises, and 82 percent said they had maintained the changes made as a result of their group participation. Compared to termination levels, the clients' self-ratings one year later also indicated that depression and anxiety were significantly lower, and that spontaneity was significantly higher. When asked to recall helpful aspects of the group, former participants most frequently mentioned trusting in the mutual support of members, encountering others who had similar problems, and having the opportunity to share feelings.

Hornblow and Sloane (1980) interviewed 214 individuals who had recently called the Christchurch (New Zealand) Life Line. The investigators compared caller responses to worker ratings and concluded that in 63 percent of the calls, the staff member had correctly identified at least one of the client's two strongest emotions. Among callers with whom a worker had negotiated a plan, 68 percent said they had begun implementation. When asked to rate the worker's understanding and helpfulness, 68 percent of the respondents assigned the maximum rating of five.

Gingerich, Gurney, and Wirtz (1988) telephoned 171 clients of a crisis service seven to fourteen days after each had called the program. Ninety-one percent said the worker had been helpful. On a rating scale measuring the quality of help received, clients were asked to label the assistance they received as being "poor," "average," "good," or "excellent." The following percentages of clients gave "good" or "excellent" ratings for the listed behavior: ability to listen, 96 percent; interest and concern, 94 percent; accuracy of information, 86 percent; and ability to understand concerns, 87 percent. At follow-up 55 percent of the clients rated their problem as less severe than when they had called, 36 percent said it had not changed, and the remainder believed conditions had worsened.

Kirk, Stanley, and Brown (1988) studied 32 walk-in clients to an outpatient crisis intervention unit at a metropolitan hospital in Australia. The researchers measured stress before and after the initial contact, then checked to see whether the client followed through with the agreed-upon plan. Ninety-three percent of the clients did carry out the plan, thereby suggesting a successful intervention. In order to study pre- and postsession stress, the investigators divided the subjects into the following three groups: (1) those whose workers were the most accurate in understanding the client's needs, (2) those whose workers were moderately accurate in their understanding, and (3) those whose workers were the least accurate. The investigators found significant postsession decreases in stress only for the clients of workers in the "most accurate" group.

At the Lafayette (Indiana) Crisis Center, Ray Young (1989) contacted 80 callers immediately after each had interacted with a crisis telephone worker. He found that 77 of the callers (96%) reported positive change. The following percentages of clients experienced moderate to extreme improvement on the category of change listed: emotions, 78 percent; thinking, 48 percent; behavioral intentions, 56 percent.

Baronet and Gerber (1997) arranged for a former employee of the Centre d'Aide in Hull (Quebec) to interview 99 of the center's clients and 25 "significant others" of those clients. For both the significant others and the clients, what they liked most about the center was the attentive listening. In addition, 83 percent of the clients indicated they were satisfied with the service.

Ben-Ari and Azaiza (2003) evaluated five help lines serving the Arabic-speaking population in Israel. Part of their study involved research interviews with 131 callers who had just completed an interaction with a volunteer worker. Thinking back to the beginning of the call, 75 percent of the callers described the problem as very severe, rating it at 8 to 10 (mean of 8.47) on a 10-point scale. When asked to rate the severity of the problem at the end of the interaction, there was a significant reduction to a mean score of 5.16. The amount of the reduction was significantly and positively correlated with the callers' perceptions of the workers' (1) degree of understanding and (2) ability to listen. Ninety-five percent of the callers said the interaction had helped them, and 92 percent said that they would use the help line again if needed and would recommend it to others.

In the previously cited research by Kalafat and his associates (2007) there were 1,617 "nonsuicidal" callers on whom information was collected during their call with one of the eight telephone crisis services. Compared to the beginning of the initial interaction, at the end of the contact the callers experienced significantly less distress, confusion, depression, anger, anxiety, hopelessness, and feelings of being overwhelmed. Researchers collected follow-up information from 801 "nonsuicidal" callers. Compared to the end of the initial phone interaction, at follow-up the callers reported significantly less distress and hopelessness. Out of the 464 callers who had developed a plan with their worker, 56 percent reported having completed or worked on the plan. When asked for feedback on what had been helpful or not helpful about the call, more than 82 percent of the respondents identified only helpful aspects of the interaction.

As previously mentioned, the same team of researchers also collected information from suicidal callers (Gould et al., 2007). There were 1,085 callers who were identified as being suicidal. Compared to the beginning of the call with the telephone crisis service, at the end of the interaction those individuals reported significantly less intent to die, hopelessness, and psychological pain. Compared to the end of the initial telephone interaction, the 380 individuals who participated in the follow-up were experiencing significantly less psychological pain and hopelessness. Among the 278 callers who had created a plan with their worker, 59 percent said they had completed or worked on the plan. When requested to give feedback on aspects of the call that had been helpful or not helpful, more than 78 percent of the participants described only helpful elements of the interaction.

In the fourteen studies reviewed that gave percentages, 83 percent of the 2,446 clients surveyed believed they had been helped. For agencies implementing the surveys, most consumers were satisfied with the crisis intervention they received.

Investigations Using Control Groups

Although client satisfaction studies support the contention that crisis intervention is effective, the best way to investigate the worth of a therapeutic endeavor is through controlled study. In such an experiment one set of subjects receives the treatment while another group of individuals does not. If the approach has an impact, one group of subjects should change more than the other.

Koocher, Curtiss, Pollin, and Patton (2001) studied patients in the Fallon Community Health Care plan who did not have a previous history of psychopathology but had been recently treated for an initial heart attack, a newly diagnosed cancer, or newly diagnosed diabetes. Patients were randomly assigned to a standard care control condition or to an experimental condition in which patients met with a clinical social worker who provided one-to-one medical crisis counseling. The intervention involved empathic listening and active problem solving that focused on issues such as control, self-image, independence, stigma, abandonment, anger, isolation, and death. The number of sessions ranged from 1 to 12, with a mean of 4.04 and a median of 3 visits. At follow-up 6 months later, the following statistically significant differences were found between the medical crisis counseling participants and the standard care control participants for the three patient groups: heart attack (12 control and 13 experimental participants)—medical crisis counseling recipients had less anxiety, depression, and psychological distress, as well as more independence and social activity; cancer (18 control and 20 experimental participants)—medical crisis counseling recipients experienced more perceived support from family and friends; diabetes (13 control and 13 experimental participants)—medical crisis counseling recipients reported less interpersonal sensitivity.

At the Memphis Center for Reproductive Health, Inc., men accompanying women seeking abortions participated in a study (Gordon, 1978) investigating the value of group crisis intervention. In the experimental condition, each of 23 male companions participated in one two-hour session with two to six other men. Another 23 men served as a control group and simply spent two hours in the waiting room of the clinic. Before their session the crisis group participants' level of anxiety was similar to the prewaiting anxiety level of the control subjects. After the meeting, however, the crisis group members' level of anxiety was significantly lower than the postwaiting anxiety level of the control subjects.

In research (Capone, Good, Westie, & Jacobson, 1980; Capone, Westie, Chitwood, Feigenbaum, & Good, 1979) conducted at the Jackson Memorial University of Miami Medical Complex, members of an experimental group of 56 patients who had genital cancer participated in at least four individual crisis intervention sessions, while a similar group of 41 patients received no such assistance. Three months after medical treatment the crisis intervention patients were significantly less confused than they had been before the intervention, and they demonstrated significantly less confusion than the control patients. Compared to the employment activity of the control subjects, twice as many of the crisis intervention patients had returned to work by the end of three months, and by the end of a year 70 percent of the crisis intervention patients had returned to their jobs while only 36 percent of the control group had gone back to work. A similar pattern of outcomes occurred with regard to frequency of sexual intercourse. Compared to control subjects, at three months almost three times as many crisis intervention patients had returned to their normal level of sexual activity. And at the end of one year 84 percent of the crisis intervention group had returned to a normal level of activity while only 43 percent of the control group had done so.

Thirty relatives accompanying seriously ill or injured patients to the emergency room were the subjects in a study at Wollongong Hospital in New South Wales (Australia). Investigators (Bunn & Clarke, 1979) randomly assigned the relatives to a control group or to an experimental group. Each of the experimental subjects received about twenty minutes of one-to-one crisis intervention. For both groups a researcher conducted an initial five-minute interview and followed with a second five-minute interview about twenty minutes later. Participants in the control group remained alone for the intervening twenty minutes while those in the experimental group received the crisis intervention. Compared to the control subjects, the crisis intervention recipients showed significantly less anxiety during the second five-minute interview. And although the subjects who waited alone experienced a slight increase in anxiety during the intervening twenty minutes, the level of anxiety among the crisis intervention participants was less than half that measured during their first five-minute interview.

Investigators (Stewart, Vockell, & Ray, 1986) at the Juvenile Division of the Superior Court of Lake County (Indiana) studied the effects of two diversionary programs for juvenile status offenders. Crisis intervention was a key component of both programs. Compared to 307 individuals in a control group, 599 juveniles in the two experimental groups made significantly fewer court appearances (a total of 40 for the two experimental groups vs. 172 for the control group). The first diversionary program limited crisis intervention to the brief time when the juvenile was in a shelter-care facility, whereas the second diversionary program provided the availability of subsequent crisis intervention contacts. Compared to the control group the 277 participants in the second program had significantly less criminal recidivism for the next two years (26 were adjudicated criminally delinquent vs. 50 for the control group).

At the Bulli Hospital in New South Wales (Australia) researchers (Viney, Benjamin, Clarke, & Bunn, 1985; Viney, Clarke, Bunn, & Benjamin, 1985) randomly assigned 298 patients to receive crisis intervention or to be in a control group. Investigators interviewed participants in the hospital at admission and at discharge, then interviewed them at home twelve to fifteen months later. Compared to the control patients, at discharge those who had received crisis intervention showed significantly greater reductions in anxiety, indirectly expressed anger, and helplessness. They also made significantly more statements of competence. After a year, the crisis intervention group was significantly less anxious than the control group. With the number of crisis contacts varying from one to four or more for those in the crisis intervention group, the researchers also discovered that the number of sessions resulted in no significant differences.

Controlled investigations have demonstrated that crisis intervention can lead to immediate reductions in anxiety, helplessness, and anger. Perhaps more importantly, these studies have also found a variety of adaptive long-term effects, including enhanced vocational functioning, greater independence, more social activity, improved marital adjustment, less criminal recidivism, decreased depression, and reduced anxiety.

WORKER PERFORMANCE

Even if crisis intervention can be a successful therapeutic technique, as the evidence indicates, it is effective only when workers implement the method in a satisfactory manner. Several studies have focused on evaluating worker performance at programs with which the researchers were affiliated.

Tanley (1972) arranged for each of 45 experienced workers at Louisiana State University's crisis telephone service to receive two simulated calls. He found that empathy was slightly below the minimum facilitative level while warmth and congruence averaged above the minimum levels.

At the crisis telephone service in Auburn (Alabama), Morgan and King (1975) placed simulated calls to 34 experienced workers. The volunteers' average communication of warmth and genuineness fell between "often" and "almost always," while their communication of empathy was between "sometimes" and "often."

Researchers (Knickerbocker, 1972; Knickerbocker & McGee, 1973) at the Suicide and Crisis Intervention Service in Gainesville (Florida) studied audio recordings of 92 interactions with actual clients in crisis who were calling for the first time. On measured empathy, workers generally scored slightly below minimum facilitative levels, whereas on genuineness and warmth they averaged above the minimum criteria. There were significant positive correlations (.25 to .36) between the demonstration of these helping skills and decreases in the callers' levels of anxiety and depression. Also, workers rated high on these facilitative conditions were able to help their clients engage in significantly more self-exploration and become significantly less anxious and depressed than the clients of workers rated low on empathy, warmth, and genuineness.

One way to study crisis intervention is for investigators to evaluate programs with which they are associated. Another approach is to evaluate multiple organizations.

Bleach and Claiborn (1974) placed 96 calls to four crisis telephone services in the Washington, D.C. area. The workers averaged levels of empathy, warmth, and genuineness that were below minimum facilitative criteria. And in 15 percent of the contacts, the caller received false or inaccurate information.

Carothers and Inslee (1974) placed a total of 23 calls to 21 different crisis telephone services. The responding workers averaged well below the minimum facilitative level of empathic understanding.

In a study of ten crisis telephone services in New England, Genther (1974) placed one simulated call to each program. On a five-point scale (1=low, 5=high) of empathy, respect, and specificity, the workers averaged 1.35, and no worker achieved level three—the minimum level for competency. Genther noted the following unhelpful behaviors: interrupting the caller in order to ask banal and irrelevant questions, placing the caller on hold in the middle of critical discussions, and abundant advice giving.

Davies (1982) used Genther's approach and placed one role-played call to each of ten hotlines in West Midlands (United Kingdom). Two of the responding workers performed at a satisfactory level. The other eight displayed a host of inappropriate behaviors. Examples included terminating the call in less than a minute, giving false reassurance, asking irrelevant questions, talking incessantly, providing inappropriate advice, and discussing the feelings of third parties rather than focusing on the feelings of the client.

The investigations reviewed to this point start at a common core, then diverge into two different sets of results. Controlled experiments demonstrate that crisis intervention can be an effective technique with persons in crisis. When researchers investigate services with which they are associated, they find that clients generally are satisfied and that experienced workers are performing above or slightly below minimum facilitative levels of helping skills that have been shown to benefit clients. But general surveys of crisis telephone services find that workers are performing at unsatisfactory levels.

Three additional studies help to explain the divergent trends in research results.

Knowles (1979) and McCarthy and Knapp (1984) discovered performance patterns very similar to those reported by Genther (1974) and Davies (1982). For example, Knowles' subjects gave advice in 70 percent of their responses, and the three top responses among the McCarthy and Knapp subjects were attempting to change the client's views, asking closed questions, and giving advice. In the Knowles (1979) and McCarthy and Knapp (1984) studies, however, the subjects displaying those poor skills were untrained individuals.

In a study cited in the previous chapter, William Doyle and his associates (1977) obtained feedback from clients at the University of Cincinnati crisis walk-in center. Thirty-six clients of 12 newly-trained workers evaluated the effectiveness of the intervention. Each client used a 5-point scale (1=low, 5=high) to assess the benefit derived from the intervention and to evaluate the worker's understanding of the problem. Part of the results were consistent with those client surveys showing consumer satisfaction, and part of the findings were in agreement with the low performance levels found in general surveys of crisis telephone services. Clients of closely supervised workers gave them ratings of 4.42 on derived benefit and 4.17 on understanding the problem. Workers receiving no supervision or supervision on a delayed basis scored significantly lower on these measures, averaging 2.63 and 2.75, respectively. In addition, closely supervised workers demonstrated significantly more empathy than did the other staff members.

The performance levels of the well-trained and closely supervised workers in the Doyle et al. (1977) study are consistent with the positive client survey results found by Getz et al. (1975), King (1977), Stelmachers et al. (1972), Speer and Schultz (1975), Preston et al. (1975), Slaikeu and Willis, (1978), Beers and Foreman (1976), Donovan et al. (1979), Hornblow and Sloane (1980), Gingerich et al. (1988), Kirk et al. (1988), Young (1989), Baronet and Gerber (1997), Ben-Ari and Azaiza (2003), Kalafat et al. (2007), and Gould et al. (2007) and with the client improvement resulting from crisis intervention in controlled investigations by Koocher et al. (2001), Gordon, (1978), Capone and her associates (1980, 1979), Bunn and Clarke (1979), Stewart et al. (1986), and Viney and her colleagues (1985, 1985). All of these researchers were collecting data from organizations with which they were affiliated. It seems reasonable to assume that if investigators associated with a crisis program expend the effort necessary to conduct a client survey or a controlled investigation, they would not have done so unless they believed an effort had also been made to offer quality services.

Recall, however, that another set of researchers conducted general surveys of crisis telephone services and did not limit their worker evaluations to programs with which the authors were associated. The low levels of performance found by Bleach and Claiborn (1974), Carothers and Inslee (1974), Genther (1974), and Davies (1982) were similar to the unsatisfactory functioning demonstrated by untrained individuals in the Knowles (1979) and McCarthy and Knapp (1984) studies and by the poorly supervised workers in the Doyle et al. (1977) investigation.

The divergent trends in research on staff performance show that some crisis personnel resemble individuals who are untrained and inadequately supervised, while other workers effectively implement crisis intervention techniques that facilitate adaptive change in their clients. Are the adequately performing workers just naturally good or does training make a difference? The next seven studies provide an answer to that question.

David Lester (1970) evaluated two actual crisis calls received by each of nine experienced workers at the Suicide Prevention and Crisis Service in Buffalo (New York). Average levels of empathy and respect were slightly below facilitative levels while average genuineness was at the minimum level. When similar evaluations were applied to an actual call received by each of 13 trainees during their first supervision shift, average empathy, respect, and genuineness did not approach minimum facilitative levels.

At the Ben Gordon Community Mental Health Center emergency service in Dekalb (Illinois), O'Donnell and George (1977) placed role-played crisis calls to ten professional staff, ten newly trained crisis line workers, ten experienced crisis line workers, and ten untrained college students. The professionals and both groups of volunteers did not differ significantly in their overall effectiveness in developing a positive relationship, engaging the client in problem solving, and using community resources. All three groups, however, performed significantly better than the untrained control subjects. In addition, all three groups of workers functioned at or above the minimum facilitative levels of empathy and genuineness.

Researchers (France, 1975a; Kalafat et al., 1979) at the Telephone Counseling Service in Tallahassee (Florida) placed two simulated crisis calls to each of 22 untrained workers, 11 individuals in the supervision phase of training, and 11 veteran workers. Thirty-four percent of the untrained workers' calls demonstrated minimum levels of warmth, and 25 percent showed facilitative levels of genuineness. For the calls to supervision and experienced workers, 43 percent had minimum levels of warmth and 64 percent contained facilitative amounts of genuineness. Only 3 of 88 calls had minimum levels of empathy. In addition to examining performance levels of empathy, warmth, and genuineness, the study evaluated the workers' ability to make a referral and to provide problem-solving assistance. Thirty-five percent of the untrained individuals' calls contained adequate referral performance, whereas minimum referral proficiency occurred in 62 percent of the calls to supervision and experienced workers. With regard to problem solving, 80 percent of the untrained workers' calls met minimum standards, while 91 percent of the calls to supervision and experienced volunteers met those minimums. In terms of statistically significant differences among groups, empathy and problem solving increased with both training and experience.

At the Phone/Baton Rouge Crisis Intervention Center, Randell Elkins and Carol Cohen (1982) measured crisis intervention counselor skills before and after a 55-hour training program. Within the pool of 27 center volunteers, posttraining counseling skills were significantly higher than pretraining skills, but there was no further improvement after five months of experience.

Thomas (1983) collected pretraining and posttraining measures from volunteer rape crisis workers at the Volunteer Supportive Advocate Program of Erie County (New York) and compared them to measures obtained from control subjects recruited in an introductory psychology course at a nearby university. Both before and after training, the 22 volunteers showed significantly more competence in crisis counseling than did the 20 psychology students. The volunteers also performed significantly better after training than before, whereas the control subjects showed no change during the intervening time period.

At a university hotline, Frauenfelder and Frauenfelder (1984) compared 17 volunteer workers to 28 control subjects from an introductory psychology course. The investigators measured the subjects' ability to respond in a supportive and reflective manner. Results followed the same pattern as in the Thomas study. The volunteers scored significantly higher than the psychology students on both pretraining and posttraining measures. And the volunteers significantly raised their scores after training, whereas the first and second scores for the control subjects were about the same.

Robert Neimeyer and William MacInnes (1981) measured the quality of pretraining and posttraining suicide intervention responses of 114 paraprofessionals in six crisis service training classes and of 13 individuals in an alcohol counseling training program. The investigators also created a control group that contained 18 introductory psychology students, 15 death education students, and 18 veteran crisis workers—all of whom took the test twice. Participants in the alcohol counseling program and in five of the six crisis worker classes scored significantly higher at the end of training, whereas the control subjects showed essentially no change on the second testing.

I believe the preceding research demonstrates that adequate training and supervision are prerequisites for the provision of acceptable crisis intervention services. And others in the field share similar opinions.

After evaluating ten British hotlines, Davies (1982) concluded that, as a group, the programs did not provide the services that they publicized to the community. To remedy the situation, he suggested that the agencies improve their basic training. Stein and Lambert (1984) made a similar suggestion.

After reviewing telephone counseling and crisis intervention research, they concluded that the typical crisis telephone worker needs additional training.

It probably is true that many crisis workers could benefit from more training. Research done in Melbourne (Australia) supports that view. Forty crisis telephone workers from a variety of programs (e.g., Lifeline, Crisis Line, Parents Anonymous, AIDS Line) were recruited by Irene Bobevski and Jim McLennan (1998) to participate in a research study that involved simulated calls. Data analysis was based on each participant receiving one scripted call portrayed by the same actor. That actor's rated effectiveness of the call (worker understanding, worker helpfulness, and caller satisfaction with the assistance) was negatively correlated with anxiety and with very high emotional involvement on the part of the worker. The authors suggested that the workers who became anxious had come to believe they were failing to achieve their objectives with the client and that the workers who experienced extremely high levels of emotional involvement probably had intrusive thoughts that were irrelevant to appropriately helping the client. There were positive correlations between caller-rated effectiveness and both worker experience and motivated effort (the amount of self-rated determined effort the worker put into the call). Seven of the workers achieved perfect scores on caller-rated effectiveness (Bobevski, Holgate, & McLennan, 1997). The actor portraying the caller expressed a variety of opinions concerning the helpfulness of the workers. She liked it when workers did the following: quickly responded to her comments; recognized and summarized issues she raised, while also encouraging her to think about their implications; helped her to consider available resources; and assisted her in the development of a more optimistic perspective that emphasized realistic and positive possibilities for gaining more control in her life. The researchers found nine of the workers formed a cluster that earned notably lower caller-rated effectiveness scores than the rest of the participants. The caller/actor did not like the following: lengthy silences; failure to respond to issues she raised; dismissal of her concerns as inconsequential; avoidance of concrete issues (e.g., finances, employment) relevant to decisions she was facing; and early in the call being asked what she was going to do about her situation. These findings suggest that there are quite a few workers who have room for substantial improvement in their skills.

RELEVANCE OF EVALUATION FOR CRISIS WORKERS

The research surveyed in this chapter demonstrates that crisis intervention can be an effective therapeutic technique. And the evidence also makes it clear that the approach is productive only when intervenors fulfill their performance responsibilities.

The studies reviewed suggest two areas in need of special vigilance on the part of workers. First, crisis intervenors must develop and maintain the communication skills necessary for creating a positive relationship. Second, workers must carefully assess the needs and values of their clients. A plan is useless if the client does not intend to implement it. When the plan includes a referral, intervenors must take care to ensure that the information provided is both accurate and appropriate.

The previously cited research highlights commonly occurring patterns. Nevertheless, the most valuable type of evaluation for you is feedback concerning your own crisis intervention efforts.

There are a variety of evaluation techniques that a program can use to assess crisis intervention (e.g., American Association of Suicidology, 2012; Bleach, 1973; Bonneson & Hartsough, 1987; Hoff & Hoff, 2012; Lester, 2002; McGee, 1974; Motto, Brooks, Ross, & Allen, 1974; Stelmachers, 1976; Stelmachers, Baxter, & Ellenson, 1978). Since a fundamental aspect of crisis intervention is the formulation of a concrete plan, one logical evaluation strategy is to assess progress in reaching specific objectives.

One of the best known systems for setting goals and measuring change is *Goal Attainment Scaling* (Kiresuk, Smith, & Cardillo, 1994). With Goal Attainment Scaling there are five levels of attainment (expected outcome, somewhat more than expected, much more than expected, somewhat less than expected, and much less than expected). Thus, change indicated by Goal Attainment Scaling is a function of the following factors: (1) future reports of the client's behavior and (2) accuracy of the staff member in defining the attainment levels. The latter factor is so crucial that Goal Attainment Scaling experts (Cardillo, 1994; Smith, 1994) recommend at least a year of direct-service experience in a relevant setting before one seeks the 14 hours of training necessary to implement the technique.

Goal Attainment Scaling experts also recommend that a minimum of three goals be established for each client and that subsequent rating interviews be conducted by uninvolved third parties. Because those procedures cost both time and money, Goal Attainment Scaling primarily has been used as a means of program evaluation rather than as a regular aspect of interventions. For example, at one crisis intervention program the typical strategy is to use the procedure with every fifteenth client (Kiresuk & Choate, 1994).

Although program evaluation is a worthy endeavor, I also believe that target setting can have important therapeutic benefits for clients. So I favor an approach I call *Observation Scaling* (France, Weikel, & Kish, 2006). If this system is used for program evaluation, then, as with Goal Attainment Scaling, the sponsoring entity must make adequate time and funding available for the setting of three targets and for the subsequent rating interviews to be conducted by uninvolved third parties.

I believe, however, that target setting can become a standard part of interventions, even when there is not time for setting three targets and when the subsequent ratings will not be done by uninvolved third parties. And rather than new staff members waiting a year before incorporating target setting into their work, as is the case with Goal Attainment Scaling, I believe such persons should be able to use target setting with their very first clients. Immediate use of this system is possible because of the way the attainment levels are defined. Unlike Goal Attainment Scaling, in which attainment levels are defined by an experienced *interviewer's predictions* of future behavior, the attainment levels in Observation Scaling are defined by the *client's observations* of past and present behavior. Consequently, it is possible for novice staff members to learn and to use Observation Scaling. (You will find the basic form in Figure 2.)

When using Observation Scaling the first step is to specify a target and its attainment levels. This endeavor requires attention to five considerations.

1. *Who develops the targets?* The staff member and the client collaborate in defining the targets.
2. *When are targets established?* Targets can be established at almost any time. If you are doing problem solving with an individual, you can discuss targets at the end of the exploration phase or later.
3. *What do the attainment levels contain?* You must write the target scales so that both the client and another staff member could ascertain the levels of attainment. In other words, the descriptions of the attainment levels should enable the collection of information that clearly indicates the current degree of success. To the best of your ability, make sure of the following: the attainment levels are concretely described; the levels do not overlap; nothing could fall between two adjacent attainment levels; the levels are defined in terms of ranges rather than specific points; the scale describes only one dimension of behavior; and the levels focus on areas that are clearly under the client's control.
4. *How many attainment levels are there?* In Observation Scaling there are four possible outcomes. Ability to cope can deteriorate, remain unchanged, return to a normal level of adjustment, or expand. The attainment levels on the Observation Scales form represent each of those possibilities—Further from Target, No Change, Normal Level of Success, and Improved Level of Coping.
5. *How many targets are there?* For program evaluation efforts, Goal Attainment Scaling experts recommend establishing at least eleven possible

Attainment Level

Name _____

	Target 1	Rated Level	Target 2	Rated Level	Target 3	Rated Level
Further from Target						
No Change						
Normal Level of Success						
Improved Level of Coping						

Figure 2. Observation Scales

steps in order to produce a summary change score that is reliable (Cardillo & Smith, 1994). If that psychometric issue is of interest to you, the minimum number of targets is three (containing a total of twelve possible steps). It is my experience, however, that setting even one target can have a positive influence by helping to focus efforts on desired change.

A good way to begin the Observation Scaling process is to ask the client, "How would you like things to be different?" It is not advisable to start by saying, "I use a process called Observation Scaling . . ." or "What would you like your target to be?" Comments such as these tend to confuse clients and may make the target-setting process unnecessarily complicated.

After getting an answer to, "How would you like things to be different?" you can summarize the response in a statement, such as, "It seems as though you would like. . . ." If the individual agrees with your comment you can say, "It sounds like a target for you would be to. . . ." (Since the process is based on the client's descriptions, it is perfectly acceptable to use the client's words and phrasing when defining targets and attainment levels.)

Write down the name of the target. Then you can ask, "Right now how would you describe (name the target area) . . . ?" Once you have a clear picture of current conditions, summarize the information and enter it in the *No Change* level.

Next you can say, "Things could get worse if (describe behavior worse than current conditions)." Enter the description in *Further from Target*.

Now say, "Within the recent past (or you may define a relevant time period) what is the best you've been able to do with regard to (name of target)?" (Throughout the discussion be sure to use the target's name, rather than referring to it as "this target.") Summarize the individual's answer, and enter the range of behavior (from current to best) in the *Normal Level of Success*.

At this point say, "Things could get better if (describe behavior above the best the client has achieved)." Write the information in the *Improved Level of Coping*.

After you have defined all of the attainment levels, review with the person the information you have collected. To do this, name the target, then describe (1) the *No Change* level by saying, "Right now. . . ," (2) the *Further from Target* level by stating, "Things could get worse if. . . ," (3) the *Normal Level of Success* by saying, "The best you've been able to do in the past was to . . ," and (4) the *Improved Level of Coping* by stating, "An improved situation would involve. . . ."

The preceding target-setting strategy helps clients focus their energy; it does not confuse them. But you *are* likely to make the process confusing if you sidetrack the interaction with technical terms by asking questions such as, "What is your normal level of success?" or by making statements like, "Your improved level of coping would be. . . ." Rather than reading the Observation Scaling labels to the client, use phrasing that will make sense to a person who has no knowledge of this target-setting procedure.

After writing down a target and its attainment levels, enter the date and your initials in the box at the top of the *Rated Level* column in the *No Change* row. During each subsequent measurement of the target, enter the date and your initials in the *Rated Level* column next to the appropriate attainment level.

Progress can be monitored as frequently as you and the client wish. Knowing that desired change has taken place provides both of you with a sense of satisfaction. Conversely, on those occasions when lack of progress becomes evident, you can help the individual consider what might be done to get things moving forward.

If you want to use Observation Scaling as an objective measure of outcome, follow-up interviews for this purpose should be conducted by a third party. The less investment the follow-up interviewer has in the outcome, the more unbiased the rating is likely to be. This final assessment can be indicated by circling the entry in the "Rated Level" column.

The case described below shows how crisis workers can implement Observation Scaling (see Figure 3).

EXAMPLE.
First contact: Saturday, November 15

Marsha Crowder came to the crisis center on Saturday morning because she said she did not have the energy to deal with the responsibilities and decisions facing her. Two months earlier she had obtained a divorce from her husband Don, and this week their house had been sold as part of the settlement. Next Saturday she would be moving to an apartment with her four-year-old son, Jake. During the last couple of weeks she had noticed herself yelling at Jake quite a bit and that worried her. She said she was finding it difficult to give him the attention he wanted, to make the preparations necessary for her move, and to maintain her full-time job. She also was anxious about Don seeing Jake. As part of the divorce settlement, Don had visitation rights, and Marsha feared he might keep Jake after one of their visits. She reported spending hours worrying about that possibility. Marsha was feeling overwhelmed and depressed, and she remained tearful during the first 25 minutes of the interview.

In collaboration with the worker, Marsha selected targets with respect to Jake, visitation, and depression. The worker encouraged her to tackle one issue at a time, and she selected child care as the first area on which to focus.

The nursery where Jake stayed while Marsha worked was not open after 6:00 p.m., so further use of that facility was not an alternative. After briefly considering several other options, Marsha decided she would call her aunt to see if Jake could stay with her in the evenings. She said that they frequently went to her aunt's house on Sunday afternoons and that Jake liked being there.

To combat feelings of depression, the worker assisted Marsha in planning several activities for the remainder of the weekend. That afternoon she would go shopping with a friend and look for a shower curtain, rug, etc., for the bathroom in her new apartment. On Sunday morning she and Jake would go to church, and in the afternoon they would visit her aunt.

At the end of the session, Marsha said she felt good about having come up with some plans, and she scheduled a walk-in contact for Sunday evening. The

Attainment Level   Name Marsha Crowder

	Target 1 Enhance relationship with son	Rated Level	Target 2 Feel settled with regard to visitation	Rated Level	Target 3 Develop realistic optimism	Rated Level
Further from Target	Most of the time find it difficult to cope with him		Entirely consumed with thoughts of dread regarding visitation		Almost never have confidence in ability to cope with the future	
No Change	Often find it difficult to cope with him	KF 11-15-14	Feel anxious and desperate regarding visitation-related possibilities	KF 11-15-14 KF 11-16-14 KF 11-19-14	Sometimes have confidence in ability to cope with the future	KF 11-15-14
Normal Level of Success	Often find coping with him to be a challenge, but generally enjoy interactions with him	KF 11-16-14 KF 11-19-14 KF 11-23-14	Feel tense about visitation-related possibilites	KF 11-23-14 (RB 12-18-14)	Usually have confidence in ability to cope with the future	KF 11-26-14
Improved Level of Coping	Generally pleased at the quality of interactions with him, and look forward to being with him	(RB 12-18-14)	Feel determined and capable when thinking about visitation-related issues		Almost always have confidence in ability to cope with the future	KF 11-19*-14 KF 11-23-14 (RB 12-18-14)

Figure 3. Observation Scales

worker gave her an agency card and encouraged her to call if she felt the need to talk again before her Sunday appointment.

Second contact: Sunday, November 16

Marsha reported that her weekend had gone OK—she had not yelled at Jake, and she was feeling less depressed. Her aunt had agreed to keep Jake in the evenings.

She said she had arranged to rent a truck to move her belongings, although she now was concerned about loading and unloading heavy objects. When she could not think of any way to get help, the worker suggested that she call a fire station to see if any of the fire fighters wanted to make some money for a couple of hours of work.

Jake was scheduled to spend Saturday with Don, and Marsha worried about the outcome of that visit. She decided to consult her attorney concerning what recourse she would have if Don failed to bring Jake back.

She arranged another walk-in for Wednesday evening. In the meantime she was to call the fire station and her attorney.

Third contact: Wednesday, November 19

Marsha began by saying there were so many boxes in her house that she had dubbed the decor "early cardboard." She had been surprised when her request for moving assistance resulted in three fire fighters agreeing to help her on Saturday.

During the conversation with her attorney, Marsha learned that if Don failed to bring Jake back, her ex-husband probably would lose his visiting privileges for a time, and he would be subject to criminal prosecution. After discussing several possibilities with the worker she decided to call Don, tell him of her desire for Jake to be returned according to their agreement, and assert her willingness to seek legal recourse if he violated the terms of the visitation.

She scheduled another walk-in for Sunday evening.

Fourth contact: Sunday, November 23

An hour before her scheduled session, Marsha called to say she would not be coming in because she wanted to continue unpacking. She reported that the move had gone as well as could be expected. And she said that although her call to Don had been bristly, she believed he understood her resolve to keep Jake. Their Saturday visit seemed to have transpired without incident, although she had worried about it some while she was moving.

She thanked the worker for his help and stated that she believed things were improving. The worker praised her progress and encouraged her to call back if she felt the need. Although the worker had mentioned follow-up during the first contact, he reminded Marsha that another staff member would be calling in about a month to see how things were going.

Follow-up contact: Thursday, December 18

Marsha said the child care arrangement with her aunt had become semipermanent; Jake now stayed with her two evenings a week so Marsha could have some time to herself. Consequently, she felt less tied down, and she enjoyed her time with Jake more.

She was pleased with the outcome of the move. In addition, during the last few weeks she had discovered that she was good at doing odd jobs such as caulking the windows and covering the air conditioner for the winter.

Don had continued to abide by the visitation agreement. Nevertheless, Marsha admitted that she still worried some when Jake was with him.

With Christmas only a week away she said it was fun being with Jake. Although at times they both felt a little down—the holiday season did not seem quite right without Don. On Christmas day she and Jake planned to open presents in the morning and then go to her aunt's for dinner.

Marsha believed the intervention had been effective in helping her to resolve her difficulties, and she said it was convenient to obtain service from the crisis center. The follow-up worker praised her continuing progress and encouraged her to call if she should need help again in the future.

DISCUSSION OF MARSHA CROWDER'S CASE. At the time of the first contact Marsha was feeling overwhelmed. The worker's response was to help her (a) sort out her problems, (b) begin to take concrete steps toward resolving a specific difficulty–child care, and (c) plan activities to help combat her depression.

By the second session she had made adequate progress in arranging child care, so the worker helped her address other issues. When she had trouble coming up with a viable way of obtaining moving help, the worker suggested an alternative. This was the only advice he gave during the contacts. Marsha generated and evaluated all of the other options discussed.

Unlike the first session, the third contact began with Marsha making a joke. Rather than feeling helpless she now had a growing self-confidence that her plans would work out.

By the fourth contact she no longer felt the need to come to the crisis center, and she decided to terminate. The worker emphasized how much she had accomplished during the past nine days, pointed out that help was still available if she should need it, and reminded her of the follow-up call she would receive.

The follow-up worker learned that Marsha had made the maximum improvement possible on two of her targets. On the remaining one she had made substantial progress, although the opportunity for further growth remained. She seemed to be coping well with the demands of being a single parent, as evidenced by her success with household maintenance tasks and by her plans for Christmas day. Overall, Marsha was pleased with the availability of the service and with the helpfulness of the intervention. The follow-up worker ended the contact by praising Marsha's accomplishments and by reminding her that help continued to be available at the crisis center.

SUMMARY

Crisis intervention is intended to help persons who are overwhelmed by a sudden upsurge in difficulties. Research demonstrates that such individuals tend to be interested in receiving help and that crisis intervention can decrease their situational distress. On the other hand, research also suggests that crisis intervention is not a sufficient response for clients with long-standing problems.

Investigators have assessed the impact of crisis intervention on clients by using referral follow-up, client satisfaction surveys, and controlled experimentation. Referral follow-up studies find that clients follow through with about half of the referrals they receive from crisis workers and that workers probably make a fair number of inappropriate referrals. In client satisfaction surveys, more than eight out of ten respondents perceive crisis intervention to have been helpful. Controlled experiments document a variety of positive outcomes following crisis intervention, including both short-term and long-term decreases in distressing emotions and increases in adaptive problem solving.

Evaluations of staff performance demonstrate that well-trained and closely supervised workers can offer quality crisis intervention services. But such research also suggests that a substantial number of programs fail to provide the necessary preparation and support for their personnel.

In addition to adequate training and supervision, ongoing evaluation is necessary in order to maintain the quality of services offered. The most valuable information for workers is feedback concerning their own crisis intervention efforts. Observation Scaling is one evaluation strategy that allows clinicians to monitor the progress of individual clients, as well as discover patterns of intervention outcomes across clients.

STUDY QUESTIONS

1. Research suggests that crisis intervention is likely to be a sufficient response for which of the following individuals?
   (A) Mary, who is anxious about her unwanted pregnancy and feels overwhelmed by the decisions facing her.
   (B) Gary, who is chronically anxious and suicidal.
2. Mary, from the previous question, strikes the worker as being in need of counseling, and they discuss the idea of psychotherapy. Although she is resistant to such a referral, the worker "talks her into it." What does research suggest about the probability of Mary following through with that referral?
3. In the client survey of hospital emergency room patients, how did the perceived helpfulness of crisis workers compare to opinions regarding other emergency room staff?
4. Research support exists for which of the following conclusions?
   (A) Crisis intervention can alleviate anxiety, anger, and helplessness.
   (B) Crisis intervention can improve performance in specific areas such as employment functioning and marital adjustment.
5. When researchers have surveyed multiple crisis intervention programs, what do their findings indicate about worker performance?
6. Jane reports that because her parents disapproved of her fiancé they forced her to leave home last month. Since moving to a nearby town

she has not heard from her family. Five days ago, Jane's brother died in an automobile accident. But she did not learn of his death until two days ago when she received a call from a girlfriend who berated her for not attending the funeral. Jane says she began an episode of uncontrollable crying when told of her brother's death.

She feels overwhelmed by events, and she is confused about what to do. So far she has not contacted her parents or visited her brother's grave. Jane says she has not slept for two days, and she reports driving for hours to no particular destination.

Several times during the interview Jane becomes tearful, and she frequently lapses into silence. Although she denies thoughts of suicide, you are concerned about her health and safety.

Using the blank Observation Scaling form, write down potential targets and attainment levels for your intervention with Jane.

REFERENCES

AAS Individual Certification Committee: *Applicant's Manual: Individual Crisis Worker Certification*. Washington, DC: American Association of Suicidology, 2005.

Adams, D.M., Overholser, J.C., and Spirito, A.: Stressful life events associated with adolescent suicide attempts. *Canadian Journal of Psychiatry, 39*: 43-48, 1994.

Al, C.M.W., Stams, G.J.J.M., van der Laan, P.H., and Asscher, J.J. The role of crisis in family crisis intervention: Do crisis experience and crisis change matter? *Children and Youth Services Review, 33*: 991-998, 2011.

Albano, R.A., and Glenwick, D.S.: Predicting the effectiveness of telephone crisis counselors: A comparison of two approaches. *Journal of College Student Development, 31*: 81-82, 1990.

Alexander, J.A.C., and Harman, R.L.: One counselor's intervention in the aftermath of a middle school student's suicide: A case study. *Journal of Counseling and Development, 66*: 283-285, 1988.

Allard, R., Marshall, M., and Plante, M.C.: Intensive follow-up does not decrease the risk of repeat suicide attempts. *Suicide and Life Threatening Behavior, 22*: 303-314, 1992.

American Academy of Child and Adolescent Psychiatry: Summary of the practice parameters for the assessment and treatment of children and adolescents with suicidal behavior. *Journal of the American Academy of Child & Adolescent Psychiatry, 40*: 495-499, 2001.

American Association of Suicidology: *Organization Accreditation Standards Manual, 11th Edition*. Washington, DC: Author, 2012.

American Psychological Association: Ethical principles of psychologists and code of conduct. *American Psychologist, 57*: 1060-1073, 2002.

Andrés, A.R., and Hempstead, K.: Gun control and suicide: The impact of state firearm regulations in the United States, 1995–2004. *Health Policy, 101*: 95-103, 2011.

Ansel, E.L.: *Correlates of Volunteer Performance in a Suicide Prevention/Crisis Intervention Service*. Unpublished doctoral dissertation. University of Florida, 1972.

Apter, A., and Wasserman, D.: Adolescent attempted suicide. In R.A. King and A. Apter (Eds.): *Suicide in Children and Adolescents*. New York: Cambridge University Press, 2003.

Asnis, G.M., Kaplan, M.L., van Praag, H.M., and Sanderson, W.C.: Homicidal behaviors among psychiatric outpatients. *Hospital & Community Psychiatry, 45:* 127-132, 1994.

269

Au, J.S.K., Yip, P.S.F., Chan, C.L.W., and Law, Y.W.: Newspaper reporting of suicide cases in Hong Kong. *Crisis, 25*: 161-168, 2004.

Augustin, D., and Fagan, T.J.: Roles for mental health professionals in critical law enforcement incidents: An overview. *Psychological Services, 8*: 166-177, 2011.

Azrael, D., Hemenway, D., Miller, M., Barber, C.W., and Schackner, R.: Youth suicide: Insights from 5 years of Arizona Child Fatality Review team data. *Suicide and Life-Threatening Behavior, 34*: 36-43, 2004.

Bailley, S.E., Kral, M .J., and Dunham, K.: Survivors of suicide do grieve differently: Empirical support for a common sense proposition. *Suicide and Life-Threatening Behavior, 29*: 256-271, 1999.

Baird, B.N., Bossett, S.B., and Smith, B .J.: A new technique for handling sexually abusive calls to telephone crisis lines. *Community Mental Health Journal, 30*: 55-60, 1994.

Ball, J.S., Links, P.S., Strike, C., and Boydell, K.M.: "It's overwhelming . . . Everything seems to be too much:" A theory of crisis for individuals with severe persistent mental illness. *Psychiatric Rehabilitation Journal, 29*: 10-17, 2005.

Barber, J.G., Blackman, E.K., Talbot, C., and Saebel, J.: The themes expressed in suicide calls to a telephone help line. *Social Psychiatry and Psychiatric Epidemiology, 39*: 121-125, 2004.

Bard, M.: The unique potentials of the police in interpersonal conflict management. *International Journal of Group Tensions, 3*: 68-75, 1973.

Bard, M., and Sangrey, D.: *The Crime Victim's Book.* New York: Basic Books, 1979.

Bard, M., and Sangrey, D.: *The Crime Victim's Book*, Second Edition. New York: Brunner/Mazel, 1986.

Baronet, A.M., and Gerber, G.J.: Client satisfaction in a community crisis center. *Evaluation and Program Planning, 20*: 443-453, 1997.

Beauford, J.E., McNiel, D.E., and Binder, R.L.: Utility of the initial therapeutic alliance in evaluating psychiatric patients' risk of violence. *American Journal of Psychiatry, 154*: 1272-1276, 1997.

Beautrais, A.L.: Further suicidal behavior among medically serious suicide attempters. *Suicide and Life-Threatening Behavior, 34*: 1-11, 2004.

Beck, A.T., Brown, G., Berchick, R.J., Stewart, B.L., and Steer, R.A.: Relationship between hopelessness and ultimate suicide: A replication with psychiatric outpatients. *American Journal of Psychiatry, 147*: 190-195, 1990.

Beck, A.T., Rush, A.J., Shaw, B.F., and Emery, G.: *Cognitive Therapy of Depression.* New York: Guilford, 1979.

Beck, A.T., Steer, R.A., Beck, J.S., and Newman, C.F.: Hopelessness, depression, suicidal ideation, and clinical diagnosis of depression. *Suicide and Life-Threatening Behavior, 23*: 139-145, 1993.

Beck, A.T., Steer, R.A, and Brown, G.: Dysfunctional attitudes and suicidal ideation in psychiatric outpatients. *Suicide and Life-Threatening Behavior, 23*: 11-20, 1993.

Beck, J.C.: Legal and ethical duties of the clinician treating a patient who is liable to be impulsively violent. *Behavioral Sciences and the Law, 16*: 375-389, 1998.

Beers, T.M., Jr., and Foreman, M.E.: Intervention patterns in crisis interviews. *Journal of Counseling Psychology, 23*: 87-91, 1976.

Bell, C.C., Jenkins, E .J., Kpo, W., and Rhodes, H.: Response of emergency rooms to victims of interpersonal violence. *Hospital & Community Psychiatry, 45*: 142-146, 1994.

Bell, J., Stanley, N., Mallon, S., and Manthorpe, J.: Life will never be the same again: Examining grief in survivors bereaved by young suicide. *Illness, Crisis & Loss, 20*: 49-68, 2012.

Ben-Ari, A., and Azaiza, F.: Effectiveness of help lines among sociopolitical minorities: A view from both sides of the line. *Families in Society: The Journal of Contemporary Human Services, 84*: 417-422, 2003.

Bengelsdorf, H., and Alden, D.C.: A mobile crisis unit in the psychiatric emergency room. *Hospital & Community Psychiatry, 38*: 662-665, 1987.

Bengelsdorf, H., Church, J.O., Kaye, R.A., Orlowski, B., and Alden, D.C.: The cost effectiveness of crisis intervention: Admission diversion savings can offset the high cost of service. *Journal of Nervous and Mental Disease, 181*: 757-762, 1993.

Bengelsdorf, H., Levy, L.E., Emerson, R.L., and Barile, F.A.: A crisis triage rating scale: Brief dispositional assessment of patients at risk for hospitalization. *Journal of Nervous and Mental Disease, 172*: 424-430, 1984.

Ben-Zur, H.: Coping, distress, and life events in a community sample. *International Journal of Stress Management, 12*: 188-196, 2005.

Berman, A.L.: Risk management with suicidal patients. *Journal of Clinical Psychology, 62*: 171-184, 2006.

Berman, A.L., Jobes, D.A., and Silverman, M.M.: *Adolescent Suicide: Assessment and Intervention.* Washington, DC: American Psychological Association, 2006.

Berman, A. and Lindahl, V.: The American Association of Suicidology: Past, present, and future. In D. Lester (Ed.): *Suicide Prevention: Resources for the Millennium.* Philadelphia: Brunner-Routledge, 2001.

Bertolote, J.M., Fleischmann, A., De Leo, D., and Wasserman, D.: Psychiatric diagnoses and suicide: Revisiting the evidence. *Crisis, 25*: 147-155, 2004.

Biggam, F.H., and Power, K.G.: Suicidality and the state-trait debate on problem solving deficits: A re-examination with incarcerated young offenders. *Archives of Suicide Research, 5*: 27-42, 1999.

Binder, R.L., and McNiel, D.E.: Application of the Tarasoff ruling and its effect on the victim and the therapeutic relationship. *Psychiatric Services, 47*: 1212-1215, 1996.

Bland, R.C., Newman, S.C., and Dyck, R.J.: The epidemiology of parasuicide in Edmonton. *Canadian Journal of Psychiatry, 39*: 391-396, 1994.

Bleach, G.: Strategies for evaluation of hotline telephone crisis centers. In G.A. Specter and W.L. Claiborn (Eds.): *Crisis Intervention.* New York: Behavioral Publications, 1973.

Bleach, G., and Claiborn, W.L.: Initial evaluation of hotline telephone crisis centers. *Community Mental Health Journal, 10*: 387-394, 1974.

Bloom, B.L.: Definitional aspects of the crisis concept. *Journal of Consulting Psychology, 27*: 498-502, 1963.

Bobevski, I., Holgate, A.M., and McLennan, J.: Characteristics of effective telephonecounseling skills. *British Journal of Guidance & Counseling, 25*: 239-249, 1997.

Bobevski, I., and McLennan, J.: The telephone counseling interview as a complex, dynamic, decision process: A self-regulation model of counselor effectiveness. *Journal of Psychology, 132*: 47-60, 1998.

Boehm, K.E., Schondel, C.K., Ivoska, W.J., Marlowe, A.L., and Manke-Mitchell, L.: Calls to Teen Line: Representative concerns of adolescents. *Adolescence, 33*: 797-803, 1998.

Boehm, K.E., Schondel, C.K., Marlowe, A.L., and Manke-Mitchell, L.: Teens' concerns: A national evaluation. *Adolescence, 34*: 523-528, 1999.

Boergers, J., and Spirito, A.: Follow-up studies of child and adolescent suicide attempters. In R.A. King and A. Apter (Eds.): *Suicide in Children and Adolescents.* New York: Cambridge University Press, 2003.

Bohanna, I., and Wang, X.: Media guidelines for the responsible reporting of suicide: A review of effectiveness. *Crisis, 33*: 190-198, 2012.

Bonanno, G.A., and Mancini, A.D.: Bereavement-related depression and PTSD: Evaluating Interventions. In L. Barbanel and R.J. Sternberg (Eds.): Psychological Interventions in Times of Crisis. New York: Springer, 2006.

Bongar, B. and Sullivan, G.: *The Suicidal Patient: Clinical and Legal Standards of Care*, 3rd Edition. Washington, DC: American Psychological Association, 2013.

Bonner, R.L.: Stressful segregation housing and psychosocial vulnerability in prison suicide ideators. *Suicide and Life-Threatening Behavior, 36*: 250-254, 2006.

Bonneson, M.E., and Hartsough, D.M.: Development of the Crisis Call Outcome Rating Scale. *Journal of Consulting and Clinical Psychology, 55*: 612-614, 1987.

Borges, G., and Rosovsky, H.: Suicide attempts and alcohol consumption in an emergency room sample. *Journal on Studies on Alcohol, 57*: 543-548, 1996.

Brenner, L.A., Breshears, R.E., Betthauser, L.M., Bellon, K.K., Holman, E., Harwood, J.E.F., et al.: Implementation of a suicide nomenclature within two VA healthcare settings. *Journal of Clinical Psychology in Medical Settings, 18*: 116-128, 2011.

Brent, D.A., and Bridge, J.: Firearms availability and suicide: Evidence, interventions, and future directions. *American Behavioral Scientist, 46*: 1192-1210, 2003.

Brent, D.A., Johnson, B.A., Perper, J., Connolly, J., Bridge, J., Bartle, S., et al.: Personality disorder, personality traits, impulsive violence, and completed suicide in adolescents. *Journal of the American Academy of Child & Adolescent Psychiatry, 33*: 1080-1086, 1994.

Brent, D.A., Kolko, D.J., Allan, M.J., and Brown, R.V.: Suicidality in affectively disordered adolescent inpatients. *Journal of the American Academy of Child & Adolescent Psychiatry, 30*: 586-593, 1990.

Brent, D.A., Perper, J.A., Goldstein, C.E., Kolko, D.J., Allan, M.J., Allman, C.J., et al.: Risk factors for adolescent suicide: A comparison of adolescent suicide victims with suicidal inpatients. *Archives of General Psychiatry, 45*: 581-588, 1988.

Brent, D.A., Perper, J., Moritz, G., Allman, C., Friend, A., Roth, C., et al.: Psychiatric risk factors for adolescent suicide: A case-control study. *Journal of the American Academy of Child & Adolescent Psychiatry, 32*: 521-529, 1993.

Brent, D.A., Perper, J., Moritz, G., Allman, C., Friend, A., Schweers, J., et al.: Psychiatric effects of exposure to suicide among the friends and acquaintances of adolescent suicide victims. *Journal of the American Academy of Child & Adolescent Psychiatry, 31*: 629-639, 1992.

Brent, D.A., Perper, J.A., Moritz, G., Baugher, M., Roth, C., Balach, L., et al.: Stressful life events, psychopathology, and adolescent suicide: A case control study. *Suicide and Life-Threatening Behavior, 23*: 179-187, 1993.

Brent, D.A., Perper, J., Moritz, G., Friend, A., Schweers, J., Allman, C., et al.: Adolescent witnesses to a peer suicide. *Journal of the American Academy of Child & Adolescent Psychiatry, 31*: 1184-1188, 1993.

Brent, D.A., Perper, J.A., Moritz, G., Liotus, L., Richardson, D., Canobbio, R., et al.: Posttraumatic stress disorder in peers of adolescent suicide victims: Predisposing factors and phenomenology. *Journal of the American Academy of Child & Adolescent Psychiatry, 34*: 209-215, 1995.

Bridge, J.A., McBee-Strayer, S.M., Cannon, E.A., Sheftall, A.H., Reynolds, B., Campo, J.V., et al.: Impaired decision making in adolescent suicide attempters. *Journal of the American Academy of Child & Adolescent Psychiatry, 51*: 394-403, 2012.

Britton, P.C., Ilgen, M.A., Rudd, M.D., and Conner, K.R.: Warning signs for suicide within a week of healthcare contact in Veteran decedents. *Psychiatry Research, 200*: 395-399, 2012.

Brockopp, G.W., and Lester, D.: The obscene caller. In D. Lester (Ed.): *Crisis Intervention and Counseling by Telephone*, 2nd Edition. Springfield, IL: Charles C Thomas, 2002.

Bronisch, T., Maragkos, M., Freyer, C., Muller-Cyran, A., Butollo, W., Weimbs. R., et al.: Crisis intervention after the tsunami in Phuket and Khao Lak. *Crisis, 27*:42-47, 2006.

Brooker, C., Ricketts, T., Bennett, S., and Lemme, F.: Admission decisions following contact with an emergency mental health assessment and intervention service. *Journal of Clinical Nursing, 16*: 1313-1322, 2007.

Brown, G.K., Jeglic, E., Henriques, G.R., and Beck, A.T.: Cognitive therapy, cognition, and suicidal behavior. In T.E. Ellis (Ed.): *Cognition and Suicide: Theory, Research, and Therapy*. Washington, DC: American Psychological Association, 2006.

Brown, G.K., Henriques, G.R., Sosdjan, D., and Beck, A.T.: Suicide intent and accurate expectations of lethality: Predictors of medical lethality of suicide attempts. *Journal of Consulting and Clinical Psychology, 72*: 1170-1174, 2004.

Brown, J.D., and Siegel, J.M.: Attributions for negative life events and depression: The role of perceived control. *Journal of Personality and Social Psychology, 54*: 316-322, 1988.

Brown, L.K., Overholser, J., Spirito, A., and Fritz, G.K.: The correlates of planning in adolescent suicide attempts. *Journal of the American Academy of Child & Adolescent Psychiatry, 30*: 95-99, 1991.

Brown, M.Z.: Linehan's theory of suicidal behavior: Theory, research, and dialectical behavior therapy. In T.E. Ellis (Ed.): *Cognition and Suicide: Theory, Research, and Therapy*. Washington, DC: American Psychological Association, 2006.

Brown, M.Z., Comtois, K.A., and Linehan, M.M.: Reasons for suicide attempts and nonsuicidal self-injury in women with borderline personality disorder. *Journal of Abnormal Psychology, 111*: 198-202, 2002.

Brown, R.M., Dahlen, E., Mills, C., Rick, J., and Biblarz, A.: Evaluation of an evolutionary model of self-preservation and self-destruction. *Suicide and Life-Threatening Behavior, 29*: 58-71, 1999.

Browning, S.L., Van Hasselt, V.B., Tucker, A.S., and Vecchi, G.M.: Dealing with individuals who have mental illness: the Crisis Intervention Team (CIT) in law enforcement. *The British Journal of Forensic Practice, 13*: 235-243, 2011.

Bryan, C.J., Clemans, T.A., and Hernandez, A.M.: Perceived burdensomeness, fearlessness of death, and suicidality among deployed military personnel. *Personality and Individual Differences, 52*: 374-379, 2012.

Bryan, C.J., and Rudd, M.D.: Advances in the assessment of suicide risk. *Journal of Clinical Psychology, 62*: 185-200, 2006.

Bryan, C.J., Stone, S.L., and Rudd, M.D.: A practical, evidence-based approach for means-restriction counseling with suicidal patients. *Professional Psychology: Research and Practice, 42*: 339-346, 2011.

Buchta, R., Wetzel, R.D., Reich, T., Butler, F., and Fuller, D.: The effect of direct contact with referred crisis center clients on outcome success rates. *Journal of Community Psychology, 1*: 395-396, 1973.

Bunn, T.A., and Clarke, A.M.: Crisis intervention: An experimental study of the effects of a brief period of counselling on the anxiety of relatives of seriously injured or ill hospital patients. *British Journal of Medical Psychology, 52*: 191-195, 1979.

Burgess, A.W.: Forward. In A.R. Roberts (Ed.): *Crisis Intervention Handbook: Assessment, Treatment, and Research.* New York: Oxford University Press, 2005.

Burgess, A.W., and Baker, T.: AIDS and victims of sexual assault. *Hospital & Community Psychiatry, 43*: 447-448, 1992.

Burgess, A.W., and Holmstrom, L.L.: Rape: Victims of Crisis. Bowie, MD: Brady, 1974. Burgess, A.W., and Holmstrom, L.L.: Rape: Sexual disruption and recovery. *American Journal of Orthopsychiatry, 49*: 648-657, 1979.

Burgess, A.W., and Holmstrom, L.L.: Rape trauma syndrome and post traumatic stress response. In A.W. Burgess (Ed.): *Rape and Sexual Assault: A Research Handbook.* New York: Garland, 1985.

Butler, W.M., Leitenberg, H., and Fuselier, G.D.: The use of mental health professional consultants to police hostage negotiation teams. *Behavioral Sciences and the Law, 11*: 213-221, 1993.

Cain, A.C., and Fast, I.: Children's disturbed reactions to parent suicide. *American Journal of Orthopsychiatry, 36*: 873-880, 1966(a).

Cain, A.C., and Fast, I.: The legacy of suicide: Observations on the pathogenic impact of suicide upon marital partners. *Psychiatry, 29*: 406-411, 1966(b).

Calhoun, L.G., and Tedeschi, R.G.: The foundations of posttraumatic growth: An expanded framework. In L.G. Calhoun and R.G. Tedeschi (Eds.): Handbook of Posttraumatic Growth: Research and Practice. Mahway, NJ: Lawrence Erlbaum Associates, 2006.

Campbell, R.: Rape survivors' experiences with the legal and medical systems: Do rape victim advocates make a difference? *Violence Against Women, 12*: 30-45, 2006.

Campbell, R.: The psychological impact or rape victims' experiences with the legal, medical, and mental health systems. *American Psychologist, 63*: 702-717, 2008.

Campbell, R.: What really happened? A validation study of rape survivors' help-seeking experiences with the legal and medical systems. *Violence and Victims, 20*: 55-68, 2005.

Campbell, R., Patterson, D., and Lichty, L.F.: The effectiveness of sexual assault nurse examiner (SANE) programs: A review of psychological, medical, legal, and community outcomes. *Trauma, Violence, & Abuse, 6*: 313-329, 2005.

Campbell, R., and Raja, S.: The sexual assault and secondary victimization of female veterans: Help-seeking experiences with military and civilian social systems. *Psychology of Women Quarterly, 29*: 97-106, 2005.

Campbell, R., Sefl, T., Barnes, H.E., Ahrens, C.E., Wasco, S.M., and Zaragoza-Diesfeld, Y.: Community services for rape survivors: Enhancing psychological well-being or increasing trauma? *Journal of Consulting and Clinical Psychology, 67*: 847-858, 1999.

Caplan, G.: A public-health approach to child psychiatry. *Mental Hygiene, 35*: 235-249, 1951.

Caplan, G.: Loss, stress, and mental health. *Community Mental Health Journal, 26*: 27-48, 1990.

Caplan, G.: *Principles of Preventive Psychiatry.* New York: Basic Books, 1964.

Caplan, G.: *Support Systems and Community Mental Health: Lectures on Concept Development.* New York: Behavioral Publications, 1974.

Caplan, G.: Foreword. In H .J. Parad, H.L.P. Resnik, and L.G. Parad (Eds.), *Emergency and Disaster Management: A Mental Health Sourcebook.* Bowie, MD: Charles Press, 1976.

Caplan, G.: Patterns of parental response to the crisis of premature birth: A preliminary approach to modifying the mental-health outcome. *Psychiatry, 23*: 365-374, 1960.

Capone, M.A., Good, R.S., Westie, K.S., and Jacobson, A.F.: Psychosocial rehabilitation of gynecologic oncology patients. *Archives of Physical Medicine and Rehabilitation, 61*: 128-132, 1980.

Capone, M.A., Westie, K.S., Chitwood, J.S., Feigenbaum, D., and Good, R.S.: Crisis intervention: A functional model for hospitalized cancer patients. *American Journal of Orthopsychiatry, 49*: 598-607, 1979.

Cardillo, J.E.: Goal setting, follow-up, and goal monitoring. In T.J. Kiresuk, A. Smith, and J.E. Cardillo (Eds.): *Goal Attainment Scaling: Applications, Theory, and Measurement.* Hillsdale, NJ: Lawrence Erlbaum Associates, 1994.

Cardillo, J.E., and Smith, A.: Reliability of goal attainment scores. In T.J. Kiresuk, A. Smith, and J.E. Cardillo (Eds.): *Goal Attainment Scaling: Applications, Theory, and Measurement.* Hillsdale, NJ: Lawrence Erlbaum Associates, 1994.

Carney, J.V., and Hazler, R.J.: Suicide and cognitive-behavioral counseling: Implications for mental counselors. *Journal of Mental Health Counseling, 20*: 28-41, 1998.

Carothers, J.E., and Inslee, L.J.: Level of empathic understanding offered by volunteer telephone services. *Journal of Counseling Psychology, 21*: 274-276, 1974.

Carter, G.L., Safranko, I., Lewin, T.J., Whyte, I.M., and Bryant, J.L.: Psychiatric hospitalization after deliberate self-poisoning. *Suicide and Life-Threatening Behavior, 36*: 213-222, 2006.

Cassells, C., Paterson, B., Dowding, D., and Morrison, R.: Long- and short-term risk factors in the prediction of inpatient suicide: A review of the literature. *Crisis, 26*: 53-63, 2005.

Catalan, J., Harding, R., Sibley, E., Clucas, C., Croome, N., and Sherr, L.: HIV infection and mental health: Suicidal behaviour–Systematic review. *Psychology, Health & Medicine: 16*: 588-611, 2011.

Catenaccio, R.: Crisis intervention with suicidal adolescents: A view from the emergency room. In J.K. Zimmerman and G.M. Asnis (Eds.): *Treatment Approaches with Suicidal Adolescents.* New York: Wiley, 1995.

Cattell, H., and Jolley, D.J.: One hundred cases of suicide in elderly people. *British Journal of Psychiatry, 166*: 451-457, 1995.

Cawunder, P., and Mohr, M.: Call length in telephone crisis intervention: Relationship with other caller and counselor characteristics. *Crisis Intervention, 11*: 66-73, 1982.

Cerel, J., Fristad, M.A., Weller, E.B., and Weller, R.A.: Suicide-bereaved children and adolescents: A controlled longitudinal examination. *Journal of the American Academy of Child & Adolescent Psychiatry, 38*: 672-679, 1999.

Chance, S.E., Kaslow, N.J., and Baldwin, K.: Anxiety and other predictors of severity of suicidal intent in urban psychiatric inpatients. *Hospital & Community Psychiatry, 45*: 716-718, 1994.

Cha, C.B., and Nock, M.K.: Emotional intelligence is a protective factor for suicidal behavior. *Journal of the American Academy of Child & Adolescent Psychiatry, 48*: 422-430, 2009.

Choi, J.W., Park, S., and Hong, J.P.: Suicide mortality of suicide attempt patients discharged from emergency room, nonsuicidal psychiatric patients discharged from emergency room, admitted suicide attempt patients, and admitted nonsuicidal psychiatric patients. *Suicide and Life-Threatening Behavior, 42*: 235-243.

Christiansen, E., and Jensen, B.F.: Risk of repetition of suicide attempt, suicide or all deaths after an episode of attempted suicide: A register-based survival analysis. *Australian and New Zealand Journal of Psychiatry, 41*: 257-265, 2007.

Chu, J.A.: Trauma and suicide. In D.G. Jacobs (Ed.) : *The Harvard Medical School Guide to Suicide Assessment and Intervention.* San Francisco: Jossey-Bass, 1999.

CIT International: Retrieved July 29, 2013 from http://www.citinternational.org/CITINT/PDF/CITIntBrochure20110408.pdf

Clark, D.C., and Goebel-Fabbri, A.E.: Lifetime risk of suicide in major affective disorders. In D.G. Jacobs (Ed.): *The Harvard Medical School Guide to Suicide Assessment and Intervention.* San Francisco: Jossey-Bass, 1999.

Clark, D.C., and Kerkhof, A.J.F.M.: No-suicide decisions and suicide contracts in therapy. *Crisis, 14*: 98-99, 1993.

Clark, L., Dombrovski, A.Y., Siegle, G.J., Butters, M.A., Shollenberger, C.L., Sahakian, B.J., et al.: Impairment in risk-sensitive decision-making in older suicide attempters with depression. *Psychology and Aging, 26*: 321-330, 2011.

Clary, E.G., and Orenstein, L.: The amount and effectiveness of help: The relationship of motives and abilities to helping behavior. *Personality and Social Psychology Bulletin, 17*: 58-64, 1991.

Claassen, C.A., Trivedi, M.H., Shimizu, I., Stewart, S., Larkin, G.L., and Litovitz, T.: Epidemiology of nonfatal deliberate self-harm in the United States as described in three medical databases. *Suicide and Life-Threatening Behavior, 36*: 192-212, 2006.

Cleary, S.D.: Adolescent victimization and associated suicidal and violent behaviors. *Adolescence, 35*: 671-682, 2000.

Cling, B .J.: Rape and rape trauma syndrome. In B.J. Cling (Ed.): *Sexualized Violence Against Women and Children.* New York: Guilford, 2004.

Cohen, D., Llorente, M., and Eisdorfer, C.: Homicide-suicide in older persons. *American Journal of Psychiatry, 155*: 390-396, 1998.

Cohen-Sandler, R., Berman, A., and King, R.: A follow-up study of hospitalized suicidal children. *Journal of the American Academy of Child Psychiatry, 21*: 398-403, 1982.

Conwell, Y., Duberstein, P.R., Connor, K., Eberly, S., Cox, C., and Caine, E.D.: Access to firearms and risk for suicide in middle-aged and older adults. *American Journal of Geriatric Psychiatry, 10*: 407-416, 2002.

Conwell, Y., Lyness, J.M., Duberstein, P., Cox, C., Seidlitz, L., DiGiorgio, A., et al.: Completed suicide among older patients in primary care practices: A controlled study. *Journal of the American Geriatrics Society, 48*: 23 29, 2000.

Cooper, J., Appleby, L., and Amos, T.: Life events preceding suicide by young people. *Social Psychiatry and Psychiatric Epidemiology, 37*: 271-275, 2002.

Cooper, J., Kapur, N., Webb, R., Lawlor, M., Guthrie, E., Mackway -Jones, K., et al.: Suicide after deliberate self-harm: A 4-year cohort study. *American Journal of Psychiatry, 162*: 297-303, 2005.

Cooperman, N.A., and Simoni, J.M.: Suicidal ideation and attempted suicide among women living with HIV/AIDS. *Journal of Behavioral Medicine, 28*: 149-156, 2005.

Corcoran, J., and Allen, S.: The effects of a police/victim assistance crisis team approach to domestic violence. *Journal of Family Violence, 20*: 39-45, 2005.

Cornelius, J.R., Salloum, I.M., Mezzich, J., Cornelius, M.D., Fabrega, H., Ehler, J.G., et al.: Disproportionate suicidality in patients with comorbid major depression and alcoholism. *American Journal of Psychiatry, 152*: 358-364, 1995.

Cornelius, L .J., Simpson, G.M., Ting, L., Wiggins, E., and Lipford, S.: Reach out and I'll be there: Mental health crisis intervention and mobile outreach services to urban African Americans. *Health & Social Work, 28*: 74-78, 2003.

Crosby, A.E., Ortega, L., and Melanson, C.: *Self-directed Violence Surveillance: Uniform Definitions and Recommended Data Elements, Version1.0.* Centers for Disease Control and Prevention, National Center for Injury Prevention and Control, Division of Violence Prevention. Atlanta, GA, 2011. Retrieved November 29, 2013 from http://www.cdc.gov/violenceprevention/pdf/self-directed-violence-a.pdf

Curphey, T.J.: The role of the social scientist in the medicolegal certification of death from suicide. In N.L. Farberow and E.S. Shneidman (Eds.): *The Cry for Help.* New York: McGraw-Hill, 1961.

Curran, D.K.: *Adolescent Suicidal Behavior.* New York: Hemisphere, 1987.

Cvinar, J.G.: Do suicide survivors suffer social stigma: A review of the literature. *Perspectives in Psychiatric Care, 41*: 14-21, 2005.

Cyr, C., and Dowrick, P.W.: Burnout in crisisline volunteers. *Administration and Policy in Mental Health, 18*: 343-354, 1991.

Daigle, M.S., and Mishara, B.L.: Intervention styles with suicidal callers at two suicide prevention centers. *Suicide and Life-Threatening Behavior, 25*: 261-275, 1995.

D'Augelli, A.R., Danish, S.J., and Brock, G.W.: Untrained paraprofessionals' verbal helping behavior: Description and implications for training. *American Journal of Community Psychology, 4*: 275-282, 1976.

D'Augelli, A.R., Handis, M.H., Brumbaugh, L., Illig, V., Searer, R., Turner, D.W., et al.: The verbal helping behavior of experienced and novice telephone counselors. *Journal of Community Psychology, 6*: 222-228, 1978.

Davies, P.G.K.: The functioning of British counselling hotlines: A pilot study. *British Journal of Guidance and Counselling, 10*: 195-199, 1982.

Deci, E.L., and Ryan, R.M.: The support of autonomy and the control of behavior. *Journal of Personality and Social Psychology, 53*: 1024-1037, 1987.

Deemer, E.D.: Ethical values and involuntary commitment: A decision-making model for consulting clinicians. *Stress, Trauma, and Crisis, 7*: 169-186, 2004.

DeJong, T.M., Overholser, J.C., and Stockmeier, C.A.: Apples to oranges?: A direct comparison between suicide attempters and suicide completers. *Journal of Affective Disorders, 124*: 90-97, 2010.

De Leo, D., Burgis, S., Bertolote, J.M., Kerkhof, A.J.F.M., and Bille-Brahe, U.: Definitions of suicidal behavior: Lessons learned from the WHO/EURO Multicentre Study. *Crisis, 27*: 4-15, 2006.

De Leo, D., and Ormskerk, S.C.R.: Suicide in the elderly: General characteristics. *Crisis, 12* (2): 3-17, 1991.

DeMaso, D.R., Ross, L., and Beardslee, W.R.: Depressive disorders and suicidal intent in adolescent suicide attempters. *Developmental and Behavioral Pediatrics, 15*: 74-77, 1994.

De Munck, S., Portzky, G., and Van Heeringen, K.: Epidemiological trends in attempted suicide in adolescents and young adults between 1996 and 2004. *Crisis, 30*: 115-119, 2009.

Dieserud, G., Roysamb, E., Ekeberg, O., and Kraft, P.: Toward an integrative model of suicide attempt: A cognitive psychological approach. *Suicide and Life-Threatening Behavior, 31*: 153-168, 2001.

Disaster Technical Assistance Center (DTAC) of the Substance Abuse and Mental Health Services Administration (SAMHSA): Crisis counseling assistance and training program Retrieved August 1, 2013 from http://www.samhsa.gov/dtac/proguide.asp

Dixon, W.A., Heppner, P.P., and Rudd, M.D.: Problem-solving appraisal, hopelessness, and suicide ideation: Evidence for a mediational model. *Journal of Counseling Psychology, 41*: 91-98, 1994.

Donegan, L.M., Sullivan, S., and McGuire, J.M.: Tolerance for ambiguity and empathic listening skills as predictors of conscientiousness in crisis service volunteers. *Crisis Intervention, 11*: 41-53, 1982.

Donovan, J.M., Bennett, M .J., and McElroy, C.M.: The crisis group–An outcome study. *American Journal of Psychiatry, 136*: 906-910, 1979.

Dori, G.A., and Overholser, J.C.: Depression, hopelessness, and self-esteem: Accounting for suicidality in adolescent psychiatric inpatients. *Suicide and Life-Threatening Behavior, 29*: 309-318, 1999.

Doyle, H., and Varian, J.: Crisis intervention in psychogeriatrics: A round-the-clock commitment? *International Journal of Geriatric Psychiatry, 9*: 65-72, 1994.

Doyle, W.W., Jr., Foreman, M.E., and Wales, E.: Effects of supervision in the training of nonprofessional crisis-intervention counselors. *Journal of Counseling Psychology, 24*: 72-78, 1977.

Drake, R.E., Gates, C., Cotton, P.G., and Whitaker, A.: Suicide among schizophrenics: Who is at risk? *Journal of Nervous and Mental Disease, 10*: 613-617, 1984.

Dunkel-Schetter, C., Folkman, S., and Lazarus, R.S.: Correlates of social support receipt. *Journal of Personality and Social Psychology, 53*: 71-80, 1987.

Dunne-Maxim, K., Godin, S., Lamb, F., Sutton, C., and Underwood, M.: The aftermath of youth suicide–Providing postvention services for the school and community. *Crisis, 13* (1): 16-22, 1992.

Dupont, R., and Cochran, S.: Police response to mental health emergencies–Barriers to change. *Journal of the American Academy of Psychiatry and the Law, 28*: 338-344, 2000.

Dyches, H., Biegel, D.E., Johnsen, J.A., Guo, S., and Min, M.O.: The impact of mobile crisis services on the use of community-based mental health services. *Research on Social Work Practice, 12*: 731-751, 2002.

Earle, K.A., Forquer, S.L., Volo, A.M., and McDonnell, P.M.: Characteristics of outpatient suicides. *Hospital & Community Psychiatry, 45*: 123-126, 1994.

Ebert, B.W.: Guide to conducting a psychological autopsy. *Professional Psychology: Research and Practice, 18*: 52-56, 1987.

Eddy, S., and Harris, E.: Risk management with the violent patient. In P.M. Kleespies (Ed.): *Emergencies in Mental Health Practice: Evaluation and Management.* New York: Guilford, 1998.

Edlis, N.: Rape crisis: Development of a center in an Israeli hospital. *Social Work in Health Care, 18* (3/4): 169-178, 1993.

Edwards, S.J., and Sachmann, M.D.: No-suicide contracts, no-suicide agreements, and no-suicide assurances. A study of their nature, utilization, perceived effectiveness, and potential to cause harm. *Crisis, 31*: 290-302, 2010.

Edwards-Stewart, A., Kinn, J.T., June, J.D., and Fullerton, N.R.: Military and civilian media coverage of suicide. *Archives of Suicide Research, 15*: 304-312, 2011.

Egan, M.P.: Contracting for safety: A concept analysis. Crisis, 18: 17-23, 1997. Elkins, R.L., and Cohen, C.R.: A comparison of the effects of prejob training and job experience on nonprofessional telephone crisis counselors. *Suicide and Life Threatening Behavior, 12*: 84-89, 1982.

Ellis, G.M.: Acquaintance rape. *Perspectives in Psychiatric Care, 30*: 11-16, 1994.

Ellis, T.E.: Psychotherapy with suicidal patients. In D. Lester (Ed.): *Suicide Prevention: Resources for the Millennium.* Philadelphia: Brunner-Routledge, 2001.

Elnour, A.A., and Harrison, J.: Lethality of suicide methods. *Injury Prevention, 14*: 39-45, 2008.

Endler, N.S., Edwards, J.M., and Kowalchuk, B.P.: The interaction model of anxiety assessed in a psychotherapy situation. *Southern Psychologist, 1*: 168-172, 1983.

Erchul, W.P.: Gerald Caplan: A tribute to the originator of mental health consultation. *Journal of Educational and Psychological Consultation, 19*: 95-105, 2009.

Erikson, E.H.: *Childhood and Society,* 2nd Edition. New York: Norton, 1963.

Esposito, C., Spirito, , A., Boergers, J., and Donaldson, D.: Affective, behavioral, and cognitive functioning in adolescents with multiple suicide attempts. *Suicide and Life-Threatening Behavior, 33*: 389-399, 2003.

Etzersdorfer, E., and Sonneck, G.: Preventing suicide by influencing mass-media reporting. The Viennese experience 1980-1996. *Archives of Suicide Research, 4*: 67- 74, 1998.

Evans, D.R., Uhlemann, M.R., and Hearn, M.T.: Microcounseling and sensitivity-training with hotline workers. *Journal of Community Psychology, 6*: 139-146, 1978.

Fakhoury, W.K.H.: Suicidal callers to a national helpline in the UK: A comparison of depressive and psychotic sufferers. *Archives of Suicide Research, 6*: 363-371, 2002.

Farberow, N.L.: Helping suicide survivors. In D. Lester (Ed.): Suicide Prevention: *Resources for the Millennium.* Philadelphia: Brunner-Routledge, 2001.

Farberow, N.L., Gallagher-Thompson, D., Gilewski, M., and Thompson, L.: The role of social supports in the bereavement process of surviving spouses of suicide and natural deaths. *Suicide and Life-Threatening Behavior, 22*: 107-124, 1992.

Farberow, N.L., and Litman, R.E.: *A Comprehensive Suicide Prevention Program. Suicide Prevention Center of Los Angeles, 1958-1969.* Unpublished final report DHEW NIMH Grants Nos. MH 14946 & MH 00128. Los Angeles: Suicide Prevention Center, 1970.

Fazel, S., Grann, M., Kling, B., Hawton, K.: Prison suicide in 12 countries: an ecological study of 861 suicides during 2003-2007. *Social Psychiatry and Psychiatric Epidemiology, 46*: 191-195, 2011.

Fawcett, J., Scheftner, W., Clark, D., Hedeker, D., Gibbons, R., and Coryell, W.: Clinical predictors of suicide in patients with major affective disorders: A controlled prospective study. *American Journal of Psychiatry, 144*: 35-40, 1987.

Fenton, W.S.: Depression, suicide, and suicide prevention in schizophrenia. *Suicide and Life-Threatening Behavior, 30*: 34-49, 2000.

Fiester, A.R.: Goal attainment and satisfaction scores for CMHC clients. *American Journal of Community Psychology, 7*: 181-188, 1979.

Fiester, A.R., and Fort, D.J.: A method of evaluating the impact of services at a comprehensive community mental health center. *American Journal of Community Psychology, 6*: 291-302, 1978.

Finn, P., and Sullivan, M.: Police handling of the mentally ill: Sharing responsibility with the mental health system. *Journal of Criminal Justice, 17*: 1-14, 1989.

Flannery, R.B., Jr., and Everly, G.S., Jr.: Crisis intervention: A review. *International Journal of Emergency Mental Health, 2*: 119-125, 2000.

Fleishman, J.A., Sherbourne, C.D., Crystal, S., Collins, R.L., Marshall, G.N., Kelly, M., et al.: Coping, conflictual social interactions, social support, and mood among HIV-infected persons. *American Journal of Community Psychology, 28*:421-453, 2000.

Fleury, R.E., Sullivan, C.M., Bybee, D.I., and Davidson, W.S., II.: "Why don't they just call the cops?": Reasons for differential police contact among women with abusive partners. *Violence and Victims, 13*: 333-346, 1998.

Folkman, S., and Lazarus, R.S.: Stress processes and depressive symptomatology. *Journal of Abnormal Psychology, 95*: 107-113, 1986.

Folkman, S., Lazarus, R.S., Dunkel-Schetter, C., DeLongis, A., and Gruen, R.J.: Dynamics of a stressful encounter: Cognitive appraisal, coping, and encounter outcomes. *Journal of Personalty and Social Psychology, 50*: 992-1003, 1986.

Forman, E.M., Berk, M.S., Henriques, G.R., Brown, G.K., and Beck, A.T.: History of multiple suicide attempts as a behavioral marker of severe psychopathology. *American Journal of Psychiatry, 161*: 437-443, 2004.

Fournier, R.R.: Group therapy and suicide. In R.I. Yufit and D. Lester (Eds.): *Assessment, Treatment, and Prevention of Suicidal Behavior.* Hoboken, NJ: Wiley, 2005.

France, K.: *Effects of Caller Value Orientation and of Worker Training and Experience on the Functioning of Lay Volunteer Crisis Telephone Workers.* Unpublished doctoral dissertation. Florida State University, 1975(a).

France, K.: Evaluation of lay volunteer crisis telephone workers. *American Journal of Community Psychology, 3*: 197-220, 1975(b).

France, K.: *The Hospital Patient: A Guide for Family and Friends.* Carlisle, PA: New Day, 1987.

France, K. and Dourte, B.: Straight Talk on Alcohol and Other Drugs / a web site for college students [On-line]. Mechanicsburg, PA: France Associates, 2014. Available: http://www.alcoholandotherdrugs.com/

France, K., Weikel, K., and Kish, M.: *Helping Skills for Human Service Workers: Building Relationships and Encouraging Productive Change,* 2nd Edition. Springfield, IL: Charles C Thomas, 2006.

Frauenfelder, K., and Frauenfelder, J.: The effect of brief empathy training for student hotline volunteers. *Crisis Intervention, 13*: 96-103, 1984.

Frazier, P.A., Mortensen, H., and Steward, J.: Coping strategies as mediators of the relations among perceived control and distress in sexual assault survivors. *Journal of Counseling Psychology, 52*: 267-278, 2005.

Fredrickson, B.L., and Branigan, C.: Positive emotions broaden the scope of attention and thought-action repertoires. *Cognition and Emotion, 19*: 313-332, 2005.

Fredrickson, B.L., Tugade, M.M., Waugh, C.E., and Larkin, G.R.: What good are positive emotions in crises? A prospective study of resilience and emotions following the terrorist attacks on the United States on September 11th, 2001. *Journal of Personality and Social Psychology, 84*: 365-376, 2003.

Freedy, J.R., Resnick, H.S., Kilpatrick, D.G., Dansky, B.S., and Tidwell, R.P.: The psychological adjustment of recent crime victims in the criminal justice system. *Journal of Interpersonal Violence, 9*: 450-468, 1994.

Frey, D.H., Motto, J.A., and Ritholz, M.D.: Group therapy for persons at risk for suicide: An evaluation using the intensive design. *Psychotherapy: Theory, Research and Practice, 20*: 281-293, 1983.

Friedmann, H., and Kohn, R.: Mortality, or probability of death, from a suicidal act in the United States. *Suicide and Life-Threatening Behavior, 38*: 287-301, 2008.

Fruehwald, S., Frottier, P., Eher, R., Gutierrez, K., and Ritter, K.: Prison suicides in Austria, 1975-1997. *Suicide and Life-Threatening Behavior, 30*: 360-369, 2000.

Furr, S.R., Westefeld, J.S., McConnell, G.N., and Jenkins, J.M.: Suicide and depression among college students: A decade later. *Professional Psychology: Research and Practice, 32*: 97-100, 2001.

Gallo, C.L., and Pfeffer, C.R.: Children and adolescents bereaved by a suicidal death: Implications for psychosocial outcomes and interventions. In R.A. King and A. Apter (Eds.): *Suicide in Children and Adolescents.* New York: Cambridge University Press, 2003.

Garland, A.F., and Zigler, E.: Adolescent suicide prevention: Current research and social policy implications. *American Psychologist, 48*: 169-182, 1993.

Garrison, C.Z., Addy, C.L., Jackson, K.L., McKeown, R.E., and Waller, J.L.: A longitudinal study of suicidal ideation in young adolescents. *Journal of the American Academy of Child & Adolescent Psychiatry, 30*: 597-603, 1991.

Genther, R.: Evaluating the functioning of community-based hotlines. *Professional Psychology, 5*: 409-414, 1974.

Gersons, B.P.R., and Carlier, I.V.E.: Plane crash crisis intervention: A preliminary report from the Bijlmermeer, Amsterdam. *Crisis, 14*: 109-116, 1993.

Getz, W.L., Fujita, B.N., and Allen, D.: The use of paraprofessionals in crisis intervention: Evaluation of an innovative program. *American Journal of Community Psychology, 3*: 135-144, 1975.

Geulayov, G., Gunnell, D., Holmen, T.L., and Metcalfe, C.: The association of parental fatal and non-fatal suicidal behaviour with offspring suicidal behaviour and depression: a systematic review and meta-analysis. *Psychological Medicine, 42*: 1567-1580, 2012.

Gibb, S.J., Beautrais, A.L., and Fergusson, D.M.: Mortality and further suicidal behaviour after an index suicide attempt: A 10-year study. *Australian and New Zealand Journal of Psychiatry, 39*: 95-100, 2005.

Gibson, C.A., Breitbart, W., Tomarken, A., Kosinski, A., and Nelson, C.J.: Mental health issues near the end of life. In J.L. Werth Jr. and D. Blevins (Eds.): *Psychosocial Issues Near the End of Life: A Resource for Professional Care Providers*, Washington, DC: American Psychological Association, 2006.

Gilbar, O.: Model for crisis intervention through group therapy for women with breast cancer. *Clinical Social Work Journal, 19*: 293-304, 1991.

Gingerich, W.J., Gurney, R.J., and Wirtz, T.S.: How helpful are helplines? A survey of callers. *Social Casework, 69*: 634-639, 1988.

Ginsberg, M.R., and Danish, S.J.: The effects of self-selection on trainees' verbal helping skills performance. *American Journal of Community Psychology, 7*: 577-581, 1979.

Gispert, M., Davis, M.S., Marsh, L., and Wheeler, K.: Predictive factors in repeated suicide attempts by adolescents. *Hospital & Community Psychiatry, 38*: 390-393, 1987.

Gordon, R.H.: Efficacy of a group crisis-counseling program for men who accompany women seeking abortions. *American Journal of Community Psychology, 6*: 239-246, 1978.

Gould, M., Jamieson, P., and Romer, D.: Media contagion and suicide among the young. *American Behavioral Scientist, 46*: 1269-1284, 2003.

Gould, M.S., Fisher, P., Parides, M., Flory, M., and Shaffer, D.: Psychosocial risk factors of child and adolescent completed suicide. *Archives of General Psychiatry, 53*: 1155-1162, 1996.

Gould, M.S., and Kramer, R.A.: Youth suicide prevention. *Suicide and Life-Threatening Behavior, 31* (Supplement): 6-31, 2001.

Gould, M.S., Harris-Munfakh, J.L., Kleinman, M., and Lake, A.M.: National Suicide Prevention Lifeline: Enhancing mental health care for suicidal individuals and other people in crisis. *Suicide and Life-Threatening Behavior, 42*: 22-35, 2012.

Gould, M.S., Kalafat, J., Harris-Munfakh, J.L., and Kleinman, M.: An evaluation of crisis hotline outcomes part 2: Suicidal callers. *Suicide and Life-Threatening Behavior, 37*: 338-352, 2007.

Gould, M.S., Shaffer, D., and Greenberg, T.: the epidemiology of youth suicide. In R.A. King and A. Apter (Eds.): *Suicide in Children and Adolescents.* New York: Cambridge University Press, 2003.

Granvold, D.K.: The crisis of divorce: Cognitive-behavioral and constructivist assessment and treatment. In A.R. Roberts (Ed.): *Crisis Intervention Handbook: Assessment, Treatment, and Research.* New York: Oxford University Press, 2005.

Greene, G.J., Lee, M.Y., Trask, R., and Rheinscheld, J.: How to work with clients' strengths in crisis intervention: A solution-focused approach. In A.R. Roberts (Ed.): *Crisis Intervention Handbook: Assessment, Treatment, and Research.* New York: Oxford University Press, 2005.

Greenhill, L.L., and Waslick, B.: Management of suicidal behavior in children and adolescents: *Psychiatric Clinics of North America, 20*: 641-666, 1997.

Greenstone, J.L.: *The Elements of Police Hostage and Crisis Negotiations: Critical Incidents and How to Respond to Them.* New York: Haworth Press, 2005.

Greenwald, D.J., Reznikoff, M., and Plutchik, R.: Suicide risk and violence risk in alcoholics: Predictors of aggressive risk. *Journal of Nervous and Mental Disease, 182*: 3-8, 1994.

Grieger, I., and Greene, P.: The psychological autopsy as a tool in student affairs. *Journal of College Student Development, 39*: 388-392, 1998.

Guidelines for the determination of death. *Journal of the American Medical Association, 246*: 2184-2186, 1981.

Guthrie, S.H.: Crisis intervention teaming: A participant's perspective. *School Counselor, 40*: 73-76, 1992.

Hall, M.H.: A conversation with the father of Rogerian therapy. *Psychology Today: 19-21,* 62-66, 1967, December.

Halpern, H.A.: Crisis theory: A definitional study. *Community Mental Health Journal, 9*: 342-349, 1973.

Halpern, H.A.: The crisis scale: A factor analysis and revision. *Community Mental Health Journal, 11*: 295-300, 1975.

Hansell, N.: *The Person-in-Distress.* New York: Human Sciences Press, 1976.

Harkavy-Friedman, J.M. and Nelson, E.A.: Assessment and intervention for the suicidal patient with schizophrenia. *Psychiatric Quarterly, 68*: 361-375, 1997(a).

Harkavy-Friedman, J.M. and Nelson, E.: Management of the suicidal patient with schizophrenia. *Psychiatric Clinics of North America, 20*: 625-640, 1997(b).

Harris, H.E., and Myers, W.C.: Adolescents' misperceptions of the dangerousness of acetaminophen in overdose. *Suicide and Life-Threatening Behavior, 27*: 274-277, 1997.

Harris, K.M., McLean, J.P., Sheffield, J., and Jobes, D.: The internal suicide debate hypothesis: Exploring the life versus death struggle. *Suicide and Life-Threatening Behavior, 40*: 181-192, 2010.

Hart, L.E., and King, G.D.: Selection versus training in the development of paraprofessionals. *Journal of Counseling Psychology, 26*: 235-241, 1979.

Hatcher, C., Mohandie, K., Turner, J., and Gelles, M.G.: The role of the psychologist in crisis/hostage negotiations. *Behavioral Sciences and the Law, 16*: 455-472, 1998.

Hayes, L.M.: Juvenile suicide in confinement – Findings from the first national survey. *Suicide and Life-Threatening Behavior, 39*: 353-363, 2009.

Hayes, L.M.: Juvenile suicide in confinement in the United States: Results from a national survey. *Crisis, 26*: 146-148, 2005.

Hayes, L.M.: National study of jail suicide: 20 years later. Journal of Correctional Health Care, 18: 233-245, 2012.

Hazell, P., and Lewin, T.: An evaluation of postvention following adolescent suicide. *Suicide and Life-Threatening Behavior, 23*: 101-109, 1993.

Heath, C., and Heath, D.: *Decisive.* New York: Crown Business, 2013.

Heckman, T.G., Anderson, E.S., Sikkema, K.J., Kochman, A., Kalichman, S.C., and Anderson, T.: Emotional distress in nonmetropolitan persons living with HIV disease enrolled in a telephone-delivered, coping improvement group intervention. *Health Psychology, 23*: 94-100, 2004.

Heckman, T.G., Miller, J., Kochman, A., Kalichman, S.C., Carlson, B., and Silverthorn, M.: Thoughts of suicide among HIV-infected rural persons enrolled in a telephone-delivered mental health intervention. *Annals of Behavioral Medicine, 24*: 141-148, 2002.

Heikkinen, M., Aro, H., and Lonnqvist, J.: Life events and social support in suicide. *Suicide and Life-Threatening Behavior, 23*: 343-358, 1993.

Heikkinen, M.E., Isometsa, E.T., Aro, H.M., Sarna, S.J., and Lonnqvist, J.K.: Age-related variation in recent life events preceding suicide. *Journal of Nervous and Mental Disease, 183*: 325-331, 1995.

Heilbron, N., Compton, J.S., Daniel, S.S., and Goldston, D.B.: The problematic label of suicide gesture: Alternatives for clinical research and practice. *Professional Psychology: Research and Practice, 41*: 221-227, 2010.

Hellman, C.M., and House, D.: Volunteers serving victims of sexual assault. *Journal of Social Psychology, 146*: 117-123, 2006.

Hembree, E.A., and Foa, E.B.: Interventions for trauma-related emotional disturbance in adult victims of crime. *Journal of Traumatic Stress, 16*: 187-199, 2003.

Hendin, H., Maltsberger, J.T., Lipschitz, A., Haas, A.P., and Kyle, J.: Recognizing and responding to a suicide crisis. *Suicide and Life-Threatening Behavior, 31*: 115-128, 2001.

Hendin, H., Maltsberger, J.T., Haas, A.P., Szanto, K., and Rabinowicz, H.: Desperation and other affective states in suicidal patients. *Suicide and Life-Threatening Behavior, 34*: 386-394, 2004.

Hendricks, J.E.: Death notification: The theory and practice of informing survivors. *Journal of Police Science and Administration, 12*: 109-116, 1984.

Herbert, H., Maltsberger, J.T., Lipschitz, A., Haas, A.P., and Kyle, J.: Recognizing and responding to a suicide crisis. *Suicide and Life-Threatening Behavior, 31*: 115-128, 2001.

Hetrick, S.E., Parker, A.G., Robinson, J., Hall, N., and Vance, A.: Predicting suicidal risk in a cohort of depressed children and adolescents. *Crisis, 33*: 13-20, 2012.

Hilarski, C.: Unresolved grief. In C.N. Dulmus and L.A. Rapp-Paglicci (Eds.): *Handbook of Preventive Interventions for Adults.* Hoboken, NJ: Wiley, 2005.

Hinduja, S., and Patchin, J.W.: Bullying, cyberbullying, and suicide. *Archives of Suicide Research, 14*: 206-221, 2010.

Hoberman, H.M., and Garfinkel, B.D.: Completed suicide in youth. *Canadian Journal of Psychiatry, 33*: 494-504, 1988.

Hoff, M.R., and Hoff, L.A.: *Crisis Education and Service Program Designs: A guide for Administrators, Educators, and Clinical Trainers.* New York: Routledge, 2012.

Holmes-Garrett, C.: The crisis of the forgotten family: A single session group in the ICU waiting room. *Social Work with Groups, 12* (4): 141-157, 1989.

Holmstrom, L.L.: The criminal justice system's response to the rape victim. In A.W. Burgess (Ed.): *Rape and Sexual Assault: A Research Handbook.* New York: Garland, 1985.

Holmstrom, L.L.: Lynda Lytle Holmstrom: Research and Publications. Retrieved August 1, 2013 from http://www2.bc.edu/~holmstro/res.htm

Holmstrom, L.L., and Burgess, A.W.: *The Victim of Rape: Institutional Reactions.* New York: Wiley, 1978.

Hopkins, C., and Niemiec, S.: Mental health crisis at home: service user perspectives on what helps and what hinders. *Journal of Psychiatric and Mental Health Nursing, 14*: 310-318, 2007.

Horacek, B .J.: A heuristic model of grieving after high-grief deaths. *Death Studies, 19*: 21-31, 1995.

Hornblow, A.R.: The evolution and effectiveness of telephone counseling services. *Hospital & Community Psychiatry, 37*. 731-733, 1986.

Hornblow, A.R., and Sloane, H.R.: Evaluating the effectiveness of a telephone counselling service. *British Journal of Psychiatry, 137*: 377-378, 1980.

Horsfall, J., Cleary, M., and Hunt, G.E.: Acute inpatient units in a comprehensive (integrated) mental health system: A review of the literature. *Issues in Mental Health Nursing, 31*: 273-278, 2010.

Huff, C.O.: Source, recency, and degree of stress in adolescence and suicide ideation. *Adolescence, 34*: 81-89, 1999.

Hung, N.C., & Rabin, L.A.: Comprehending childhood bereavement by parental suicide: A critical review of research on outcomes, grief processes, and interventions. *Death Studies, 33*: 781-814, 2009.

Hutchinson, G., Daisley, H., Simeon, D., Simmonds, V., Shetty, M., and Lynn, D.: High rates of paraquat-induced suicide in southern Trinidad. *Suicide and Life-Threatening Behavior, 29*: 186-191, 1999.

Hutchinson, R.L., Tess, D.E., Gleckman, A.D., and Spence, W.C.: Psychosocial characteristics of institutionalized adolescents: Resilient or at risk? *Adolescence, 27*: 339-356, 1992.

Isometsa, E.T., and Lonnqvist, J.K.: Suicide attempts preceding completed suicide. *British Journal of Psychiatry, 173*: 531-535, 1998.

Jacobs, D.G., Brewer, M., and Klein-Benheim, M.: Suicide assessment: An overview and recommended protocol. In D.G. Jacobs (Ed.): *The Harvard Medical School Guide to Suicide Assessment and Intervention.* San Francisco: Jossey-Bass, 1999.

Jacobs, G.A.: The development of a national plan for disaster mental health. *Professional Psychology: Research and Practice, 26*: 543-549, 1995.

James, R.K., Logan, J., and Davis, S.A.: Including School Resource Officers in school-based crisis intervention: Strengthening student support. *School Psychology International, 32*: 210-224, 2011.

Janoff-Bulman, R.: Schema-change perspectives on posttraumatic growth. In L.G. Calhoun and R.G. Tedeschi (Eds.): *Handbook of Posttraumatic Growth: Research and Practice.* Mahwah, NJ: Lawrence Erlbaum Associates, 2006.

Jayaratne, S., Croxton, T.A., and Mattison, D.: A national survey of violence in the practice of social work. *Families in Society, 85*: 445-453, 2004.

Jobes, D.A.: Collaborating to prevent suicide: A clinical-research perspective. *Suicide and Life-Threatening Behavior, 30*: 8-17, 2000.

Jobes, D.A., Berman, A.L., and Martin, C.E.: Adolescent suicidality and crisis intervention. In A.R. Roberts (Ed.): *Crisis Intervention Handbook: Assessment, Treatment, and Research.* New York: Oxford University Press, 2005.

Jobes, D.A., Jacoby, A.M., Cimbolic, P., and Hustead, L.A.T.: Assessment and treatment of suicidal clients in a university counseling center. *Journal of Counseling Psychology, 44*: 368-377, 1997.

Jobes, D.A., and Mann, R.E.: Reasons for living versus reasons for dying: Examining the internal debate of suicide. *Suicide and Life-Threatening Behavior, 29*: 97-104, 1999.

Jobes, D.A., Rudd, M.D., Overholser, J.C., and Joiner, T.E. Jr.: Ethical and competent care of suicidal patients: Contemporary challenges, new developments, and considerations for clinical practice. *Professional Psychology: Research and Practice, 39*: 405-413, 2008.

Johnson, D.W.: *Reaching Out: Interpersonal Effectiveness and Self-Actualization,* 11th Edition. Boston: Pearson, 2014.

Johnson, S.L., McMurrich, S.L., and Yates, M.: Suicidality in Bipolar I Disorder. *Suicide and Life-Threatening Behavior, 35*: 681-689, 2005.

Joiner, T.: New life in suicide science. In T. Joiner and M.D. Rudd (Eds.): *Suicide Science: Expanding the Boundaries.* Boston: Kluwer Academic Publishers, 2000. Joiner, T.: *Why People Die by Suicide.* Cambridge, MA: Harvard University Press, 2005.

Joiner, T.E., Kalafat, J., Draper, J., Stokes, H., Knudson, M., Berman, A.L., et al.: Establishing standards for the assessment of suicide risk among callers to the National Suicide Prevention Lifeline. *Suicide and Life-Threatening Behavior, 37*: 353-365, 2007.

Joiner, T.E., Jr., Pettit, J.W., Walker, R.L., Voelz, Z.R., Cruz, J., Rudd, M.D., et al.: Perceived burdensomeness and suicidality: Two studies on the suicide notes of those attempting and those completing suicide. *Journal of Social and Clinical Psychology, 21*: 531-545, 2002.

Joiner, T.E., and Rudd, M.D.: Disentangling the interrelations between hopelessness, loneliness, and suicidal ideation. *Suicide and Life-Threatening Behavior, 26*: 19-26, 1996.

Joiner, T.E., Jr., and Rudd, M.D.: Intensity and duration of suicidal crises vary as a function of previous suicide attempts and negative life events. *Journal of Consulting and Clinical Psychology, 68*: 909-916, 2000.

Joiner, T.E., Jr., Rudd, M.D., and Rajab, M.H.: Agreement between self- and clinician-rated suicidal symptoms in a clinical sample of young adults: Explaining discrepancies. *Journal of Consulting and Clinical Psychology, 67*: 171-176, 1999.

Joiner, T.E., Jr., Rudd, M.D., and Rajab, M.H.: The Modified Scale for Suicidal Ideation: Factors of suicidality and their relation to clinical and diagnostic variables. *Journal of Abnormal Psychology, 106*: 260-265, 1997.

Joiner, T.F., Jr., Walker, R.L., Rudd, M.D., and Jobes, D.A.: Scientizing and routinizing the assessment of suicidality in outpatient practice. *Professional Psychology: Research and Practice, 30*: 447-453, 1999.

Jones, R.M., Hales, H., Butwell, M., Ferriter, M., and Taylor, P.J.: Suicide in high security hospital patients. *Social Psychiatry and Psychiatric Epidemiology, 46*: 723-731, 2011.

Jordan, J.R., and McMenamy, J.: Interventions for suicide survivors: A review of the literature. *Suicide and Life-Threatening Behavior, 34*: 337-349, 2004.

Kalafat, J.: Crisis intervention and counseling by telephone: An update. In D. Lester (Ed.): *Crisis Intervention and Counseling by Telephone*, 2nd Edition. Springfield, IL: Charles C Thomas, 2002(a).

Kalafat, J.: Training telephone counselors. In D. Lester (Ed.): *Crisis Intervention and Counseling by Telephone*, 2nd Edition. Springfield, IL: Charles C Thomas, 2002(b).

Kalafat, J., Boroto, D.R., and France, K.: Relationships among experience level and value orientation and the performance of paraprofessional telephone counselors. *American Journal of Community Psychology, 7*: 167-180, 1979.

Kalafat, J., Gould, M.S., Harris-Munfakh, J.L., and Kleinman, M.: An evaluation of crisis hotline outcomes part 1: Nonsuicidal crisis callers. *Suicide and Life-Threatening Behavior, 37*: 322-337, 2007.

Kalafat, J., and Underwood, M.M.: Crisis intervention in the context of outpatient treatment of suicidal patients. In R.I. Yufit and D. Lester (Eds.): *Assessment, Treatment, and Prevention of Suicidal Behavior*. Hoboken, NJ: Wiley, 2005.

Kallert, T.W., Leisse, M., and Winiecki, P.: Suicidality of chronic schizophrenic patients in long-term community care. *Crisis, 25*: 54-64, 2004.

Katz, B.L., and Burt, M.R.: Self-blame in recovery from rape: Help or hindrance? In A.W. Burgess (Ed.): *Rape and Sexual Assault II*. New York: Garland, 1988.

Kernic, M.A., and Bonomi, A.E.: Female victims of domestic violence: Which victims do police refer to crisis intervention. *Violence and Victims, 22*: 463-473, 2007.

Kienhorst, I.C.W.M., De Wilde, E.J., Diekstra, R.F.W., and Wolters, W.H.G.: Adolescents' image of their suicide attempt. *Journal of the American Academy of Child &Adolescent Psychiatry, 34*: 623-628, 1995.

Kimerling, R., and Calhoun, K.S.: Somatic symptoms, social support, and treatment seeking among sexual assault victims. *Journal of Consulting and Clinical Psychology, 62*: 333-340, 1994.

King, C.A., Hill, E.M., Naylor, M., Evans, T., and Shain, B.: Alcohol consumption in relation to other predictors of suicidality among adolescent inpatient girls. *Journal of the American Academy of Child & Adolescent Psychiatry, 32*: 82-88, 1993.

King, E.: Suicide in the mentally ill: An epidemiological sample and implications for clinicians. *British Journal of Psychiatry, 165*: 658-663, 1994.

King, G.D.: An evaluation of the effectiveness of a telephone counseling center. *American Journal of Community Psychology, 5*: 75-83, 1977.

King, R., Nurcombe, B., Bickman, L., Hides, L., and Reid, W.: Telephone counselling for adolescent suicide prevention: Changes in suicidality and mental state from beginning to end of a counselling session. *Suicide and Life-Threatening Behavior, 33*: 400-411, 2003.

Kingsbury, S.J.: Clinical components of suicidal intent in adolescent overdose. *Journal of the American Academy of Child & Adolescent Psychiatry, 32*: 518-520, 1993.

Kinyanda, E., Hjelmeland, H., and Musisi, S.: Negative life events associated with deliberate self-harm in an African population in Uganda. *Crisis, 26*: 4-11, 2005.

Kiresuk, T.J., and Choate, R.O.: Applications of Goal Attainment Scaling. In T.J. Kiresuk, A. Smith, and J.E. Cardillo (Eds.): *Goal Attainment Scaling: Applications, Theory, and Measurement.* Hillsdale, NJ: Lawrence Erlbaum Associates, 1994.

Kiresuk, T.J., Smith, A., and Cardillo, J.E. (Eds.): Goal Attainment Scaling: Applications, Theory, and Measurement. Hillsdale, NJ: Lawrence Erlbaum Associates, 1994.

Kirk, A.K., Stanley, G.V., and Brown, D.F.: Changes in patients' stress and arousal levels associated with therapists' perception of their requests during crisis intervention. *British Journal of Clinical Psychology, 27*: 363-369, 1988.

Kisely, S., Campbell, L.A., Peddle, S., Hare, S., Pyche, M., Spicer, D., and Moore, B.: A controlled before-and-after evaluation of a mobile crisis partnership between mental health and police services in Nova Scotia. *The Canadian Journal of Psychiatry, 55*: 662-668, 2010.

Kleespies, P.M., and Dettmer, E.L.: An evidence-based approach to evaluating and managing suicidal emergencies. *Journal of Clinical Psychology, 56*: 1109-1130, 2000.

Kleespies, P.M., Hughes, D.H., and Gallacher, F.P.: Suicide in the medically and terminally ill: Psychological and ethical considerations. *Journal of Clinical Psychology, 56*: 1153-1171, 2000.

Kleespies, P.M.: *Decision Making in Behavioral Emergencies: Acquiring Skill in Evaluating and Managing High-Risk Patients.* Washington, DC: American Psychological Association, 2014.

Klingman, A.: Emotional first aid during the impact phase of a mass disaster. *Emotional First Aid, 3* (3): 51-57, 1986.

Knickerbocker, D.A.: *Lay Volunteer and Professional Trainee Therapeutic Functioning and Outcomes in a Suicide and Crisis Intervention Service.* Unpublished doctoral dissertation. University of Florida, 1972.

Knickerbocker, D.A., and McGee, R.K.: Clinical effectiveness of nonprofessional and professional telephone workers in a crisis intervention center. In D. Lester and G.W. Brockopp (Eds.): *Crisis Intervention and Counseling by Telephone.* Springfield, IL: Charles C Thomas, 1973.

Knowles, D.: On the tendency for volunteer helpers to give advice. *Journal of Counseling Psychology, 26*: 352-354, 1979.

Koocher, G.P., Curtiss, E.K., Pollin, I.S., and Patton, K.E.: Medical crisis counseling in a health maintenance organization: Preventive intervention. *Professional Psychology: Research and Practice, 32*: 52-58, 2001.

Kosky, R.: Childhood suicidal behavior. *Journal of Child Psychology and Psychiatry, 24*: 457-468, 1983.

Kovacs, M., Goldston, D., and Gatsonis, C.: Suicidal behaviors and childhood-onset depressive disorders: A longitudinal investigation. *Journal of the American Academy of Child & Adolescent Psychiatry, 32*: 8-20, 1993.

Kranz, P.L.: Crisis intervention: A new approach to crisis intervention: A mentor trained mode. *Crisis Intervention, 14*: 107-114, 1985.

Kroon, M.B.R., and Overdijk, W.I.E.: Psychosocial care and shelter following the Bijlmermeer air disaster. *Crisis, 14*: 117-125, 1993.

Kruesi, M .J.P., Grossman, J., Pennington, J.M., Woodward, P.J., Duda, D., and Hirsch, J.G.: Suicide and violence prevention: Parent education in the emergency department. *Journal of the American Academy of Child & Adolescent Psychiatry, 38*: 250-255, 1999.

Lamb, H.R., Weinberger, L.E., and Gross, B.H.: Mentally ill persons in the criminal justice system: Some perspectives. *Psychiatric Quarterly, 75*: 107-126, 2004.

Lammers, J. C.: Attitudes, motives, and demographic predictors of volunteer commitment and service duration. *Journal of Social Service Research, 14 (3/4)*: 125-140, 1991.

Lanceley, F.J.: *On-Scene Guide for Crisis Negotiators*, 2nd Edition. Boca Raton, FL: CRC Press, 2003.

Langsley, D.G.: Crisis intervention for the chronic mental patient. In B.S. Comstock, W.E. Fann, A.D. Pokorny, and R.L. Williams (Eds.): *Phenomenology and Treatment of Psychiatric Emergencies*. New York: Spectrum Publications, 1984.

Large, M., Smith, G., and Nielssen, O.: The epidemiology of homicide followed by suicide: A systematic and quantitative review. *Suicide and Life-Threatening Behavior, 39*: 294-306, 2009.

Lazar, A., and Erera, P.I.. The telephone helpline as social support. *International Social Work, 41*: 89-101, 1998.

Lazarus, R.S.: *Stress and Emotion: A New Synthesis*. New York: Springer, 1999.

Ledray, L.E.: Evidence collection: An update. *Journal of Child Sexual Abuse, 2*: 113-115, 1993.

Leenaars, A.A.: *Psychotherapy with suicidal people: A person-centered approach*. West Sussex, England: Wiley, 2004.

Leenaars, A.A.: Suicide prevention in schools: Resources for the millennium. In D. Lester (Ed.): *Suicide Prevention: Resources for the Millennium*. Philadelphia: BrunnerRoutledge, 2001.

Lester, D.: Steps toward the evaluation of suicide prevention centers: Part four. *Crisis Intervention, 2* (Supplement): 20-22, 1970.

Lester, D.: Challenges in preventing suicide. *Crisis, 14*: 187-189, 1993.

Lester, D.: Challenges in preventing suicide. *Death Studies, 18*: 623-639, 1994.

Lester, D.: Resources and tactics for preventing suicide. *Clinical Neuropsychiatry, 2*: 32-36, 2005a.

Lester, D.: The effectiveness of suicide prevention and crisis intervention services. In D. Lester (Ed.): *Crisis Intervention and Counseling by Telephone,* 2nd Edition. Springfield, IL: Charles C Thomas, 2002.

Lester, D.: The classic systems of psychotherapy and suicidal behavior. In R.I. Yufit and D. Lester (Eds.): *Assessment, Treatment, and Prevention of Suicidal Behavior.* Hoboken, NJ: Wiley, 2005b.

LeVine, E.S. Facilitating recovery for people with serious mental illness employing a psychobiosocial model of care. *Professional Psychology: Research and Practice, 43*: 58-64, 2012.

Levinson, D., Haklai, Z., Stein, N., and Gordon, E.S.: Suicide attempts in Israel: Age by gender analysis of a national emergency departments database. *Suicide and Life-Threatening Behavior, 36*: 97-102, 2006.

Lewinsohn, P.M., Rohde, P., and Seeley, J.R.: Psychosocial risk factors for future adolescent suicide attempts. *Journal of Consulting and Clinical Psychology, 62*: 297-305, 1994.

Lewinsohn, P.M., Rohde, P., and Seeley, J.R.: Adolescent suicidal ideation and attempts: Prevalence, risk factors, and clinical implications. *Clinical Psychology: Science and Practice, 5*: 25-46, 1996.

Lewis, S.J.: The Crisis State Assessment Scale: Development and psychometrics. In A.R. Roberts (Ed.): *Crisis Intervention Handbook: Assessment, Treatment, and Research.* New York: Oxford University Press, 2005.

Lewis, S.J., and Harrison, D.M.: Crisis intervention with HIV positive women. In A.R. Roberts (Ed.): *Crisis Intervention Handbook: Assessment, Treatment, and Research.* New York: Oxford University Press, 2005.

Ligon, J.: Mobile crisis units: Frontline community mental health services. In A.R. Roberts (Ed.): *Crisis Intervention Handbook: Assessment, Treatment, and Research.* New York: Oxford University Press, 2005.

Lindemann, E.: Symptomatology and management of acute grief. *American Journal of Psychiatry, 101*: 141-148, 1944.

Linehan, M.M., Goodstein, J.L., Nielsen, S.L., and Chiles, J.A.: Reasons for staying alive when you are thinking of killing yourself: The reasons for living inventory. *Journal of Consulting and Clinical Psychology, 51*: 276-286, 1983.

Links, P.S., Eynan, R., Ball, J.S., Barr, A., and Rourke, S.: Crisis occurrence and resolution in patients with severe and persistent mental illness: The contribution of suicidality. *Crisis, 26*: 160-169, 2005.

Litt, I.F., Cuskey, W.R., and Rudd, S.: Emergency room evaluation of the adolescent who attempts suicide: Compliance with follow-up. *Journal of Adolescent Health Care, 4*: 106-108, 1983.

Logan, T.K., Walker, R., Jordan, C.E., and Leukefeld, C.G.: *Women and Victimization: Contributing Factors, Interventions, and Implications.* Washington, DC: American Psychological Association, 2006.

Lubin, G., Werbeloff, N., Halperin, D., Shmushkevitch, M., Weiser, M., and Knobler, H.Y.: Decrease in suicide rates after a change of policy reducing access to firearms in adolescents: A naturalistic epidemiological study. *Suicide and Life-Threatening Behavior, 40*: 421-424.

Lynch, T.R., Cheavens, J.S., Morse, J.Q., and Rosenthal, M.Z.: A model predicting suicidal ideation and hopelessness in depressed older adults: The impact of emotion inhibition and affect intensity. *Aging & Mental Health, 8*: 486-497, 2004.

MacLeod, A.K., Tata, P., Evans, K., Tyrer, P., Schmidt, U., Davidson, K. et al.: Recovery of positive future thinking within a high-risk parasuicide group: Results from a pilot randomized controlled trial. *British Journal of Clinical Psychology, 37*: 371-379, 1998.

Madonia, J.F.: Clinical and supervisory aspects of crisis intervention. S*ocial Casework, 65*: 364-368, 1984.

Maltsberger, J.T.: Suicide danger: Clinical estimation and decision. *Suicide and Life-Threatening Behavior, 18*: 47-54, 1988.

Maltsberger, J.T., Hendin, H., Haas, A.P., and Lipschitz, A.: Determination of precipitating events in the suicide of psychiatric patients. *Suicide and Life-Threatening Behavior, 33*: 111-119, 2003.

Mann, J.J., Waternaux, C., Haas, G.L., and Malone, K.M.: Toward a clinical model of suicidal behavior in psychiatric patients. *American Journal of Psychiatry, 156*: 181-189, 1999.

Margolis, C.G., Edwards, D.W., Shrier, L.P., and Cramer, M.: Brief hotline training: An effort to examine impact on volunteers. *American Journal of Community Psychology, 3*: 59-67, 1975.

Maris, R.W., Berman, A.L., and Silverman, M.M.: *Comprehensive Textbook of Suicidology.* New York: Guilford, 2000.

Marttunen, M.J., Aro, H.M., and Lonnqvist, J.K.: Adolescent suicide: Endpoint of long-term difficulties. *Journal of the American Academy of Child & Adolescent Psychiatry, 31*: 649-654, 1992.

Marttunen, M.J., Aro, H.M., and Lonnqvist, J.K.: Precipitant stressors in adolescent suicide. *Journal of the American Academy of Child & Adolescent Psychiatry, 32*: 1178-1183, 1993.

Marzuk, P.M., Hartwell, N., Leon, A.C., and Portera, L.: Executive functioning in depressed patients with suicidal ideation. *Acta Psychiatrica Scandinavica, 112*: 294-301, 2005.

McCarthy, P.R., and Knapp, S.L.: Helping styles of crisis intervenors, psychotherapists, and untrained individuals. *American Journal of Community Psychology, 12*: 623-627, 1984.

McMahon, E.M., Corcoran, P., McAuliffe, C., Keeley, H., Perry, I.J., and Arensman, E.: Mediating effects of coping style on associations between mental health factors and self-harm among adolescents. *Crisis, 34*: 242-250, 2013.

McFarlane, A.C.: Psychiatric morbidity following disasters: Epidemiology, risk and protective factors. In J.J. Lopez-Ibor, G. Christodoulou, M. Maj, N. Sartorius, and A. Okasha (Eds.) *Disasters and Mental Health.* New York: Wiley, 2005.

McGee, R.K.: *Crisis Intervention in the Community.* Baltimore: University Park Press, 1974.

McGee, R.K., and Jennings, B.: Ascending to "lower" levels: The case for nonprofessional crisis workers. In D. Lester (Ed.): *Crisis Intervention and Counseling by Telephone*, 2nd Edition. Springfield, IL: Charles C Thomas, 2002.

McMyler, C., and Pryjmachuk. S.: Do "no-suicide" contracts work? *Journal of Psychiatric and Mental Health Nursing, 15*: 512-522, 2008.

Meichenbaum, D.: *Cognitive-Behavior Modification.* New York: Plenum, 1977.

Meichenbaum, D.: *Stress Inoculation Training.* New York: Pergamon, 1985.

Michel, K.: Suicide risk factors: A comparison of suicide attempters with suicide completers. *British Journal of Psychiatry, 150*: 78-82, 1987.

Miller, J.S., Segal, D.L., and Coolidge, F.L.: A comparison of suicidal thinking and reasons for living among younger and older adults. *Death Studies, 25*: 357-365, 2001.

Miller, A.L., and Glinski, J.: Youth suicidal behavior: Assessment and intervention. *Journal of Clinical Psychology, 56*: 1131-1152, 2000.

Miller, K.E., King, C.A., Shain, B.N., and Naylor, M.W.: Suicidal adolescents' perceptions of their family environment. *Suicide and Life-Threatening Behavior, 22*: 226-239, 1992.

Miller, M.C.: Suicide-prevention contracts. In D.G. Jacobs (Ed.): *The Harvard Medical School Guide to Suicide Assessment and Intervention.* San Francisco: Jossey-Bass, 1999.

Miller, W.R.: Motivational interviewing: Research, practice, and puzzles. *Addictive Behaviors, 21*: 835-842, 1996.

Miller, W.R., and Rollnick, S.: *Motivational Interviewing: Preparing People for Change*, 2nd Edition. New York: Guilford Press, 2002.

Miller, W.R., and Rose, G.S.: Toward a theory of motivational interviewing. *American Psychologist, 64*: 527-537, 2009.

Mishara, B.L., Chagnon, F., Daigle, M., Balan, B., Raymond, S., Marcoux, I., et al.: Comparing models of helper behavior to actual practice in telephone crisis intervention: A silent monitoring study of calls to the U.S. 1-800-SUICIDE Network. *Suicide and Life-Threatening Behavior, 37*: 291-307, 2007 (a).

Mishara, B.L., Chagnon, F., Daigle, M., Balan, B., Raymond, S., Marcoux, I., et al.: Which helper behaviors and intervention styles are related to better short-term outcomes in telephone crisis intervention? Results from a silent monitoring study of calls to the U.S. 1-800-SUICIDE Network. *Suicide and Life-Threatening Behavior, 37*: 308-321, 2007 (b).

Mishara, B.L., and Daigle, M.S.: Effects of different telephone intervention styles with suicidal callers at two suicide prevention centers: An empirical investigation. *American Journal of Community Psychology, 25*: 861-885, 1997.

Mishara, B.L., and Giroux, G.: The relationship between coping strategies and perceived stress in telephone intervention volunteers at a suicide prevention center. *Suicide and Life-Threatening Behavior, 23*: 221-229, 1993.

Mishara, B.L., and Weisstub, D.N.: Resolving ethical dilemmas in suicide prevention: The case of telephone helpline rescue policies. *Suicide and Life-Threatening Behavior, 40*: 159-169, 2010.

Mitchell, A.M., Kim, Y., Prigerson, H.G., and Mortimer, M.K.: Complicated grief and suicidal ideation in adult survivors of suicide. *Suicide and Life-Threatening Behavior, 35*: 498-506, 2005.

Mitchell, A.M., Kim, Y., Prigerson, H.G., and Mortimer-Stephens, M.K.: Complicated grief in survivors of suicide. *Crisis, 25*: 12-18, 2004.

Modai, I., Hirschmann, S., Hadjez, J., Bernat, C., Gelber, D., Ratner, Y., et al.: Clinical evaluation of prior suicide attempts and suicide risk in psychiatric inpatients. *Crisis, 23*: 47-54, 2002.

Monteith, L.L., Menefee, D.S., Pettit, J.W., Leopoulos, W.L., and Vincent, J.P.: Examining the interpersonal-psychological theory of suicide in an inpatient veteran sample. *Suicide and Life-Threatening Behavior, 43*: 418-428, 2013.

Montross, L.P., Zisook, S., and Kasckow, J.: Suicide among patients with schizophrenia: A consideration of risk and protective factors. *Annals of Clinical Psychiatry, 17*: 173-182, 2005.

Morgenstern, J., Kuerbis, A., Amrhein, P., Hail, L., Lynch, K., and McKay, J.R.: Motivational interviewing: A pilot test of active ingredients and mechanisms of change. *Psychology of Addictive Behaviors, 26*: 859-869, 2012.

Morgan, J.P., and King, G.D.: The selection and evaluation of the volunteer paraprofessional telephone counselor. *American Journal of Community Psychology, 3*: 237-249, 1975.

Morris, A.J.F.: Psychic aftershocks: Crisis counseling and disaster relief policy. *History of Psychology, 14*: 264-286, 2011.

Morris, C.A.W., and Minton, C.A.B: Crisis in the curriculum? New counselors' crisis preparation, experiences, and self-efficacy. *Counselor Education and Supervision, 51*: 256-269, 2012.

Moskos, M., Olson, L., Halbern, S., Keller, T., and Gray, D.: Utah youth suicide study: Psychological autopsy. *Suicide and Life-Threatening Behavior, 35*: 536-546, 2005.

Motto, J.A.: Critical points in the assessment and management of suicide risk. In D.G. Jacobs (Ed.): *The Harvard Medical School Guide to Suicide Assessment and Intervention.* San Francisco: Jossey-Bass, 1999.

Motto, J.A., Brooks, R.M., Ross, C.P., and Allen, N.H.: *Standards for Suicide Prevention and Crisis Centers.* New York: Behavioral Publications, 1974.

Murphy, G.E., Wetzel, R.D., Swallow, C.S., and McClure, J.N.: Who calls the suicide prevention center: A study of 55 persons calling on their own behalf. *American Journal of Psychiatry, 126*: 314-324, 1969.

Myer, R.A., and Moore, H.B.: Crisis in context theory: An ecological model. *Journal of Counseling & Development, 84*: 139-147, 2006.

Myers, K., McCauley, E., Calderon, R., and Treder, R.: The 3-year longitudinal course of suicidality and predictive factors for subsequent suicidality in youths with major depressive disorder. *Journal of the American Academy of Child & Adolescent Psychiatry, 30*: 804-810, 1991.

Myers, W.C., Otto, T.A., Harris, E., Diaco, D., and Moreno, A.: Acetaminophen overdose as a suicidal gesture: A survey of adolescents' knowledge of its potential for toxicity. *Journal of the American Academy of Child & Adolescent Psychiatry, 31*: 686-690, 1992.

Neimeyer, R.A., Fortner, B., and Melby, D.: Personal and professional factors and suicide intervention skills. *Suicide and Life-Threatening Behavior, 31*: 71-82, 2001.

Neimeyer, R.A., and MacInnes, W.D.: Assessing paraprofessional competence with the Suicide Intervention Response Inventory. *Journal of Counseling Psychology, 28*: 176-179, 1981.

Neimeyer, R.A., and Pfeiffer, A.M.: Evaluation of suicide intervention effectiveness. *Death Studies, 18*: 131-166, 1994.

Nelson, R.H.: *The Analysis of a Crisis Call Center: An Examination of Both Its Function and Meaning Within the Mental Health Community.* Unpublished doctoral dissertation. George Peabody College for Teachers, 1972.

Newgass, S., and Schonfeld, D.J.: School crisis intervention, crisis prevention, and crisis response. In A.R. Roberts (Ed.): *Crisis Intervention Handbook: Assessment, Treatment, and Research.* New York: Oxford University Press, 2005.

Niederkrotenhaler, T., and Sonneck, G..: Assessing the impact of media guidelines for reporting on suicides in Austria: Interrupted time series analysis. *Australian and New Zealand Journal of Psychiatry, 41*: 419-428, 2007.

Nock, M.K., and Marzuk, P.M.: Murder-suicide: Phenomenology and clinical implications. In D.G. Jacobs (Ed.): *The Harvard Medical School Guide to Suicide Assessment and Intervention.* San Francisco: Jossey-Bass, 1999.

Norris, F.H., Hamblen, J.L., Watson, P.J., Ruzek, J.I., Gibson, L.E., Pfefferbaum, B .J., et al.: Toward understanding and creating systems of postdisaster care: A case study of New York's response to the World Trade Center disaster. In E.C. Ritchie, P.J. Watson, and M.J. Friedman (Eds.): *Interventions Following Mass Violence and Disasters: Strategies for Mental Health Practice.* New York: Guilford, 2006.

O'Carroll, P.W., Berman, A.L., Maris, R.W., Moscicki, E.K., Tanney, B.L., and Silverman, M.M.: Beyond the Tower of Babel: A nomenclature for Suicidology. *Suicide and Life-Threatening Behavior, 26*: 237-252, 1996.

Occupational Safety and Health Administration. *Guidelines for preventing work-related violence for health care and social service workers* (OSHA Publication No. 3148-01R). Washington, DC: Author, 2004.

O'Donnell, J.M., and George, K.: The use of volunteers in a community mental health center emergency and reception service: A comparative study of professional and lay telephone counseling. *Community Mental Health Journal, 13*: 3-12, 1977.

Olfson, M., Gameroff, M .J., Marcus, S.C., Greenberg, T., and Shaffer, D.: National trends in hospitalization of youth with intentional self-inflicted injuries. *American Journal of Psychiatry, 162*: 1328-1335, 2005.

Olivero, J.M., and Hansen, R.: Linkage agreements between mental health and law enforcement agencies: Managing suicidal persons. *Administration and Policy in Mental Health, 21*: 217-225, 1994.

Olsson, M.: Social support in bereavement crisis - A study of interaction in crisis situations. *Social Work in Health Care, 25*: 117-130, 1997.

Orbach, I.: *Children Who Don't Want to Live.* San Francisco: Jossey-Bass, 1988.

Orbach, I.: Suicide prevention for adolescents. In R.A. King and A. Apter (Eds.): *Suicide in Children and Adolescents.* New York: Cambridge University Press, 2003.

Orbach, I., Bar-Joseph, H., and Dror, N.: Styles of problem solving in suicidal individuals. *Suicide and Life-Threatening Behavior, 20*: 56-64, 1990.

Orbach, I., Mikulincer, M., Blumenson, R., Mester, R., and Stein, D.: The subjective experience of problem irresolvability and suicidal behavior: Dynamics and measurement. *Suicide and Life-Threatening Behavior, 29*: 150-164, 1999.

Orbach, I., Mikulincer, M., Gilboa-Schechtman, E., and Sirota, P.: Mental pain and its relationship to suicidality and life meaning. *Suicide and Life-Threatening Behavior, 33*: 231-241, 2003.

Orbach, I., Mikulincer, M., Sirota, P., and Gilboa-Schechtman, E.: Mental pain: A multidimensional operationalization and definition. *Suicide and Life-Threatening Behavior, 33*: 219-230, 2003.

Osman, A., Downs, W.R., Kopper, B.A., Barrios, F.X., Baker, M.T., Osman, J.R., et al.: The Reasons for Living Inventory for Adolescents (FFL-A): Development and psychometric properties. *Journal of Clinical Psychology, 54*: 1063-1078, 1998.

Overholser, J.C., Braden, A., and Dieter, L.: Understanding suicide risk: Identification of high-risk groups during high-risk times. *Journal of Clinical Psychology, 68*: 334-348, 2012.

Parad, H.J., and Caplan, G.: A framework for studying families in crisis. *Social Work, 5*: 3-15, 1960.

Parikh, S.J.T., and Morris, C.A.W.: Integrating Crisis Theory and Individual Psychology: An application and case study. *The Journal of Individual Psychology, 67*: 364-379, 2011.

Parry, J.K.: Death review: An important component of grief resolution. *Social Work in Health Care, 20* (2): 97-107, 1994.

Paterson, H., Reniers, R., and Vollm, B.: Personality types and mental health experiences of those who volunteer for helplines. *British Journal of Guidance & Counselling, 37*: 459-471, 2009.

Paukert, A., Stagner, B., and Hope, K.: The assessment of active listening skills in helpline volunteers. *Stress, Trauma, and Crisis, 7*: 61-76, 2004.

Peck, D.L.: Completed suicides: Correlates of choice of method. *Omega, 16*: 309-322, 1986.

Perls, F.S.: Four lectures. In J. Fagen and I.L. Shepherd (Eds.): *Gestalt Therapy Now.* New York: Harper & Row, 1970.

Peterson, C., Maier, S.F., and Seligman, M.E.P.: *Learned Helplessness: A Theory for the Age of Personal Control.* New York: Oxford University Press, 1993.

Peterson, J., Skeem, J., and Manchak, S.: If you want to know, consider asking: How likely is it that patients will hurt themselves. *Psychological Assessment, 23*: 626-634, 2011.

Petit, J.R.: Management of the acutely violent patient. *Psychiatric Clinics of North America, 28*: 701-711, 2005.

Pfeffer, C.R.: Diagnosis of childhood and adolescent suicidal behavior: Unmet needs for suicide prevention. *Biological Psychiatry, 49*: 1055-1061, 2001.

Pfeffer, C.R., Klerman, G.L., Hurt, S.W., Kakuma, T., Peskin, J.R., and Siefker, C.A.: Suicidal children grow up: Rates and psychosocial risk factors for suicide attempts during follow-up. *Journal of the American Academy of Child & Adolescent Psychiatry, 32*: 106-113, 1993.

Pfeffer, C.R., Klerman, G.L., Hurt, S.W., Lesser, M., Peskin, J.R., and Siefker, C.A.: Suicidal children grow up: Demographic and clinical risk factors for adolescent suicide attempts. *Journal of the American Academy of Child & Adolescent Psychiatry, 30*: 609-616, 1991.

Pfeffer, C.R., Normandin, L., and Kakuma, T.: Suicidal children grow up: Suicidal behavior and psychiatric disorders among relatives. *Journal of the American Academy of Child & Adolescent Psychiatry, 33*: 1087-1097, 1994.

Piacentini, J., Rotheram-Borus, M .J., Gillis, J.R., Graae, F., Trautman, P., Cantwell, C., et al.: Demographic predictors of treatment attendance among adolescent suicide attempters. *Journal of Consulting and Clinical Psychology, 63*: 469-473, 1995.

Pierpont, J.H., and McGinty, K.: Suicide. In C.N. Dulmus and L.A. Rapp-Paglicci (Eds.): *Handbook of Preventive Interventions for Adults.* Hoboken, NJ: Wiley, 2005.

Pietromonaco, P.R., and Rook, K.S.: Decision style in depression: The contribution of perceived risks versus benefits. *Journal of Personality and Social Psychology, 52*: 399-408, 1987.

Pitcher, G.D., and Poland, S.: *Crisis Intervention in the Schools.* New York: Guilford, 1992.

Plutchik, R.: Aggression, violence, and suicide. In R.W. Maris, A.L. Berman, and M.M. Silverman. *Comprehensive Textbook of Suicidology.* New York: Guilford, 2000.

Poindexter, C.C.: In the aftermath: Serial crisis intervention for people with HIV. *Health and Social Work, 22*: 125-132, 1997.

Poland, S.: The role of school crisis intervention teams to prevent and reduce school violence and trauma. *School Psychology Review, 23*: 175-189, 1994.

Preston, J., Schoenfeld, L.S., and Adams, R.L.: Evaluating the effectiveness of a telephone crisis center from the consumer's viewpoint. *Hospital & Community Psychiatry, 26*: 719-720, 1975.

Prochaska, J.O., and Prochaska, J.M.: Why don't continents move? Why don't people change? *Journal of Psychotherapy Integration, 9*: 83-102, 1999.

Prochaska, J.O., Norcross, J.C., and DiClemente, C.C.: *Changing for Good.* New York: Morrow, 1994.

Purselle, D.C., Henninger, M., Hanzlick, R., and Garlow, S.J.: Differential association of socioeconomic status in ethnic and age-defined suicides. *Psychiatry Research, 167*: 258-265, 2009.

Puryear, D.A.: *Helping People in Crisis.* San Francisco: Jossey-Bass, 1979.

Range, L.M.: No-suicide contracts. In R.I. Yufit and D. Lester (Eds.): *Assessment, Treatment, and Prevention of Suicidal Behavior.* Hoboken, NJ: Wiley, 2005.

Rauch, S.A.M., and Foa, E.B.: Sexual trauma: Impact and recovery. In B.T. Litz (Ed.): *Early Intervention for Trauma and Traumatic Loss.* New York: Guilford, 2004.

Reed, M.D., and Greenwald, J.Y.: Survivor-victim status, attachment, and sudden death bereavement. *Suicide and Life-Threatening Behavior, 21*: 385-401, 1991.

Reilly, J., Newton, R., and Dowling, R.: Implementation of a first presentation psychosis clinical pathway in an area mental health service: The trials of a continuing quality improvement process. *Australasian Psychiatry, 15*: 14-18, 2007.

Reinecke, M.A.: Problem solving: A conceptual approach to suicidality and psychotherapy. In T.E. Ellis (Ed.): *Cognition and Suicide: Theory, Research, and Therapy.* Washington, DC: American Psychological Association, 2006.

Reinecke, M.A., and Didie, E.R.: Cognitive-behavioral therapy with suicidal patients. In R.I. Yufit and D. Lester (Eds.): *Assessment, Treatment, and Prevention of Suicidal Behavior.* Hoboken, NJ: Wiley, 2005.

Reinherz, H.Z., Giaconia, R.M., Silverman, A.B., Friedman, A., Pakiz, B., Frost, A.K., et al.: Early psychosocial risks for adolescent suicidal ideation and attempts. *Journal of the American Academy of Child & Adolescent Psychiatry, 34:* 599-611, 1995.

Resick, P.A., and Ellis, E.M.: Victims of rape: Repeated assessment of depressive symptoms. *Journal of Consulting and Clinical Psychology, 50:* 96-102, 1982.

Reyes, G., and Elhai, J.D.: Psychosocial interventions in the early phases of disasters. *Psychotherapy: Theory, Research, Practice, Training, 41:* 399-411, 2004.

Ribeiro, J.D., Bodell, L.P., Hames, J.L., Hagan, C.R., and Joiner, T.E.: An empirically based approach to the assessment and management of suicidal behavior. *Journal of Psychotherapy Integration, 23:* 207-221, 2013.

Richman, J.: Psychotherapy with suicidal older adults. *Death Studies, 18:* 391-407, 1994.

Rigby, K. and Slee, P.: Suicidal ideation among adolescent school children, involvement in bully victim problems, and perceived social support. *Suicide and Life-Threatening Behavior, 29:* 119-130, 1999.

Riskind, J.H., Long, D.G., Williams, N.L., and White, J.C.: Desperate acts for desperate times: Looming vulnerability and suicide. In T. Joiner and M.D. Rudd (Eds.): *Suicide Science: Expanding the Boundaries.* Boston: Kluwer Academic Publishers, 2000.

Ritter, C., Teller, J.L.S., Marcussen, K., Munetz, M.R., and Teasdale, B.: Crisis intervention team officer dispatch, assessment, and disposition: Interactions with individuals with severe mental illness. *International Journal of Law and Psychiatry, 34:* 30-38, 2011.

Robbins, D.R., and Alessi, N.E.: Depressive symptoms and suicidal behavior in adolescents. *American Journal of Psychiatry, 142:* 588-592, 1985.

Roberts, A.R.: The ACT model: Assessment, crisis intervention, and trauma treatment in the aftermath of community disaster and terrorism attacks. In A.R. Roberts (Ed.): *Crisis Intervention Handbook: Assessment, Treatment, and Research.* New York: Oxford University Press, 2005(a).

Roberts, A.R.: Bridging the past and present to the future of crisis intervention and crisis management. In A.R. Roberts (Ed.): *Crisis Intervention Handbook: Assessment, Treatment, and Research.* New York: Oxford University Press, 2005(b).

Roberts, A.R.: Introduction. In A.R. Roberts (Ed.): *Crisis Intervention Handbook: Assessment, Treatment, and Research.* New York: Oxford University Press, 2005(c).

Roberts, A.R., and Yeager, K.R.: Lethality assessment and crisis intervention with persons presenting with suicidal ideation. In A.R. Roberts (Ed.): *Crisis Intervention Handbook: Assessment, Treatment, and Research.* New York: Oxford University Press, 2005.

Roehl, J.E. and Gray, D.: The crisis of rape: A guide to counseling victims of rape. *Crisis Intervention, 13:* 67-77, 1984.

Rosenberg, H.J., Jankowski, M.K., Sengupta, A., Wolfe, R.S., Wolford, G.L., and Rosenberg, S.D.: Single and multiple suicide attempts and associated health risk factors in New Hampshire adolescents. *Suicide and Life-Threatening Behavior, 35*: 547-557, 2005.

Rosenberg, J.I.: Suicide prevention: An integrated training model using affective and action-based interventions. *Professional Psychology: Research and Practice, 30*: 83-87, 1999.

Rotheram-Borus, M .J., Trautman, P.D., Dopkins, S.C., and Shrout, P.E.: Cognitive style and pleasant activities among female adolescent suicide attempters. *Journal of Consulting and Clinical Psychology, 58*: 554-561, 1990.

Rotheram-Borus, M .J., Walker, J.U., and Ferns, W.: Suicidal behavior among middle-class adolescents who seek crisis services. *Journal of Clinical Psychology, 52*: 137-143, 1996.

Roy, A.: Consumers of mental health services. *Suicide and Life-Threatening Behavior, 31* (Supplement): 60-83, 2001.

Royce, T.: The negotiator and the bomber: Analyzing the critical role of active listening in crisis negotiations. *Negotiation Journal, 21*: 5-27, 2005.

Rubenstein, J.L., Heeren, T., Housman, D., Rubin, C., and Stechler, G.: Suicidal behavior in "normal" adolescents: Risk and protective factors. *American Journal of Orthopsychiatry, 59*: 59-71, 1989.

Rubonis, A.V., and Bickman, L.: Psychological impairment in the wake of disaster: The disaster-psychopathology relationship. *Psychological Bulletin, 109*: 384-399, 1991.

Rudd, M.D.: Fluid vulnerability theory: A cognitive approach to understanding the process of acute and chronic suicide risk. In T.E. Ellis (Ed.): *Cognition and Suicide: Theory, Research, and Therapy*. Washington, DC: American Psychological Association, 2006.

Rudd, M.D., and Joiner, T.: The assessment, management, and treatment of suicidality: Toward clinically informed and balanced standards of care. *Clinical Psychology: Science and Practice, 5*: 135-150, 1998.

Rudd, M.D., Joiner, T.E., Jr., Jobes, D.A., and King, C.A.: The outpatient treatment of suicidality: An integration of science and recognition of its limitations. *Professional Psychology: Research and Practice, 30*: 437-446, 1999.

Rudd, M.D., Joiner, T.E., Jr., and Rajab, M.H.: Help negation after acute suicidal crisis. *Journal of Consulting and Clinical Psychology, 63*: 499-503, 1995.

Rudd, M.D., Joiner, T., and Rajab, M.H.: Relationships among suicide ideators, attempters, and multiple attempters in a young-adult sample. *Journal of Abnormal Psychology, 105*: 541-550, 1996.

Rudd, M.D., Mandrusiak, M., and Joiner, T.E. Jr.: The case against no-suicide contracts: The commitment to treatment statement as a practice alternative. *Journal of Clinical Psychology, 62*: 243-251, 2006.

Rudd, M.D., Rajab, M.H., and Dahm, F.P.: Problem-solving appraisal in suicide ideators and attempters. *American Journal of Orthopsychiatry, 64*: 136-149, 1994.

Runeson, B.S., Beskow, J., and Waern, M.: The suicidal process in suicides among young people. *Acta Psychiatrica Scandinavica, 93*: 35-42, 1996.

Russell, R.K., and Petrie, T.: Issues in training effective supervisors. *Applied & Preventive Psychology, 3*: 27-42, 1994.

Sakowitz, M.L., and Hirschman, R.: Paraprofessional selection–myth or safeguard? *Journal of Community Psychology, 5*: 340-343, 1977.

Sandoval, J., and Brock, S.E.: The school psychologist's role in suicide prevention. *School Psychology Quarterly, 11*: 169-185, 1996.

Sayil, I., and Devrimci-Ozguven, H.: Suicide and suicide attempts in Ankara in 1998: Results of the WHO/EURO Multicentre Study of Suicidal Behaviour. *Crisis, 23*: 11-16, 2002.

Schinke, S.P., and Rose, S.D.: Interpersonal skill training in groups. *Journal of Counseling Psychology, 23*: 442-448, 1976.

Schinke, S.P., Smith, T.E., Myers, R.K., and Altman, D.C.: Crisis-intervention training with paraprofessionals. *Journal of Community Psychology, 7*: 343-347, 1979.

Schonfeld, D.J., and Kline, M.: School-based crisis intervention: An organizational model. *Crisis Intervention, 1*: 155-166, 1994.

Schotte, D.E., and Clum, G.A.: Problem-solving skills in suicidal psychiatric patients. *Journal of Consulting and Clinical Psychology, 55*: 49-54, 1987.

Schuster, J.M.: Psychiatric consultation in the general hospital emergency department. *Psychiatric Services, 46*: 555-557, 1995.

Schwartz, A.J.: Rate, relative risk, and method of suicide by students at 4-year colleges and universities in the United States, 2004-2005 through 2008-2009. *Suicide and Life-Threatening Behavior, 41*: 353-371.

Schwartz, R.C., and Cohen, B.N.: Psychosocial correlates of suicidal intent among patients with schizophrenia. *Comprehensive Psychiatry, 42*: 118-123, 2001.

Schwartz, R.C., and Rogers, J.R.: Suicide assessment and evaluation strategies: A primer for counseling psychologists. *Counselling Psychology Quarterly, 17*: 89-97, 2004.

Segal, S.P., and Dittrich, E.A.: Quality of care for psychiatric emergency service patients presenting with substance use problems. *American Journal of Orthopsychiatry, 71*: 72-78, 2001.

Seguin, M., Lesage, A., and Kiely, M.C.: Parental bereavement after suicide and accident: A comparative study. *Suicide and Life-Threatening Behavior, 25*: 489-498, 1995.

Semke, J., Brown, L., Sutphen-Mroz, J., Cox, G.B., Gilchrist, L.D., Allen, D.G., et al.: Impact of mental health reform on service use. *Evaluation and Program Planning, 17*: 73-79, 1994.

Sethi, S., and Bhargava, S.C.: Child and adolescent survivors of suicide. *Crisis, 24*: 4-6, 2003.

Shafii, M., Carrigan, S., Whittinghill, J.R., and Derrick, A.: Psychological autopsy of completed suicide in children and adolescents. *American Journal of Psychiatry, 142*: 1061-1064, 1985.

Shah, S., Hoffman, R.E., Wake, L., and Marine, W.M.: Adolescent suicide and household access to firearms in Colorado: Results of a case-control study. *Journal of Adolescent Health, 26*: 157-163, 2000.

Shahar, B., Carlin, E.R., Engle, D.E., Hegde, J., Szepsenwol, O., and Arkowitz, H.: A pilot investigation of emotion-focused two-chair dialogue intervention for self-criticism. *Clinical Psychology and Psychotherapy, 19*: 496-507, 2012.

Shamai, M.: Family crisis intervention by phone: Intervention with families during the Gulf War. *Journal of Marital and Family Therapy, 20*: 317-323, 1994.

Shaw, J., Baker, D., Hunt, I.M., Moloney, A., and Appleby, L.: Suicide by prisoners: National clinical survey. *British Journal of Psychiatry, 184*: 263-267, 2004.

Shelby, J.S., and Tredinnick, M.G.: Crisis intervention with survivors of natural disaster: Lessons from Hurricane Andrew. *Journal of Counseling & Development, 73*: 491-497, 1995.

Sherr, L., Lampe, F., Fisher, M., Arthur, G., Anderson, J., Zetler, S., et al.: Suicidal ideation in UK HIV clinic attenders. *AIDS, 22*: 1651-1658, 2008.

Shiho, Y., Tohru, T., Shinji, S., Manabu, T., Yuka, T., Eriko, T., et al.: Suicide in Japan: Present condition and prevention measures. *Crisis, 26*: 12-19, 2005.

Shneidman, E.: Perturbation and lethality: A psychological approach to assessment and intervention. In D.G. Jacobs (Ed.): *The Harvard Medical School Guide to Suicide Assessment and Intervention.* San Francisco: Jossey-Bass, 1999.

Shneidman, E.S.: *Comprehending Suicide: Landmarks in 20th-century Suicidology.* Washington, DC: American Psychological Association, 2001.

Shone, L.P., King, J.P., Doane, C., Wilson, K.M., and Wolf, M.S.: Misunderstanding and potential unintended misuse of acetaminophen among adolescents and young adults. *Journal of Health Communication, 16*: 256-267, 2011.

Shrivastava, A.K., Johnston, M.E., Stitt, L., Thakar, M., Sakel, G., Iyer, S., et al.: Reducing treatment delay for early intervention: Evaluation of a community based crisis helpline. *Annals of General Psychiatry, 11*: 1-6, 2012.

Silver, T., and Goldstein, H.: A collaborative model of a county crisis intervention team: The Lake County experience. *Community Mental Health Journal, 28*: 249-256, 1992.

Silverman, D.C.: Sharing the crisis of rape: Counseling the mates and families of victims. *American Journal of Orthopsychiatry, 48*: 166-173, 1978.

Silverman, M.M.: Helping college students cope with suicidal impulses. In R.I. Yufit and D. Lester (Eds.): *Assessment, Treatment, and Prevention of Suicidal Behavior.* Hoboken, NJ: Wiley, 2005.

Simon, R.I.: Gun safety management with patients at risk for suicide. *Suicide and Life-Threatening Behavior, 37*: 518-526, 2007.

Simon, T.R., and Crosby, A.E.: Suicide planning among high school students who report attempting suicide. *Suicide and Life-Threatening Behavior, 30*: 213-221, 2000.

Simon, T.R., Swann, A.C., Powell, K.E., Potter, L.B., Kresnow, M., and O'Carroll, P.W.: Characteristics of impulsive suicide attempts and attempters. *Suicide and Life-Threatening Behavior, 32* (Supplement): 49-59, 2001.

Simonds, J.F., McMahon, T., and Armstrong, D.: Young suicide attempters compared with a control group: Psychological, affective, and attitudinal variables. *Suicide and Life-Threatening Behavior, 21*: 134-151, 1991.

Slaby, A.E.: Outpatient management of suicidal patients. In B. Bongar, A.L. Berman, R.W. Maris, M.M. Silerman, E.A. Harris, and W.L. Packman (Eds.): *Risk Management with Suicidal Patients.* New York: Guilford, 1998.

Slaikeu, K.A., Lester, D., and Tulkin, S.R.: Show versus no show: A comparison of referral calls to a suicide prevention and crisis service. *Journal of Consulting and Clinical Psychology, 40*: 481-486, 1973.

Slaikeu, K.A., Tulkin, S.R., and Speer, D.C.: Process and outcome in the evaluation of telephone counseling referrals. *Journal of Consulting and Clinical Psychology, 43*: 700-707, 1975.

Slaikeu, K.A., and Willis, M.A.: Caller feedback on counselor performance in telephone crisis intervention: A follow-up study. *Crisis Intervention, 9*: 42-49, 1978.

Smith, A.: Introduction and overview. In T.J. Kiresuk, A. Smith, and J.E. Cardillo (Eds.): *Goal Attainment Scaling: Applications, Theory, and Measurement.* Hillsdale, NJ: Lawrence Erlbaum Associates, 1994.

Smith, E.M., North, C.S., McCool, R.E., and Shea, J.M.: Acute postdisaster psychiatric disorders: Identification of persons at risk. *American Journal of Psychiatry, 147*: 202-206, 1990.

Solomon, P.L., Gordon, B.H., and Davis, J.M.: *Community Services to Discharged Psychiatric Patients.* Springfield, IL: Charles C Thomas, 1984.

Sonneck, G., and Horn, W.: Contribution to suicide risk assessment: I. A simple method to predict crises after suicide attempts (parasuicides). *Crisis, 11* (2): 31-33, 1990.

Speckens, A.E.M., and Hawton, K.: Social problem solving in adolescents with suicidal behavior: A systematic review. *Suicide and Life-Threatening Behavior, 35*: 365-387, 2005.

Speer, D.C., and Schultz, M.: An instrument for assessing caller-reported benefits of calls to a telephone crisis service. *Journal of Consulting and Clinical Psychology, 43*: 102, 1975.

Spirito, A., Bond, A., Kurkjian, J., Devost, L., Bosworth, T., and Brown, L.K.: Gender differences among adolescent suicide attempters. *Crisis, 14*: 178-184, 1993.

Spirito, A., Plummer, B., Gispert, M., Levy, S., Kurkjian, J., Lewander, et al.: Adolescent suicide attempts: Outcomes at follow-up. *American Journal of Orthopsychiatry, 62*: 464-468, 1992.

Stack, S.: Media coverage as a risk factor in suicide. *Journal of Epidemiology and Community Health, 57*: 238-240, 2003.

Stanton, A.L., Bower, J.E., and Low, C.A.: Posttraumatic growth after cancer. In L.G. Calhoun and R.G. Tedeschi (Eds.): *Handbook of Posttraumatic Growth: Research and Practice.* Mahwah, NJ: Lawrence Erlbaum Associates, 2006.

Steadman, H.J., Stainbrook, K.A., Griffin, P., Draine, J., Dupont, R., and Horey, C.: A specialized crisis response site as a core element of police-based diversion programs. *Psychiatric Services, 52*: 219-222, 2001.

Steenbarger, B.N.: Duration and outcome in psychotherapy: An integrative review. *Professional Psychology: Research and Practice, 25*: 111-119, 1994.

Stefanowski-Harding, S.: Child suicide: A review of the literature and implications for school counselors. *School Counselor, 37*: 328-336, 1990.

Stein, D.M., and Lambert, M.J.: Telephone counseling and crisis intervention: A review. *American Journal of Community Psychology, 12*: 101-126, 1984.

Steinglass, P., and Gerrity, E.: Natural disasters and Post-traumatic Stress Disorder: Short-term versus long-term recovery in two disaster-affected communities. *Journal of Applied Social Psychology, 20*: 1746-1765, 1990.

Steley, J.R.: Sexually abusive callers in the context of crisis agencies: A literature review. *Australian Journal of Marriage & Family, 11* (1): 19-27, 1990.

Stellrecht, N.E., Gordon, K.H., Van Orden, K., Witte, T.K., Wingate, L.R., Cukrow-icz, K.C. et al.: Clinical applications of the interpersonal-psychological theory of attempted and completed suicide. *Journal of Clinical Psychology, 62*: 211- 222, 2006.

Stelmachers, Z.T.: Current status of program evaluation efforts. *Suicide and Life-Threatening Behavior, 6*: 67-78, 1976.

Stelmachers, Z.T., Baxter, J.W., and Ellenson, G.M.: Auditing the quality of care of a crisis center. *Suicide and Life-Threatening Behavior, 8*: 18-31, 1978.

Stelmachers, Z.T., Lund, S.H., and Meade, C.J.: Hennepin County Crisis Interven-tion Center: Evaluation of its effectiveness. *Evaluation*: 61-65, Fall, 1972.

Stewart, C.D., Quinn, A., Plever, S., and Emmerson, B.: Comparing cognitive be-havior therapy, problem solving therapy, and treatment as usual in a high risk population. *Suicide and Life-Threatening Behavior, 39*: 538-547, 2009

Stewart, M .J., Vockell, E.L., and Ray, R.E.: Decreasing court appearances of juve-nile status offenders. *Social Casework, 67*: 74-79, 1986.

Stravynski, A., and Boyer, R.: Loneliness in relation to suicide ideation and parasui-cide: A population-wide study. *Suicide and Life-Threatening Behavior, 31*: 32-40, 2001.

Strauss, G., Chassin, M., and Lock, J.: Can experts agree when to hospitalize ado-lescents? *Journal of the American Academy of Child & Adolescent Psychiatry, 34*: 418-424, 1995.

Strauss, G., Glenn, M., Reddi, P., Afaq, I.., Podolskaya, A., Rybakova, T. et al.: Psy-chiatric disposition of patients brought in by crisis intervention team police offi-cers. *Community Mental Health Journal, 41*: 223-228, 2005.

Strentz, T.: *Hostage/Crisis Negotiations: Lesson Learned from the Bad, the Mad, and the Sad.* Springfield, IL: Charles C Thomas, 2013.

Strentz, T.: *Psychological Aspects of Crisis Negotiation*, 2nd Edition. Boca Raton, FL: Tay-lor & Francis, 2012.

Streufert, B .J.: Death on campuses: Common postvention strategies in higher edu-cation. *Death Studies, 28*: 151-172, 2004.

Tanley, J.C.: *Use of Personality and Interest Measures in Predicting Crisis Phone Counselor Effectiveness.* Unpublished doctoral dissertation. Louisiana State University and Agricultural and Mechanical College, 1972.

Tapp, J.T., Slaikeu, K.A., and Tulkin, S.R.: Toward an evaluation of telephone coun-seling: Process and technical variables influencing "shows" and "no-shows" for a clinic referral. *American Journal of Community Psychology, 2*: 357-364, 1974.

Tatum, P.T., Canetto, S.S., and Slater, M.D.: Suicide coverage in U.S. newspapers following publication of the media guidelines. *Suicide and Life-Threatening Behav-ior, 40*: 524-534.

Taylor, W., and Furlonger, B., A review of vicarious traumatisation and supervision among Australian telephone and online counselors. *Australian Journal of Guidance and Counselling, 21*: 225-235, 2011.

Teller, J.L.S., Munetz, M.R., Gil, K.M., and Ritter, C.: Crisis intervention team train-ing for police officers responding to mental disturbance calls. *Psychiatric Services, 57*: 232-237, 2006.

Thigpen, J.D., and Jones, E.: The crime victim advocate program: A new service for crisis intervention services. *Crisis Intervention, 8*: 25-32, 1977.

Thomas, R.: Training volunteers to provide crisis counseling to rape victims: An evaluation. *Crisis Intervention, 12*: 43-59, 1983.

Tidemalm, D., Elofsson, S., Stefansson, C.G., Waern, M., and Runeson, B.: Predictors of suicide in a community-based cohort of individuals with severe mental disorder. *Social Psychiatry and Psychiatric Epidemiology, 40*: 595-600, 2005.

Tidwell, R.: Crisis counseling: A right and a necessity for members of the underclass. *Counselling Psychology Quarterly, 5*: 245-249, 1992.

Trautman, P.D., Rotheram-Borus, M.J., Dopkins, S., and Lewin, N.: Psychiatric diagnoses in minority female adolescent suicide attempters. *Journal of the American Academy of Child & Adolescent Psychiatry, 30*: 617-622, 1991.

Trautman, P.D., Stewart, N., and Morishima, A.: Are adolescent suicide attempters noncompliant with outpatient care? *Journal of the American Academy of Child & Adolescent Psychiatry, 32*: 89-94, 1993.

Truscott, D., Evans, J., and Mansell, S.: Outpatient psychotherapy with dangerous clients: A model for clinical decision making. *Professional Psychology: Research and Practice, 26*: 484-490, 1995.

Tugade, M.M., Fredrickson, B.L., and Barrett, L.F.: Psychological resilience and positive emotional granularity: Examining the benefits of positive emotions on coping and health. *Journal of Personality, 72*: 1161-1190, 2004.

Ullman, S.E.: Social reactions, coping strategies, and self-blame attributions in adjustment to sexual assault. *Psychology of Women Quarterly, 20*: 505-526, 1996.

Van Hasselt, V.B., Baker, M.T., Romano, S.J., Sellers, A.H., Noesner, G.W., and Smith, S.: Development and validation of a role-play test for assessing crisis (hostage) negotiation skills. *Criminal Justice and Behavior, 32*: 345-361, 2005(a).

Van Hasselt, V.B., Baker, M.T., Romano, S.J., Schlessinger, K.M., Zucker, M., Dragone, R. et al.: Crisis (hostage) negotiation training: A preliminary evaluation of program efficacy. *Criminal Justice and Behavior, 33*: 56-69, 2006.

Van Hasselt, V.B., Flood, J.J., Romano, S.J., Vecchi, G.M., de Fabrique, N., and Dalfonzo, V.A.: Hostage-taking in the context of domestic violence: Some case examples. *Journal of Family Violence, 20*: 21-27, 2005(b).

Van Heeringen, C., Jannes, S., Buylaert, W., Henderick, H., de Bacquer, D., and van Remoortel, J.: The management of non-compliance with referral to out-patient after-care among attempted suicide patients: a controlled intervention study. *Psychological Medicine: 25*, 963-970, 1995.

Van Orden, K.A., Witte, T.K., Cukrowicz, K.C., Braithwaite, S.R., Selby, E.A., and Joiner, T.E. Jr.: The interpersonal theory of suicide. *Psychological Review, 117*: 575-600, 2010.

Vecchi, G.M., Van Hasselt, V.B., and Romano. S.J.: Crisis (hostage) negotiation: Current strategies and issues in high-risk conflict resolution. *Aggression and Violent Behavior, 10*: 533-551, 2005.

Vijayakumar, L., John, S., Pirkis, J., and Whiteford, H.: Suicide in developing countries (2). *Crisis, 26*: 112-119, 2005.

Viney, L.L., Benjamin, Y.N., Clarke, A.M., and Bunn, T.A.: Sex differences in the psychological reactions of medical and surgical patients to crisis intervention counseling: Sauce for the goose may not be sauce for the gander. *Social Science & Medicine, 20*: 1199-1205, 1985.

Viney, L.L., Clarke, A.M., Bunn, T.A., and Benjamin, Y.N.: Crisis-intervention counseling: An evaluation of long- and short-term effects. *Journal of Counseling Psychology, 32*: 29-39, 1985.

Waern, M., Rubenowitz, E., and Wilhelmson, K.: Predictors of suicide in the old elderly. *Gerontology, 49*: 328-334, 2003.

Wagner, B.M., and Zimmerman, J.H.: Developmental influences on suicidality among adolescents: Cognitive, emotional, and neuroscience aspects. In T.E. Ellis (Ed.): *Cognition and Suicide: Theory, Research, and Therapy.* Washington, DC: American Psychological Association, 2006.

Waldron, H.B., Turner, C.W., Barton, C., Alexander, J.F., and Cline, V.B.: Therapist defensiveness and marital therapy process and outcome. *American Journal of Family Therapy, 25*: 233-243, 1997.

Walfish, S., Tapp, J.T., Tulkin, S.R., Slaikeu, K., and Russell, M.: The prediction of "shows" and "no-shows" to a crisis center: A replication. *American Journal of Community Psychology, 3*: 367-370, 1975.

Wallace, M.D.: The origin of suicide prevention in the United States. In D. Lester (Ed.): *Suicide Prevention: Resources for the Millennium.* Philadelphia: BrunnerRoutledge, 2001.

Wark, V.: A look at the work of the telephone counseling center. *Personnel and Guidance Journal, 61*: 110-112, 1982.

Warman, D.M., Forman, E.M., Henriques, G.R., Brown, G.K., and Beck, A.T.: Suicidality and psychosis: Beyond depression and hopelessness. *Suicide and Life-Threatening Behavior, 34*: 77-86, 2004.

Watson, A.C., Ottati, V.C., Morabito, M., Draine, J., Kerr, A.N., and Angell, B.: Outcomes of police contacts with persons with mental illness: The impact of CIT. *Administration and Policy in Mental Health, 37*: 302-317, 2010.

Way, B.B., and Banks, S.: Clinical factors related to admission and release decisions in psychiatric emergency services. *Psychiatric Services, 52*: 214-218, 2001.

Wenzel, A., Berchick, E.R., Tenhave, T., Halberstadt, S., Brown, G.K., and Beck, A.T.: Predictors of suicide relative to other deaths in patients with suicide attempts and suicide ideation: A 30-year prospective study. *Journal of Affective Disorders, 132*: 375-382, 2011.

Werlang, B.S.G., and Botega, N.J.: A semistructured interview for psychological autopsy: An inter-rater reliability study. *Suicide and Life-Threatening Behavior, 33*: 326-330, 2003.

Westefeld, J.S., and Heckman-Stone, C.: The Integrated Problem-Solving Model of crisis intervention: Overview and application. *The Counseling Psychologist, 31*: 221-239, 2003.

Westheide, J., Quednow, B.B., Kuhn, K.U., Hoppe, C., Cooper-Mahkorn, D., Hawellek, B. et al.: Executive performance of depressed suicide attempters: The role of suicidal ideation. *European Archives of Psychiatry and Clinical Neuroscience, 258*: 414-421, 2008.

Westmarland, N., and Alderson, S.: The health, mental health, and well-being benefits of rape crisis counseling. *Journal of Interpersonal Violence, 28*: 3265-3282, 2013.

Widmer, C.: Volunteers with the dual roles of service provider and board member: A case study of role conflict. *Organization Development Journal, 14*: 54-61, 1996.

Wiener, R.L., Wiley, D., Huelsman, T., and Hilgeman, A.: Needs assessment: Combining qualitative interviews and concept mapping methodology. *Evaluation Review, 18*: 227-240, 1994.

Wilcox, H.C., Kuramoto, S.J., Lichenstein, P., Langstrom, N., Brent, D.A., and Runeson, B.: Psychiatric morbidity, violent crime, and suicide among children and adolescents exposed to parental death. *Journal of the American Academy of Child & Adolescent Psychiatry, 49*: 514-523, 2010.

Williams, J.M.G., Barnhofer, T., Crane, C., and Duggan, D.S.: The role of overgeneral memory in suicidality. In T.E. Ellis (Ed.): *Cognition and Suicide: Theory, Research, and Therapy*. Washington, DC: American Psychological Association, 2006.

Williams, M.: *Suicide and Attempted Suicide*. London: Penguin Books, 2002.

Wills, T.A.: Help-seeking as a coping mechanism. In C.R. Snyder and C.E. Ford (Eds.): *Coping With Negative Life Events: Clinical and Social Psychological Perspectives*. New York: Plenum, 1987.

Wilson, A., and Marshall, A.: The support needs and experiences of suicidally bereaved family and friends. *Death Studies, 34*: 625-640, 2010.

Wilson, K.G., Stelzer, J., Bergman, J.N., Kral, M.J., Inayatullah, M., and Elliott, C.A.: Problem solving, stress, and coping in adolescent suicide attempts. *Suicide and Life-Threatening Behavior, 25*: 241-252, 1995.

Winkler, G.E.: Assessing and responding to suicidal jail inmates. *Community Mental Health Journal, 28*: 317-326, 1992.

Winogrond, I.R., and Mirassou, M.M.: A crisis intervention service: Comparison of younger and older adult clients. *Gerontologist, 23*: 370-376, 1983.

Wirtz, P.W., and Harrell, A.V.: Effects of postassault exposure to attack-similar stimuli on long-term recovery of victims. *Journal of Consulting and Clinical Psychology, 55*: 10-16, 1987(a).

Wirtz, P.W., and Harrell, A.V.: Victim and crime characteristics, coping responses, and short- and long-term recovery from victimization. *Journal of Consulting and Clinical Psychology, 55*: 866-871, 1987(b).

Witte, T.K., Gould, M.S., Munfakh, J.L.H., Kleinman, M., Joiner, T.E. Jr., and Kalafat, J.: Assessing suicide risk among callers to crisis hotlines: A confirmatory factor analysis. *Journal of Clinical Psychology, 66*: 941-964, 2010.

Wolitzky-Taylor, K.B., Resnick, H.S., Amstadter, A.B., McCauley, J.L., Rugiero, K.J., and Kilpatrick, D.G.: Reporting rape in a national sample of college women. *Journal of American College Health, 59*: 582-587, 2011 (a).

Wolitzky-Taylor, K.B., Resnick, H.S., McCauley, J.L., Amstadter, A.B., Kilpatrick, D.G., and Rugiero, K.J.: Is the reporting of rape on the rise? A comparison of women with reported with unreported rape experiences in the National Women's Study-Replication. *Journal of Interpersonal Violence, 26*: 807-832, 2011 (b).

Woody, J.D., and Beldin, K.L.: The mental health focus in rape crisis services: Tensions and recommendations. *Violence and Victims, 27*: 95-108, 2012.

Young, B.H.: The immediate response to disaster: Guidelines for adult psychological first aid. In E.C. Ritchie, P.J. Watson, and M.J. Friedman (Eds.) *Interventions Following Mass Violence and Disasters: Strategies for Mental Health Practice*. New York: Guilford, 2006.

Young, R.: Helpful behaviors in the crisis center call. *Journal of Community Psychology, 17*: 70-77, 1989.

Zealberg, J.J., Hardesty, S.J., and Tyson, S.C.: Mental health clinicians' role in responding to critical incidents in the community. *Psychiatric Services, 49*: 301-303, 1998.

Zealberg, J.J., Santos, A.B., and Fisher, R.K.: Benefits of mobile crisis programs. *Hospital & Community Psychiatry, 44*: 16-17, 1993.

Zimmerman, J.K.: Treating suicidal adolescents: Is it really worth it? In J.K. Zimmerman and G.M. Asnis (Eds.): *Treatment Approaches with Suicidal Adolescents.* New York: Wiley, 1995.

Zimmerman, J.K., Asnis, G.M., and Schwartz, B.J.: Enhancing outpatient treatment compliance: A multifamily psychoeducational intake group. In J.K. Zimmerman and G.M. Asnis (Eds.): *Treatment Approaches with Suicidal Adolescents.* New York: Wiley, 1995.

Zinner, E.S.: Group survivorship: A model and case study application. In E.S.

Zinner (Ed.): *Coping with Death on Campus.* San Francisco: Jossey-Bass, 1985.

Zinner, E.S.: Responding to suicide in schools: A case study in loss intervention and group survivorship. *Journal of Counseling and Development, 65*: 499-501, 1987.

NAME INDEX

H

SUBJECT INDEX

319